DETECTING
MALINGERING
— AND —
DECEPTION

Forensic Distortion
Analysis (FDA)

DETECTING
MALINGERING
——— AND ———
DECEPTION

Forensic Distortion
Analysis (FDA)

Harold V. Hall
David A. Pritchard

1996

S^t_L

St. Lucie Press
Delray Beach, Florida

Direct all inquiries to:
St. Lucie Press, Inc.
100 E. Linton Blvd., Suite 403B
Delray Beach, Florida, 33483.
Phone: (407) 274-9906
Fax: (407) 274-9927

St. Lucie Press
Delray Beach, Florida

To my wife, Jerilynn Ono Hall
H.V.H.

To the memory of my mother and father
D.A.P.

"Tell a man there are 300 billion stars in the universe and he'll believe you. Tell him a bench has wet paint on it and he'll have to touch it to be sure."

Jaeger's Facts

"Trust everybody; but always cut the cards."

Finley Peter Dunne's Credo

"No matter where or what, there are makers, takers, and fakers."

Kegley's Principle of Observation

"Toothaches tend to occur on Saturday nights."

Johnson-Laird's Law

"Tell the truth and you won't have so much to remember."

Abraham Lincoln

"An honest answer can get you into a lot of trouble."

Welch's Caution

"I have seen the truth, and it makes no sense."

G. K. Chesterton's Observation

TABLE OF CONTENTS

About the Authors

Harold V. Hall is the Director of Psychological Consultants, Inc. He has served as a consultant for a wide variety of criminal and civil justice system agencies, including the Federal Bureau of Investigation, the National Bureau of Prisons, the U. S. Secret Service, and district and circuit courts at both the state and federal levels. Dr. Hall is a Diplomate in both Forensic Psychology and Clinical Psychology from the American Board of Professional Psychology and is a Fellow of the American Psychological Association. He has investigated and trained others in deception analysis and violence assessment and prediction since 1969 in Hawaii, on the continental United States, and in Europe.

David A. Pritchard is Chairman of the Advisory Board of Psychological Consultants, Inc. and in the private practice of forensic psychology in several southern states. He has served as a professor of clinical psychology at the University of Mississippi, Chief Forensic Psychologist for the State of Arkansas, and consultant to trial courts at both the state and federal level. He has published numerous research articles and books on psychological assessment and on forensic psychology. Dr. Pritchard is certified in Forensic Psychology by the American Board of Professional Psychology. He is currently employed at the Atlanta Rehabilitation Center in Atlanta, Georgia.

Psychological Consultants (PSYCON) is approved by the American Psychological Association to offer Category I Continuing Education to psychologists. The APA-approved sponsor maintains responsibility for the program. PSYCON is dedicated to the understanding and control of human violence, and currently has advisory board members from Hawaii, the mainland United States, Germany, and Poland.

PREFACE

Scholars and clinicians have commented on deception for at least two millennia. What new things do we have to offer in this book? Perhaps an awareness of the evolution in this field is our contribution. Three generations of deception-detecting methods can be identified, two of which are utilized today by most practitioners. The first generation consists of all those judgmental methods which rely on observing/talking to the possible deceiver and/or significant others. Observation of the person's behavior in different contexts is part of this basic method. Accuracy rates for this first generation set of measures range from almost zero to somewhat better than chance, depending upon a host of situational and interpersonal factors.

The second generation of deception detection includes objective methods with accuracy rates substantially and consistently above chance. However, they are still by no means awe-inspiring, falling somewhere in the 60% to 85% accuracy range. The validity indices of the Minnesota Multiphasic Personality Inventory and the polygraph for arousal responses to crime-related stimuli are two examples in this category.

A third generation of methods has recently emerged in focal areas such as forced choice testing and neurocognitive assessment. Accuracy rates exceed 90% under the right conditions. In addition, models which may eventually lead to a general theory of deception have been created.

Although this book is more of an applied book than a learned treatise, a model of deception which has utility for the evaluator is presented. The proposed model covers (a) targets of the faker, (b) response styles shown, and (c) methods to detect the deception. It will take the reader far beyond the basic differentiation between malingering versus defensiveness as the two modes of distortion. The model proposes, for example, a fluctuating response mode as a distinct possibility, where the assessee may shift faking strategies during a single evaluation period. Hopefully, the forensic evaluator will find useful methods which can be applied to a variety of deception-related settings and situations.

This book has three general aims: 1) to summarize current information on distortion detection; 2) to present guidelines for detecting distortion which take into account the variable accuracy rates for different methods of deception detection and which consider the varying contexts in which distortion analysis may be relevant; and 3) to stimulate further research on effective methods of deception detection. The review of current detection methods includes experimental and judgemental methods as well as replicated and objective methods. The inclusion of these less accurate methods is not intended as an endorsement of their use by the practicing clinician, but rather as an impetus for refinement and development which may eventuate in more useful methods.

The data base of the authors consists of a review of several hundred articles and books on deception and direct evaluation of several thousand forensic clients over the last quarter century. New areas of deception have continued to emerge, with a reading list of source material now numbering over a thousand. This book attempts to address the focal issue of detecting distortion in forensic contexts, yet it is the writers' sense that all of the material included in the book contributes to a vigorous discussion of deception detection.

Several caveats are in order:

1. All cases in this book, are disguised to protect the identification of relevant parties.

2. Legal citations are included to illustrate trends and controversies in the law and are not intended to represent precedents in any particular jurisdiction. Locally applicable law should be reviewed to determine practices and standards in particular cases.

3. The state of the art in deception analysis is crude. It is tempting to press current methods into immediate service, yet caution should reign. This book is as much about prospects for the future as it is about practical guidelines for the present. Nevertheless, recommendations and guidelines for the practicing clinician are offered throughout the book, even when such counsel is simply to ignore a particular method.

4. This book requires readers to examine their own decision processes in regard to deception. Yet, many forensic professionals are reluctant to change their biases and values in regards to deception, especially when loss of self-esteem or prestige is equated with giving up cherished beliefs.

5. A common complaint is that proper deception analysis requires much time and effort, burdening the busy professional even more. This is true, but the authors have no sympathy for this problem. The days of administering an MMPI and a Rorschach to a client and thereby knowing everything there is to know about the person are gone forever.

The authors acknowledge the following individuals, many of whom have generously supplied time, ideas, manuscript reviews, and encouragement: (a) Marvin Acklin, Ph.D., Independent Practice, Honolulu, Hawaii; (b) Steven Alm, Esq., U.S. Attorney, Honolulu, Hawaii; (c) Edward C. Brennan, Ph.D., Social Security Administration, Scranton, Philadelphia; (d) James Craine, Ph.D., Consultant, Hawaii State Neuropsychology Service; (e) Frederick Lee Hall III, Esq., Veterans' Administration, Honolulu, Hawaii; (f) William Kilauano, Pacific Center for Post-Traumatic Stress Disorder, Honolulu, Hawaii; (g) James I. Morrow, MGySgt, USMC (Ret.), Vet Center, Hilo, Hawaii; (h) Terri Needels, Ph.D., Dean, American School of Professional Psychology, Kaneohe, Hawaii; (i) Eugene Shooter, Ph.D., Windward Counseling Center, Kaneohe, Hawaii; and (j) Udo Undeutsch, Ph.D., University of Cologne, Germany.

Permission was gratefully received from *Child Development* and *Forensic Reports*, the source of a number of data-based articles relevant to faked memory, to reproduce a variety of tables and figures. Contents of several other articles first appeared in the *American Journal of Forensic Psychology* and are so indicated. The American Psychiatric Press agreed to allow presentation of base-rate data on hysterical pseudoseizures, a vexing problem in deception analysis. John E. Reid and Associates allowed the reproduction of "The 9 Steps of Interrogation, In Brief," even though the authors have pronounced misgivings about deception to uncover deception (*see* Chapter 10). Scrutinizing methods at close quarters represents the first step toward understanding and limiting those techniques.

Many thanks are due to students and colleagues who have attended workshops and case conferences on deception. Appreciation is expressed to the staff of the National Institute of Justice, which has spent much time and effort in generating deception-related, base-rate data, especially in regard to violence and substance abuse.

Jerilynn Ono Hall, Esq. supplied many fruitful ideas on points of law and procedure. Lastly, special recognition is due to Helen H. Hashizume, who was extremely helpful in the preparation of this manuscript.

Harold V. Hall	David A. Pritchard
Kamuela, HI	Atlanta, GA

Introduction

Deception refers to inducing a false belief in another. Often successful and rewarded when undetected, victims of deception are subject to its influence even when they know they are being duped. False praise and adoration, as well as concealing dislike and loathing, allow smooth interaction with others—a social lubricant. Lovers and family members lie to one another in abundance. Business people and politicians distort as part of their natural interactions with others. "In everyday life it is usually possible for the performer to create intentionally almost any kind of false impression without putting himself in the indefensible position of having told a clear-cut lie. Communication techniques such as innuendo, strategic ambiguity, and crucial omissions allow the misinformer to profit from lies without, technically, telling any" (Goffman, 1959, p. 62).

Deception is learned early in life. Lying begins at a very early age, cuts across all socioeconomic statuses and educational groupings, and continues unabated into adolescence and young adulthood. Between one-third and two-thirds of high school and college students cheat (Collison, 1990a, 1990b), with the majority of college faculty observing cheating (Jendrek, 1989). More than 85% of college students were found to be deceptive to their partners, almost all in regard to other relationships and with the justification that they wanted to protect their partners (Shusterman & Saxe, 1990). In the writers' experience, much research with human subjects incorporates misleading, incomplete, or blatantly false instructions, rationalized by the belief that true knowledge of experimental procedures by subjects would bias results.

Almost all violence involves deception. In burglary, concealment, hiding the real, and blending into the environment are commonplace. Robbery often involves faking good, shown by innocuous approach behaviors, followed by faking bad (e.g., when the robber pretends to hold a pistol to the victim's back.) Kidnapping also uses a combination of faking good and bad, as when the location of the victim is concealed, coupled with threats to harm the victim for noncompliance. Victims and their significant others can ill-afford to test whether the perpetrators are bluffing.

Rape often involves substantial stalking and verbiage designed to lull the victim into complacency, and usually occurs at night or behind visual barriers. Date rape involves considerable trauma to the victim in spite of being acquainted with the rapist. Some serial rapists use a combination of faking good and bad, as Ted Bundy did when he concealed his intent to kill and had victims carry his books to his car because of his "broken" arm.

Deception is successful in many types of violence, perhaps partially explaining why the report rate is so low. People do not report what they believe will not result in direct action by authorities. Many violent offenders interviewed by the writers speak of how easy it is to commit violence and get away with it. They usually get caught when they don't practice deception, when they become substance intoxicated or impulsive, and the critical processes necessary for high-grade deception are impaired. Even murder, usually considered a crime of passion and therefore easily solved, has a 70% to 80% clearance rate—where the probable perpetrator is identified and brought into custody. Right off the top, this means that about 20% to 30% of the murders in this country are successfully concealed in terms of the identity of the killers.

Confidence games and white-collar crimes include forgery, counterfeiting, fraud, embezzlement, bribery, theft of services and trade secrets, smuggling, tax evasion, and now computer fraud. Always, the deceiver's position of fiduciary trust, power, or influence has provided the opportunity for exploitation. The Dictionary of Criminal Justice Data Terminology (U. S. Department of Justice, 1981), defines white-collar crime as:

> ...nonviolent crime for financial gain committed by means of deception by persons whose occupational status is entrepreneurial, professional or semiprofessional and utilizing their special occupational skills and opportunities. Also, nonviolent crime for financial gain utilizing deception and committed by anyone having special technical and professional knowledge of business and government, irrespective of the person's occupation.

The natural history of confidence games in America is provided by Nash (1976). Documented accounts include that of Dr. John Tennant of Virginia, one of a long line of "quacks" in this country, who provided rattlesnake root to cure pleurisy (1800). Some of the more bizarre, but successful, medical schemes in the 19th century included the two-part pill for tuberculosis. Here, the first part of the pill turned the urine bright green and frightened the person into taking the second part, made of licorice and saw palmetto. The litany of fraud continued with feeding bone-thin cattle herds salted food to fatten them before a sale (1815), fake inheritance con games (1835), bogus stock issuances (1854), police payoffs (1870), selling "sucker lists" to mail order houses (1881), and the start of the "wire"—obtaining the results of a horse race before the bookmakers (1898). David Mauer's *The American Confidence Man* (1974), A. A. Leff's *Swindling and Selling* (1976), and Darwin Ortiz's *Gambling Scams* (1990) each provide additional descriptions of how the con game works.

Base-rate studies of theft-at-work problems indicate that 26% to 42% of employees admit to stealing from their job, depending on whether the setting is a retail business, hospital, manufacturing company, fast-food restaurant, or supermarket (*see review by* Jones & Terris, 1990). These investigators cite statistics that show (a) a $1.8 billion increase in industry shrinkage from 1982 to 1987 and (b) a 50% reduction in shrinkage over an 18-month period during which integrity testing was initiated in a home improvement center (Jones & Terris, 1990). This finding has since been replicated by the authors. In general, employees who steal are very common, cause a huge amount of financial loss, and are almost never caught (Slora, 1989).

False presentations of self and deliberate distortions of intentions are part of the fabric of social life. From innocuous efforts to "make a good impression," to complicated schemes of fraud, to terrifying acts of violence, deception is an integral part of social interaction. The social science literature is replete with analyses of, and commentaries on, the varieties of human deception.

Detecting Malingering and Deception: Forensic Distortion Analysis (FDA) focuses on the detection of deception in one important situation: the forensic evaluation. To date, the clinical-forensic literature has not yielded a lucid, organized approach to the overall analysis and detection of faked behavior in forensic situations. Although individual techniques for detecting deception in the forensic evaluation have been evaluated (Rogers, 1988), no organized plan of detection has been offered.

This book discusses and demonstrates individual clinical and testing methods which may be applied readily to a wide variety of forensic situations. But, more importantly, it suggests a framework for integrating data on deception from multiple sources. Application guidelines and common errors to avoid in deception analysis are presented to forensic evaluators of various disciplines in the civil and/or criminal justice systems. The focus is on the overall problems of detecting deception, supporting one's conclusions and communicating findings rather than on specific techniques alone.

A sound method of deception analysis is proposed whereby the most likely target symptoms and response styles of the client are scrutinized, which then suggest specific detection methods. Topics in this book include (a) a general model of deception analysis; (b) applications in civil and criminal law; (c) psychometrics and structured interviewing; (d) forms and report language; (e) denied or minimized conditions: amnesia, dangerousness, sensory loss; (f) specific malingered conditions: pain, psychosis, post-traumatic stress; and (g) recent advances in the detection of deception (e.g., forced choice, explicit alternative testing, neurocognitive assessment).

Forensic Distortion Analysis (FDA) is defined generically as a set of interlocking procedures designed to answer focal questions relevant to deception. The definitional inclusion of "forensic" in FDA refers to the application of psychological principles to civil and criminal law; the word "distortion" suggests that nondeliberate distortion must be considered before offering statements regarding intentional deception.

The purposes of FDA are as follows:

1. To examine the reliability and validity of database information.
2. To detect the possible existence of misrepresentation.
3. To determine the response style(s) utilized by the client.
4. To determine the magnitude of distortion.
5. To place symptoms, behaviors, or mental conditions associated with deception into clear perspective.
6. To generate hypotheses for further evaluation/investigation.
7. To communicate the decision path and the findings of FDA to the referral source.
8. To eventually standardize the deception analysis process.

Metaphorically, FDA is an attempt to induce meaning from nebulous forms within shadows, an effort to validly and reliably distinguish illusive response styles within equally illusive mental conditions and psychological patterns. As difficult as it may sound, however, distortion analysis is possible.

PROFESSIONAL MISCONCEPTIONS REGARDING DECEPTION

Throughout the history of the mental health-law disciplines, beliefs about faking have been characterized by ignorance and vanity. We are naive about deception. We believe that we can tell if someone is deceiving us and that it does not happen very often. Actually, people are lousy at lie-catching. That is why deception is generally successful.

Although successive advances in distortion analysis have dispelled some misconceptions, others persist as follows:

1. Most spoken words and behavior can be taken at face value. Actually, as we shall see, most people distort, either unintentionally or intentionally. Popular surveys reveal that over 90% of average Americans say that they lie regularly (Gates, 1991). Many forensic professionals believe that distortion does not usually occur. They do not look for it. In the helping disciplines, false negatives may be less of an issue, but it is a problem when forensic issues are involved. Malingering has been confirmed or suspected in more than 20% of criminal defendants, with another 5% showing substantial unintentional distortion (Rogers, 1988). The deception rates for litigants in civil actions may be even higher.

2. Malingering, when it does occur, means that the faker is mentally sick. Desperate people often resort to desperate measures to survive or adapt. A person who fakes insanity is not necessarily mentally ill, but may want to avoid prison, a soul-destroying place under the best of conditions. As will be discussed, malingerers in general have good reality contact and are not psychotic. This myth may have been reinforced by the need to see psychopathology in liars when defendants or clients are misdiagnosed.

3. The evaluator cannot be fooled (other people can). A favorite trick in cross-examination of experts is the following (Ziskin, 1981, p. 100):
   Q. And it is possible for an individual to deceive you, isn't it?
   A. Yes, it is possible, but I don't think that I am fooled very often.
   Q. Well, if someone was successful in fooling you, you wouldn't know that he or she had fooled you, would you?

   Melvin Belli, the famed litigator attorney, recounted a case where a woman allegedly slipped on a greasy sauce on the floor of a restaurant, suffering a crippling hand injury. She was the ideal witness, "everybody's grandmother," giving a pitiful account about how she could no longer play the church organ until she bolted out the courtroom when the defense attorney showed how she collected $500,000 on a similar case in Florida. Belli used this case to illustrate how honest his clients are, and how he was duped for the first time in 60 years of practicing law. (Honolulu Star-Bulletin, January 25, 1991).

In general, health and legal professionals are not good at detecting faking (Ekman & O'Sullivan, 1991). Worse yet, an inverse relationship is suggested from research: the greater the confidence, the lower the accuracy in detecting faking.

The writers would like to believe that they are not fooled by forensic clients, given their experience and knowledge of the literature. The fact is that they would be fooled frequently without cross-validating data and standardized testing. A recent case illustrates this point:

Defendant Stardowsky, examined for criminal responsibility, stated to the examiner that the "glow" in the right side of his brain was quite clearly unequal to that in the left hemisphere. Forces of good (FOG) and forces of the enemy (FOE) operated in the jail where he was incarcerated for robbery. "The police hacked off my arms and legs; it's a good thing I didn't try to get away." Visual hallucinations of personages were affirmed, providing the basis for his Prolixin medication and schizophrenic diagnosis by the correctional facility medical staff. Several days later, the investigating probation officer revealed that the defendant's mental problems had never been raised as an issue in his 100-plus burglaries and robberies over the last 10 years. His parents pointed out that the accused had been playing the FOG and FOE story since the fourth grade, but only when he wanted to get out of trouble.

4. DSM-IV allows for deception analysis. DSM-IV states that malingering should be diagnosed if any combination of the following is shown (American Psychiatric Association [APA], 1994, p. 297):
    (1) medicolegal context of presentation (e.g., the person's being referred by his or her attorney to the physician for examination);
    (2) marked discrepancy between the person's claimed stress of disability and the objective findings;
    (3) lack of cooperation during the diagnostic evaluation and in complying with the prescribed treatment regimen;
    (4) the presence of Antisocial Personality Disorder.

However, these criteria are clinically inadequate. They fail to distinguish distorting influences such as evaluation-anxiety and fatigue from deliberate deception; they emphasize exaggeration and fabrication of symptoms to the neglect of denial and defensiveness; they associate deliberate deception with a personality type rather than with a person-in-a-situation. The reader is cautioned not to use the DSM-IV operational definition of malingering.

5. Some conditions (e.g., amnesia, hallucinations, post-traumatic reactions) are easily faked and nearly impossible to

prove. As will be presented, empirical methods can detect faked amnesia with promising degrees of accuracy. Hallucinations are hard to disprove, yet base rates for comparison and decision criteria are available to assist the evaluator. Post-Traumatic Stress Disorder (PTSD) can be assessed by psychometrics or arousal methods with built-in features to assess deception.

6. Detecting faking is an art and cannot be taught. Actually, the reverse appears to be true. Following a few simple rules increases the accuracy rate substantially. Deception analysis is a trainable skill. Workshops and clinical experiences over the years reveal that the average professional can be taught to adequately detect faking in a relatively short time.

Instructional material on deception analysis is embedded in the evaluation of (a) fitness to proceed and criminal responsibility (Hall, 1985, 1986); (b) post-traumatic stress disorder (Hall & Hall, 1987); (c) neuropsychological impairment (Hall & McNinch, 1988; Hall & Sbordone, 1993); (d) mitigating defenses to murder (Hall, 1990); and (e) dangerousness (Hall, 1982, 1984; Hall, Catlin, Boissevain, & Westgate, 1984). Detection tools include the MMPI and MMPI-2 as part of a comprehensive evaluation (Shooter & Hall, 1989), as well as process guidelines for deception analysis as a specific focus of inquiry (Hall, 1985; Paulsen & Hall, 1991).

Forced choice testing for deception provides a quick example of teaching others to detect deception. Learning a few statistical decision rules allows the evaluator to obtain a high degree of accuracy in assessing faked memory deficits. A series of investigations highlights the ease of learning how to administer the procedure and to interpret results (Hall & Shooter, 1989; Shooter & Hall, 1990; Hall, Shooter, Craine, & Paulsen, 1991). Figure I.1 shows the cumulative (non-overlapping) accuracy with which pseudo-malingering subjects in these three studies can be classified. Using one decision rule, only 58% of the subjects were correctly identified as "malingering." However, using multiple decision rules in a sequential strategy increased the positive hit rate to 95%.

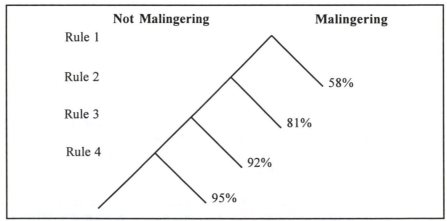

Fig. I.1 Classification of Pseudo-malingerers Using Multi-stage Rules

Table I.1 Applications of Deception Analysis		
Criminal	**Civil**	**Clinical**
Identification of perpetrators	Competency exams	Selection for treatment
Competency to proceed	Witness credibility	Readiness for discharge
Criminal responsibility	Child custody and divorce actions	Treatment motivation
Dangerousness prediction	Personal injury and wrongful death	Transference and countertransference
	Employment screening and dishonesty	Honesty of collaterals
	Eligibility for disability benefits	Community monitoring of treatment

APPLICATIONS

Deception analysis is a foundational issue in applied forensics. Table I.1 presents a number of clinical-forensic situations in which deception is a key issue (Hall, 1990). The emphasis of this book is on civil and criminal law applications.

DECEPTIVE SIGNS

What are the signs of deception? For what do evaluators look? Traditionally, the two most common factors are consistency and history. Does the subject present an inconsistent story of relevant events? Is there a positive history of misrepresentation? Unless specific and replicable, inconsistency as a factor is of small value in demonstrating deception.

Knowing that the assessee deceived others in the past is likewise of little help. Almost everyone has a substantial history of misrepresentation. High achievement-oriented children (i.e., future leaders of our society) actually seem to cheat more than their peers, perhaps to maintain their high status and other rewards that come from performing well academically (Grinder, 1961; Mischel & Gilligan, 1964). Adults are no better, as the above surveys demonstrated. Modern society appears to offer daily opportunities for distortion of the truth. Skill at faking may even be positively related to success in some professions, at least in western society.

Too many false positives emerge when applying the historical criteria—erroneously describing individuals as deceptive. This holds true when there is a history of criminality. Previous arrests, charges, convictions, or incarceration for crimes may not be helpful in determining whether the individual is presently deceiving in a specific context. Associating a history of maladaptive behavior with current faking is conceptually hazardous in another sense. A circular quality to utilizing history and mental illness or criminality emerges. Faking is seen as a symptom of maladaptation; proof that a person is mentally ill or criminal is taken as an indication of a tendency to distort and deceive. All this violates a basic premise of this book—that deception is adaptive and both cross- and intra-situation specific.

History, however, can be validly scrutinized in two ways. Are there contradictions between the reported and actual history of an individual? Differences are suspicious after mitigating factors, such as head trauma or drunkenness are taken into account.

The second way history can be scrutinized concerns whether or not a close "goodness of fit" exists between the relevant act and method (e.g., providing drugs to minors to obtain sex) and previous acts of the same kind.

A model of deception is presented in this book. Briefly, target symptoms of the faker selected in congruence with goal achievement are first considered by the evaluator. A veteran may malinger the intensity of his or her PTSD to obtain a higher service-connected compensation. A defendant may deny a history of violence to receive a lighter sentence for assault. A plaintiff may fake memory loss to obtain a large monetary settlement. A defendant may fake insanity to achieve exculpation and, hence, avoid penal incarceration. The task for the evaluator is to tap into these cognitive targets in order to determine whether they have led to faked or honest behavior.

The second part of the model deals with the response patterns of the deceiver, which fortunately cluster into variations of concealing the real or presenting the fake. The following response patterns seem most indicative of faking:

1. **A rapid improvement when external incentives change or when weak environmental triggers are presented**. A waxing or waning of response intensity is suspicious when it is in harmony with environmental events as when the deceiver knows he or she is being observed.

2. **Response patterns not congruent with neuropsychological or psychological conditions or symptoms**. This often involves the violation of anatomical laws (e.g., loss of feeling across widely separated sites allegedly due to spinal injury rather than according to expected deficits). Neuropsychological principles may also be suspiciously disregarded (e.g., loss of crystallized knowledge in presence of ability to learn and short-term recall skills).

3. **Critical behaviors during the interview such as absurd responses, unlikely combinations, and contradictory responses**. While not definitive by themselves, these critical behaviors should alert the evaluator to conduct a more intensive search for indicators of deception.

Detection methods are the third and last part of the FDA model. These include (a) variation from expected performance (e.g., errors on simple questions, violation of learning curves, deviant scores on parallel testing); (b) validity indicators (e.g., random patterns, subtle versus obvious discrepancies); and (c) failure on tests specifically designed to assess deception (e.g., Explicit Alternative Testing, tests of illusory difficulty).

For each faked condition discussed in this book, a synopsis of methods is provided at the end of the chapter. This will provide explicit guidelines on detecting deception. New directions which may have fundamental impact on the FDA are discussed. This includes neurocognitive assessment and computerized versions of forced choice, utilizing multiple decision rules. In the final analysis, it is hoped that a practical method of detecting deception will emerge from this inquiry.

As a starting point, this book attempts to equip the evaluator with data and procedures to answer relevant questions concerning deception. Several critical questions in every assessment of deception are as follows:

1. Am I properly trained to conduct an FDA? Have ethical issues in this case been considered?
2. What events triggered a referral for a deception analysis? What happened at that time?
3. Did unintentional distortion occur during the critical forensic event or evaluation? What is the source of that distortion and how was it measured?
4. Has the assessee engaged in deliberate deception? How is that known? Is the deception associated with the past or the present, or both?
5. What is the magnitude of the faking? Quantitatively or qualitatively, how can I demonstrate the degree of faking uncovered?
6. Does present deception differ from that shown previously by the assessee? What is the assessee's history of deception in similar situations?
7. What are the possible inducements to deceive for this particular forensic situation?
8. What is the deception response style shown by the client? Behaviorally, which variation of malingering or defensiveness is shown?
9. Who were, are, or will be the most likely targets of deception?
10. Which feedback mechanism can I suggest to assist future evaluators of this person's possible deception?
11. How can I fairly and accurately represent this person's possible deception to the referring party or trier of fact?

REFERENCES

American Psychiatric Association. (1994). *Diagnostic and statistical manual of mental disorders* (4th ed., revised). Washington, DC: Author.

Collison, M. N-K. (1990a, January 17). Apparent rise in students' cheating has college officials worried. *Chronicle of Higher Education*, A33-A34.

Collison, M. N-K. (1990b, October 24). Survey at Rutgers suggests that cheating may be on the rise in large universities. *Chronicle of Higher Education*, A31-A32.

Ekman, P., & O'Sullivan, M. (1991). Who can catch a liar? *American Psychologist, 46*(9), 913-920.

Gates, M. (1991, May 14). It's healthy to always be honest (Wait, we lied!). *Newhouse News Service*, Honolulu Star-Bulletin, Honolulu, HI.

Goffman, E. (1959). *The presentation of self in everyday life.* Garden City, NY: Doubleday.

Grinder, R. (1961). New techniques for research in children's temptation behavior. *Child Development, 32*, 679-688.

Hall, H. V. (1982). Dangerousness prediction and the maligned forensic professional: Suggestions for estimating true basal violence. *Criminal Justice and Behavior, 9*, 3-12.

Hall, H. V. (1984). Predicting dangerousness for the courts. *American Journal of Forensic Psychology, 2*, 5-25.

Hall, H. V. (1985). Cognitive and volitional capacity assessment: A proposed decision tree. *American Journal of Forensic Psychology, 3*, 3-17.

Hall, H. V. (1986). The forensic distortion analysis: A proposed decision tree and report format. *American Journal of Forensic Psychology, 4*, 31-59.

Hall, H. V. (1990). *Truth or lies: Guidelines for detecting malingering and deception.* Psychological Consultants and Forest Institute of Professional Psychology Workshop, East-West Center, University of Hawaii, Honolulu, Hawaii.

Hall, H. V., Catlin, E., Boissevain, A., & Westgate, J. (1984). Dangerous myths about predicting dangerousness. *American Journal of Forensic Psychology, 2*, 173-193.

Hall, H. V., & Hall, F. L. (1987). Post-traumatic stress disorder as a legal defense in criminal trials. *American Journal of Forensic Psychology, 5*, 45-53.

Hall, H. V., & McNinch, D. (1988). Linking crime-specific behavior to neuropsychological impairment. *International Journal of Clinical Neuropsychology, 10*, 113-122.

Hall, H. V., & Sbordone, R. (Eds.). (1993). *Disorders of executive function: Civil and criminal law applications.* Delray Beach, FL: St. Lucie Press, Inc.

Hall, H. V., & Shooter, E. (1989). Explicit alternative testing for feigned memory deficits. *Forensic Reports, 2*, 277-286.

Hall, H. V., Shooter, E., Craine, J., & Paulsen, S. (1991). Explicit alternative testing for claimed visual recall deficits: A trilogy of studies. *Forensic Reports, 4*, 29-37.

Jendrek, M. P. (1989). Faculty reactions to academic dishonesty. *Journal of College Student Development, 30*, 401-406.

Jones, J. J., & Terris, W. (1990). Integrity testing for personnel selection: An overview. *Forensic Reports, 4*, 117-140.

Leff, A. A. (1976). *Swindling and selling.* New York: The Free Press.

Mauer, D. (1974). *The American confidence man.* Springfield, IL: Charles C. Thomas.

Mischel, W., & Gilligan, C. (1964). Delay of gratification, motivation for the prohibited gratification, and response to temptation. *Journal of Abnormal Social Psychology, 4*, 411-417.

Nash, J. R. (1976). *Hustlers and con men.* New York: M. Evans & Co., Inc.

Ortiz, D. (1990). *Gambling scams.* New York: Carol Publishing.

Paulsen, S., & Hall, H. V. (1991). Common sense process factors in deception analysis. *Forensic Reports, 4*, 37-39.

Rogers, R. (Ed.). (1988). *Clinical assessment of malingering and deception.* New York: Guilford Press.

Rogers, R. (1990). Models of feigned mental illness. *Professional Psychology: Research and Practice, 21*(3), 182-188.

Shooter, E., & Hall, H. V. (1989). Distortion analysis on the MMPI and MMPI-2. *Bulletin of the American Academy of Forensic Psychology, 10*, 9.

Shooter, E., & Hall, H. V. (1990). Explicit alternative testing for deliberate distortion: Towards an abbreviated format. *Forensic Reports, 4*, 45-49.

Shusterman, G., & Saxe, L. (1990). *Deception in romantic relationships.* Unpublished manuscript. Brandeis University.

Slora, K. (1989). An empirical approach to determining employee deviance base rates. *Journal of Business and Psychology, 4*, 199-219.

U. S. Department of Justice. (1981). *Bureau of Justice Statistics* (2nd ed., NCJ-76939), p. 215. Washington, DC.

Ziskin, J. (1981). *Coping with psychiatric and psychological testimony* (2nd ed., Vols. 1-2). Beverly Hills, CA: Law and Psychology Press.

PART I

Background, Theory, and Method in Deception Analysis

FOUNDATIONAL ISSUES IN DECEPTION

Deception is widespread in human affairs. From the con man, to the crooked politician, to the cheating spouse, to the military strategist, making things appear other than what they actually are has been raised to an art form. In this chapter, we explore a variety of perspectives on deception, which help to define the scope, context, and study of human deception. First, we examine deception in non-human organisms in order to understand the most rudimentary features of deception. Second, we describe military deception as an example of the most developed, systematic use of deception. Then, we briefly discuss deception in the socialization process and its pervasive effect on personality. Fourth, we look at the ethics of deception as debated by moral philosophers and professional organizations. Last, we present suggestions for evaluating and using research results on deception.

A single, coherent field theory of deception is possible if it can cut across disciplines and account for the entire range of faking and falsehood. Once classification and theory-building have begun, application and prediction can better proceed. Thus, in this chapter, we will consider deception from a variety of perspectives. Examination of deception in nonhumans will help us to understand the purposes of deception; the strategies of military planners provide us with a systematic description of successful deception; discussion of our socialization in deceptive practices will remind us that we are all both givers and receivers of deception; the views of ethicists will aid us in evaluating the use of deception to detect the deceivers; and a review of principles of research interpretation will help us to distinguish theory-building from applied detection.

There can be no deception without an entity to deceive. As a corollary, all falsehood is interactional and all interpersonal transactions are subject to deception. Intentional deception always involves misrepresenting some aspect of the interaction and keeping it apart from the truth.

Psychologists, psychiatrists, and others in the helping professions have, with few exceptions, performed miserably in understanding this phenomenon. Typically, researchers in the social sciences have ignored deception or have viewed it as situation-dependent. Other investigators see it as a stable trait cutting across many contexts. Actually, it may be both. Trait conceptualizations of human behavior have validity. Crime profiling is built entirely on trait descriptors of the perpetrator from crime scene characteristics, for example, and has yielded some remarkable solutions in individual cases.

Cross-disciplinary concepts and methods are utilized in this book in order to understand deception. These include ideas from biology, philosophy, neuropsychology, cognitive science, and sociology. Statistics and probability theory are employed when appropriate. The binomial probability distribution, for example, provides the underpinnings for forced choice testing. Thus, as expanded upon later, if a claimant asserts loss of sensory ability as a compensable disorder due to an auto accident, the evaluator can compare total responses to expected responses. Detection rates for faking are quite favorable, now in excess of 90% for a variety of subpopulation groups.

Most investigation in deception, to date, has been in detection technology—observational schemes, paper-and-pencil tests, polygraph, "truth" serum, and so forth. The justification ranges from the cost of dishonest employees to the need of governments to conceal information for security reasons. In mental health, the justification is to provide better treatment. In forensic contexts, the evaluation of litigants is justified by the need to provide the trier-of-fact with accurate information.

The assertion by some that near absolute accuracy can never be achieved may be a dangerous untruth. Saxe (1991) predicted, for example, that such development is a fantasy because honesty is situational and because "[i]ndividuals have too many options available to encode their thoughts for us to be able to probe what they choose to hide." Recent technologies (e.g., DNA finger-printing, P300 wave analysis) are nearly 100% accurate. The latter method is based on brain waves associated with stimulus familiarity rather than arousal, as in polygraphy, voice stress analysis, and penile plethysmography (Farwell, 1990; Farwell & Donchin, 1986, 1988, 1989).

Indeed, forensic professionals and investigators face a moral dilemma much like researchers and practitioners in the physical sciences in their development of more accurate technologies. Given the increased tendency to exploit others through deceptive means on the parts of both institutions and individuals, this should cause real concern to the practicing professional. This issue of "too little" versus "too much" accuracy in detecting deception suggests both balance issues and ethical mandates, and will be reiterated as a central issue throughout this book.

PROTO-THEORY AND EARLY WORK ON DECEPTION

Deception has traditionally been seen as ubiquitous and adaptive in nature (see Dessoir, 1893; Binet, 1896; Jastrow, 1900). Some early conceptualizations viewed deception as originating in a universal instinct in the context of natural selection. Triplett (1900), a fellow at Clark University, explored magical tricks as his model for deception, stating that conjuring "...rests upon a universal instinct of deception—a biological tendency appearing throughout the animal world from simple forms to the highest orders, which acts as a constant force in the process of natural selection—as a means of preserving the self or species. This instinct, blind enough at the beginning, and to be classed as a deception only by reason of its effect, in the higher orders becomes implicated with an ever-increasing intelligence, ending with the conscious deceptions of man which in him, find their widest range and their highest form."

According to Triplett (1900), human deception traces its roots to mimicry, and conjuring is just one manifestation. In addition to revealing the secrets to known magical tricks in specific detail, Triplett commented on deceiver and target characteristics. The production of passive attention in the target was seen as essential for effective deception, implying that successful deception covaried with increased suggestibility of the target. The effect of conjuring should never be announced, and no trick should be presented twice, lest the target "catch on."

The best deceivers were seen as self-confident, highly disciplined and competent, socially graced, and given to planning. They should never rest on their laurels, and to achieve the best effect, should present deceptions in graduated form—each one having more impact than the previous. Thus, a strong achievement orientation is required. Every teacher was seen as some sort of conjurer by Triplett. Presaging qualities found in today's successful professionals, the same traits are mentioned today in describing excellent therapists, investigators, and forensic professionals across many disciplines.

Psychological work on deception emerged in the early 1900s before its promise faded. In a thought-provoking review of the deception literature, Hyman (1989) described the demise and resurgence of interest in this area as follows:

> Human deception deals with the correspondences between internal representations and external reality. The behavioristic psychology that dominated American psychology from the early 1900s until the cognitive revolution in the late 1950s had no room for mentalism of any kind, including the intentionalism inherent in psychology of deception.... Although those early accounts relied heavily on the prevailing associationalistic psychology, the principles they illustrate have aged surprisingly well and harmonize with the contemporary view of cognitive psychology. (p. 36)

Principles of deception discussed by Hyman (1989) from the early works include:

1. Perceptions are inferred from sensory input and are therefore subject to distortion. People have perceptual guidelines as to what constitutes reality, usually based on the most probable event, and these are capitalized upon by deceivers.
2. Knowledge of deception does not equal action to escape, avoid, or expose falsehood. The early literature is replete with examples in which deception was seen as positive (e.g., "white lies") or actually sought after (e.g., as in a magic show).
3. The notion of the invited inferences has relevance. A deceiver should lead targets into the desired outcome rather than tell them what they should believe or what the result will be.

More recently, Rogers (1990) has restated the adaptive nature of deception:

> Inclusion criteria for the classification of malingering are shaped and largely predetermined by our explanatory theories. Current theories have postulated the motivation to malinger is either the product of underlying psychopathology (pathogenic model) or criminal backgrounds (DSM III-R model). I have proposed a third model that malingering is typically an adaptive response to adverse circumstances which may best be understood in the context of decision theory. (p.27)

NONHUMAN DECEPTION

Animal investigation leads to implications for theory and practice; all forms of animal deception appear to have a parallel in human faking. Findings allow us to tighten up the behavioral factors in our descriptions of deception and to elucidate the cognitive-intent factors that may be employed. Lastly, principles from animal deception can be integrated into an overall theory.

A simple model of consummated deception involves the following sequence (Hyman, 1989; Mitchell, 1986; Whaley, 1982):

1. Organism "A" emits or conceals a stimulus.
2. Organism "B" picks up or misses the input. Misperception takes place.
3. Organism "A" obtains a favorable outcome or avoids an unpleasant consequence.

Here, "A" communicates to "B" a false or distorted message by emitting or concealing information. It is an untruthful message because it suggests an event of importance to "B" that will or will not occur. Successful deception results in a desirable outcome for "A," depending on whether the message is misperceived by "B," thus sustaining the deceptive patterns of "A."

An apparently desirable outcome for both "A" and "B" results from our preliminary analysis. Our simplest example actually comes from plant life. In Hawaii, a variety of plant, commonly called "sleeping grass," folds up when touched, assuming the appearance of limp, dead vegetation. While no one would suggest that the plant is deliberately distorting, apparent reward for both plant and possible eater of vegetation are operative. The plant stays alive and the eater avoids ostensibly unattractive food. In successful deception, the deceived behaves as if the false state of affairs had rewarding or punishing consequences.

Insects, such as butterflies with predator eyes on their wings, may fool their would-be eaters into believing that they are a danger, thus living to fly another day. The butterfly's predators may employ deception applicable to their own species.

Birds that "cry wolf" (Munn, 1986) provide another example of mutual possible reward. Two species of birds, *Lanio Versicolor* and *T. Schistogynus*, give a predator alarm call to scare off other birds, thus obtaining an unrestricted access to anthropoids in the area. Here, "A" gets food and "B" expects to preserve its life by escape.

The message by "A" must be believed to be effective. A balance between truth and falsehood must be achieved. Bond (1989), an ethnologist who writes of animal conflict, asserted that:

> ...the information in aggressive displays may not be strictly truthful, but may instead represent an "optimal deceit," a balance between the advantages of deceit or bluffing and the disadvantages of selecting for skepticism in the receiver.

Bond (1989) received corroborating data for his hypothesis by using a numerical simulation model, finding that an equilibrium level of deceit was described, even when "B" was unaware of the degree of deception by "A."

Deception among birds may be unintentional, yet effective. Already mated male Pied Flycatchers hide their mating status by singing in a secondary (nonnest) territory, thus increasing the probability of obtaining a second mate (Stenmark, Slagsvold, & Lifjeld, 1988). Not to be outdone, male chickens use food calling when no edible food is present to attract hens to the area (Gyger & Marler, 1988). Trained pigeons misreported the correct color of a light associated with a reward to a fellow pigeon also taught the procedure, thus obtaining more reward for themselves (Lanza, Starr, & Skinner, 1982).

Subtlety may increase as mammals are scrutinized, illustrated by the following:

> Cougar, the cat of the writer and his wife, is allowed to remain on a ledge along side the dining table provided she does not attempt to obtain food from the table. She has been well-trained in this "paws off" behavior over the years. When a particularly tasty fish dinner was served one evening, Cougar's attention was riveted at once. She moved toward the fish, only to be verbally admonished, so she returned to her original sitting position on the ledge. Feigning indifference and immobility, her eyes on the wall, she lay down and opened her mouth in a wide yawn. Her front left paw reached up as in a stretch, but instead of retracting it, her paw came to rest on the fish, paws spread out in a gripping posture. Her eyes, by this time, were on the fish, the yawn no longer in evidence.

Is this deception? Perhaps Cougar merely wished to stretch and found herself in a good position to obtain food. We don't know, yet the writer believes that deception did indeed take place. This belief appears to have predictive power in regard to Cougar's behavior in similar situations. She cannot be trusted totally to act in a nondeceitful fashion when her keeper's food is available.

Intentionality becomes more probable when lower primates are scrutinized for deception. The tactical deception of familiar baboons *Papio Ursinus* by peers has been illustrated (Bryne & Whiten, 1985). Deception in apes has been observed to include (a) use of camouflage, (b) feigning moods and curiosity, and (c) giving false motor signals to others (De Waal, 1986).

More ominously, there is now evidence that lower primates can and have engaged in warfare and murder with their own kind. Invasion of another territory, use of surprise and concealment, attacks on other chimpanzees using superior methods (e.g., coordinated movements, group attacks), and eventual extermination or chasing away of all males in the conquered territory have been documented.

The perpetrators were all chimpanzees of the famous Gombe Colony in Tanganyika, studied by primatologist Jane Goodall for over 10 years. Chimps in captivity at the famous Arnheim Zoo in the Netherlands have been shown to murder other chimps (Greene & Dewar, 1985). Deception and planning appeared to play an integral part of the violence.

Animal deception reveals two primary response tendencies—faking good and faking bad, both of which operate in any given deception to varying degrees. The former occurs when organisms deny, minimize, or conceal traits/events that would be noxious, dangerous, or otherwise unpleasant to the target, and/or pretend to have traits that are positive. Tiger stripes blending this predator into the background, an alligator hiding all but its nose and eyes under the water, and apes using foliage to conceal their presence from an enemy—all fit this criterion. Hiding the real, masking, camouflaging, blurring old patterns, and subtracting from the customary are further possibilities. Faking good always involves looking benign, better, or more attractive than one is in order to achieve a given outcome.

Faking bad is showing the false by pretending to have negative traits, or denying the genuinely positive to obtain a particular goal. Other descriptors include fabrication, exaggeration, conjuring, and mimicking, keeping in mind that a new pattern is copied or invented. Harmless snakes with skin patterns of poisonous vipers, birds that "cry wolf," and buffalo that stamp their feet and snort before a fight with a peer in mating season may fit this criterion. Faking bad always involves looking worse, more dangerous, sick, or negative than one is to accomplish some task or to obtain a desired outcome.

Presenting the false and concealing the real are present to some degree in both faking good and faking bad. For deception of either type to occur, the deceived must have engaged in withdrawal or approach, depending on its perception of the false event. Mixed forms of faking good and bad appear with regularity. The fox may fake good by concealment and hiding, only to feign death when trapped and exhausted.

Playing dead or wounded may be the prototype of human malingering. Common observation and the clinical lore on animals presents data across the phylogenetic scale:

- Plants which appear lifeless and limp when touched
- Spiders, coleoptera, and caterpillars which roll up into a ball when trapped
- Fish that appear dead when caught, only to swim away if set back in the water
- Plovers and other birds that feign a broken wing to draw predators away from the nest
- Opossums, foxes, and red squirrels feigning death when no escape seems possible
- Monkeys, chimpanzees, apes, and baboons playing dead when defeated by others of a similar species

In sum, the literature on animal deception provides a partial base upon which to build a general theory of human deception. The range and diversity of deceptive responses and the conditions under which they occur are paralleled in humans. A microanalysis of deceptive animal behavior also leads us into potentially fruitful areas such as primal response tendencies involving all deception—faking good and faking bad. By necessity, deception, in its simplest form, represents an interactional phenomenon—there must be another organism that will hopefully react in a desired manner. Table 1.1 illustrates a model of animal deception.

DECEPTION IN THE MILITARY

Table 1.1 Deceptive Styles in Animals		
Action	**Faking Good**	**Faking Bad**
D presents stimulus (shows the false)	T sees reward if deception true (e.g., cat "playing" with mouse)	T sees a punishment if deception true (e.g., birds that "cry wolf")
D removes stimulus (hides the real)	T sees no punishment if deception believed (e.g. tiger stripes)	T sees a punishment if deception true (e.g., opossum feigning death)

D = Deceiver
T = Target

Deceptive practices in the military provide an excellent example of deception in contemporary society (Handel, 1977, 1982; Reit, 1978; Whaley, 1969, 1982). Vast sums of money have been spent by the federal government in the systematic study of operational deception, principles of which have been applied in modern American wars.

The roots of current military thinking have their basis in the Old Testament of the Bible, Carl von Clausewitz' *On War* (translated in 1976), Chinese philosophers such as Sun Tzu's *Art of War* (translated in 1973), psychophysics and psychometrics, magic, and other sources.

Deception is viewed favorably by the military. It serves as a force multiplier by magnifying the ostensible strength of friendly forces, or by misdirecting the enemy in some other advantageous manner: cunning may be the only hope when friendly forces are under-strength. An inverse relationship is usually found between the amount of deception employed and the strength of the military force. Deception is cheap in terms of labor and capital.

Finally, deception seems to work in most cases, given adequate planning, which accounts for its high favor and continued use. Handel (1982, p. 145) stated:

> Since no effective measures to counter or identify deception have yet
> been developed, the inevitable conclusion is that deception—even if
> it does not achieve its original goals—almost never fails and will
> therefore always favor the deceiver, the initiating party.... Perceptual

and cognitive biases strongly favor the deceiver as long as the goal of deception is to reinforce a target's preconceptions or simply create ambiguity and doubt about the deceiver's intention.... Rationality dictates that a move which involves little cost and little risk of failure should always be included in one's repertoire.

The process of deceptive operations is most relevant to this book. Whaley (1982), and to some extent Handel (1982), described a sequence of successful deceptive operations involving deception by hiding (i.e., termed *masking, repackaging, dazzling*) and by presenting the false (i.e., termed *mimicking, inventing, decoying*). The following descriptive sequence is presented with illustrations for military and forensic evaluations from the viewpoint of the litigant:

1. Select a long-range goal with a definable outcome.
   a. Military strategists try to win a war; tactically, a surprise invasion may be a long-range goal.
   b. Litigants in criminal settings may attempt to escape the consequences of their conduct; those in civil settings may desire a substantial cash settlement.
2. Determine how the target should respond and what they should think as a consequence.
   a. Movement in a certain direction to violate concentration and economy of forces may be a military objective. The enemy should think that a distinct advantage will accrue, such as cutting off opposing forces.
   b. Defendants in insanity trials may want the trier-of-fact to award them the Not Guilty by Reason of Insanity (NGRI) verdict. The trier-of-fact should think that the defendant is in need of psychiatric help but is not a criminal in personality or deed.
3. Decide what is to be hidden and what is to be falsely shown about the facts. Hiding and showing are best when they are presented simultaneously.
   a. Hiding the real involves passive deception. Descriptors include *covert, obscure, deny, minimize, mask, camouflage,* and others.
      1) Masking: Real objects or activities are put out of sight in this type of deception.
         - Smoke screens cover activities in combat.
         - Past violence consisting of predatory aggression may be denied by the defendant.
      2) Repackaging: Disguise hides the real in this fakery.
         - A warship may be disguised as a freighter.
         - Conventional clothes may be worn by the defendant for a forensic evaluation in hopes of leading the examiner to conclude that one is not associated with a criminal subculture.
      3) Dazzling: Hides the real by confusion; the attempt is to blur a true pattern of events or responses.
         - Zigzag patterns are painted on war vessels.
         - Random patterns on testing or feigning confusion is sometimes seen in forensic clients.
   b. Presenting the false involves active attention and focused behaviors. Descriptors include *pretend, portray, profess, exaggerate, fabricate, invent,* and others. Successfully presenting the false is always based on successfully hiding the real.

1) Mimicking: Involves fake imitation or copying.
   - Cooks posted as infantrymen bolster the apparent strength of combatants.
   - Forensic clients may learn symptoms from actual patients.
2) Inventing: Presents or creates something entirely new.
   - Rubber tanks and wooden guns may mislead the enemy into believing in a false capability.
   - Fabricating visual hallucinations may convince evaluators of a psychotic process.
3) Decoying: Inverts and distracts the attention of the opposition by falsely presenting a second pattern.
   - Diversion in one battle zone with an attack in another is frequently, almost routinely, employed by the military.
   - Entering psychotherapy to create a basis for civil litigation is frequently suggested to plaintiffs by retained attorneys.
4. Consider opportunity variables to set the plan into operation.
   a. Ordnance and back-up equipment are made available for military operations.
   b. Factitious patients acquire the means to falsely portray illness; some aggressive defendants seek out the victim or witness to limit damaging testimony, or go to certain doctors whose outcomes are largely known beforehand.
5. Effect execution.
   a. Command and control units direct subordinate organizations to set the deceptive plan into action.
   b. Civil and criminal litigants execute the deception themselves; significant others occasionally attempt to deceive the evaluator at the behest of the defendant.
6. Send the distorted input to the target.
   a. Surrender leaflets must be read, seen as relevant, and construed with the intended meaning.
   b. The forensic evaluator must notice and see as genuine faked messages sent by the faker. Planning and rehearsal help increase believability.
7. Seek feedback on effectiveness of the deception effort.
   a. Outcome of battle and questioning of prisoners provide valuable insight into efficacy.
   b. Fakers frequently ask for feedback regarding how they have performed.

According to various commentators on military deception, personality traits associated with good deceivers include imagination, practicality, knowledge of the relevant culture and history, and empathy, with the ability to see things from the target's viewpoint. Other traits include a high degree of competitiveness, individualism, and asociality, with operators and planners not being the traditional "company" person. Trait analysis appears to be ad hoc in the military studies and may actually have a weak or absent association with successful deception.

The dangers of military deception are much more convincing. The biggest error is self-deception—believing and acting on one's own distortions. Time and again, individuals and countries are seen to display unjustified arrogance because of a few initial successes. Military lore reveals frequent examples of the deceived

party recovering and eventually achieving the upper hand. Targets usually re-
double their efforts when "faked out," improve their skills, and react to the adver-
sary with greater determination. The deceiver's bluff may even be called and
weaknesses exposed, their forces eventually defeated. A very real danger, then, is
short-term success with deception, followed by a negative long-term impact.

Paradoxical findings emerge from the military literature, which have relevance for the forensic evaluator. The more alert military planners are to deception, the more likely they are to be eventually deceived. Most evaluators have
been fooled by targets, creating skepticism about the truthfulness of the subjects.
The more skeptical we are of the data, the more we rely on preconceptions which
may or may not be accurate in particular cases. Conversely, once a source is seen
as credible, the harder it is for evaluators to disregard the data.

Countermeasures are possible, based on the assumption that deception can
never be 100% successful. The first is to keep open all channels of observation in
regard to a situation. This corresponds in forensic evaluations to having a large
and varied database, as clients may produce a consistent set of (distorted) data on
one or two measures. This strategy increases "noise," or extra nonusable data, but
the evaluator can sift through this excess information with a variety of sound
decision paths.

Generally, the better the reputation for honesty, the easier it is for countries,
military personnel, or individuals to lie. Frequent use of deception is associated
with loss of credibility. This yields another paradoxical finding. Honest and high
status people are the best liars in that they are believed the most. Military officers
and high-ranking civilian employees would fit into this category. Thus, they would
be good deceivers in any planned operation.

In sum, the military literature on deception has some important lessons for
the forensic evaluator. The military has clearly described the steps necessary to
successful deception and has cataloged a variety of deceptive tactics which may be
employed.

Socialization in Deception

American society is characterized by ambivalence regarding deception and
lying. Whereas misrepresentation in business is condemned, undercover tactics
and "sting" operations by law enforcement agencies are tolerated and even ap-
plauded. Lying in the name of national security is an acceptable practice, while
lying to protect one's privacy is a reason for dismissal from employment. Lying
during union negotiations or budget hearings is a common, even expected, practice, for which adjustments are automatically made. Social scientists are gaining
a reputation for deceptive research practices, while their students are soundly
punished for cheating in their classes. Electronic evangelists preach a rigid morality, while converting donations to the maintenance of a hypocritical lifestyle.

Deception in contemporary America is both tolerated and condemned. We
transmit this ambivalence to our children and it is reinforced throughout development by cultural practices. Lying is one of the first interactive verbal behaviors to
develop (Stouthammer-Loeber, 1986); it continues to be displayed and denied in
adolescence and adulthood (Shusterman & Saxe, 1990).

One early influence on deception may come from fairy tales and fables. Children are taught early on the values of good and evil by their caretakers, as well as about distortion and deception. In *Puss and Boots* (Charles Perrault), a fake drowning is concocted to convince a king that Puss's master, the Marquis de Carabas, needed to be saved. Puss subsequently threatens to "chop into fine pieces" any worker in the area who would not lie by affirming that the Marquis indeed owned a large, attractive tract of land. Puss then murders the real land owner, pretending to be awed by the latter's abilities. The Marquis, who is aware of the deception, is rewarded with the land, marries the murdered king's daughter, and makes Puss the prime minister.

Faking bad is illustrated by the heroine's sisters in *Beauty and the Beast* (Madame Leprince de Beaumont), who rubbed onions in their eyes in order to cry. In *Cinderella*, also by Charles Perrault, the wicked stepmother pretends to be nice to Cinderella until she marries Cinderella's father, then heaps work and abuse on her. Not to be outdone, Cinderella yawns and pretends to have been asleep when opening the door for her stepfamily returning from the ball, when in actuality, she had just returned from the ball herself.

Deception is presented in children's stories in other cultures as well. In the Russian fable, *Finn, the Keen Falcon*, the heroine attempts to hide a diamond pin in a piece of pie dough, but is observed by her jealous sisters. The Sea King's daughter in the Japanese fable, *Urashima and the Turtle*, changes into a turtle to see if a fisherman would eat her, thereby proving that he had a good heart when he did not do so.

Virtually all popular fairy tales and fables told to children by their caretakers contain substantial deception by one or more of the principal actors. In those stories, deception is usually successful for those who initiate it. "Bad" deception is done by bad people, usually involving those with self-centered or base motives; "good" deception is performed by the heroes and heroines and is justified in terms of their righteousness and object goal. "Good" faking always triumphs over "bad" deception.

Children may be fed powerful messages about deception at a critical time in their development—when they form their notions about interactions with others and work through the Ericksonian issues of trust, autonomy, and initiation (Erickson, 1968). Identification with the hero or heroine who deceives may allow children to successfully work through basic mistrust, shame, doubt, and guilt by creating illusions of reality upon which they can operate. A smoother fit into the adult world can be anticipated and perhaps is the principal function of learning fables.

Negative side effects emerge from this incidental learning. The differences between good and evil, base and altruistic, crazy and normal are not at all clear and appear to vary as a function of antecedents, the act itself, and the consequences of the deed, whether intended or not. Without ascribing to a relativistic view of morality, children taught the absolutes of virtue and favorable outcome, and provided with role models who have the same characteristics (and win on top of that) may lack flexibility of thought and action when encountering reality. Unlike our view of Pinocchio's nose, much deception is nonverifiable, with unintentional distortion and deliberate deception merging together in overlapping and unmeasurable ways.

More insidiously, an identification of self with the good—the hero or hero-ine—may take place from exposure to these fairy tales and fables. One may come to believe that deception is carried as a virtuous by-product of this basic goodness. Self-righteousness may result.

Forensic professionals risk carrying these myths from childhood. Our decep-tion in investigation is justified because it is performed by an ethical person and leads to a worthy end. Deception by offenders, in comparison, is loathsome. When they fool us, we become indignant. From a logical, as well as phylogenetic, per-spective, it is incredible to believe that defendants would not engage in deception to avoid imprisonment or some other aversive outcome.

In civil contexts, personal injury and workers' compensation plaintiffs may feel that they not only deserve the possible financial reward, but that they need it to survive. Deception is not surprising.

Anger at being deceived may say more about the evaluator's self-beliefs than about the deceiver. It may also reflect overexposure to mythology in one's culture, providing the basis for a rigid and judgmental cognitive style.

In sum, the widespread ambivalence towards deception in American society likely pervades our perceptions, attitudes, beliefs, and behaviors. Detecting decep-tion in others requires a candid appraisal of its presence in our own lives and practices.

DECEPTION AND MORAL PHILOSOPHY

No one would argue that deception in plants and animals is immoral. Their deception can be evaluated solely on its consequences: it either has adaptive value and ensures survival or it does not. In humans, however, deception can become immoral in spite of advantageous consequences. Forgery, impersonation, consumer fraud, and perjury may all be adaptive and advantageous, but are nonetheless regarded as immoral and sometimes illegal.

Moral philosophers generally agree that deception which produces intended or foreseen harm is wrong. The deceptive act itself may be morally neutral—as in keeping a secret (Bok, 1989b), but the intentional harm that follows condemns the entire enterprise. Failing to reveal defects in a car, switching brand labels on a consumer product or concealing limitations in one's skills are not immoral *per se*, but become wrong from the harm that follows. At the very least, deceptive practices unfairly alter the choices of the deceived by obscuring alternatives, the costs/benefits of those alternatives or the probabilities of desired outcomes. Thus, potentially injurious consequences are one basis for evaluating the ethics of hu-man deception.

A more hotly debated issue is whether or not certain deceptions by humans are wrong in themselves, irrespective of their intended or foreseeable consequences. The debate has focused on deceptive statements (i.e., lying) rather than on all types of deception. St. Augustine, Immanuel Kant, and John Wesley are among those who have argued that lying is always wrong and admit of no exceptions. Statements made with the intent to deceive may differ in the harm they cause, but they are always wrong, even if just in a technical sense. The condemnation of all forms of lying generally rests on its violation of natural law, its threat to interper-sonal trust which is necessary for society's survival or its affront to the dignity of other persons (Fagothey, 1967). Each of these arguments elevates a greater good above any outcome which might accrue from a lie.

The sweeping rejection of all lies has led to provocative debates about its implications. Why, for example, is it justifiable to use force in self-defense, while it is unjustifiable to lie for the same reason? Should a would-be assassin be directed to his intended target to avoid lying to him about the victim's whereabouts? Should a lie be avoided, if it would ensure the salvation of a million souls?

Such debate has produced logical subdivisions of lies, which allow important distinctions among lies, while at the same time preserving the categorical condemnation. St. Thomas Acquinas, for example, distinguished mortal from venial lies and argued that forgiveness of the latter is easier than of the former. Some scholastics have defined lies strictly in terms of the discrepancy between one's "mind" and one's statements. This distinction permits liars to use silent statements to themselves to reverse the apparent intent of their spoken words (akin to crossing one's fingers behind one's back while lying to another). Still other philosophers define a group of intentional misstatements which are justified because the deceived has no right to know the truth.

Utilitarian philosophers, on the other hand, do not categorically censure lying. For them the ethics of a lie are determined by balancing the positive and negative consequences of the lie. Some deceptive statements to some people under some circumstances are morally acceptable (even preferable) and other lies to other people under other circumstances are morally repugnant. This situational ethic avoids the machinations needed to apply a categorical condemnation of lying to the real world.

However, the utilitarian view of lying has its own problems. First, it is frequently difficult in the real world to estimate the complex costs and benefits associated with a lie. Complex issues, like nuclear power, abortion, and the death penalty, do not easily lend themselves to the simple calculation of costs and benefits; lies about these issues do not make the calculations any easier. Second, the situational justification of lying provides no mechanism for correcting the biases of the liar. Since the justification is essentially private, it is too easy for the would-be liar to first settle on the desired outcome (to lie or not lie) and then to adjust the calculations to support that alternative. Third, the utilitarian view of lying assumes that lying *per se* is morally neutral and is not accorded an initially negative weight (cost) which must be overcome by especially positive benefits. This neutral view of lying *per se* overlooks the inherent harm done to society when even justifiable lies are offered.

The moral philosophers have not provided a simple checklist or set of rules for evaluating lies. But, their discussion, disagreement, and analysis have provided a perspective which must be considered in any discussion of human deception. Bok (1989a) offered a contemporary application of this perspective which may serve as a guide to discussions throughout this book:

> ...we must ask, first, whether there are alternative forms of action which will resolve the difficulty without the use of a lie; second, what might be the moral reasons brought forward to excuse the lie, and what reasons can be raised as counter-arguments. Third, as a test of these two steps, we must ask what a public of reasonable persons might say about such lies. (pp. 105-106)

These three questions assume that lying is a last resort which must be justified by moral reasons acceptable to reasonable persons other than the would-be liar. While not resolving the centuries-old debates in moral philosophy, this perspective demands a stringent accounting of lying in strictly moral terms.

The authors are especially interested in applying the moral perspective to the methods used by professionals to detect deception and lying in others. Must clients be informed that one purpose of an evaluation is to assess the genuineness of their self-presentations? Should clients be informed that a particular test's sole purpose is to detect malingering? Is it ethical for professionals to lie in order to detect deception in clients?

Perhaps the published ethical statements of leading professional organizations will provide guidance on these questions. The *Ethical Principles of Psychologists* (American Psychological Association, 1989) states:

> Principle 8a. In using assessment techniques, psychologists respect the right of clients to have **full explanations of the nature and purpose of the techniques** [emphasis added] in language the clients can understand, unless an explicit exception to this right has been agreed upon in advance.

The proposed revision of the *Ethical Principles of Psychologists* (American Psychological Association, 1992) states:

> Standard 1.7(a). When psychologists provide assessment, evaluation, treatment, counseling, supervision, teaching, consultation, research, or other psychological services to an individual, a group, or an organization, they first provide the patient or client with **appropriate information about the nature of such service** [emphasis added], and they later provide appropriate information about results and conclusions.

The *Specialty Guidelines for Forensic Psychologists* (Committee on Ethical Guidelines for Forensic Psychologists, 1991) states:

> IV.E. Forensic psychologists have an obligation to ensure that prospective clients are informed of their legal rights with respect to the anticipated forensic service, of **the purposes of any evaluation, of the nature of procedures to be employed** [emphasis added], of the intended uses of any product of their services, and of the party who has employed the forensic psychologist.

The *American College of Physicians Ethics Manual* (American College of Physicians, 1989), in discussing disclosures to patients, states:

> In general, **full disclosure is a fundamental ethical requirement** [emphasis added]. However, ethicists recognize the "therapeutic privilege," which is an exemption from the most detailed disclosure when such disclosure might inflict serious emotional damage, impair rational decision-making, or otherwise harm the patient. **On balance, the therapeutic privilege should be interpreted narrowly** [emphasis added]; if it is invoked without justification, it can undermine the whole concept of informed consent.

These excerpts offer varying advice to the practicing professional. The 1989 statement by the American Psychological Association requires a "full explanation" of assessment services and techniques. This position would appear to prohibit both deceptive practices (e.g., nondisclosure) as well as outright lying to clients. However, the revised statement by the same organization requires only "appropriate information about the nature of such services." Presumably the practitioner is to decide personally what is appropriate for disclosure and what is not. This revised statement appears to allow nondisclosure of information to a client, if the practitioner deems such nondisclosure appropriate, but does not specifically address the ethics of lying to a client, even if such lying is deemed appropriate. The Forensic Psychologists' Ethical Standards (1991) statement obliges, without exception, the practitioner to inform clients of both the purpose of an assessment and the nature of procedures to be used. This position leaves little room for either nondisclosure or lying. The American College of Physicians' (1989) statement requires full disclosure to patients, except when the patient may be personally harmed by such disclosure. This statement seems to allow nondisclosure under limited circumstances, but to prohibit nondisclosure in general. The statement is ambiguous regarding the ethics of intentional misstatements to clients.

This variety of opinion represents the full spectrum of moral positions on full disclosure, from categorical rejection of deception by a practitioner to utilitarian acceptance of deception depending on the judgment of the practitioner. There appear to be no easy answers to the moral questions posed by deception and no agreement among thoughtful practitioners. Perhaps the most that individual practitioners can do is (1) be sensitive to the moral issues involving the detection of deception, (2) consult with colleagues on the ethics of particular practices, and (3) adopt consistent procedures which address the ethical issues involved.

In summary, the ethics of human deception can always be evaluated in terms of its consequences, while the ethics of lying (as a special case of deception) must be evaluated differently. Before adopting deceptive practices (e.g., nondisclosure), the individual practitioner must evaluate the potential harm which the practice may cause. However, lying (i.e., intentional misstatement) has such general, negative consequences that it requires extraordinary justification before reasonable persons will condone it. The statements of various professional organizations all differ on the ethics of deceiving clients through nondisclosure and are generally silent on the ethics of lying to clients.

EVALUATING AND USING RESEARCH RESULTS ON DECEPTION

Forensic experts commonly refer to the wealth of research supporting their conclusions, predictions, and opinions. Little distinction is made between research which supports a particular theory or conceptualization and research which supports an applied prediction or classification.

Any discussion of research on deception must carefully separate that research which supports "theories" of deception and deception-detection from that which supports actual predictions of deception. Research on theories relevant to deception focuses on the validity of hypotheses regarding the process of deception or the process of deception-detection, while research on the prediction of deception focuses on the validity of predictions of deception.

The practitioner, concerned with detecting deception in particular cases, needs to review the available research on deception. But only some of that research is immediately useful in the individual case. The following guidelines should be considered in evaluating research studies:

1.   **A significant relationship between a variable and deception does not necessarily indicate that the variable is a good predictor of deception.** Some research findings bear on the processes of deception and deception-detection rather than on the outcomes of deception-detection. Research on impression management and self-presentation (e.g., Schlenker & Weigold, 1992) is clearly relevant to deception, but only some of the research is relevant to the accurate identification of individual deceivers. Ekman (1985) described how nonverbal behaviors (e.g., posture, tone of voice, facial expression) may leak information about the truthfulness of a person. Such findings provide valuable information about the processes of deception, but do not provide reliable clues to deception in individual cases. Ekman (1985), for example, warned that these clues may be related in individual cases to genuine emotions or to the person's feelings about being suspected of lying. The practitioner is cautioned that "behavioral clues to deceit should only serve to alert you to the need for further information and investigation" (p. 189).

In general, research reports of mean differences between groups of "deceivers" and "nondeceivers" or of correlations between test scores and malingering do not provide justification for use of the reported measures for detection of deception in individual cases. Such group differences and correlations do not address the important question of predictive accuracy. Group differences on Rorschach variables, for example, do not reflect the accuracy of predictions made with a particular cut-off score.

Even when a research finding focuses on individual prediction rather than group correlates, a statistically significant relationship does not necessarily indicate a good predictor. The value of a variable as a predictor of deception is determined by its effect size not by its statistical significance (Cohen, 1977). Since the significance of a statistical relationship is determined in part by the sample size of the study, it is possible for a weak relationship (small effect size) to attain statistical significance. Such weak predictors will not prove useful in the prediction of individual cases. Good overall predictors of deception are those which show a large difference (effect size) between deceivers and nondeceivers.

2.   **Some good predictors of deception are "locally" rather than "generally" valid.** For example, being bald is a good predictor that one is male, but having a full head of hair is not a good predictor of being female. Amount of head hair is a poor general predictor of sex, but being bald is a good local predictor of being male. In general, a variable may be unrelated to a criterion throughout its entire range, but still be related to the criterion within a local region of its range.

In deception research, a low value on a scale or the absence of a "sign" may be unrelated to truthfulness, while a high value or the presence of the "sign" may indicate deception. A low MMPI F-scale score, for example, tells us nothing about deceptiveness, but a high score increases the likelihood of deception. An anatomically impossible symptom predicts deception, but the presence of a plausible symptom does not predict a genuine disorder.

Such asymmetrical relationships between predictors and deception function to lower overall tests of statistical significance, which are based on the entire range of values of the predictor. Thus, it is possible for research results which yield nonsignificant or small effects nonetheless to discover good predictors of deception.

These "local" predictors of deception are most clearly revealed in decision tables rather than in t-tests or correlation coefficients. Decision tables relate ranges of values on the predictor (e.g., high, medium, low) to values on the criterion (e.g., deceptive, nondeceptive) (Wiggins, 1973). Such classification tables permit analysis of the relationship between successive local ranges of the predictor and the criterion rather than just the overall relationship between predictor and criterion.

3. **Different research comparisons have differing practical implications**. Published research on malingering typically involves group comparisons between (1) normal subjects instructed to "fake bad" and normal subjects instructed to respond normally; (2) normal subjects instructed to "fake bad" and genuine patients instructed to respond normally; or (3) patients suspected of malingering instructed to respond normally and genuine patients instructed to respond normally. These three types of comparisons yield widely varying accuracy rates and resulting scales, patterns, and cut-off scores are applicable to widely different evaluation situations.

For example, Leavitt (1987) reported that a measure of pain was 82% accurate in detecting normal subjects instructed to fake pain, but only 64% accurate in detecting genuine pain patients who were instructed to exaggerate their pain. Similarly, Berry, Baer, and Harris (1991) reported in a meta-analysis of MMPI indicators of malingering that the mean effect size for studies comparing normal subjects with normal subjects instructed to "fake bad" was 2.66, the mean effect size for studies comparing genuine patients with normal subjects instructed to "fake bad" was 1.86, the mean effect size for studies comparing genuine patients with patients instructed to exaggerate was 1.48, and the mean effect size for groups inferred to be malingering with other groups was .83. Thus, the accuracy of detection methods varies greatly with the type of discriminations being made.

The results of studies which compare normal subjects with normal subjects instructed to "fake bad" are most relevant to evaluation situations which themselves involve this comparison (e.g., detecting malingerers among job applicants). The results of studies which compare genuine patients with normals instructed to "fake bad" are most relevant to situations where malingerers are seeking admission to patient status. The results of studies which compare genuine patients with other patients instructed to exaggerate their symptoms are most relevant to situations where current patients are seeking additional treatment attention benefits. In terms of the MMPI results reported by Berry et al. (1991), MMPI indices of malingering are likely to be most accurate in situations where they are least needed (e.g., distinguishing genuine normals from faking normals) and to be less accurate in situations where they are needed most (e.g., distinguishing suspected malingerers from genuine patients).

4. **A good predictor is not necessarily a useful one**. Discovery of a good overall or local predictor of deception is necessary but not sufficient for useful predic-

tion of deception. It must also be shown that the predictor is useful in the situation in which it is applied. Meehl and Rosen (1955) discussed the influence of base rates (prior probabilities) on errors in prediction. If deception is very rare or very frequent in a particular situation, a good predictor will nevertheless produce a large number of incorrect predictions. Indeed, if the base rate is low enough, a good predictor with even a low error rate can produce more incorrect than correct predictions!

Even a predictor which produces more correct than incorrect predictions in a particular situation may not be useful. A false prediction in one situation is not necessarily as serious as a false prediction in a different situation. Falsely predicting malingering in a neurological case may have more dire consequences than falsely predicting dishonesty in hiring. Indeed, Swets (1992) has argued that the best decision rule for any given test is strictly a function of the base rate of the condition being evaluated and the relative costs of false positive and false negative decisions. Without knowing anything at all about the accuracy of a particular test, sign, or other decision rule, it is possible to define its usefulness in given situations. In general, assessment procedures for malingering will be less useful in situations with a low base rate for malingering than in situations with a higher base rate for malingering. "That is, one should not make the positive decision very readily when the chances are great that the negative alternative will actually occur" (Swets, 1992, p. 525). In addition, conservative rules for predicting malingering will be more useful than liberal rules when the relative cost of falsely calling someone "malingering" is greater than the relative cost of falsely calling someone "genuine." These costs of misclassification may differ considerably from one situation to another, even when the assessment decision (e.g., neurological malingering vs. genuine impairment) and base rates are the same. For example, it can be argued that the costs of falsely calling some "malingering" is greater when the decision is irreversible (e.g., in courtroom testimony) than when the decision is reversible (e.g., in treatment where new information continuously updates treatment plans).

Of course, evaluation of the costs of predictive errors depends on one's values and one's investment in the outcome. Whether refusal to hire an applicant falsely labeled as "dishonest" is evaluated positively or negatively depends on whether you are the employer or the applicant. But the difficulty of balancing competing interests does not minimize the effect of those disparate values on the prediction process. What would be helpful is a public discussion of the relative costs of mispredicting "malingering" and of mispredicting "genuineness" in real-world situations (e.g., medical diagnosis, eligibility for disability, need for involuntary treatment) as perceived by consumers, decisionmakers, institutions, and society in general. Such discussion would help to define the type of decision rules (conservative vs. liberal) appropriate to situations with different base rates of "malingering" (low vs. medium vs. high) and with different costs of misclassification (high false positive costs vs. high false negative costs).

A final factor in determining the usefulness of a malingering assessment procedure is the cost of administering the procedure. A procedure which appropriately minimizes costs of misclassifications for a given situation may not be useful if it is prohibitively expensive to administer. Most clinicians would be unwilling to spend three hours assessing the "genuineness" of a one-hour screening evaluation. However, the same three-hour assessment may be a bargain when the relative cost of a misclassification is high enough (e.g., selection of astronauts for long-term space missions). Similarly, equipment costs may offset the value of accurately classifying subjects. Buchwald (1965) presented a discussion of the impact of the cost of testing on decisions whether or not to use a test at all. In some situations, the cost of detecting "malingering" may be greater than the cost of tolerating undetected "malingerers."

5. **The accuracy of an individual prediction is all-or-none.** Statistics on the accuracy of predictions and classifications (e.g., valid positive rates, positive hit rates) always reflect the results of a series of decisions. An assessment procedure is used with a group of people and the accuracy of the procedure is determined for the entire group (i.e., for the series of individual decisions). This type of accuracy information provides an empirical basis for deciding which procedures, cutting scores, signs, or other decision rules to use for particular purposes. For a particular purpose, the procedure with higher accuracy is preferable to one with lower accuracy; for a particular assessment situation, one cutting score is more accurate than another cutting score; for a given set of classificatory costs, a less costly procedure is preferable to a more costly procedure.

However, none of these statistics reflect the accuracy of a prediction in an individual case. When an assessment procedure for "malingering" has a positive hit rate of 80% (for a particular base rate), the probability that a person with a positive score on the procedure is actually malingering is not .80. The probability of an individual prediction being correct is always either 1.0 or 0.0. A prediction in an individual case is always either correct or incorrect. The positive hit rate, valid positive rate, etc. associated with a particular procedure refer only to the relative frequency of correct decisions among a series of decisions, not to the probability of being correct in a particular case.

However, the accuracy statistics associated with a particular procedure in a particular situation can be used in a logical argument to support the decision in a particular case (Movahedi & Ogles, 1976). Given that 80% of persons with a positive score on a malingering test are in fact malingering and given that Mr. Jones has a positive score on the test, it is "80% logical" that Mr. Jones is malingering. In other words, the claimed probability is a measure of the logical relationship between the premises and the conclusion and not a measure of the empirical truth of the conclusion. Given the following premises:

Seventy-five percent of persons with X, Y, and Z are malingering and Mr. Jones possess X, Y, and Z, the proper conclusion is not that "There is a 75% chance that Mr. Jones is malingering," but rather that "It is 75% logical that Mr. Jones is malingering."

Alternatively, accuracy statistics can be regarded as a measure of the decisionmaker's confidence in an individual conclusion rather than as a statement about reality. A rational decisionmaker would have more confidence, for example, in an individual prediction based on a procedure with a positive hit rate of 80% than in an individual prediction based on a procedure with a positive hit rate of 50%. The proper conclusion in the above syllogism is that "I am willing to bet that Mr. Jones is malingering."

With either interpretation, an individual decision is empirically either correct or incorrect, but the decisionmaker has a rational basis for acting on the decision in this particular case.

In summary, research on deception is relevant to the actual detection of deception only when it presents results on the predictive accuracy of general or local predictors of deception in research groups similar to those with whom the detection method will actually be used. These results are best evaluated in decision or classification tables which allow determination of the error rates associated with the predictor. Predictors with low error rates must then be evaluated in terms of their usefulness in particular situations. The usefulness of a procedure involves considerations of (1) the base rate of the condition being assessed in the situation where the procedure will be used, (2) the relative costs associated with false positive and false negative classifications, and (3) the cost of administering the procedure. The accuracy statistics for a given procedure can be used in a logical argument that assessment results in individual cases should be used as if they were empirically true.

SYNTHESIS

This chapter asserts that deception is an ubiquitous, adaptive, and potentially detectable phenomenon. Discussions are presented on deception in nonhumans, deception in the military, deception during socialization, deception and ethics, and research findings on deception detection.

Deception in its most rudimentary form in animals involves either presentation of the false or concealment of the true by the deceiver and induces either attraction or avoidance in the deceived. The goal of animal deception is always adaptive. In its more developed forms in humans, deception has been elaborated into a systematic strategy for achieving specific objectives. In between these two extremes are shades of distortion which are nondeliberate and unintentional, but which nonetheless obscure the truth.

The spectrum of deception among humans may be evaluated for its adaptive or strategic consequences, but must also be considered from an ethical perspective. Even if deception produces important outcomes, can it be recommended as a moral practice to be encouraged by society? Both ethicists and professional organizations disagree on the morality of deception in general and lying in particular.

This ambivalence towards deception is reflected throughout our culture. Socialization practices, as illustrated in the fables and fairy tales communicated to our children, glorify the use of deception by the "good guys" and vilify its use by the "bad guys." As adults, we are quick to justify our deceptions in terms of our good intentions.

The forensic expert is not immune from these ambiguities and contradictions. Should a subject's deception be viewed as adaptive or immoral? Is the deception intentional or nondeliberate? Is it justifiable to lie to a subject to unmask his pretense? How can the expert be "objective" in evaluating the deceit of another? Does scientific research really support his opinion?

Although this book cannot answer these difficult questions, it can provide a framework for detecting deception in others. This framework makes explicit the data, assumptions, and decisions of the expert and therefore, makes them available to public scrutiny. Others will then be in a position to agree, criticize, argue, and debate the expert's opinion.

REFERENCES

American College of Physicians. (1989). American College of Physicians Ethics Manual. *Annals of Internal Medicine, 111*(3), 245-251.

American Psychological Association. (1989). *Ethical principles of psychologists.* Washington, DC: Author

American Psychological Association. (1992, May). Ethics code. *APA Monitor,* 30-35.

Berry, D., Baer, R., & Harris, M. (1991). Detection of malingering on the MMPI: A meta-analysis. *Clinical Psychology Review, 11,* 585-598.

Binet, A. (1896). Psychology of prestidigitation. *Annual Report of the Board of Regents of the Smithsonian Institution* (pp. 555-571). Washington, DC: Government Printing Office.

Bok, S. (1989a). *Lying: Moral choice in public and moral life.* New York, NY: Vintage Books.

Bok, S. (1989b). *Secrets: On the ethics of concealment and revelation.* New York, NY: Vintage Books.

Bond, A. B. (1989, January). Toward a resolution of the paradox of aggressive displays: I. Optimal deceit in the communication of fighting ability. *Ethology, 81*(1), 29-46.

Buchwald, A. M. (1965). Values and the use of tests. *Journal of Consulting Psychology, 29,* 49-54.

Byrne, R. W., & Whiten, A. (1985, May). Tactical deception of familiar individuals in baboons (Papio ursinus). *Animal Behavior, 33*(2), 669-673.

Cohen, J. (1977). *Statistical power analysis for the behavioral sciences.* New York, NY: Academic Press.

Committee on Ethical Guidelines for Forensic Psychologists. (1991). Specialty guidelines for forensic psychologists. *Law and Human Behavior, 15,* 655-666.

Dessoir, M. (1893). The psychology of legedermain. *The Open Court, 7,* 3599-3602, 3608-3611, 3616-3619, 3626-3627, 3633-3634.

De Waal, F. (1986). Deception in the natural communication of chimpanzees. In R. Mitchell & N. Thompson (Eds.), *Deception: Perspective on humans and nonhuman deceit* (pp. 527-529). Albany, NY: State University of New York.

Ekman, P. (1985). *Telling lies: Clues to deception in the market place, politics, and marriage.* New York: W. W. Norton and Company.

Erickson, E. (1968). *Identity: Youth and crisis.* New York, NY: W. W. Norton & Co.

Fagothey, A. (1967). *Right and reason: Ethics in theory and practice.* St. Louis, MO: C. V. Mosby.

Farwell, L. A., & Donchin, E. (1986). The "brain detector": P300 in the detection of deception [Abstract]. *Psychophysiology, 23*(4), 434.

Farwell, L. A., & Donchin, E. (1988). Event-related potentials in interrogative polygraphy: Analysis using bootstrapping [Abstract]. *Psychophysiology, 25*(4), 445.

Farwell, L. A., & Donchin, E. (1989). Detection of guilty knowledge with ERPs [Abstract]. *Supplement to Psychophysiology, 26*(4A), 439.

Farwell, L. A. (1990). Personal communication.

Green, C., & Dewar, S. (1985). *The ascent of the chimps.* Film by New Wilderness III, Inc. Distributed by Prism Entertainment Corp., Los Angeles, CA.

Gyger, M., & Marler, P. (1988, April). Food calling in the domestic fowl. Gallus gallus: The role of external referents and deception. *Animal Behavior, 36*(2), 358-365.

Handel, M. I. (1977, September). The Yom Kippur War and the inevitability of surprise. *International Studies Quarterly, 21*(3), 461-502.

Handel, M. I. (1982, March). Intelligence and deception. *The Journal of Strategic Studies, 5,* 122-154.

Hyman, R. (1989). The psychology of deception. *Annual Review of Psychology, 40,* 133-154.

Jastrow, J. (1900). *Fact and fable in psychology.* Cambridge, MA: Riverside Press.

Lanza, R. P., Starr, J., & Skinner, B. F. (1982, September). Lying in the pigeon. *Journal of the Experimental Analysis of Behavior, 38*(2), 201-203.

Leavitt, F. (1987). Detection of simulation among persons instructed to exaggerate symptoms of low back pain. *Journal of Occupational Medicine, 29*(3), 229-233.

Meehl, P., & Rosen, A. (1955). Antecedent probability and the efficiency of psychometric signs, patterns or cutting scores. *Psychological Bulletin, 52,* 194-216.

Mitchell, R. W. (1986). A framework for discussing deception. In R. W. Mitchell & N. S. Thompson (Eds.), *Deception: Perspective on human and nonhuman deceit* (pp. 3-40). Albany, NY: State University of New York.

Movahedi, S., & Ogles, R. (1976). Prediction and inference in criminology. *Criminology, 14*(2), 177-188.

Munn, C. A. (1986, January). Birds that "cry wolf." *Nature, 319*(6049), 143-145.

Reit, S. (1978). *Masquerade: The amazing camouflage deceptions of World War II.* New York: Hawthorn.

Rogers, R. (1990). Development of a new classification model of malingering. *Bulletin American Academy of Psychiatry and the Law, 18*(3), 323.

Saxe, L. (1991, April). Lying: Thoughts of an applied social psychologist. *American Psychologist, 46*(4), 409-415.

Schlenker, B., & Weigold, M. (1992). Interpersonal processes involving impression regulation and management. In M. Rosenzweig & L. Porter (Eds.), *Annual Review of Psychology* (pp. 133-168). Palo Alto, CA: Annual Reviews, Inc.

Shusterman, G., & Saxe, L. (1990). *Deception in romantic relationships*. Unpublished manuscript. Brandeis University.

Stenmark, G., Slagsvold, T., & Lifjeld, J. T. (1988). Polygyny in the pied flycatcher. Ficedula hypoleuca: A test of the deception hypothesis. *Animal Behavior, 36*(6), 1646-1657.

Stouthammer-Loeber, M. (1986). Lying as a problem behavior in children: A review. *Clinicial Psychology Review, 6*, 267-289.

Swets, J. A. (1992). The science of choosing the right decision threshold in high-stakes diagnostics. *American Psychologist, 47*(4), 522-532.

Triplett, N. (1900). The psychology of conjuring deceptions. *The American Journal of Psychology, 11*(4), 439-510.

Tzu, Sun (1973). *The art of war* (translated by S. B. Griffith), p. 133. New York: Oxford University Press.

von Clausewitz, C. (1976). *On war* (edited and translated by M. Howard & P. Paret), p. 203. Princeton, NJ: Princeton University Press.

Whaley, B. (1969). *Stratagem: Deception and surprise in war*. Cambridge, MA: Center for International Studies, MIT.

Whaley, B. (1982). Toward a general theory of deception. *The Journal of Strategic Studies, 5*, 178-192.

2

Involuntary Distortion

Generally, all information relevant to Forensic Distortion Analysis (FDA) comes from the actor, the one acted upon, and the context in which it occurs. Interdisciplinary and multisourced in nature, no discipline or school of thought has cornered the market on deception analysis. This does not mean that the information must be gathered first-hand by the evaluator; rather, the issues surrounding FDA make it impossible for one discipline or individual to answer all the biological, psychological, and social questions in deception analysis.

The Evaluator's Database

An adequate database for FDA requires information relevant both to the times of the evaluation and to the time of some past event. Thus, at the very least, the examiner must scrutinize two time periods. This is particularly important in light of the tendency of clients to fake differentially depending on the time period involved. Many criminal offenders, for example, fake bad for the time of the alleged crime only to fake good for the present (e.g., when applying for release from hospital incarceration). The database continues to expand until all referral questions are addressed. It is secured, protected against scrutiny, utilized again if needed, and eventually destroyed.

As an initial step, the evaluator must gather information. Possible sources include:

1. Interviews of significant/knowledgeable others;
2. Behavioral observations of the possible deceiver in individual and group, structured and unstructured, stressful and nonstressful situations;
3. Functional analysis of previous (i.e., historical) deception;
4. Analysis of validity indicators on psychological testing;
5. Analysis of learning curves and expected performance in intellectual and neuropsychological methods;
6. Competence assessment;
7. Medical and laboratory analysis;

8. Neurological testing using PET, CAT, and MRI technologies;
9. Semantic and transcript analysis;
10. Body "leakage" analysis;
11. Autobiographical materials (e.g., diaries, letters);
12. Records produced by others (e.g., military, school, job);
13. "Expunged" records in the state or federal archives;
14. Intervention paradigms designed to assess deceit by changing it; and
15. Base-rate analysis for traits of groups in which the deceiver holds membership.

The analysis then proceeds to a synthesis of the findings. All known factors are considered; weights, if estimable, are given to the various factors. A judgment is rendered in terms of the evaluator's confidence in the findings and possible degree of accuracy. Hopefully, the synthesis is verifiable and replicable by independent examiners. A good working rule is that deception must be demonstrated, not simply arrived at by ruling out other possibilities.

The evaluator should recognize that *ground truth* for any event, free of camouflage and faking, stands by itself and can be measured. Murders do happen and can be solved despite some "actors" attempts to conceal or disguise their occurrence. Auto accidents may cause genuine neurological damage for the plaintiff, who might exaggerate the symptoms in an effort to collect compensation. Normal persons have faked their way into hospitals (and residential programs) for various reasons (Rosenhan, 1973); abnormal individuals have faked their way out of these settings. Some people even fake symptoms in others, for example, in Munchausen by Proxy, in which a person (typically a parent) induces or claims a physical problem in another (typically a child). In all of these situations, a reality exists separate from the faking. We call this reality *ground truth*.

Deception manifests itself in the ways the deceiver attempts to fool others within a certain context. Ground truth always represents itself as an interaction of actor, acted upon, and context; deception represents a departure from what actually transpired in this three-entity interaction. Unfortunately for the deceiver, deliberate deception takes energy and thought and often times reveals inconsistency. This can be uncovered with diligence and method.

Nondeliberate Distortion

Unintentional distortion of words or behavior is common. It must be considered before the individual's behaviors are understood, and placed into perspective prior to the examiner concluding that deliberate deception has taken place.

Nondeliberate distortion can be analyzed in terms of (a) the reporting person, (b) the reported event, and (c) evaluation methods. Table 2.1 presents the more common nondeliberate distortion factors. The examiner should scan this list routinely in every assessment of deception before conclusions are rendered.

For example, in a recent case that involved the defendant shooting a police officer in the abdomen with a large caliber pistol, the officer experienced a gross stress reaction. The forensic report read as follows:

Nondeliberate distortion due to stress and other factors appears to have been operative to a significant degree.

Officer Jones reported, for example, during the instant offense, perceiving his alleged assailant as between 5'7" to 5'10" tall and weighing "far more" than 200 pounds (actually, the perpetrator stood 5'4" and weighed 180 pounds). Temporal events were seen as stretched out in duration (the victim estimated 10 minutes for the entire time span of the violence; actually, it was more like two or three minutes at most). Some relevant details were not recalled (e.g., the license plate number of the vehicle allegedly belonging to the defendant, the behavior of the nearby witness during the time of the shooting). This is not surprising. Research has shown that as people switch from normal states into General Adaptational Syndrome (GAS) behaviors which may be associated with threats to their lives or well-being, they become less attuned to details because they are more concerned with immediate safety needs. Generally, memory for details and sequences can be demonstrated, but recall is less clear than normal. Time estimates are especially vulnerable to exaggeration—in some studies by a factor of two and a half to one (e.g., see Buckhout [1980]). Size and weight of the defendant are usually overestimated with poor recall of perpetrator's clothing, as with the officer-victim.

Table 2.1
Nondeliberate Distortion Factors

1. Reporting Person
   a. Stress
   b. Physical disability
   c. Limited intelligence
   d. Inattention
   e. Recall problems
   f. Psychosis
2. Reported Event
   a. Too brief
   b. Physical barriers
   c. Weak intensity
   d. Distractions
   e. Figure-ground merging
   f. No stimulus uniqueness
3. Evaluation Errors
   a. Unreliable measures
   b. Invalid measures
   c. Inadequate training
   d. Leading questions/procedures
   e. Emotional evaluation contexts
   f. Assessed event in remote past

DISTORTION GUIDELINES

A dozen guidelines for the evaluation of unintentional distortion should be considered:

1. **Use multimodel methods.** Standardized interviews, observation, review of records, and interviews of significant others can yield valid results; however, the evaluator should not rely on insight alone based upon these traditional sources of information. If psychometric tests are administered, a battery of tests should be utilized. This addresses the issue of single tests versus a composite battery. Often, evaluators search for a quick sample of faking on a standardized instrument. It is highly unlikely that all parameters of deception will be covered by a single test instrument. In addition, an inordinate amount of false negatives and positives may be generated.

The choice of a battery should typically include measures for possible genuine problems as well as for deliberate deception. Faking often accompanies nondeliberate distortion, as the evaluation of the defendant who shot the police officer revealed:

> Nondeliberate distortion for the defendant may include a chronic condition of borderline retardation with specific learning disabilities. Specific chronic deficits noted on standardized testing two weeks before the instant offense included (a) a short attention span, (b) a borderline level of memory for general information, (c) a low average word knowledge (vocabulary) and social comprehension (common sense), and (d) an inability to cognitively process visual stimuli due to selecting specific visual cues in a maladaptive or inaccurate manner.
>
> He was unable to effectively handle selective visual cues. He experienced excessive anxiety, tension, and emotional conflict. Results on another test indicated a limited visual awareness for noting essential details of the human figure and social immaturity, and (e) confusion when listening. The Detroit Tests of Learning Aptitude showed problem areas in auditory sequencing and vocabulary skills.
>
> The Durrell Listening Comprehension results were at the third grade level. In general, results from the most recent testing are in accord with 10 years of previous evaluation results which suggest significant problems in attention, both visual and auditory stimulus processing and recall, and language comprehension.
>
> The defendant admitted lying to the police officer when he stated he had not been drinking beer and in regard to the ownership of the assault weapon. After the shooting, the defendant told bystanders that a nearby witness was the actual perpetrator. He then drove from the scene, covered his car with bushes in a ravine, and attempted to hide in the mountains.

A standard clinical battery—Wechsler Adult Intelligence Scale-Revised (WAIS-R), Minnesota Multiphasic Personality Inventory-2 (MMPI-2), Sentence

Completion Test (SCT), Bender-Gestalt Visual-Motor Test (BGVMT), and an interview—consistently revealed faking in this case. Tests designed specifically to detect faking can be included in a composite battery of tests in spite of the possibility that the assessee has considerable nondeliberate distortion.

2. **Start with the most valid information first**. Data considered first most influences the evaluator. Premature closure and/or attempts to confirm what the evaluator already believes may lead to incorrect conclusions. The evaluator can consider data with the highest "hit rates" for accuracy first and suspend his or her conclusions (e.g., lab data for substance consumption at the time of the relevant event) until all data is analyzed.

3. **Adhere to validated decision rules even when tempted to abandon them for a particular case**. Decision rules are more accurate than clinical judgment. The evaluator should ask why he or she is tempted to abandon the validated decision rules in the first place. What biasing factors may be operating?

4. **Think base-rates**. Knowledge of base-rates alerts the evaluator of deception as to the general chances that certain events will occur. Literature will be cited later to provide base-rate information in deception analysis. It would be helpful, for instance, if the evaluator knew that between one-third and one-half of defendants malinger memory problems in murder cases, with a 25% overall rate of such malingering when pleading insanity.

Studies show, almost 50% of substance use is verbally underreported compared to the results of urinalysis, yet the percentages differ depending on the particular locality and substance involved. On a test of remote memory, people generally do not err on autobiographical questions even if they are brain-injured. Further, base-rate information is all that may be available to the evaluator in certain types of crimes, (e.g., serial homicides where the perpetrator is unknown). For some types of unverifiable problems (e.g., suicide ideation, command hallucinations), base-rate information may be the only data available to the evaluator as a springboard for deception analysis.

5. **Do not become overly focused on unique, salient, or unusual case features**. Some evaluators consider the behavior in question to be genuine when a psychopath cries during the rendition of the instant offense. Conversely, evaluators have viewed a rape victim as not being credible because she was a prostitute and a belly dancer.

6. **Do not fall prey to illusory associations between evaluation responses and supposed faking**. These unfounded associations include the following:
   a. From the ancient literature, a burnt tongue from a hot sword indicates deception.
   b. Responses to white spaces on the Rorschach means oppositional tendencies.
   c. A lucid and reasonable account of the crime under hypnosis spells genuineness.

Evaluators should be wary of meaningless scores on tests measuring deception. Recall that:

a. Scores regress toward the mean with extreme scores showing the greatest change upon retesting.
b. Small samples frequently misrepresent population parameters.Unfortunately, most of the specific tests for malingering fall into this category.
c. Scatter can be due to chance and, thus, not indicate deception or other relevant dimensions.
d. Chance occurrences can be seen as ordered.
e. The year when a test is normed affects the scoring pattern.
f. Reliance on highly intercorrelated measures is frequent. Evaluators tend to confirm same problems when they use redundant testing. For example, administration of the MMPI and the California Personality Inventory (CPI) produces the same results in deception analysis.

7.   **Do not assess deception from DSM-IV criteria**. Making incorrect associations between a diagnosis and certain traits may result in falsely attributing faking or honesty. For instance, a diagnosis of Antisocial Personality Disorder does not always imply lying and a diagnosis of Adjustment Disorder does not automatically mean that the labeled person is telling the truth. In general, no mental condition automatically indicates deception or honesty.

As discussed in the Introduction, the DSM-IV criteria for malingering are fatally flawed. Any forensic problem could be seen as malingered if the assessee was uncooperative or happened to be diagnosed as Antisocial Personality Disorder. The need for a marked discrepancy between the subject's presented deficits and outside findings is important. Unfortunately, DSM-IV provides no threshold criteria for evaluating such discrepancies.

8.   **Do not fail to consider triggers to ostensibly concealing or uncooperative behavior**. Clients have bad days. The need to assess over several sittings is important. Evaluators may have atypical days. Frustration or stress unrelated to the evaluation may be communicated to the assessee, who may show countertransference as a result. The cause and effect relationship may be overlooked by the evaluator, who may report distorted results.

One trigger to distortion is commitment bias—the tendency to repeat a wrong answer if given a second chance to respond. It is operative when the subject wants to please the evaluator and believes that the assessor thinks a certain choice is correct. The client, for example, may pick out the wrong face again in a photo line-up due to this bias. Unconscious transference is another trigger. This occurs when a person seen in one situation is confused with another, such as when one sees the partial face of a person in a subway and concludes it was the defendant's face.

9.   **List alternative hypotheses and seek evidence for each**. The evaluator should systematically list disconfirming and confirming data for each conclusion rendered. This may result in more accuracy; there is some evidence that evaluators who deliberate longer are most accurate.

10.   **Do not fail to limit and operationalize conclusions**. The evaluator should note the confidence in results as well as indicate the degree of defendant distortion which may have occurred. A feedback mechanism to reassess results should be specified—for example, a readministration of the same measures when a forensic issue reemerges.

11. **Do not overload the referring party or trier-of-fact with data**. The average working memory holds about seven bits of information at a time. There may be a decrease in accuracy in most people due to overload after that point. The writers try to give jurors no more than about one-half dozen critical points in their attempts to synthesize overall presentation in court.

12. **Make a deliberate effort to get feedback**. At a bare minimum, cross-validating information should validate findings on deception. Normative data regarding distortion and deception for one's area, practice, or circumstances should be systematically collected. Age, sex, educational level, and ethnic differences should be noted.

Hindsight bias should be avoided. This occurs when an evaluator believes, after the fact, that the outcome could have been easily detected. It can be demonstrated by asking evaluators to estimate their own accuracy levels and comparing them with known results. Foresight in FDA focuses instead on what comes next in a deception problem.

SYNTHESIS

Generally, nondeliberate distortion needs to be ruled out or taken into account before deception is considered. Ground truth may be misrepresented by both nondeliberate and deliberate deception.

The issues in separating deliberate from nondeliberate distortion are important for both the individual and society. In criminal trials, jurors appear less willing to exculpate and judges may be harsher in sentencing when the defendant has been caught at deception. In civil cases, awards may be reduced (or eliminated) for behavior seen as deceptive.

Evaluators should know the behavioral-science literature on deception to reduce their own nondeliberate distortion. This exercise will serve to keep one humble. The literature on deception is incomplete and fragmentary up to 1990. Even worse, there is a persistent use of invalid or marginally acceptable techniques to establish that deception has occurred. These include the traditional clinical interview, forensic hypnosis, drug-assisted interviews, and some arousal methods (e.g., the voice stress analyzer, penile plethysmograph). These methods are not held in high esteem in this book mainly because, for the most part, their scientific validity is lacking or disappointing.

The purpose of this chapter will be well-served if the evaluator of deception follows a few simple guidelines as presented. Ground truth is that abstract absolute in forensics; it is the Holy Grail which we all seek. Separating us from ground truth is distortion, both intentional and unintentional. In a post hoc analysis of deception, unintentional distortion must be ruled out or accounted for first, as it may explain the evaluation findings. The forensic evaluator should routinely check for factors and events associated with nondeliberate distortion and report upon these in consultation or trial testimony. Failure to do so renders conclusions regarding intentional deception meaningless.

REFERENCES

Buckhout, R. (1980). Eyewitness identification and psychology in the courtroom. In G. Cooke (Ed.), *The role of the forensic psychologist* (pp. 335-339). Springfield, IL: Charles C. Thomas.

Rosenhan, D. L. (1973). On being sane in insane places. *Science, 179,* 250-358.

3

THE APPLIED FORENSIC DISTORTION ANALYSIS MODEL

Forensic Distortion Analysis (FDA) mandates a close scrutiny of the actor, yourself as evaluator, and the context in which the distortion occurs. To comment upon possible faking by a murderer, you must be intimately familiar with the homicide. To state that cerebral insult stems from a car accident, you should know how the person typically behaved prior to the alleged trauma. To claim that a rehabilitation client is deliberately sabotaging therapy due to secondary motives, you must be aware of your own countertransference, an insidious and often overlooked source of self-deception.

This chapter focuses further on the FDA model by discussing (a) the symptoms targeted for deception which may reflect goal formulation and perhaps planning on the part of the faker; (b) behavioral output in the form of typical styles of deceptive responding; and (c) the means used to understand and measure these response patterns. Figure 3.1 presents these aspects of deception analysis.

TARGET SYMPTOMS

As a rule, fakers choose target symptoms in accordance with the direction of their vested interests. People choose what they think will work to accomplish their goals. Much knowledge of psychological and medical conditions has been publicized in the media. Thus, actual neuropsychological symptoms may be selected for bogus head trauma. Amnesia may be chosen when a gap in memory is self-serving in a violent crime. Targets are not to be confused with goals, which may include anything from avoiding prison to obtaining a monetary reward. Targets are short-term in nature; goals represent the ultimate objective of the faker.

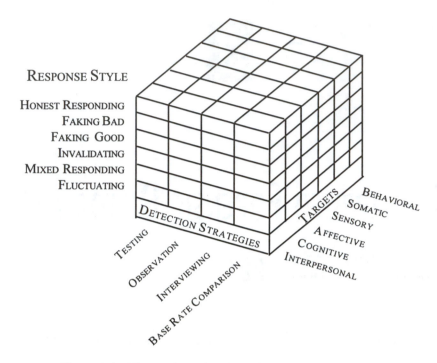

Figure 3.1. Three Dimensional Model of Distortion Analysis

Selecting a target means that the faker makes assumptions about both ground truth and distortion. Psychosis cannot be faked without having an idea of how a psychotic person behaves. This gives the evaluator an advantage by putting the onus for performing on the deceiver.

Targets can change as a function of many factors such as opportunity, fatigue, and evaluator behavior. The goal, however, usually remains the same (e.g., wanting compensation for a back injury). Some targets are nonverifiable, particularly suicidal ideation, pain, hearing voices, and trauma-related nightmares. Finally, targets are often based on partially real deficits and represent an exaggeration of deficits rather than pure fabrication. The best lie is the partial truth.

A simple method for listing cognitive targets is presented in Table 3.1. All the major dimensions of deception in terms of targets are covered. The *behavioral* category includes verbal or motor acts as targets. *Somatic or psychosomatic* targets and symptoms include a broad-band category of physical signs. *Sensation* refers to faked deficits in vision, hearing, smell, taste, touch, temperature, pressure, balance, and pain. *Affect* can involve autonomic and/or emotional events which may be distorted. *Cognitive* problems include deficits in attention, memory, language, and thinking. *Interpersonal* deficits involve faking when reporting upon the interaction with others. Table 3.1 presents clinical examples of target symptoms.

In sum, targets involve any short-term objective which, when reached, are in the direction of the faker's vested interest. The targets (a) may change over time, during the evaluation, and/or subsequent to the evaluation; (b) may be specific or broad-band in focus (e.g., tics, dementia); (c) are based upon cognitive schemes, experience, sophistication, and available disguises; (d) must be differentiated from nonfaked behaviors; and (e) can be translated into discrete response styles which can be measured.

+---+

Table 3.1
Targets of Deception

Category	Examples
Behavioral	
Motor	Slowness/agitation
Verbal	Mutism; aphonia
Somatic/Psychosomatic	
Central nervous System	Epileptic seizures; paralysis
Other Systems	Factitious arthritis; muscle weakness
Sensation	
Visual	Visual hallucinations; partial blindness
Auditory	Hearing voices; deafness
Tactile	Intense or persisting pain
Taste	Gustatory insensitivity
Smell	Olfactory hallucinations; loss of smell
Imagery	
Perception	Flashbacks; illusions
Dreaming	Nightmares; night terrors
Affect	
Autonomic	Anxiety; rage
Emotional	Lability; major depression
Cognitive	
Attention	Stupor; unconsciousness
Memory	Amnesia; recall problems
Language	Aphasia; word salad
Thinking	Schizophrenia; dementia
Interpersonal	
Social	Imposture; Munchausen by proxy

+---+

RESPONSE STYLES OF DECEPTIVE BEHAVIOR

Response styles are the second part of the FDA model. The heart of FDA is in the analysis of response styles. Only through behavior can we infer deception. Response styles are connected to targets in the nature of cause and effect even though targets can be quickly conceived of or yield poor (i.e., detectable) patterns of behavior.

The basic response styles for deception are presented in Table 3.2

Table 3.2 Basic Response Styles	
Response Styles	
1. Honest Responding	Attempts to be accurate within own frame of reference; may show nondeliberate distortion.
2. Faking bad	Exaggeration of fabrication of symptoms and negative features; denial and/or minimization of positive traits/events; misattribution of deficit to false cause.
3. Faking good	Minimization and/or denial of symptoms and behaviors; exaggeration or fabrication of positive points; misattribuation of blame to outside source.
4. Invalidating	Attempts to render the evaluation meaningless.
5. Mixed Responding	Combination of styles within same evaluation period.
6. Fluctuating	Change of style within or between evaluation period(s).

HONEST RESPONDING

Despite the focus of this book, most individuals have built-in prohibitions against deliberate deception. In forensic intervention settings, many clients are distressed psychologically or physically and just want to be well again. Returning to work or a meaningful lifestyle is a powerful reinforcer; most clients believe that nondeceptive behavior is proper and essential to achieve these goals.

In the criminal arena, defendants, witnesses, and significant others are reminded of their moral duty, which is reinforced by legal sanction, for truth-telling. Possible charges relating to perjury and hindering prosecution add incentive to tell the truth. For defendants, malingering is strongly suspected in about 20% of the cases (Rogers, 1988). This means that the vast majority of defendants are not engaging in blatant deception, even when their liberty is at stake.

In the civil arena, the most notorious of settings for deception for monetary gain, there may be a fear of being detected for one's fakery. Depositions are taken and oaths are administered in a judicial attempt to reduce deception. For some situations, such as workers' compensation, a theoretical question emerges as to why persons would fake in order to obtain a fraction of their normal pay.

Honest responding does not equal cooperation with the evaluator. Noncooperation can occur for a variety of reasons—from dislike of the evaluator to circumstances of the setting. Witnesses and significant others are often only minimally cooperative. They may claim that they are too busy, or make it clear that they do not want to become involved, or may be biased in favor of or against the accused.

Nondeliberate distortion does occur in the presence of truth-telling. The brain-damaged or psychotic subject may give what he or she believes to be an accurate portrayal of events. Recall that nondeliberate distortion caused by stress may occur in the majority of people (Buckhout, 1980).

The following case illustrates honest responding for an individual who admitted to attempting to sexually assault a 25-year-old school teacher.

> Mr. Tanaka displayed few evidences of deliberate deception as suggested by (a) the congruence between pathological test signs and clinical behavior (e.g., both showing perseveration, bizarre statements); (b) acceptable range of responses on measures helpful in detecting faking bad and faking good (e.g., MMPI, forced choice testing); (c) expected learning deficits with increased task difficulty (e.g., on neuropsychological testing); (d) similarity of scores on different subtests or test items of equal difficulty (e.g., digits forward and backward obtained on WAIS-R); (e) congruence of volunteered information with the physical evidence, and victim and witness statements; (f) concordance of mental condition at the time of assessment with crime behavior, and (g) volunteering of much self-incriminating data.
>
> There were suggestions of considerable nondeliberate distortion for both the time of the evaluation and the alleged offenses. Immediate, short-term, and long-term recall showed contamination with psychotic features when compared to cross-validating data. Concrete answers were given to many queries with prompting needed to extract responses which were later determined to be correct. His sense of time was substantially impaired compared to cross-validating data. He also displayed an inability to see his mistakes during testing, corresponding to historical behavior which showed poor judgment at home and on the job. His WAIS-R score revealed borderline intelligence with deficits in all areas of intellectual functioning, including vocabulary, computational, informational, and verbal associational skills.
>
> In general, for both the time of the evaluation and the instant offenses, the accused showed little deliberate, but considerable nondeliberate, distortion. Cross-validation with other data base sources was necessary to determine credibility parameters.

FAKING BAD

Faking bad, also known as *malingering*, *false imputation*, and *simulation*, always involves fabrication of nonexistent problems or the exaggeration of actual pathology. Denial or minimization of good points in an attempt to look worse than one actually is may also occur. As with any response style, malingering can coexist with genuine deficits. The writers' experience is that malingering is often associated with genuine deficiencies.

Many faking bad patterns are possible. Table 3.3 presents a dozen of the more common patterns of faking bad encountered in clinical-forensic evaluation.

Frequency data is lacking for most of these faking subtypes. Data on faked recall problems using a forced choice format, however, suggest that many of the

Table 3.3
Faking Bad Responses Styles

Style	Behavioral Strategy	Examples
1. Verbal fabrication	Claims a nonexistent problem	"I hear voices."
2. Verbal exaggeration	Amplifies real problem	"I have terrible memory problems."
3. Verbal denial	Disclaims an ability	"I can't smell anything."
4. Verbal minimizing	Downplays an ability	"I can walk only one block."
5. Misattribution	States deficit due to false cause rather than true etiology	Claiming developmental learning disability caused by a vehicular accident
6. Behavioral fractionalizing	Shows crudely estimated fraction of ability	Hand grip scores only 1/2 of ability
7. Behavioral approximating	Gets a close, but not exact, answer	"6+6=13; 7x3=22"
8. Behavioral infrequency	Sprinkles errors throughout performance on graduated scale	Errors on WAIS-R Comp. and Vocab. on initial items
9. Behavioral disengagement	Shows confusion and frustration–may give up	Claims total inability during blindfolded period of TPT testing
10. Impulsivity	Answers quickly, presents first thing on mind	Poor on Arith. and Block Design compared to untimed performance
11. Perseveration	Persists with one response mode regardless of feedback	Alternates errors on WCST or Explicit Alternative Testing
12. Randomizing	No consistent pattern of errors.	Speech Perception Test errors due to deliberate inattention.

subtypes are common among successful fakers (Hall & Shooter, 1989; Shooter & Hall, 1990). These include randomizing (28%), perseveration (19%), fabrication (16%), fractionalizing (9%), and disengagement (9%). For unsuccessful fakers, the same response subtypes emerged, but in a different order or magnitude. Results showed that randomizing (9%), perseveration (5%), fabrication (41%), fractionalizing (20%), and disengagement (13%) were clearly detectable as response strategies. For both successful and unsuccessful fakers, the full gamut of the subtypes presented on Table 3.3 were represented.

FAKING GOOD

Also known as *defensiveness* and *dissimulation*, faking good is the exact opposite of faking bad. Faking good always involves denial or minimization of problems in the direction of one's vested interests. Fabricating and exaggerating positive points are also frequent.

Second to honest responding, faking good is probably the most common distortion strategy utilized. Indeed, most people minimize and deny or exaggerate their positive points to adapt to the social environment. Otherwise, most marriages, businesses, and other relationships involving people would not last.

In faking good, the deceiver cannot do better than his or her true ability. Thus, faking good cannot occur on intelligence, neuropsychological, and other ability tests because clients cannot do better than their true best performance. The exception to this rule is taking performance-enhancing drugs, (e.g., anabolic steroids, stimulants) to increase vigilance, strength, and motor speed. Some substances (e.g., anti-anxiety drugs), are occasionally used to cover anxiety during an interview and to project an image of confidence to the evaluator.

It is possible to fake good on personality measures and in interviews. One may affirm a fraction of the pathological items on the MMPI, or engage in self-praise during an interview. In general, the five most commonly used methods of faking good are:

1. Denial: "I didn't drink alcohol."
                  "I don't have a memory problem."
2. Minimizing: "I snort coke only on Wednesday nights."
                  "I do poorly on tests like this."
3. Fabrication: "I have run a mile in less than four minutes."
                  "I have a parasensory ability which allows me to discern the truth."
4. Exaggeration: "Nobody cooks as well as I."
                  "I'm considered a virtuous person."
5. Misattribution: "I beat my wife because I was grieving over my friend's death."

Faking good is difficult to demonstrate when it involves concealing the real. It places the onus on the evaluator to demonstrate the existence of that which is denied or minimized. Cross-validation is essential in these cases. The following illustrates defensiveness in a case involving a 26-year-old defendant accused of savagely beating his ex-girlfriend into a coma.

During the second interview on October 9, 1990, the defendant blamed the victim, acquaintances of the victim, his own attorney, and the court for slanting the "truth" and refusing to allow him to tell the whole story. He declined to take psychological tests, citing issues of trust. Intellectually bright, verbal, and persistent in his efforts to dominate the interview, this brown-haired, brown-eyed male utilized cognitive strategies of minimization, denial, and withholding of information to convey a picture that this whole affair (i.e., the instant offense and events leading up to it) was a romantic feud that should best be simply forgotten by the court so he can go on with his life.

In regards to minimization and denial, examples include stating that (a) he hit the victim only once, consisting of an open-handed slap with his left hand, during the February 3, 1990 assault which caused brain damage to the victim, despite statements by two witnesses to the contrary; (b) he has never "attacked" the victim, only "hit" her on occasion. He affirmed the December 1988 assault, but stated that he hit the victim in the ribs two to three times at that time because she allegedly told him she had been sexually unfaithful with a previous boyfriend; (c) he placed an ice pick through a jacket on the victim's door, stating to the examiner that he was only returning the jacket and that no threat was intended. In retrospect, he can now see how the victim reacted with fright; (d) he threw a rock through the victim's window in October 1989 only to "wake her up," not to frighten her; (e) he never intended to pull the victim's hair out on October 6, 1989 and that he grabbed her head to get her attention; earlier in the day, the victim had reportedly walked into his apartment and destroyed two or three paintings with an umbrella. Even though he was angry at the victim, the hair-pulling allegedly occurred because the victim pushed his hand away, thus in essence pulling her own hair out; and (f) he has never had a really serious drug problem; however, he stated later that while in California, he injected heroin 15 to 20 times, smoked it many other times, and committed crimes with eventual incarceration for drug procurement activities. Records from California revealed that his daily heroin addiction cost about $200.

Many other examples exist. Suffice it to say that the defendant may not be a credible source of information due to distortion methods of (a) minimization, (b) denial, (c) projection of blame, and (d) withholding information in order to project a positive picture of himself. He denied feelings of anger towards the victim. Finally, he stated that he did not want his relatives contacted in connection with this case.

INVALIDATION

The evaluator may not know the reasons for a client invalidating the evaluation by some tactic(s), thus rendering it meaningless. Conclusions cannot be reached when this occurs. Examples include (a) not reporting for the evaluation; (b) reporting for the evaluation, but having to leave after one-half hour to avoid being fired from work or because of a sick spouse; (c) showing up substance-intoxicated; (d) becoming nauseous and sick in the middle of an interview; or (e) leaving too many unanswered items on MMPI. The evaluator must then perform the evaluation at another time or change data collection strategies to counter attempts at invalidation.

MIXED RESPONSE STYLES

Mixed response styles within one evaluation involves faking good and faking bad. How is it possible to have both malingering and defensiveness within one evaluation? The person may be extraordinarily sensitive about sexual behavior, for example, thinking (wrongly, of course) that this is none of the evaluator's business, yet attempting at the same time to exaggerate pain reactions to reap a financial reward in a civil suit.

Clinically, they may say, "I am here to assess my pain, not my lifestyle." On the MMPI, over-endorsed depression and other traits associated with pain may be seen, but anger, distrust, and suspicion may be downplayed.

FLUCTUATING RESPONSE STYLES

Suggestions are beginning to emerge that changes in response strategies occur within the same evaluation period. A common one, found in testing for feigned amnesia, is faking bad at the beginning of evaluation and showing honest responding, as fatigue sets in or as clients begin to believe that they have given themselves away. Honesty in the beginning of the interview, with faking bad as the evaluation progresses, is occasionally seen. This is a sign that the client may think the examiner can be duped.

A second fluctuating style involves presenting different styles during different time periods. The defendant may claim psychosis at the time of the instant offense to escape criminal liability, yet deny problems for the present to obtain release from hospitalization. A civil litigant may fake good concerning problems previous to an accident but fake bad for the present to assert damages. This suggests that evaluation procedures must be geared toward both the past and the present.

DETECTION STRATEGIES

The last part of the FDA model deals with detection methods. The overall strategy of the evaluation is to gather information about the actor, the one acted upon, and the context of deception, all within a systematic, comprehensive approach, which is then tailored to the assessment needs of the individual examined.

For example, in testing for claimed cerebral deficits as a result of an auto accident involving the loss of specific sensory skills (e.g., numbness, agnosia), the evaluator would first use a neuropsychological battery. Specific claimed problems not measured on the battery, such as loss of smell and "frontal" problems, would then be tested.

Nontesting approaches that yield high reliability can be utilized. Structured interviews and interviews of significant/knowledgeable others for cross-validation of claimed deficits, for example, are very helpful. Observation, to determine whether or not claimed deficits correspond to actual behavior, may be utilized. Inpatient hospitalization for observation of deceptive response patterns is held in high regard by the forensic community. This method builds in multiple measures over time to evaluate the assessee. Figure 3.2 presents the authors' opinions of the clinical efficacy of selected methods for detecting deception.

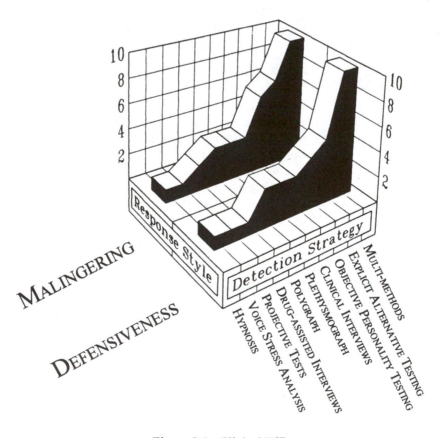

Figure 3.2. Clinical Efficacy

In regard to detection methods, the evaluator should keep in mind that no one method is 100% accurate; they should be used in combination with one another. The examiner should use methods that are broad-banded, standardized, and flexible. Methods must eventually be geared specifically towards symptoms/targets. As discussed, they are operative for at least two time periods. Few referral sources are particularly interested in deception only at the time of the evaluation. Lastly, built-in feedback and replication features are necessary to assess the effectiveness of the methods.

SYNTHESIS

In sum, the FDA model may assist the evaluator in focusing on the possible deceiver's target symptoms and response patterns. Detection methods can be broad-banded in order to illuminate targets and responses, and to provide testable hypotheses for further inquiry. Evaluation for deception must be general in the beginning and tailored to individual and specific questions as they arise.

REFERENCES

Buckout, R. (1980). Eyewitness identification and psychology in the courtroom. In G. Cooke (Ed.), *The role of the forensic psychologist.* Springfield, IL: Charles C. Thomas.

Cooke, G. (Ed.). (1980). *The role of the forensic psychologist.* Springfield, IL: Charles C Thomas.

Hall, H. V., & Shooter, E. (1989). Explicit alternative testing for feigned memory deficits. *Forensic Reports, 2,* 277-286.

Rogers, R. (Ed.). (1988). *Clinical assessment of malingering and deception.* New York: Guilford Press.

Shooter, E., & Hall, H. V. (1990). Explicit alternative testing for deliberate distortion: Towards an abbreviated format. *Forensic Reports, 4,* 45-49.

EVALUATION PROCESS GUIDELINES

Successful FDA requires proper preparation for the evaluation, proper conduct of the evaluation, and proper follow-up after the evaluation. A set of process guidelines by Paulsen and Hall (1991) is recommended and presented in Table 4.1.

BEFORE THE EVALUATION

The following case, which won a $500,000 award for the plaintiff, illustrates errors on the part of the defendant, the State of Hawaii Health Department, which could have been avoided with proper preparation before an evaluation of a patient's readiness for discharge:

> A 28-year-old White male paranoid schizophrenic began hallucinating, hearing the voice of a spirit urging him to hurt people, particularly his family members who were responsible for his involuntary hospitalization. There was a history of repeated assaults on family members with threats to kill. After two weeks, the patient was partially stabilized on antipsychotic medication. However, episodic outbursts of rage, shown by head banging and chair throwing, continued. The patient was overheard saying that he belonged in the hospital and that, if released, he would physically hurt his family. For the next three days, he went to great lengths to deny and minimize symptoms, finally stating that he had "learned his lesson" and was ready to return home.
>
> The psychiatrist noted that the patient had "achieved insight" and made arrangements for discharge, which unfortunately did not include informing the patient's parents of his return to the community. The patient went to his family's home unannounced, refused to take his medication, and quickly deteriorated. One week later, he stabbed his mother in the heart with a 12-inch kitchen knife, lacerated his niece and nephew on the legs and arms, and plunged the knife into his sister's torso, leaving the blade imbedded.

Table 4.1 Process Factors in Deception Analysis	
SUGGESTION	**RATIONALE**
Prior to the Evaluation	
1. Remain vigilant to possibility of assessee distortion.	Knowledge of high risk groups and distortion literature is essential.
2. Assess examiner distortion, including that which is unintended.	Examiner distortion is common (e.g., wrong assumptions, bias).
3. Maintain independence from referral party.	Closeness with referral party suggests bias.
4. Gather source data relevant to subject/incident.	Objective data must be reviewed in order to ask incident-specific questions.
5. Prepare a standardized distortion battery.	There is no substitute for evaluation completeness.
6. Schedule the evaluation.	Generally, distortion increases with time since the incident.
During the Evaluation	
7. Orient client to evaluation process and disposition.	Written and signed orientation forms are recommended to refute later claims of evaluation bias.
8. Tape the evaluation, with knowledge of client.	This assists evaluator's recall and is the basis for possible replication.
9. Conduct an open-ended interview.	Broad questions force assessee to work out details.
10. Eventually focus on critical distortion issues.	Binary-type questions force assessee to take a stand.
11. Sprinkle questions with known answers throughout interview.	Known deviation from "ground truth" is helpful to assess distortion style.
12. Use multiple assessment methods	Validity and examiner credibility will be increased.
13. Modify the evaluation as appropriate.	Flexibility of examiner response may increase database (e.g., quickly presented questions).
14 Confront client with suggestions of distortion.	Providing opportunity to change story may resolve discrepancies.
After the Evaluation	
15. Evaluate validity of each data source.	Cross-validating sources are subject to distortion.
16. Assess nondeliberate distortion of client.	Rule out unintentional distortion before deception is ruled in.
17. Rule in deliberate distortion.	Deception should be explicitly demonstrated.

(continued on next page)

Table 4.1	
Process Factors in Deception Analysis *(continued)*	
SUGGESTION	**RATIONALE**
18. Differentiate between incident and evaluation distortion.	Distortion always refers to two different points in time.
19. Identify distortion along different points of time subsequent to incident.	Fluctuating response styles suggest deception.
20. Report incomplete or invalid data.	Referral source needs to know if complete database is utilized.
21. Determine whether uncovered distortion is relevant to referral questions.	Genuine impairments are often associated with deception.
22. Reflect the decision process in the report.	How the examiner arrived at conclusions is central to distortion.
23. Describe adequacy of process.	Explicitly stating that distortion data warrant conclusions is helpful.
24. Delimit scope of distortion-related conclusions.	Degree of certainty and temporal limitations should be specified.
25. Make recommendations for case disposition.	Further evaluation may be indicated (e.g., inpatient observation).
26. Identify a feedback mechanism.	Later retesting for distortion is a frequent issue.
27. Retain all data regarding distortion.	Baseline materials may be used for reanalysis.

The forensic report submitted in this case concluded with the following:

> In sum, a prediction of violent behavior with a decision to continue preventive hospitalization was expected, required, and approved behavior by the authorities. There was no way for the State Hospital to escape the obligation of assessing the risk of violence prior to the patient's release from the hospital. Dr. Trevane should have been aware of a multitude of signals from the patient and from other sources that the patient posed a substantial risk of violence at the time of release. Dr. Trevane further ignored the extant professional literature on the subject, disregarded his own observations in deciding to release the patient, and used factors in his decision-making process that bore little, if any, relationship to whether future violence would occur.
>
> The staff did not have in their possession, or were otherwise not aware of, the contents of retrievable documentation regarding the patient's past violence and, thus, completely failed to uncover a history of dangerousness, escapes from previous inpatient psychiatric programs, noncompliance in taking medication, and other critical factors that must be considered in predicting dangerousness.

They believed the patient when presented with his falsehoods and did not believe or ignored him when he stated that he should not return to his family upon release. The staff should have known that he was a substantial risk of danger to his family in particular, that the opportunity to inflict violence through the use of a knife was available and precedented in both the patient's recent and remote history, and that consideration of inhibitory factors such as preparing or even notifying the family of his release and insuring treatment compliance was important in preventing and/or controlling violence. The acute and chronic physical and mental trauma suffered by the victims were created by the patient's violence of May 15, 1988 in the nature of cause and effect.

In this case, a number of factors were neglected. First, hospital staff should have been alerted to the possibility of defensiveness, particularly after the patient changed his mind and stated that he wanted to go home. Florid psychosis usually does not disappear in several days; rather it dissipates gradually. The basal history of violence was neglected, and there was strong evidence that the staff was unaware of the patient's previous dangerousness and/or future anticipated triggers of violence. No psychometric testing was conducted. Ward notes by nursing and social work staff did not appear to have been read by program planners. In sum, very basic errors in evaluating the patient's claim of readiness for release were made through inadequate preparation before the formal evaluation for release.

DURING THE EVALUATION

One of the factors to be dealt with during an evaluation is the occurrence of disruptions, distractions, and sabotage of the evaluation process.

A 38-year-old White male defendant reported for the sanity evaluation with his (loud) wife, a neighbor, and a friend, despite specific instructions to come alone.

A review of court records had revealed a lengthy criminal past with known attempts to manipulate evaluators in the direction of leniency.

The solution to this problem involved psychometrically testing the accused while his significant others were being interviewed individually. They were also given instructions to write down what they knew of the accused's history and the instant offense involving an alleged assault on the wife.

After three hours of evaluation and the collection of much forensic data, the accused and his significant others were released from evaluation.

Significant others are often given checklists to complete in addition to their other tasks. These include the Mooney Problem Checklist, Post-Traumatic Stress Disorder checklists, and a structured history form, all regarding the accused. Basic background information is collected about the party supplying the information to assess his or her credibility. Orientation procedures, of course, are followed in gleaning information from significant others to counteract later claims of examiner distortion. The evaluator is advised to treat these individuals with the same rights and privileges as the defendant, including the right to cease questioning.

The evaluation should begin on a general level in order to tap into the assessee's stream of consciousness and style of thinking. Police commonly interrupt the interrogation of the accused before obtaining broad-banded information, thus losing the chance to observe the arrestee mentally working out details to the questions.

Sometime during the initial part of the evaluation, the first in a pair of parallel test forms can be administered, followed by the second test toward the end of the session. These parallel test procedures include repeated measures of receptive vocabulary (e.g., Peabody Picture Vocabulary Test), visual recall (e.g., California Memory Test), and auditory discrimination (e.g., Auditory Discrimination Test), or other tests if the skills tapped by those tests are relevant to the issue of deception in a particular case. For example, the Shipley Institute of Living Scale or the Ravens Standard Progressive Matrices can be administered to the accused in a sanity screening. This provides for parallel administration later or for comparison with WAIS-R scores. Regression equations permit prediction of WAIS-R IQ scores from both the Shipley and the Ravens tests.

Flexibility of response is especially important. One client refused to operate the hand dynamometer, claiming that it was a test for "physical therapy," but he agreed to do finger tapping. Although these tests are not sensitive to the same parts of the motor cortex, both yield an indication of motor ability. One individual refused a recommended CAT scan but are agreeable to the MRI, which is more sensitive to cerebral injury.

The authors start with a structured interview format in order to lower the feeling of threat in the assessee. In sanity evaluations, the accused is oriented to the task, asked about identifying information, questioned on fitness to proceed, and then asked to describe the day of the instant offense in detailed sequence. The instant offense is probed again to fill in missing time periods, behaviors, and other important details.

Confrontation is used to allow the assessee a chance to resolve discrepancies. The evaluator should understand that the purpose of confrontation is to obtain more information, not to present an overview of evaluation findings. Table 4.2 presents five methods of confrontation, and examples of each.

In sum, it is acceptable to ask the defendant to resolve discrepancies between the following:

1. What is written versus what is stated orally; and
2. What was said or done earlier in evaluation versus what is being said or done now.

AFTER THE EVALUATION

A retrospective check for completeness is essential before the assessee is dismissed. A common problem by examiners is failure to recognize that data about deception must be relevant to time periods other than that of the evaluation.

Table 4.2
Confrontation During Analysis for Deception

1. Assessor summarizes evaluation behaviors.

"Are you saying that you do not recall anything about what happened on that night?"

2. Eliciting more complete information.

"Tell me more about the reasons for your earlier [psychiatric] hospitalization."

3. Giving a chance to change self-report.

"Looking back on what you said about the voices, do you obey them all the time? When don't you do what they say?"

4. Giving a chance to resolve discrepancies.

"I'm wondering why you don't remember what you said yesterday about the accident."

5. Allowing client to admit to distortion.

"If your ex-wife (boss, victim, etc.) were to describe your truthfulness, what would she say and why?"

Table 4.3
Retrospective Forensic Decision Analysis Steps

A. Forensic Database
  1. Multisourced
  2. Interdisciplinary
B. Rule Out/Account for Nondeliberate Distortion
  1. Reporting person
  2. Reported event
  3. Evaluation errors
C. Rule in Deliberate Distortion
  1. Examiner factors
  2. Individual examined
  3. Cross-validating sources
D. Determination of Response Style
  1. Honest responding
  2. Faking good
  3. Faking bad
  4. Invalidating results
  5. Mixed style
  6. Fluctuating style
E. Conclusions
  1. Sufficiency of data
  2. Degree of deception
  3. Confidence in judgement
  4. Likely targets of deception
  5. Temporal limits
  6. Feedback mechanism
  7. Intervention recommendations

Many forensic evaluations reviewed by the writers for various purposes have large amounts of data on distortion for the time of the evaluation but very little on that which connects to the critical event in question. Information relevant to distortion about the critical incident includes (a) verbal statements about capacities versus self-control at the time of the instant offense, (b) blood alcohol concentration (BAC) versus self-reported alcohol ingestion, (c) comparing observations of witnesses to those provided by the client, and (d) statements about past behavior which violate known diagnostic criteria, or can be demonstrated to be false. Table 4.3 lists other process factors when assessing for deception.

Table 4.3 is an important tool for the forensic examiner of deception and distortion. Retrospectively, the examiner ensures that he or she has covered all the bases in deception analysis.

As always, an adequate database is essential. The evaluator must be familiar with all data before proceeding through the post-hoc decision tree. Next, nondeliberate distortion must be ruled out or taken into account.

Deliberate distortion must then be examined in witnesses and significant others, the accused, and the evaluator. Eventually, the subject's deception style must be identified. Lastly, conclusions regarding deception are presented.

The evaluator's report should state explicitly that the database was sufficient to draw conclusions to a reasonable degree of psychological certainty. Second, the degree of deception uncovered should also be specified.

Table 4.4 presents degree factors for faking bad and faking good. Whatever the response style, the degree of deception uncovered must be specified.

Table 4.4 Degree of Deception Uncovered		
	Faking bad	**Faking good**
1. Negligible	No evidence of deception.	No evidence of deception.
2. Minimal	Basically honest but with some exaggeration of symptoms or minimization of strengths.	Basically honest with some minimization of negative behaviors and/or exaggeration of positive attributes.
3. Mild	Exaggeration of several critical symptoms and/or minimization of several positive behaviors.	Minimization of several critical symptoms or exaggeration of several critical positive attributes.
4. Moderate	Creation or fabrication of several critical symptoms or denial of several critical positive behaviors.	Denial of several critical factors or fabrication of several critical positive attributes.
5. Considerable	Creation or fabrication of wide range of critical symptoms or denial of a wide range of positive behaviors.	Denial of a wide range of critical behaviors or fabrication of a wide range of positive attributes.
6. Extreme	Faked or denied behaviors are absurd with absolutely no basis in reality.	Denied or fabricated behaviors are patently obvious and can be easily demonstrated.

Third, the confidence level of the evaluator's judgment about deception needs to be specified. Base-rates and empirical support, as Table 4.5 shows, should support one's conclusions whenever possible.

Table 4.5 Confidence in Evaluation Findings	
1. Negligible	The examiner has no confidence in evaluation findings. The probability of valid findings in terms of accurately classifying the person is 0-10%.
2. Minimal	Findings are congruent with theory and yield some information about distortion, but there is much conflicting and/or insignificant data. The probability of valid findings in terms of accurately classifying the person is 11-25%.
3. Mild	The probability of valid findings in terms of accurately classifying the person is 26-50%.
4. Moderate	The probability of valid findings in terms of accurately classifying the person is 51-75%.
5. Considerable	The probability of valid findings in terms of accurately classifying the person is 76-89%.
6. Near certain	Findings are supported by research and theory and can be replicated upon re-evaluation, using the same test procedures. Accuracy is from 90-100%.

Intervention recommendations are given when appropriate. The assessee should be treated for nondeliberate distortion as deficits may affect the ability and motivation to deceive. It is highly recommended that a professional other than the evaluator provide the intervention, in order to avoid claims of bias should a forensic issue re-emerge.

Examples where treatment would be appropriate include:

1. Intensive psychotherapy for a child sex victim evaluated for credibility.
2. Some fakers have severe associated problems such as psychosis, borderline retardation, and brain damage.
3. Factitious disorders, variants of faking bad, are almost always associated with severe psychopathology, such as willingness to chemically alter the body to assume the role of a hospitalized patient. Table 4.6 illustrates the diversity and seriousness of factitious disorders.

Evaluators should keep gathered data for as long as necessary—usually for a minimum of five to 10 years after an evaluation. Following a criminal or civil action, data should not be released to anyone unless written permission from the original referring party is obtained.

Table 4.6
Factitious Disorders

Targets	Response Style	Detection Method	References
Bereavement	Overdose, depression, etc.	Interview/Observation (denial of medical history with familiarity of routines).	Snowdon, Solomons, & Druce (1978)
Hyperamylasuria (Pancreatis)	Altered urine sample (introduction of saliva into sample).	Lab analysis (inconsistency between urine sample produced by patient and catheter).	Robison, Gilton, Morrelli, & Mann (1982)
Fever	Manipulating thermometers (switching/warming).	Observation.	Aduan, Dale, Herzberg, & Wolff (1979)
Myopathy	Self-induced lesions by paraffin injections.	Follow-up on the patient revealed that she was admitted shortly thereafter with similar symptoms to another medical center.	Cramer, Gershberg, & Stern (1971)
Porphyria (disturbance of a group of complex cyclic compounds)	Overdose, acute alcohol intoxication.	Investigation of past records and history. Recognition by staff that patient was a well-known faker.	Cramer, Gershberg, & Stern (1971)
Duodenal Ulcer	Verbal complaints only.	Confessed to feigned illnesses.	Cramer, Gershberg, & Stern (1971)
Renal Colic	Pricked finger and placed blood in urine sample.	Requested psychiatric help and confessed to factitious complaints.	Spiro (1968)
Ecchymosis and Cardiac Arrest	Took an excessive does of lithium, causing cardiac arrest. Took 60 aspirins, causing capillary fragility which turned to ecchymosis.	Psychiatric consultation with both his and her parents.	Stone (1977)
Sepsis	Injection/insertion of contaminated substances.	Searches of personal belongings and confronting patient with suspicion.	Reich & Gottfried (1983)

REFERENCES

Aduan, A., Dale, D. C., Herzberg, J. H., & Wolff, S. M. (1979). Factitious fever and self-induced infection. *Annals of Internal Medicine, 90*, 230-242.

Cramer, B., Gershberg, M. R., & Stern, M. (1971). Munchausen syndrome: Its relationship to malingering, hysteria, and the physician-patient relationship. *Archives of General Psychiatry, 24*, 573-578.

Paulsen, S., & Hall, H. V. (1991). Commonsense clinical process factors in deception analysis. *Forensic Reports, 4*, 37-39.

Reich, P., & Gottfried, L. A. (1983). Factitious disorders in a teaching hospital. *Annals of Internal Medicine, 99*, 240-247.

Robison, J. C., Gitlin, N., Morrelli, H. F., & Mann, L. J. (1982). Factitious hyperamylasuria: A trap in the diagnosis of pancreatitis. *The New England Journal of Medicine, 306*, 1211-212.

Snowdon, J., Solomons, R., & Druce, H. (1978). Feigned bereavement: Twelve cases. *British Journal of Psychiatry, 133*, 5-19.

Spiro, H. R. (1968). Chronic factitious illness: Munchausen's syndrome. *Archives of General Psychiatry, 18*, 569-579.

Stone, M. H. (1977). Factitious psychological findings and treatment recommendations. *Bulletin of the Menninger Clinic, 41*, 239-254.

PART II

DECEPTION ANALYSIS IN CIVIL CONTEXTS

5

Civil Law and Deception

Deception is relevant to all forensic settings and situations where expert opinions on mental state are proffered. All legal forums require a valid foundation (database) for expert opinions; deception by a client affects the validity of that foundation. This chapter considers applications of deception analysis in civil law. Specific techniques for assessing faked organic deficits, pain, and post-trauma reactions—common targets of civil claims—are addressed in subsequent chapters.

Civil claims of mental injury or defect may be categorized into tort claims and eligibility claims. Tort claims allege that an injury was caused to the plaintiff by the negligence or intentional infliction of the defendant. Such injuries are compensable through awards for the actual damages sustained and, sometimes, for punitive damages as well. Eligibility claims allege that the claimant satisfies current criteria for special assistance from a government program. Examples of disability assistance programs include Social Security Supplemental Income for disabled persons, workers' compensation, and Veterans Administration programs.

Tort claims are originally tried in state and federal inferior courts, while eligibility claims are originally heard before administrative boards or tribunals. The threshold legal questions, rules of evidence, rules of procedures, and burdens of proof differ between these two types of forums.

The following discussion broadly outlines the features of these two classes of claims. Special attention is given to issues involving claims of psychological injury or disability (Hall, 1990, 1991).

Tort Claims

A tort is simply an injury to one's person, interests, reputation, or property. The successful prosecution of a tort claim requires proof (a) that a personal injury occurred, (b) that the injury was the result of the defendant's negligence or intentional act, and (c) that the injury should have been foreseen by the defendant.

The issue of deception in tort claims speaks to the question of the existence or severity of the alleged injury. If the defendant can show that no injury was actually suffered, then the claim has been successfully defended. If the defendant can show that the actual injury suffered is less severe than claimed, then the size of any damages may be reduced accordingly.

Civil courts have shown a combination of reluctance and fear in accepting opinions that a plaintiff is malingering. In *Miller v. United States Fidelity and Guaranty Co.*, 99 So., 2d 511, 516 (La. App. 1957), the court stated:

> The principle that courts will stigmatize a claimant as a malingerer only upon positive and convincing evidence justifying such a conclusion is so well embedded in our jurisprudence as to preclude the necessity for specific citations.

The damage done to the plaintiff's reputation is one reason for this reluctance to accept opinions of malingering. Another is the logic of the economic situation. In both *King Mining Co. v. Mullins*, 252 S.W.2d 871 (Ky. App. 1952) and *Sutcliffe v. E. I. Dupont De Nemours & Co.*, 36 So.2nd 874 (La. App. 1948), the courts found it difficult to believe that the plaintiffs would sacrifice relatively well-paying jobs to fake an injury for a mere fraction of the amount of their pay.

The courts want neither to label one as a malingerer, nor to allow recovery for malingering to take place. This dilemma is partially resolved by a strategy adopted by many courts:

> The common law has long been wary of permitting recovery for mental or emotional injuries because of the fear that an absence of demonstrably verifiable injuries posed a risk of fraud to which the courts could not effectively respond. One aspect of a gradual diminution of that fear is that a plaintiff may now recover damages for mental or emotional injuries, in all jurisdictions, if these are proximately related to compensable physical injuries. The presence of related physical injuries serves two purposes. First, the physical injuries are thought to provide some safeguard against fraud by demanding some demonstrable evidence that the plaintiff has actually been injured. Second, courts have come to accept that physical trauma may have an emotional consequence and are, therefore, more willing to permit recovery in these instances (Shuman, 1986).

However, courts have made clear that, absent evidence of malingering, awards can be made under many conditions for psychological trauma in the absence of physical injury. Table 5.1 lists several principles which have emerged in case law over the years.

An inspection of this table reveals that considerable conceptual latitude is shown toward the plaintiff when he or she is attempting to recover for nonverifiable (i.e., mental) states. Juries appear to become very rigid, however, when they feel the plaintiff may have attempted to dupe them. In *Freeman v. Bandlow*, 143 So.2d 547 (2d DCA Fla. 1962), a 37-year-old passenger in a bus was hit by the defendant's auto. The jury awarded the plaintiff only $280—the amount of a doctor's bill. The court noted as follows (pp. 548-549):

> The plaintiff alleged that he was severely injured in the area of the neck and back, suffered great physical and mental pain which will continue in the future, and sustained temporary and permanent dimi-

Table 5.1	
Personal Injury Litigation	
Principle	**Representative Case**
Recovery of damages possible for mental or emotional injuries if linked to compensable physical truama.	*Sinn v. Byrd,* 486 Pa. 146, 404 A.2d 672 (1979).
Physical truama frequently causes emotional sequelae.	*Murphy v. Penn Fruit Co.,* 274 Pa. Sup. 427, 418 A.2d 480 (1980).
Physical trauma frequently causes associated residual pain.	*Tramutola v. Bortine,* 63 NJ 9, 304 A.2d 197 (1973).
Expert testimony required if physical trauma or associated psychological injuries are not a matter of common knowledge.	*Foley v. Kibrick,* 12 Mass.App. Ct. 382, 425 N.E.2d 376 (1981).
Expert psychiatric/psychological testimony required to establish link between physical injury and schizophrenia.	*Pagan v. Dewitt P. Henry Co.,* 27 Pa. Commw. 495, 365 A.2d 463 (1976).
Expert psychiatric/psychological testimony required to establish link between physical injury and psychoneurosis.	*Hess v. Philadelphia Transp. Co.,* 358 Pa. 144, 56 A.2d 89 (1948).
Expert testimony not required for pain and suffering.	*Jones v. Miller,* 290 A.2d 587 (DC 1972).
Successful cases depend on requirement of reasonable medical certainty.	*Bell v. New York City Health & Hosp. Corp.,* 104 N.E.2d 872, 456 NYS 2d 787 (1982).
Psychologists can relate pain to organic cause if malingering ruled out.	*Buckler v. Sinclair Ref. Co.,* 68 Il. App.2d 283 216 N.E.2d 14 (1966).
Recovery for psychological injuries in absence of physical injury possible if intentionally inflicted.	*Nickerson v. Hodges,* 146 La. 735, 84 So. 37 (1920).
Recovery for psychological injuries in absence of physical traumata possible if another party injured or died.	*Landreth v. Reed,* 570 S.W.2d 486 (Tex. Civ. App. 1978).
Recovery for psychological injuries in absence of physical traumata possible injured party in "zone of risk."	*Tobin v. Grossman,* 24 NY2d 609, 249 N.E.2d 419, 301 NYS2d 554 (1969).
Neuropsychologist can testify to organic basis of cognitive deficits caused by exposure to toxic chemicals.	*Morris V. Chandler Exterminators,* 409 S.E. 2d 677 (Ga. Ct. App.) (1991).

nution of income and earning capacity. There was little doubt as to
defendant's negligence, but the record reflects considerable doubt as
to the cause, nature, and extent of plaintiff's pathological condition
during the two year interim between the collision and the trial of the
case early in 1961.

[and]

Thus there was substantial expert opinion testimony tending to show
that plaintiff's injuries were grossly exaggerated and that he was largely
a malingerer and was not, in fact, appreciably disabled as a result of
his mishap.

ELIGIBILITY CLAIMS

Eligibility claims require evidence that the claimant satisfies current criteria
for admission to special government programs developed to assist eligible persons. These programs differ from entitlement programs, since the applicant must
prove that special eligibility criteria are satisfied. The largest eligibility programs
include the Social Security Supplemental Security Income Program, the Social
Security Disability Insurance Program, Worker's Compensation Programs, and
Veterans Administration Disability Assistance Programs.

The Social Security Disability Program provides cash assistance to currently
disabled workers and their dependents who have contributed to social security
taxes in the past. The Social Security Supplemental Security Income Program
provides a minimum income to the needy disabled (regardless of whether or not
they paid social security taxes in the past). Both programs require proof that the
applicant has a *medically determinable impairment*, which interferes with the
ability to engage in substantial gainful work and which can be expected to last for
at least 12 months (Social Security Administration, 1986). Original decisions
regarding eligibility are made by each state's Disability Determination Service.
Adverse decisions are appealable to the federal court system.

Some, but not all, mental disorders are considered impairments for purposes
of determining eligibility for these Social Security programs. Organic mental
disorders, schizophrenic, paranoid and other psychotic disorders, affective disor-
ders, mental retardation and autism, anxiety-related disorders, somatoform dis-
orders, personality disorders, and substance addiction disorders are eligible dis-
orders in adults. Chronic brain syndrome, psychosis of infancy and childhood,
functional nonpsychotic disorders, and mental retardation are eligible disorders
in children. However, the criteria used to define these categories are not necessarily the same as those in related categories of the DSM-IV.

Workers' Compensation Programs provide compensation or insurance for
injuries arising in the course and scope of employment, regardless of whether the
injury was due to the negligent or intentional fault of the employer. The amount
of compensation is set by a fixed schedule according to the degree of loss.

Federal employees are covered under the Federal Employees Compensation
Act; seaman are covered by the federal Jones Act; longshoremen are covered by
the federal Longshoremen's and Harbour Workers' Compensation Act. In addition, each state has its own employee compensation program with varying cover-
age, rules, and compensation schedules. These local acts should be consulted for

specific information on the operation of workers' compensation programs in each locale. Adverse decisions are appealable to either the federal or state court systems.

The Veterans Administration (VA) offers programs of medical and mental health treatment to honorably discharged veterans on a priority basis. The availability of these services depends on current VA resources and eligibility depends on one's status at the time of discharge and whether or not the disorder is "service-connected." In addition, the VA administers a program of monetary payments to veterans (and their dependents) who are partially or totally disabled by a service-connected disability. Eligibility for disability payments and the degree of disability are determined by regional Offices of Jurisdiction, whose decisions are appealable to the Board of Veterans Appeals. Decisions of the Board of Veterans Appeals are appealable to the U. S. Court of Veterans Appeals.

All of these types of eligibility claims are vexed with problems of malingering (Beal, 1989; Braverman, 1978; Hall, 1990; Hall & Hall, 1991; Lipman, 1962; Rickarby, 1979; Wasyliw & Cavanaugh, 1989). For example, the U. S. Department of Veterans Affairs, *Physician's Guide for Disability Evaluations*, Ch. 1, Sec. II, Para. 1.14, 1.16 and 13.6(f), 13.6(g) (1985), 1B11-56, states as follows:

> Physicians encounter some veterans or other claimants who are not capable of reliably participating in examinations because they are too ill physically or mentally to provide an accurate report of current symptoms or current level of functioning. Some veterans may exaggerate their disabilities, while others, particularly older veterans, may deny or be unrealistic in reporting the extent of their disablement.

A selection of cases and holdings for Social Security and Workers' Compensation determinations are presented in Tables 5.2 and 5.3.

Generally, the claimant in administrative hearings is given much leeway in demonstrating disability. Although malingering, per se, is not grounds for denial of eligibility, it is likely to be a contentious element in many claims. In *Board of Trustees of Fire and Police Employees Retirement System of City of Baltimore v. Ches*, 436 A.2d 1131 (Md. 1981), a police officer claimant was held to be disabled from an August 1, 1977 rear-end accident in his police car despite medical testimony of his malingering (pretending to be ill or injured to avoid work). In *Transit Authority of River City v. Vinson*, 703 S.W.2d 482 (Ky. App. 1985), collateral evidence of social security, disability, and insurance benefits paid to a plaintiff after an accident was excluded where the court felt that the jury would be misled by evidence of malingering. In *Cockrell v. U. S.*, 74 F.2d 151 (8th Cir. 1934), the plaintiff's deliberate failure to obtain work to avoid discontinuance of a VA disability was admissible as evidence of malingering, and in *Board of Veterans Appeals* (BVA) decision of March 17, 1978, Docket No. 77-36-991, feigned reactive depression was admissible evidence in a VA case.

The essential feature of most eligibility programs is the adversarial nature of the disability determination evaluation. Claimants are presumed to be ineligible for services unless they can prove that their injury/disability satisfies current eligibility criteria.

Table 5.2
Social Security Disability

Principle	Representative Case
Ultimate test for compensation is whether claimant unable to engage in substantial gainful activity.	*Lewis v. Weinberger*, 541 F2d 417, 420 (4th Cir. 1976).
Inability to work must be supported by objective clinical evidence; claimant's statements alone are insufficient.	*Underwood v. Ribicoff*, 298 F2d 850, 851 (4th Cir. 1962).
Objective criteria for mental disorders exist infrequently.	*Branham v. Gardner*, 383 F2d 614 (6th Cir. 1967).
Preference by review boards of opinions by treaters over Social Security consultants manifest.	*Wiggins v. Schweiker*, 679 F2d 1387 (11th Cir. 1982).
Opinions by mental/health treaters which reach disability standard require substantial opposition data in order to deny claim.	*Aubeuf v. Schweiker*, 649 F2d 107 (2nd Cir. 1981).
Weight accorded psychiatric opinion a function of database utilized.	*Richardson v. Perales*, 402 U.S. 389 (1971).
Administrative hearings to appeal adverse determination are not adversarial, with SSA not represented.	*Ware v. Schweiker*, 651 F2d 408 (5th Cir. 1981), cert. denied, 455 U.S. 912 (1982).
Qualifications of psychologist or psychiatrist should be provided if opinions only based on written report, and do affect weight given that report.	*Alvaredo v. Weinberger*, 511 F2d 1046 (1st Cir. 1975).

TARGETS

Any deficit may be faked in the civil claim of psychological damage. Although monetary compensation may be the prime motive for civil litigation, other motives are suggested by case law, behavioral science research, and the authors' clinical experience. One such incentive is the preservation of self-esteem in the face of the possible loss of major supports in life—work and physical/mental health. Loss of function is generally associated with diminution in self-esteem. This triggers a search to rectify the situation or to at least place the disability in a different and less threatening perspective. For many cases of malingering, unintentional distortion may occur.

Table 5.3 Workers' Compensation	
Principle	**Representative Case**
Conversion reactions with unknown physical etiology recoverable.	*American Smelting & Ref. Co. v. Industrial Commn.,* 59 Ariz. 87, 123 P.2d 163 (1942).
No difference seen between physical and psychological injury if end result is disability.	*Carter v. General Motors,* 361 Mich. 577, 106 N.W.2d 105 (1960).·
Recovery possible for psychological injuries in absence of physical trauma if another party injured or died.	*Bailey v. American General Insurance Co.,* 154 Tex. 430, 279 S.W.2d 315 (1955).
Recovery for psychological injuries possible if another party committed suicide.	*Wolfe v. Sibley, Lindsay & Curr & Co.,* 36 NY 505, 330 N.E.2d 603, 369 NYS2d 637 (1975).
Malingering is not compensable.	*Swift & Co. v. Ware,* 53 Ga.App. 500, 186 S.E. 452 (1936).
PTSD is compensable if related to relevant injury.	*Allis Chalmers Mfg. Co. v. Industrial Commn.,* 57 Il.2d 257, 312 N.E.2d 280 (1974).
Expert testimony necessary to link mental diagnoses to injury claimed.	*Andrus V. Rimmer & Garrett, Inc.,* 316 So.2d 433 (La. Ct. App. 1975).
Direct examination of claimant of mental injury by psychiatrist or psychologist required as a minimum.	*Texas Employers Assn. v. Thames,* 236 S.W.2d 203 (Tex.Civ.App., Ft. Worth 1951).
Rules of evidence are generally more relaxed.	*Thom v. Callahan,* 97 Idaho 151, 540 P.2d 1330 (1975).
Requirement of reasonable medical certainty not necessary with opinions expressed in terms of probability.	*Schope v. Red Owl Stores, Inc.,* 323 N.W.2d 801 (Minn. 1982).

Paul Lees-Haley (1988, p. 196) described these nondeliberate factors in civil claims in terms of the following progression: 1) a physical or psychological trauma occurs; 2) this trauma causes genuine transient effects such as pain, anxiety and depression; 3) the patient develops a combination of reactions during treatment, including (a) hysterical reactions to real and imagined problems, (b) hypochondriacal reactions to real and imagined problems, (c) genuine side effects of prescribed medications, (d) hysterical and hypochondriacal reactions to the side effects; and (e) secondary gain. Throughout this process, the patient learns the "language" of stress disorder claims through interactions with attorneys, relatives, friends, health care providers, and others, including popular magazines. This knowledge influences the patient's view of symptoms and interpretations of other, irrelevant experiences.

Thus, fakers who are wholly conscious of their deception and who target specific symptoms for deception may be in the minority. Malingering associated with real conditions, representing an exaggeration rather than a fabrication, may represent the norm. Keep in mind that disability may be represented for several time periods (e.g., for the time of an evaluation, for the past or future), adding to the difficulty of assessing disability claims.

RESPONSE STYLES

In a typology of deceivers within an industrial injury context, Braverman (1978) described several styles of malingering:

1. **"True," deliberate, or fraudulent malingerer**. This type comprised less than 1% of Braverman's 2,500 clients. Detection was simple as they were all persons with (a) gross psychopathology, (b) no binding ties within a migratory pattern, (c) all men from 25-37, (d) intolerance for long diagnostic testing, and (e) a quick termination of the case once confronted with the possibility of malingering.

2. **Cover-up or decoy malingerer**. Here, the faker experienced real trauma (most likely to the head). The compensable disease (e.g., cancer) is misattributed to the genuine injury. Fear of death and a family history of the disease emerged as central dynamics. About 3% of Braverman's sample is accounted for by this type of deception.

3. **The hysterical malingerer**. Comprising about 31% of the patients and the largest proportion of the sample, malingering in this type stems from a hysteric process culminating in loss of hope and victim distress.

Braverman stated (1978, p. 38):

> By "hysteric malingering" reference is made to a condition which emerges following objective or threatened injury after the affected person (a) loses all hope of recovery to pre-injury status; (b) begins to perceive himself with a new identification, namely, as "the injured," in which development of the "part" (injured) becomes more important than the "whole" (the intact residual). Reaction to the injured "part" may pervade the "intact residual"; and (c) becomes aware that his very sustenance is to be determined no longer by his previous capacity to work (now lost), but by the obligation the effects of his injury and incapacity impose upon society.

4. **The psychotic malingerer**. Comprising about 2% of the sample, this type usually has paranoid and bizarre features to his or her disability.

5. **The organic malingerer**. Comprised largely of Korsakoff patients and consisting of 2% of the sample, this type invents pathology due to the organic condition. Associated features included hypersuggestibility, shifting of symptoms, and uncertainty about the symptoms.

Braverman (1978) makes the valid point that work-related malingering is seldom planned in advance and is usually concocted after genuine injury and attendant loss of face occur. In anticipation of fluctuating response styles, he stated that malingering, like most other defenses to loss of face, waxes and wanes in accordance with environmental stimuli. Overall, as the above percentages suggest, Braverman found that about one-third of his 2,500 clients engaged in psychotraumatic malingering.

Four types of response styles have been described by Lipman (1962, p. 143):

1. *Invention* - the patient has no symptoms, but fraudulently represents that he has;
2. *Perseveration* - genuine symptoms formerly present have ceased, but are fraudulently alleged to continue;
3. *Exaggeration* - genuine symptoms are present, but the patient fraudulently makes these out to be worse than they are; and
4. *Transference* - genuine symptoms are fraudulently attributed to a cause other than the actual cause in fact.

In general, the response styles delineated by investigators describe one or more of the classic types described in this book. Applied to civil situations, these are as follows:

1. *Honesty*. Attempts to be accurate within one's own frame of reference and perceptions. Here, deficits are portrayed as they are seen, even though nonintentional distortion, such as caused by stress, may be operative to a considerable degree.
2. *Faking bad.* Exaggeration or fabrication of symptoms and behaviors, or denial/minimization takes place in order to look worse than one is. Exaggerated back injuries, common and difficult to disprove, are placed into this category.
3. *Faking good.* Minimization or denial of symptoms and behaviors, or exaggeration/fabrication of symptoms in order to look good. The claimant may try to hide the fact that illicit substances contributed to an auto accident or that safety equipment was not operative.
4. *Invalidation.* Attempts to render the evaluation meaningless (e.g., irrelevant, random responding). The claimant may feign cooperation with the retained expert but not report for appointments with the opposition expert.
5. *Mixed Responding.* Combination of above within same evaluation period. The claimant may exaggerate back injury but deny alcohol problems.
6. *Fluctuating.* Change of response styles between or within evaluation periods. The claimant may start off honestly in order to become familiar with testing procedures, then switch to mixed responding, then to random responding as tiredness sets in.

DETECTION METHODS

Lees-Haley (1990, 1991a, 1991b) has proposed several existing (Ego Strength) or new (Fake Bad, Credibility) scales from the Minnesota Multiphasic Personality Inventory item pool for use with civil litigants. However, these scales have not been widely used or cross-validated. In general, a large database is suggested for the detection of both intentional and unintentional distortion among civil litigants. The FDA model suggests that any combination of methods—interviewing, testing, observation, base-rate comparison—can be utilized. The next three chapters on faked brain damage, pain, and post-trauma reactions review techniques which may be used in the detection of deception in civil cases.

LEGAL REFERENCES

Allis Chalmers Mfg. Co. v. Industrial Commn., 57 Ill.2d 257, 31 N.E.2d 280 (1974).
Alvaredo v. Weinberger, 511 F.2d 1046 (1st Cir. 1975).
American Smelting & Ref. Co. v. Industrial Commn., 59 Ariz. 87, 23 P.2d 163 (1942).
Andrus v. Rimmer & Garrett, Inc., 316 So.2d 433 (La.Ct.App.975).
Aubeuf v. Schweiker, 649 F.2d 107 (2nd Cir. 1981).
Bailey v. American General Insurance Co., 154 Tex. 430, 279 S.W.2d 315 (1955).
Bell v. New York City Health & Hosp. Corp., 104 N.E.2 872, 456 NYS2d 787 (1982).
Blackmar v. U. S., 120 F.Supp. 408 (Court of Claims 1954).
Board of Trustees of Fire and Police Employees Retirement System of City of Baltimore v. Ches, 436 A2d 1131 (1981), affd. 452 A2d 422 (1982).
Board of Veterans Appeals Decision, March 17, 1978, Docket No. 77-36-991.
Branham v. Gardner, 383 F.2d 614 (6th Cir. 1967).
Buckler v. Sinclair Ref. Co., 68 Ill.App. 2d 283, 216 N.E.2d 14 (1966).
Carter v. General Motors, 361 Mich. 577, 106 N.W.2d 105 (1960).
Cockrell v. U. S., 74 F.2d 151 (8th Cir. 1934).
Foley v. Kibrick, 12 Mass.App.Ct. 382, 425 N.E.2d 376 (1981).
Freeman v. Bandlow, 143 So.2d 547 (2d DCA Fla. 1962).
Hess v. Philadelphia Transp. Co., 358 Pa. 144, 56 A.2d 89 (1948).
Hughes v. Moore, 214 Va. 27, 197 S.E.2d 214 (1973).
Jones v. Miller, 290 A.2d 587 (DC 1972).
King Mining Co. v. Mullins, 252 S.W.2d 871 (Ky, App. 1952).
Landreth v. Reed, 570 S.W.2d 486 (Tex. Civ. App. 1976).
Lewis v. Weinberger, 541 F.2d 417, (4th Cir. 1976).
Miller v. United States Fidelity and Guaranty Co., 99 So.2d, 516 (La. App. 1957).
Murphy v. Penn Fruit Co., 274 Pa.Super. 427, 418 A.2d 480 (1980).
Nickerson v. Hodges, 146 La. 735, 84 So. 37 (1920).
Pagan v. Dewitt P. Henry Co., 27 Pa.Commw. 495, 365 A.2d 46 (1976).
Richardson v. Perales, 402 U.S. 389, (1971).
Schope v. Red Owl Stores, Inc., 323 N.W.2d 801 (Minn. 1982).
Sinn v. Byrd, 486 Pa. 146, 404 A.2d 672 (1979).
Sutcliffe v. E. I. Dupont De Nemours & Co., 36 So.2d 874, (La. App. 1948).
Swift & Co. v. Ware, 53 Ga.App. 500, 186 S.E. 452 (1936).
Texas Employers Assn. v. Thames, 236 S.W.2d 203 (Tex. Civ. App. Ft. Worth 1951).
Thom v. Callahan, 97 Idaho 151, 540 P.2d 1330 (1975).
Tobin v. Grossman, 24 N.Y.2d 609, 249 N.E.2d 419, 301 NYS2d 554 (1969).
Tramutola v. Bortine, 63 NJ 9, 304 A.2d 197 (1973).
Transit Authority of River City v. Vinson, 703 S.W.2d 482 (Ky. App. 1985).
Underwood v. Ribicoff, 298 F.2d 850, (4th Cir. 1962).
Ware v. Schweiker, 651 F.2d 408 (5th Cir. 1981), cert. denied, 455 U. S. 912 (1982).
Wiggins v. Schweiker, 679 F.2d 1387 (11th Cir. 1982).
Wolfe v. Sibley, Linday & Curr & Co., 36 N.Y. 505, 330 N.E.2d 603, 369 NYS 2d 637 (1975).

REFERENCES

Beal, D. (1989). Assessment of malingering in personal injury cases. *American Journal of Forensic Psychology, 7*(4), 59-65.

Braverman, M. (1978). Post-injury malingering is seldom a calculated ploy. *Occupational Health and Safety, 47*(2), 36-48.

Hall, F. L. III (1990). *Materials on law of malingering.* Unpublished manuscript.

Hall, F. L. III, & Hall, H. V. (1991). *The law and psychology of malingering.* Unpublished manuscript.

Lees-Haley, P. (1988, April). Unintentionally fraudulent claims for stress disorders. *Defense Counsel Journal,* 194-197.

Lees-Haley, P. (1990). Provisional normative data for a credibility scale for assessing personal injury claimants. *Psychological Reports, 66*(3), 1355-1360.

Lees-Haley, P. (1991a). A fake bad scale on the MMPI-2 for personal injury claimants. *Psychological Reports, 68*(1), 203-210.

Lees-Haley, P. (1991b). Ego strength denial on the MMPI-2 as a clue to simulation of personal injury in vocational neuropsychological and emotional distress. *Perceptual and Motor Skills, 72*(3), 815-819.

Lipman, F. D. (1962). Malingering in personal injury cases. *Temple Law Quarterly, 35*(2), 141-162.

Rickarby, G. A. (1979). Compensation-neurosis and the psycho-social requirements of the family. *British Journal of Medical Psychology, 52,* 333-338.

Shuman, D. W. (1986). *Psychiatric and psychological evidence* (Trial practice series). Colorado Springs: Shepard's/ McGraw-Hill.

Social Security Administration. (1986). *Disability Evaluation under Social Security.* Social Security Administration Publication No. 64-039.

U. S. Dept. of Veterans Affairs. (1985). *Physician's guide for disability evaluations* (1B11-56). Washington, DC: U.S. Government Printing Office.

Wasyliw, O. E., & Cavanaugh, J. L., Jr. (1989). Simulation of brain damage: Assessment and decision rules. *Bulletin of the American Academy of Psychiatry & Law, 17*(4), 373-386.

6

Malingered Neuropsychological Deficits

Greg Lance is a 22-year-old single, White male acquitted by reason of insanity and civilly committed to the state hospital for the attempted murder, rape, and sodomy of a female tourist.

He had an extensive history of assaultive behavior and other antisocial behavior extending back to early adolescence.

Exculpation was granted in 1988 on the basis of claimed epilepsy with associated amnesia at the time of the instant offenses, although this was never substantiated by the defense or proven otherwise by the prosecution.

Ward notes during hospitalization contain examples of serious prevarication in order to leave the hospital grounds, have sex with incompetent psychotic patients, and "con" money from his peers. In examining his history, significant distortion of facts by Mr. Lance appears to have occurred since at least 1988. When questioned in 1989 about previous alleged suicide gestures, he finally admitted that the only instance occurred while in custody in 1988 as a ruse to change cells. During that year, the forensic hospital social worker, during a social intake, noted: "...he has been observed in animated interaction and activity with other patients, but when speaking to staff, assumes a 'depressive' attitude" (July 29, 1988). He played the role of a depressed individual to the staff over a one-half-year period. During that time, Dr. Smith observed that "recent MMPI findings would strongly indicate that the patient is faking the symptoms of isolation and impoverishment of emotional experience. This evidence is supported by the fact that in unguarded moments, the patient exhibits the full range of affective state" (August 18, 1988).

Other suggestions of faking bad included (a) obtaining better scores on some intellectual subtests when allegedly mentally retarded than when "normal" —his Wechsler Adult Intelligence Test Full Scale IQs rose from 57 to 116 over three separate administrations, from mentally defective to bright normal in 25 months; (b) during administration of different tests during the same general time period, showing the ability to perform multiplication and other complex mathematical manipulations on one test while exhibiting the inability to do simple addition problems on another test; (c) correctly identifying words such as "kayak," "descend," "bereavement," "appraising," and "amphibian" while showing the inability to define simpler words such as "winter," "slice," "conceal," and "enormous"; (d) exhibiting inconsistent memory skills (digits forward, digits backward) over time instead of a consistently poor performance; and (e) reversing Performance and Verbal IQs as the superior mode of functioning at different times, instead of showing improvement within the dominant factor upon retesting.

Faking cerebral dysfunction has a long and infamous history. In civil law, faking central nervous system (CNS) damage is discussed by Miller & Cartlidge (1972):

Simulation and accident neurosis following injuries to the head and the spinal cord on a large scale are really disorders of the Industrial Revolution. Attention was first directed to them in Prussia, where the introduction of a national railway system evoked the first accident-insurance laws in 1871 and 1884. Within a few years professional attention was drawn to the frequency with which malingering was encountered in civilians claiming severe disablement after minor industrial injury, and to the importance of financial gain as a motive. In Britain an exactly similar situation followed the Employers Liability Act of 1880 and the Workmen's Compensation Acts of 1898 and 1906. The epidemic of functional complaints that arose as a byproduct of this socially admirable legislation attracted the attention of many of the most eminent neurologists of the period. In less sophisticated hands it led to the creation of a group of new syndromes such as railway spine, which enjoyed a remarkable vogue for a few decades, until the courts tumbled to its nature and it promptly disappeared.

Successfully faking CNS deficits is predicated on knowledge of the characteristics and types of brain damage. The four main categories of organic brain syndromes (OBS) (Strub & Black, 1981) are (a) the acute confusional states, (b) the dementias, (c) the focal brain syndromes, and (d) the "symptomatic functional syndromes." The latter are organically based and resemble psychopathology (e.g., schizophrenic behavior in temporal lobe epilepsy; schizophreniform syndrome in chronic LSD abuse).

Subclinical pathology is often underdiagnosed or regarded as faked (Boll, 1985; Parker, 1990). The post-concussive syndrome (PCS), for example, is commonly mistaken for "compensation neurosis" despite the cluster of symptoms that appear with regularity whether or not economic gain is realized (Binder,1986). The cluster of post-concussive symptoms includes headache, labile behavior, concentration problems, sleep disturbances, and diffuse residential effects. Normal people under high stress may also show OBS-like symptoms. Subsequent deficits remit quickly as the stress is eliminated.

Malingering brain damage has long been recognized in criminal-forensic settings, despite an unwarranted belief that neuropsychological tests could not be malingered (Heaton, Smith, Lehman, & Vogt, 1978; Ziskin & Faust, 1988). This acceptance of the nonfakability of tests used to assess brain-behavior relationships occurred at a time when neuropsychologists were being granted expert witness status (*Jenkins v. United States*, 1961, *Buckler v. Sinclair Ref. Co.*, 1966. Despite recent challenges to neuropsychologists in court, their role remains crucial to the understanding of cerebral dysfunctions in defendants.

MODELS

Few models of feigning cerebral dysfunctions have been offered. One model is provided by Freedland (1982) who stated:

> The model proposes that patterns of faking on neuropsychological test batteries can be analyzed in terms of relationships among (a) the sophistication of the subject; (b) the events to which the subject attributes his or her apparent dysfunctions; (c) the symptoms and problems which the subject intends to fake; (d) strategies used in attempting to fake believable deficits without getting caught; and (e) the perceived risks and potential benefits of faking. The model predicts that subjects tend to selectively fake only tests which are perceived as being relevant to the intended symptoms, implying that the results of tests used to detect faking (such as the MMPI) may not correlate with patterns of faking on other tests in the battery. An alternative approach would be to develop measures of faking which are intrinsic to the tests of interest, based upon principles of faking detection.

This chapter incorporates Freedland's (1982) concepts and focuses on the model presented in Chapter 3, which scrutinizes targets of the faker, response styles employed, and the detection strategies used to uncover feigned neuropsychological dysfunctions.

TARGETS

As an illustration, let's look at the criminal-civil case at the beginning of this chapter. First, Lance could have chosen a multitude of targets in the direction of his vested interest. For example, to obtain his not guilty by reason of insanity (NGRI) verdict, Lance might have chosen to excuse the perpetrated violence by a condition known to create brain insult. The range of conditions causing (blameless) violence include (Hall & McNinch, 1989): (a) acute confusional states; (b) some degenerative conditions (e.g., Huntington's Disease, Alzheimer's Disease, alcoholic dementia); (c) head trauma, post-concussive syndrome; (d) toxic conditions caused by drugs, alcohol, medications, and some heavy metals; (e) neoplastic disease processes of the central nervous system; (f) seizure disorders (e.g., psychomotor, complex-partial, temporal lobe epilepsy); and (g) "borderland" organic mental disorders (c.f. Strub & Black, 1981) such as the episodic dyscontrol syndrome.

As a working hypothesis, a seizure disorder may have been selected by the defendant. In order to obtain the NGRI verdict, he then faked bad on a wide range of intellectual, achievement, and ability tests. Lance may not have known that virtually any target can be selected and that it may change over time and be combined with other conditions such as a thought disorder. Yet, pathology was seen on both neuropsychological and psychological testing. The professional attempting to understand faked OBS in a particular person must realize that targets themselves are cognitive events which are nonverifiable in nature. Thus, for the first part of the model, the basic questions are:

> Does the individual have a motive for faking?
> What are the most likely targets of deception?

In the instant case, the defendant had a motive for faking and, in fact, achieved his goal of admission to the state hospital as opposed to receiving a sentence of 20 years to life in prison. He appeared to choose targets that were broad-banded, conformed in part to his history, and were largely unverifiable.

In a study using the Halstead-Reitan Neuropsychological Battery (HRNB) on 52 brain-impaired patients and 202 normal subjects, Goebel (1989) determined the following strategies for faking from debriefing his 141 faking subjects:

Giving the wrong answer	30%
Slowing performance or looking dull or confused	36%
Showing motor incoordination	14%
Simulating memory impairment	2%
Ignoring stimuli	2%
Changing emotional state	1.5%
Stuttering	.5%

Deterrents to faking are also important to consider. In all of the writers' investigations on deception with subjects instructed to fake, a small but significant proportion of the sample showed no deception. About 10% of Goebel's (1989) subjects did not fake despite instructions to do so, and 92% believed they could have done a better job of faking. Reasons for not faking or for thinking they could have done better include:

Unfamiliar with and unprepared for task	60%
Presence of the examiner	21%
Tests too easy to allow faking	20%
Got too involved to fake	30%

As a final note in regard to targets, the evaluator is urged to take into account a general caution by fakers in reaching their long-term goals. Freedland (1982) stated:

> The fear of getting caught may also affect the selection of faking criteria. This occurs for two different reasons.
>
> First, mild deficits are easier to fake than severe ones; therefore a mild faking criterion is less likely to be questioned by an examiner. Second, choices of criteria may be influenced by the effects they will have on the patient's lifestyle. For example, fake unilateral deafness is seen more often than fake bilateral deafness. Bilateral deafness might merit a larger compensatory settlement, but the patient wishing to avoid later charges of fraud might have to feign total deafness indefinitely. Unilateral deafness is worth less money but the patient is able to engage in most of his or her favorite activities without arousing suspicion.

RESPONSE STYLES

The following is a generic summary of strategies that fakers, including the defendant in the instant case, may employ in attempts to feign believable deficits on neuropsychological evaluations (Craine, 1981, 1990; Hall, 1985, 1990):

1. **Present realistic symptoms.** A deceiver will employ a "common sense" or "popular" schema of what brain-damaged persons are like and will select symptoms which accord with that "naive" view (e.g., Aubrey, Dobbs, & Rule, 1989). Although the symptoms may appear realistic from this unsophisticated point of view, the expert evaluator will (hopefully) have a more objective and detailed view of "realistic" neurological symptoms.

2. **Distribute errors**. To cover their targets, fakers tend to make a deliberate number of mistakes throughout the evaluation rather than miss only difficult items. A balance is sought between appearing fully functional (missing too few items) and appearing too impaired (missing too many items). Fakers attempt to control their errors as much as possible, but, in practice, they fail to maintain a "realistic" percentage of errors.

3. **Protest that tasks are too difficult and/or feign confusion and frustration.** The faker may feign confusion, anger, or other emotions superimposed upon adequate cooperation and task compliance. For example, a 22-year-old man convicted of rape and assault was observed by the neuropsychological technician on the Tactile Performance Test (TPT) as follows (total time = 21.9; memory = 5; localization = 1):

> Constantly complaining–"It's too hard" "This is too much"- Rt Block in hand–moving block over board–doing some exploration of spaces –getting fairly good messages–after 1st block inserted. Began to explore the whole board–getting fairly good messages but taking a lot of time locating the correct block, thereby losing the location and needs to start again feeling the spaces [sic].

4. **Perform at a crudely estimated fraction of actual ability**. Speed may be deliberately decreased. The faker is generally knowledgeable of his or her true rate of responding but may decide to show a partial performance. The following evaluation illustrates this point for a 35-year-old Portuguese man accused of murder:

> The scores obtained on the neuropsychological battery would be compatible with a diagnosis of brain dysfunction, except that we have some grave doubts as to how motivated Jim was for these particular tests. He appears to have adequate fine motor speed, for example, but when he is given a test of Fine Finger Dexterity (manipulating small pegs), he is noted to purposely work very slow in order to appear somewhat damaged in this respect. On most tasks that required speed, this client was noted to purposely work quite slowly in order to give a poor picture of his abilities. It may well be that he does have some minor brain dysfunction, but once we have noted that he has purposely performed poorly on some of these tests, we have serious doubts as to the legitimacy of any of the scores we obtained after that point.

The evaluator needs to search for other types of failures on easy test items. The WAIS-R items, for example, generally progress from easy to difficult. Fakers may try to distribute their errors throughout the subtest (or battery), not realizing that, for some tasks, successive items increase in difficulty.

Failure on easy items, according to Freedland and Craine (1981), also occurs on graduated forced-choice tests. Deliberate errors are made on the (easy) items to which the answers are known. Random responses may occur when the faker encounters difficult items to which the answers are unknown. This means that the point between the known (and deliberately faked) items and the unknown items is very difficult to estimate. Thus, the evaluator needs to weight easily missed items more heavily than mistakes on difficult items.

Easy items on the Aphasia Screening Test which are particularly sensitive to faking include (a) mispronounced words, (b) misspelled words, and (c) acalculia. All items on the Aphasia Screening Test, or a similarly constructed scale, should be passed by a normal person. If a client has difficulty with these easy items, other tests tapping the same skills should also show deficit responding.

DETECTION STRATEGIES

The search for detection measures has been slowed by discipline-specific practices and concerns. Freedland (1982) comments:

> Most of the techniques published to date were intended for use with specific symptoms such as various types of hearing or vision impairment. It has rarely been suggested that techniques designed to assess one type of symptom might also be useful with very different types of symptoms. The special lenses and filters used to detect faking in optometric examinations, for example, have no apparent relevance to the diagnostic challenges facing audiologists. There has accordingly been relatively little pooling of ideas across specialties in which malingering is an issue. A review of these diverse techniques suggests, however, that *most of them are variations on the same few underlying strategies*. [emphasis added]

Detection strategies fall into several categories (Craine, 1990a; Freedland & Craine, 1981; Hall, Shooter, Craine, & Paulsen, 1991). These include (a) lack of neurological fit, (b) searching for patterns of failures on easy items, (c) administering easy versus difficult versions of similar tasks; (d) searching for departures from expected levels of accuracy on forced choice tests, and (e) examining for test inconsistencies.

1. **Lack of neurological fit:** The question of neurological fit is whether reported history, presenting symptoms, or responses on neuropsychological tests or on individual test items make sense compared to what is known about the functional neurological systems involved. For single items or symptoms, does the assessee present signs which do not make sense neurologically, (e.g., glove amnesia, hemiparesis ipsilateral to a supposedly involved hemisphere)? On multidimensional tests, does the assessee produce a pattern of scores (profile) which is consistent with known neuropsychological syndromes?

Lack of neurological fit as a detection method for malingering is described in the manual for VA evaluators of service disability (U.S. Department of Veterans Affairs, 1985) as follows:

13.6 Neurologic Examination

f. Abnormalities in motor performance observed on examination, particularly incoordination, weakness, and decreased range of motion, not associated with supporting or confirmatory signs (atrophy, reflex changes, abnormal tone, automatic compensatory actions, etc.) require special consideration. Often such abnormalities will be present when the patient perceives the performance is being specifically tested but absent when the performance is part of a larger, more spontaneous action, or when the patient's attention is distracted. A common example is the patient who, while standing with heels together sways wildly when asked to close his/her eyes (Romberg's sign). Yet the patient does not sway when asked to close the eyes in the same standing posture but is distracted by doing rapid alternating finger-to-nose movements. Another common example is the patient who demonstrates marked weakness of some muscles (or muscle groups) when they are tested individually, yet shows no dysfunction in using the same muscles during other parts of the examination, or in dressing, etc., when the examination is "over." *Such performances strongly suggest hysteria or malingering but by themselves alone do not warrant a diagnosis of either. Unless such diagnoses are confirmed by more positive and definitive findings, it is best not to speculate but simply to report the observed discrepancies.*[emphasis added]

g. Hysterical weakness (or malingering), however, should not be confused with apraxia. Associated with disease of one or both cerebral hemispheres, apraxia is the loss of the ability to perform complex, often symbolic, acts at will or on command, without specific paralysis of the invoked parts.

Generally the apractic patient will attempt the movement, but cannot complete it and appears perplexed and frustrated. It is as if he/she has "forgotten" how to do the act. Simpler voluntary and associated movements may be normal, and individual muscles (or muscle groups) are not affected. As with aphasia, apraxia is worsened by fatigue and improved by the presence of environmental clues. Also as with aphasia, the type and degree of apraxia observed depends in part on the methods by which it is sought.

A comparison of epileptic seizures with faked seizures (Roy, 1989) illustrates the strategy of evaluating neurological fit. Feigned epilepsy is often superimposed on a history of genuine seizures. This accords with studies which show that simulation of brain and spinal cord injuries are frequently superimposed on tangible organic pathology (Miller & Cartlidge, 1972). Morgan, Manning, Williams, and Rosenbloom (1984) discovered disparities in eight (child) patients between the clinical description and frequency of seizures at home versus school. Fabrication of seizures began for some as early as age five. The characteristics of genuine and faked seizures in this small sample are listed in Table 6.1.

Generally, persons who pseudo-seize compared to those with genuine seizures have (a) a greater history of other relatives with mental illness; (b) a greater personal history of psychiatric disorder, including attempted suicide and sexual maladjustment; and (c) more claimed health problems, depression, anxiety, and an increased likelihood of an affective disorder (Roy, 1979). Thus, there are many differences in history and symptoms which helped to differentiate genuine from malingered seizures in this sample. These features, while not definitive, should raise suspicions of exaggeration or fabrication of seizures.

Another strategy is to compare the test profile of the assessee with that of a comparison group from the research literature. Is there goodness of fit between the claimant's profile and that of either "genuine" or "faking" research groups reported in the neuropsychological literature? Smith, Nelson, Sadoff, and Sadoff (1989) used a hand dynamometer connected to a computer to measure peak force and force-time curves for subjects instructed to fake bad. These faked performances could be distinguished from normative performance with between 92% and 100% accuracy, depending on the particular statistic used for comparison.

Heaton et al. (1978) used an expanded Halstead-Reitan Neuropsychological Battery to distinguish between 16 volunteer malingerers and 16 genuine brain-injured patients. Stepwise discriminant analysis for this sample of subjects yielded two functions that achieved a hit rate of 100% (neuropsychological tests) and 94% (MMPI scales). However, when Thompson and Cullum (1991) applied these discriminant functions to a new sample, they were unable to discriminate between patients judged to have put forth their best efforts on the tests and patients judged not to have tried their best. The lack of replication is not surprising given the small number of subjects in the study and the small subject-to-variable ratio in the multivariate analysis.

Although the Heaton et al. (1978) discriminant functions do not appear to be generally useful, their results suggested particular tests which may be especially prone to faking. They reported the following differences on individual tests:

Worse with Head-Injury Group	Worse With Malingerers
Category Test	Speech-Sounds Perception Test
TMT, Part B (errors)	Finger tapping
TPT (Total time, memory, location)	Finger agnosia, sensory suppressions, hand grip
	WAIS Digit Span
	Higher F scale and six clinical scales on MMPI

Thompson and Cullum (1991) also found individual tests capable of distinguishing faked from genuine performances. These include measures of sensory-perceptual, learning and memory abilities (Cullum, Heaton, & Grant, 1991). In a study of these same tests, Trueblood and Schmidt (in press) compared eight patients in a neuropsychological practice who failed a stringent test of malingering with eight patients who passed the test of malingering. They found that their malingering patients performed significantly worse than their matched controls on the WAIS-R Digit Span, Finger Tip Number Writing, and Speech Perception tests, but not on Finger Tapping, Finger Agnosia, Sensory Suppressions, or hand grip tests.

Mensch and Woods (1986) found that normal subjects instructed to "fake bad" on the Luria-Nebraska Neuropsychological Battery showed a discrepancy between the number of elevated clinical scales and the elevation of the Pathognomic

Table 6.1
Main Characteristics of Epileptic Fits and
Hysterical Pseudoseizures

	Epilepsy	Hysteria
Attack pattern	Similar	Variable
Apparent cause	Absent	Emotional disorder
Frequency	Rarely more than one a day, except petit mal	Several a day
Others present?	Sometimes when alone; can be nocturnal	Only when other people are present; rarely nocturnal
Where?	Anywhere	Indoors, usually at home
Warning	If present, often stereotyped	Variable, sometimes over-breathing
Onset	Sudden	Gradual
Scream	At onset	During attack
Convulsion	Stereotyped tonic-clonic phase	Variable, rigidity with random struggling movement
Biting	Tongue	Of lips, hands, and other people
Micturition	Very common	Rarely
Injury	Fairly frequent	Infrequently
Talking during attack	Never	Frequently
Duration	A few minutes	Many minutes, but sometimes much longer
EEG	Abnormal during and between seizures	Normal during and between attacks

Reprinted with permission from Roy, A. (1989). Pseudoseizures: A psychiatric perspective. *Journal of Neuropsychiatry, 1*,69-71.

Scale. The subjects generally showed more cerebral pathology on scales measuring specific neuropsychological functions than they did on the single scale most sensitive to brain dysfunction. Like the subjects in the Heaton et al. (1979) study, subjects performed most poorly on tests of sensory and motor functions and displayed longer response times. It is possible that impairment on sensory-motor and timed tasks is most consistent with laymens' conceptions of how brain-injured patients perform.

The following case illustrates the above detection methods for a 45-year-old taxicab driver involved in litigation after an accident. Malingering was diagnosed based upon the following:

a. On the WAIS-R, he obtained a VIQ of 65 and a PIQ of 70. Several years before, he achieved an FSIQ of 110 with comparable verbal and performance abilities.

b. On an auditory discrimination test, he obtained a score equal to that of a six-year-old child. Upon retesting with a parallel form one hour later, he obtained a normal score, showing a 300% improvement.

c. On a memory test, he displayed an inability to remember his age and the institution and city in which he was evaluated, responses obtained by less than 1% of the normative sample.

d. He obtained the minimal possible score on a test tapping visual, logical, verbal, and other kinds of memory. This score is compatible with such conditions as severe diffuse brain damage, but not with the memory skills the accused clinically demonstrated outside the test context.

e. He obtained a score on a forced-choice scale designed to test deception that was compatible with recognizing the visual stimulus but choosing not to report it.

f. There was a lack of fit between his clinical demeanor and a condition of dementia.

g. He previously exhibited faking while being tested for cerebral impairment similar to that claimed in the present case.

In this case the lack of fit between expected neurological performance and 1) presenting symptoms and 2) obtained test results revealed so many inconsistencies that the cumulative weight of the evidence supported a diagnosis of malingering.

2. **Retesting or comparison strategies.**

a. Easy versus difficult versions of similar tests. The faker may not understand that a second testing may be easier or more difficult than the first. Thus, fakers may perform similarly on the two versions whereas nonfakers would perform differently.

The Dot Counting Test (DCT) illustrates this method. Cards A, B, and C (consisting of massed dots) are more difficult than their counterparts, Cards, D, E, and F (consisting of clusters of dots), even though the two sets have the same number of dots to count. Administration of the two sets of the Dot Counting Test may yield such inconsistent results that only a conscious attempt to control performance can explain them.

Another test with built-in easy versus difficult items is the Auditory Discrimination Test (ADT) (Language Research Institute, 1958). Initial administration of the ADT involves informing the assessee that words will be read, two at a time, and that the task is to say whether the two words are the same or different (e.g., tub - tub, lack - lack, web - wed, leg - led, chap - chap). A second form presents same or different word pairs of similar difficulty and number (N = 40) as the first form (e.g., gear - beer, cad - cab, bug - bud). In terms of threshold values, the faker may not realize that normals can miss many of the "same" items (< 15), but should miss only a few of the "different" items (> 4) before the performance appears suspicious. Comparison of the "hit rates" for same versus different items may detect a suspicious asymmetry in the types of items missed.

> Claiming brain damage and psychosis in connection with the alleged murder of his cellmate, defendant Marcos was tested four times with both forms of the ADT. His performance ranged from normal to markedly impaired, with proportionally more "different" than "same" items missed in the abnormal performances. During the testing, he would interrupt the evaluator, saying it was time for him to see his other doctor.

Caution should be exercised, however, in deciding that failure of "easy" items within a test are more characteristic of deliberate distortion than of genuine responding. Mittenberg, Hammeke, and Rao (1989) examined the distribution of intratest scatter among brain-damaged and normal subjects on the Vocabulary, Comprehension, and Similarities subtests of the WAIS-R. Their results suggested quite high cut-off scores (e.g., more than six failed items interpolated among passed items) for distinguishing brain-damaged subjects from normal subjects. If intratest scatter is to be used as an index of "faking bad" as well as an index of brain damage, then the cut-off scores for distinguishing actual brain-damage from malingered brain damage would have to be even higher than those for distinguishing brain-damaged from normal subjects.

Whether failing more "easy" items than "difficult" items on a particular test is indicative of "faking bad" is, despite its common sense appeal, always an empirical question. The distributions of intratest scatter among normal subjects, genuinely impaired subjects and "faking" subjects must be explicitly compared to determine the usefulness of intratest scatter as an indicator of "faking." Gudjonsson and Shackleton (1986) described a statistical method for analyzing responses to easy versus difficult subtests on the Ravens Standard Progressive Matrices (RSPM) and present cut-off scores for distinguishing faked from nonfaked performances. Their technique tests for a lack of expected decrease in subtest scores across the five, increasingly more difficult subtests, of the RSPM. Their technique may have applicability to other tests with subtests differing in difficulty level or with "easy" and "difficult" forms.

b. Parallel testing. Repeat administrations of the same test or administration of a parallel form of a test should yield similar performances. The faker may not understand that a repeat of the test will be given and, therefore, may have difficulty replicating the previous performance. Faked scores in general are less stable than genuine scores.

The Peabody Picture Vocabulary Test (PPVT) as a test of receptive vocabulary is an example. Clients often have difficulty obtaining the same score on a parallel form even when the testing is administered a short time later.

c. Deviations from predicted scores. The evaluator can compare performance on predicted scores on a test with actual performance on that test. For example, regression equations have been developed to predict WAIS-R scores from scores on the Shipley-Hartford Institute of Living Scale (Zachry, 1986; Weiss & Schell, 1991), Ravens Standard Progressive Matrices (O'Leary, Rusch, & Guastello, 1991) and the National Adult Reading Test (Willshire, Kinsella, & Pryor, 1991). A faker's obtained score on the WAIS-R may fall outside the confidence interval predicted from one of these three other tests.

The Shipley-Hartford and Ravens Matrices in particular are useful screening measures of intelligence because they take only a short time to administer. In addition, the Shipley-Hartford provides alternate forms which will yield information on test-retest performance as well as giving an estimated WAIS-R IQ. Impaired, nonfaking subjects should obtain WAIS-R IQ scores similar to those predicted by these two tests.

3. **Certain test characteristics.**

a. Inconsistencies across similar items or tasks. Within the same test, the faker may not pay attention to item similarity and, therefore, not perform in an identical fashion. A less stable performance on similar items is frequently seen in fakers, just as with parallel tests. On tests with repeated trials of the same task (e.g., finger tapping, dynamometer), intertrial variability also increases with faking. However, it should be remembered that the reliability of item-level scores is much lower than the reliability of scale-level scores. Therefore, less confidence should be placed in item-level or trial-level inconsistencies than in scale-level inconsistencies.

b. Failure to show learning. Fakers often do not show expected learning curves (or may perhaps even show deterioration) across repeated trials of a task. The Mirror Tracing Test (Andreas, 1960; Millard, 1985) illustrates this expectation. The subject is told to trace the path between the two solid lines of a maze while viewing the maze in a mirror. An error is counted each time the subject's pencil touches a guideline. If the subject crosses the line, he or she must reenter at the same point; otherwise, a reentry counts as a second error. Faking may be suspected if the expected bilateral transfer of training (improved performance with the opposite hand after training with one hand) does not occur, if the expected improvement over trials (learning curve) is not apparent or if the total time exceeds five minutes.

4. **Departures from expected accuracy.** Forced-choice testing and forced-choice reaction time testing provide powerful methods of assessing deception of deficits. These tasks are all so easy that even severely impaired persons should perform satisfactorily. Departures from expected levels of performance provide a measure of a conscious attempt to manipulate performance.

Jensen (1980, pp. 686-698) described the use of forced-choice reaction time (RT) as a measure of faking. The subject is presented with an apparatus containing a push-type microswitch ("home") with eight additional push-switches arranged in a semi-circle above the "home" button. Above each of the eight switches is a signaling light. The subject is instructed to depress the "home" button and wait for a warning tone. Within one to four seconds of the warning tone, one of the signal lights is illuminated and the subject is asked to move "as quickly as possible" the finger from the "home" button to the switch below the illuminated light. The subject's reaction time (measured in milliseconds) is the time between the onset of the signal light and the decompression of the "home" button.

Since a subject's average reaction time is considerably less than the recognition threshold (approximately .5 seconds), any intentional attempt to delay responding will dramatically and obviously shift the distribution of reaction times in the direction of longer latencies. Preliminary research showed that "when subjects are instructed to attempt voluntarily to fake less than their "best" RT performance, they are remarkably unsuccessful. The subject's least conscious intention to respond less quickly than his or her "best" RT puts the RT into an entirely different distribution with *a median about eight standard deviations removed from the median of the distribution of the subject's normal, unfaked RT. Faked RTs do not even fall within the normal distribution of individual differences in RT*" (emphasis added) (Jensen, 1980, p. 691).

These faked choice reaction times are clearly distinguishable not only from the performances of normal subjects, but also from the performances of even severely retarded subjects (IQ < 40). They are also distinguishable from the large day-to-day variations in reaction times displayed by all subjects. Thus, the forced-choice reaction time test may provide nearly 100% accuracy in distinguishing persons who are consciously slowing their response times from even severely retarded persons whose reaction times are slower than normal.

It has yet to be determined how distinct deliberately slowed RTs are from those of patients with various neuropsychological deficits. Although Miller (1970) and van Zomeren and Deelman (1976, 1978) presented simple and forced-choice reaction times for groups of brain-injured patients, no study has yet compared such patients with other patients, with normal subjects or with malingerers on the same reaction time task. Do apraxic patients perform similarly to severely retarded persons or are they more similar to deliberate fakers? Where does the distribution of RTs among patients with Alzheimer's disease fall in relation to normal and faked RTs? If RTs are as discriminating between known neurological groups and fakers as they are between severely retarded persons and fakers, a simple and effective (unfakeable?) detection method would be available to the practicing neuropsychologist.

Symptom Validity Testing (SVT) or Explicit Alternative Testing (EAT) attempts to measure faked sensory and recall deficits (Grosz & Zimmerman, 1965; Hall & Shooter, 1989; Pankratz, 1979, 1983, 1988; Pankratz, Fausti, & Peed, 1975; Theodor & Mandelcorn, 1973). EAT involves the presentation of stimuli, whose perception or recognition is either affirmed or denied by the assessee. An interference period may be added if recall, rather than sensory perception, is the target of evaluation (see Chapter 15).

Almost no one should miss the presented items unless a genuine impairment exists. In the case of total impairment (e.g., total blindness), one's performance should approximate chance responding (50% accuracy with two-choice tasks). A significant deviation from chance responding is defined as an accuracy score with a probability less than some specified level (e.g., p < .05 or p < .01) as determined by the binomial distribution. For example, the one-tailed probability of obtaining less than 40 correct responses in 100 trials of a two-choice task is less than 2%. Achieving less than 36 correct answers would occur by chance less than twice in a thousand tests (p = < .0019).

Fakers usually assume that impaired performance requires less than 50 % accuracy (Haughton, Lewsley, Wilson, & Williams, 1979; Pankratz, 1988). Persons genuinely impaired will usually guess randomly on EAT testing. Fakers do worse than chance because they intentionally suppress the correct answers on items to which they know the answers. Pankratz (1988, p. 185) explains the basic problem for the faker on an EAT task:

> A 50% hit rate is expected from any patient who declares at the outset that he or she cannot perceive the test stimuli in a two-alternative procedure. The untruthful patient is in a dilemma when confronted with repeated trials. If he or she holds to the denial and tries to manage the impression of a disability, then he or she runs the risk of revealing too much. On the other hand, if the deceptive patient properly identifies the cues, he or she openly admits that the deficit is not as severe as first claimed. In most clinical situations deceptive patients "guess" wrong too frequently.
>
> In doing this, the final results are often below the probabilities of chance. Even when the final score is within normal limits, the response pattern may be incompatible with the notion that the stimulus did not register at all.

Pritchard (1992) has developed a computerized version of EAT which examines faked hearing, visual, or mnestic deficits. This is a 72-item forced-choice test which utilizes three sets of 24 trials each (Hiscock & Hiscock, 1989). A subject's total and subset performance may be compared with expected (theoretical) levels based on the binomial probability distribution. In comparing the performance of normal subjects instructed to feign a sensory or memory deficit and hospitalized psychiatric patients (including patients with organic mental disorders) instructed to try their best on this computerized version of EAT, Pritchard and Moses (1992) found that 66% of the pseudo-malingerers performed below expectation while 0% of the patients performed this poorly.

Evaluators can improvise applications of the EAT methodology for particular clinical problems. For example, in testing a 56-year-old male VA patient for alleged numbness of the entire body except for the spine, which was tender to touch, Pankratz, Binder, and Wilcox (1987) stated:

> The patient was asked to close his eyes and guess which hand the examiner touched. After 34 trials he refused to continue; he made 27 errors. Application of the binomial theorem resulted in a score of 3.25, P = <.0006, one-tailed test.

A table of binomial probability values is presented in Appendix H. The reader is encouraged to use this table when constructing specially adapted, binary-choice forms of EAT.

One problem with EAT methodology is that it is too conservative. By considering as "faked" only those performances which are significantly below chance levels of responding, one is assuming that the person is attempting to mimic a complete loss of the tested function. For example, a completely blind person or a totally deaf person would respond with around 50% accuracy on a binary forced-choice test and performances significantly below this level would indicate an intentional underreporting of actual perceptions. However, most subjects do not claim a total loss of function and, therefore, would not be expected to perform significantly below chance levels. Hart, Guilmette, and Elliott (1991) reported that only 38% of their pseudo-malingerers performed significantly below chance as defined by the binomial distribution. Pritchard and Moses (1992) found that only 66% of normal subjects instructed to feign a deficit performed below expectation. Similarly, Bickart, Meyer, and Connell (1991); Brandt, Bubinsky, and Lassen (1985); Haughton et al. (1979); and Iverson, Franzen, and McCracken (1991); found large false negative rates when referring the performances of pseudo-malingerers to the binomial distribution.

To detect those fakers who are presenting only a partial loss of function, Pritchard (1992) provided three alternative sets of interpretation rules. One set compared the subject's performance with chance levels based on the binomial distribution; a second set was empirically defined to maximize the positive hit rate (percentage of fakers who are called faking by the test); the third set was empirically defined to maximize the negative hit rate (percentage of nonfakers who are called not faking by the test). This combination of theoretical and empirical rules may prove more useful in actual clinical practice than the sole use of interpretations based on the binomial probability distribution.

The Smell Identification Test (SIT) provides an illustration of forced choice testing of faked sensory deficits. Developed by Doty, Shaman, and Dann (1984) at the University of Pennsylvania, the 40-item SIT provides a quantitative measure of smell function in less than 15 minutes. Doty et al. (1984) note that problems with the sense of smell are frequently associated with head trauma, with anosmia found in between 7% and 8% of cases.

The SIT may be useful when the assessee is suspected of malingering in regard to his or her sense of smell, such as when insurance/accident claims are filed. Four choices of smells are presented upon release of an odorant, yielding a 25% chance of accuracy in correctly identifying the designated smell, given total anosmia (10 out of 40). Most nonfaking patients will correctly identify 35 or more of the 40 odorants with females generally outscoring males at all age levels. Zero was the modal number of correct guesses for 158 men and women instructed to fake bad in the Doty et al. (1984) study. Doty (1991) notes that under the assumption that p = 0.25, the probability of obtaining a score of zero by chance is one in 100,000; the chance of obtaining five or less correct on the SIT is less than five in 100. Those with genuine problems reflecting total loss of smell (i.e., anosmia) generally score around 10 at chance level due to essentially random responding. Patients with partial dysfunction have intermediate SIT scores. Patients with multiple sclerosis yield scores slightly above average; Parkinson's or Alzheimer's patients produce scores that are significantly lower than average, but that are still substantially above the expected range for random responding.

CAVEATS

Forensic professionals attempting to understand faked brain damage do not appear to be aware of the rudimentary state of the art. Studies generally show that clinicians perform at chance to slightly above chance levels when asked to detect neuropsychological malingering (Heaton et al., 1978; Faust et al., 1988). Standard neuropsychological training is *not* sufficient to detect faking in spite of the usually high confidence neuropsychologists place on their opinions. Heaton et al. (1978, p. 900) state:

> On virtually all ability tests, the subject is told what is required in order to do well. At the same time, it usually becomes obvious what a bad performance entails, for example, be slow, make errors, fail to solve problems. Therefore, neuropsychological tests would seem intrinsically vulnerable to faking.

Although this holds true for sensory and mental status evaluation by neuropsychologists and psychiatrists, the courts generally hold neuropsychological testing in high esteem (Ziskin & Faust, 1988). Yet, neuropsychologists need to learn that their training poorly prepares them for deception analysis. Neuropsychological tests can and have been faked and it is quite possible (and even likely) that those most prone to faking may have some genuine impairments. The question is not simply one of either faking or nonfaking; rather, the two coexist in many cases.

In comparison, neuropsychologists' training does prepare them to read the literature and apply statistical guidelines. The clinical judgment of neuropsychologists in regard to detecting faking is poor while statistical decision-making may not be. The development and cross-validation of such statistical decision rules should become a high priority in neuropsychological research and the use of such rules by clinical neuropsychologists should become commonplace.

A second caveat is that the evaluator should be wary of the traditionally accepted signs of hysteria and malingering, which actually may reflect cerebral dysfunction. Gould, Miller, Goldberg, and Benson (1986) surveyed the literature and found that the majority of clients (60% to 80%) thought to be hysteric or presenting neurological problems due to secondary gain, actually suffered brain damage. In their own study of 30 consecutive neurology service admissions with acute structural brain disease, the encephalopathies confirmed by CT scans and other evidence, the following signs were revealed by the patients:

- history of hypochondriasis
- secondary gain
- *la belle indifference*
- nonanatomical sensory loss
- split of mid-line by pain or vibratory stimulation
- changing boundaries of hypalgesia
- give-away weakness

All subjects showed at least one of the above signs, with most exhibiting three to four of them. The presence of these "malingering" signs in genuine patients means that they may be worthless for discriminating malingering. The lack of a comparison group in this study, however, prohibits the clear conclusion that these signs are not indicative of exaggerated or fabricated symptoms.

A third caveat concerns the need for multiple measures of distortion. When evaluating neuropsychological patients for forensic purposes, the authors use specific devices for detecting deception, in addition to a composite neuropsychological battery and as much historical and premorbid information as is available. Recall that the Bender-Gestalt Test has been inappropriately used for decades by clinicians (and APA-approved training programs) as a sole measure of cerebral impairment. Bigler and Ehrfurth (1981) and others present convincing evidence, supported by CT scans, that this test misses genuine cerebral impairment. The high false negative rate suggests the need for broad-banded neuropsychological testing with built-in devices for detecting deception. A further problem with the Bender-Gestalt is false positives. Bruhn and Reed (1975) found that the Pascal-Suttell and Canter scoring methods failed to differentiate fakers from those who are genuinely impaired. Since any distorted response is scored by these systems, they fail to differentiate among genuine disorders, situational influences (e.g., fatigue, or boredom), peripheral disorders (e.g., peripheral neuritis) and malingering. Similarly, Mattarazzo (1990) and Ryan, Paolo, and Smith (1992) cogently argue that WAIS-R Verbal-Performance discrepancies and subtest scatter are inadequate signs by themselves of cerebral dysfunction. The only adequate database for assessing neuropsychological deception is one that includes test and non-test data, contemporary and historical information, and third-party as well as first-person reports.

Further cautions for neuropsychological assessment are presented by Wasyliw and Cavanaugh (1989), who state that evaluators should avoid:

> ...(1) blind testing and interpretation (i.e., using a stock procedure regardless of the specifics or without review of prior history and evaluation); (2) lack of personality and psychopathology evaluation; (3) "gut" impressions of diagnosis or issues of malingering without clear objective or observational data; (4) conclusions as to organicity or malingering based on single tests, intelligence testing alone or performance on personality tests; (5) conclusions that loss or reduction in functioning has occurred without historical assessment of prior functioning; (6) prognostic conclusions based on testing performed prior to maximum recovery; (7) conclusions as to degree of recovery based on the client's self-description alone; and (8) conclusions that deficits were due to a specific historical incident, based on test data alone.

Relevant to civil forensic practice, Wasyliw and Cavanaugh (1989) point out that to prove a personal injury case, the evaluator must demonstrate (a) the presence of encephalopathy; (b) damages in the form of behavioral, cognitive, or affective deficits; (c) a connection between the deficits and the encephalopathy, and (d) a causal connection between the encephalopathy and the allegedly tortious incident. Refutation of any of the four elements is sufficient to refute the total claim.

The same general requirements are found in criminal-forensic neuropsychology. To demonstrate mental incapacity under the American Law Institute Standard of insanity, for example, the neuropsychologist must (a) diagnose an organic mental condition operative at the time of the instant offense, (b) demonstrate a cognitive and/or volitional impairment at the time of the alleged crime, and (c) connect the mental condition to the cognitive and/or volitional impairment. Refutation of any of these three factors suffices to disprove insanity.

SUMMARY AND SUGGESTIVE SIGNS OF FAKING

Neuropsychological testing lends itself well to deception analysis. Fruitful areas of inquiry are plentiful within a composite battery, whose findings can then be integrated with data from other sources. Tests for cerebral functioning can be combined with personality tests, clinical observation, and cross-validating sources to provide conclusions regarding faking.

The following list presents signs suggestive of deception:

- Failure on specific measures adapted to assess faking of cerebral impairment (e.g., illusorily difficult tests)
  - (a) Inconsistency between clinical/test behaviors and known neuropsychological syndromes (i.e., goodness of neurological fit)
  - (b) Failure to exhibit impaired function outside the context of evaluation
- Skill performance changes on parallel testing
- Anterograde better than retrograde memory
- Approximate answers in interviews when concurrent testing reveals adequate skills
- Neuropsychological test results consistent with statistical rules for detecting malingering
- Similar or better performance on easy compared to difficult versions of the same test
- Less than accurate performance on forced-choice sensory, recall, and reaction-time tests
- No improvement where expected (e.g., absence of learning curve)
- Test scores outside of predicted confidence intervals (e.g., actual WAIS-R Full Scale IQ outside the confidence interval predicted by the score on the Ravens Progressive Matrices).

While not definitive in themselves, these factors are suggestive enough of distorted performance to justify a more intensive investigation of the possibility of malingering.

LEGAL REFERENCES

Buckler v. Sinclair Ref. Co., 68 Ill.App.2d 283, 216 N.E.2d 14 (1966).
Jenkins v. United States, 307 F.2d 637, 651 (D.C. Cir. 1961).

REFERENCES

Andreas, B. G. (1960). *Experimental psychology*. New York: Wiley.

Aubrey, J., Dobbs, A., & Rule, B. (1989). Laypersons' knowledge about the sequelae of minor head injury and whiplash. *Journal of Neurology, Neurosurgery, & Psychiatry, 52*(7), 842-846.

Bickart, W., Meyer, R., & Connell, D. (1991). The symptom validity technique as a measure of feigned short-term memory deficit. *American Journal of Forensic Psychology, 9*(2), 3-11.

Bigler, E., & Ehrfurth, J. (1981). The continued inappropriate singular use of the Bender Visual Motor Gestalt Test. *Professional Psychology, 12*, 562-569.

Binder, L. W. (1986). Persisting symptoms after mild head injury: A review of the postconcussive syndrome. *Journal of Clinical and Experimental Neuropsychology, 8*, 323-346.

Boll, T. (1985). Developing issues in neuropsychology. *Journal of Clinical and Experimental Neuropsychology, 7*, 473-484.

Brandt, J., Rubinsky, E., & Lassen, G. (1985). Uncovering malingered amnesia. *Annals of the New York Academy of Science, 44*, 502-503.

Bruhn, A., & Reed, M. (1975). Simulation of brain damage on the Bender-Gestalt Test by college students. *Journal of Personality Assessment, 39*, 244-255.

Craine, J. (1981). *Faking on neuropsychological tests*. Presented at Hawaii Psychological Association, Honolulu, Hawaii.

Craine, J. (1990a, April). Minimizing and denying: A testing approach to feigned amnesia. In *Truth or lies: Guidelines for detecting malingering and deception*. Workshop by Psychological Consultants and Forest Institute of Professional Psychology, Honolulu, Hawaii.

Craine, J. (1990b). Personal communication. Hawaii State Hospital, Kaneohe, Hawaii.

Cullum, C., Heaton, R., & Grant, I. (1991). Psychogenic factors influencing neuropsychological performance: Somatoform disorders, factitious disorders and malingering. In H. Doerr & A. Carlin (Eds.), *Forensic neuropsychology: Legal and scientific bases* (pp. 195-196). New York: The Guilford Press.

Doty, R. L. (1991). Personal communication. University of Pennsylvania Smell and Taste Center, Philadelphia, PA.

Doty, R. L., Shaman, P. S., & Dann, M. (1984). Development of the University of Pennsylvania Smell Identification Test: A standardized microencapsulated test of olfactory function. *Physiology & Behavior, 32*, 489-502.

Doty, R. L., Shaman, P. S., & Kimmelman, C. P. (1984). University of Pennsylvania smell identification test: A rapid quantitative olfactory function test for the clinic. *Laryngoscope, 94*, 176-178.

Faust, D., & Ziskin, J. (1988). The expert witness in psychology and psychiatry. *Science, 241*, 31-35.

Freedland, K. (1982). *The detection of faking on neuropsychological tests*. Unpublished doctoral dissertation, University of Hawaii, Manoa.

Freedland, K., & Craine, J. (1981). Personal communication.

Goebel, R. (1989). Detection of faking on the Halstead-Reitan Neuropsychological Test Battery. *Journal of Clinical Psychology, 39*, 731-742.

Gould, R., Miller, B., Goldberg, M., & Benson, D. (1986). The validity of hysterical signs and symptoms. *Journal of Nervous & Mental Diseases, 174*, 593-597.

Grosz, H., & Zimmerman, J. (1965). Experimental analysis of hysterical blindness: A follow-up report and new experiment data. *Archives of General Psychiatry, 13*, 255-260.

Gudjonsson, G., & Shackelton, H. (1986). The pattern of scores on Ravens' Matrices during 'faking bad' and 'nonfaking' performance. *British Journal of Clinical Psychology, 25*(1), 35-41.

Hall, H. V. (1985). Cognitive and volitional capacity assessment: A proposed decision tree. *American Journal of Forensic Psychology, 3*, 3-17.

Hall, H. V. (1990a, April). Faking good and faking bad. In *Truth or lies: Guidelines for detecting malingering and deception*. Workshop by Psychological Consultants and Forest Institute of Professional Psychology, Honolulu, Hawaii.

Hall, H. V. (1990b). Extreme emotion. *University of Hawaii Law Review, 12*, 39-82.

Hall, H. V., & McNinch, D. (1989). Linking crime-specific behavior to neuropsychological impairment. *International Journal of Clinical Neuropsychology, 10*, 113-122.

Hall, H. V., & Shooter, E. (1989). Explicit alternative testing for feigned memory deficits. *Forensic Reports, 2*, 277-286.

Hall, H. V., Shooter, E. A., Craine, J., & Paulsen, S. (1991). Explicit alternative testing: A trilogy of studies on faked memory deficits. *Forensic Reports, 4*(3), 259-279.

Hart, K., Guilmette, T., & Elliott, M. (1991). *Symptom validity testing as a method for malingering detections.* Paper presented at the 11th Annual Conference of the National Academy of Neuropsychology, Dallas, TX.

Haughton, P. M., Lewsley, A., Wilson, M., & Williams, R. G. (1979). A forced-choice procedure to detect feigned or exaggerated hearing loss. *British Journal of Audiology, 13,* 135-138.

Heaton, R., Smith, H., Lehman, R., & Vogt. A. (1978). Prospects for faking believable deficits on neuropsychological testing. *Journal of Consulting and Clinical Psychology, 46,* 892-900.

Hiscock, M., & Hiscock, C. (1989). Refining the forced-choice method for the detection of malingering. *Journal of Clinical and Experimental Neuropsychology, 11,* 967-974.

Iverson, G., Franzen, M., & McCracken, L. (1991). Evaluation of an objective assessment technique for the detection of malingered memory deficits. *Law and Human Behavior, 15*(6), 667-676.

Jensen, A. (1980). *Bias in mental testing.* New York: The Free Press.

Language Research Association. (1958). *The Auditory Discrimination Test.* Chicago, IL: Author.

Mattarazzo, J. (1990). Psychological assessment versus psychological testing: Validation from Binet to the school, clinic, and courtroom. *American Psychologist, 45,* 999-1016.

Meusch, A. & Woods, D. (1986). Patterns of feigning brain damage on the LNNB. *International Journal of Clinical Neuropsychology, 8,*2, 59-63.

Millard, R. W. (1985). *Application of selected measures for detecting neuropsychological impairment among alcoholics.* Unpublished doctoral dissertation, University of Hawaii, Manoa.

Miller, E. (1970). Simple and choice reaction time following severe head injury. *Cortex, 6*(1), 121-127.

Miller, H., & Cartlidge, N. (1972). Simulation and malingering after injuries to the brain and spinal cord. *Lancet, 1,* 580-584.

Mittenberg, W., Hammeke, T., & Rao, S. (1989). Intrasubtest scatter on the WAIS-R as a pathognomonic sign of brain injury. *Psychological Assessment: A Journal of Consulting and Clinical Psychology, 1,* 273-276.

Morgan, M., Manning, D., Williams, W., & Rosenbloom, L. (1984). Fictitious epilepsy. *Lancet,* 232-233.

O'Leary, U. Rusch, K., & Gudstello, S. (1991). Estimating age-stratified WAIS-R IWs from scores on the Ravess Standard Progressive Matrices. *Journal of Clinical Psychology, 47,*2, 277-284.

Pankratz, L. (1979). Symptom validity testing and symptom retraining: Procedures for the assessment and treatment of functional sensory deficits. *Journal of Consulting and Clinical Psychology, 47,* 409-410.

Pankratz, L. (1983). A new technique for the assessment and modification of feigned memory deficits. *Perceptual and Motor Skills, 57,* 367-372.

Pankratz, L. (1988). Malingering on intellectual and neuropsychological measures. In R. Rogers (Ed.), *Clinical assessment of malingering and deception* (pp. 169-192). New York: Guilford Press.

Pankratz, L., Binder, L. M., & Wilcox, L. M. (1987). Evaluation of an exaggerated somatosensory deficits with symptom validity testing (Letter to the editor). *Archives of Neurology, 44,* 798.

Pankratz, L., Fausti, S. A., & Peed, S. (1975). A forced-choice technique to evaluate deafness in a hysterical or malingering patient. *Journal of Consulting and Clinical Psychology, 43,* 421-422.

Parker, R. (1990). *Traumatic brain injury and neuropsychological impairment.* New York: Springer-Verlag.

Pritchard, D. (1992). *Tests of neuropsychological malingering.* Delray Beach, FL: St. Lucie Press, Inc.

Pritchard, D., & Moses, J. (1992). Tests of neuropsychological malingering. *Forensic Reports, 5,* 287-290.

Ryan, J., Paolo, A., & Smith, A. (1992). Wechsler Adult Intelligence Scale - Revised intersubtest scatter in brain-damaged patients: A comparison with the standardization sample. *Psychological Assessment, 4*(1), 63-66.

Roy, A. (1989). Pseudoseizures: A psychiatric perspective. *Journal of Neuropsychiatry, 1,* 69-71.

Smith, G., Nelson, R., Sadoff, S., & Sadoff, A. (1989). Assessing sincerity of effort in maximal grip strength tests. *American Journal of Physical Medicine & Rehabilitation, 68*(2), 73-80.

Strub, R., & Black, F. (1981). *Organic brain syndromes.* Philadelphia, PA: F. A. Davis Company.

Theodor, L. H., & Mandelcorn, M. S. (1973). Hysterical blindness: A case report and study using a modern psychophysical technique. *Journal of Abnormal Psychology, 82,* 552-553.

Thompson, L., & Cullum, C. (1991). *Pattern of performance on neuropsychological tests in relation to effort in mild head injury patients.* Paper presented at the 1991 meeting of the National Academy of Neuropsychology, Reno, Nevada.

Trueblood, W., & Schmidt, M. (in press). Malingering and other validity considerations in the neuropsychological evaluation of mild head injury. *Journal of Clinical and Experimental Neuropsychology.*

U. S. Department of Veterans Affairs. (1985). *Physician's Guide for Disability Evaluation, 1B,* 11-56. Washington, DC: U.S. Government Printing Office.

van Zomeren, A., & Deelman, B. (1976). Differential effects of simple and choice reaction after closed head injury. *Journal of Clinical Neurology and Neurosurgery, 79*(2), 81- 90.

van Zomeren, A., & Deelman, B. (1978). Long-term recovery of visual reaction time after closed head injury. *Journal of Neurology, Neurosurgery and Psychiatry, 1978*(41), 452-457.

Wasyliw, O., & Cavanaugh, J. (1989). Simulation of brain damage: Assessment and decision rules. *Bulletin of American Academy of Psychiatry and Law, 17,* 373-386.

Weiss, J., & Schell, R. (1991). Estimating WAIS-R IQ from the Shipley Institute of Living Scale: A replication. *Journal of Clinical Psychology, 47*(4), 558-562.

Willshire, D., Kinsella, G., & Pryor, M. (1991). Estimating WAIS-R IQ from the National Adult Reading Test: A cross-validation. *Journal of Clinical and Experimental Neuropsychology, 13*(2), 204-216.

Zachry, R. (1986). *Manual for Shipley Institute of Living Scale.* Los Angeles, CA: Western Psychological Services.

Ziskin, J., & Faust, D. (1988). *Coping with psychiatric and psychological testimony* (4th ed.). Los Angeles: Law and Psychology Press.

7

FAKED PAIN AND LOSS OF SENSATION

According to Stein (1972), professionals should be cautious in concluding that feigned pain indicates malingering:

> An expert may properly state his opinion that the pain is real, imagined or feigned. However, a claim that the plaintiff is malingering must be approached with great caution, since it necessarily implies that the plaintiff is practicing willful deception, if not perjury. "Malingering" may be defined as the deliberate, conscious feigning of pain by one who knows that he has no pain. The fact that there is no objective basis for the pain which the plaintiff claims falls far short of proving malingering.
>
> According to this view, purely subjective claims of pain should not automatically be construed as fabricated or exaggerated. Imputation of conscious, intentional faking of pain requires more than the absence of tissue pathology or of functional impairment.

In *Boyd v. General Industries* (1987), the court held that a 47-year-old assembly line worker who injured her back on the job in 1980 could recover for increased or prolonged disability due to subjective pain in view of the testimony of doctors that her experience of pain was real to her. Furthermore, plaintiffs may recover damages even if they engaged in willful deception, based on the principle that genuine deficits (e.g., psychological pain) can be accompanied by unrelated lying and distortion. The court stated as follows (p. 755):

> We have also said, however, that the Commission may not refuse compensation to a claimant simply because he is untruthful *(Guidry v. J & Eads Const. Co.*, 11 Ark. App. 219, 669 S.W.2d 483 [1984]). In the case at bar, Boyd's credibility is only relevant on the issue of whether she is malingering, and the Commission's decision carries

with it an implicit finding that she is malingering. As the Supreme
Court stated in *Wilson & Co. v. Christman*:

> It goes without saying, and without the necessity for citation of
> cases, that true malingering is not a form of disability of any sort. It is
> a form of ability rather than disability.

> It is a form of ability to feign injury or disability that does not
> exist. Had [the] appellee in this case been malingering his disability,
> the Commission might well have determined that he had none.

The Boyd Court continued:

> Here, there is no substantial evidence to support a finding of
> malingering. Dr. Hutt, upon whose testimony the Commission par-
> ticularly relied, said that Boyd's perceptions of pain are "very real to
> her," and that there was no evidence of malingering or intentional
> distortion of perceived severity of pain. Dr. Bevilacqua stated that
> Boyd appeared "very sincere and reliable" and that "she has abso-
> lutely no insight into her obvious emotional conflicts."

> Dr. Kaczenski said Boyd was not malingering. None of the many
> doctors who have seen Boyd have so much as suggested that she might
> be malingering. Although compensation claims predicated upon mental
> disorders must be carefully scrutinized in order to protect the em-
> ployer against unwarranted claims, the danger of denying recovery to
> a deserving claimant must be guarded against with equal enthusiasm.
> *Royer v. Cantrelle*, 267 So.2d 601 (La.Ct. App. 3rd 1972), writ de-
> nied, 263 La. 626, 268 So.2d 680 (1972). (p. 755)

To summarize, the evidence in this case clearly established that:

1. Boyd suffered a compensable but relatively minor back injury in 1980, which has now completely healed;
2. At the time of the injury she was neurotic, but without symptoms;
3. She now suffers pain which causes her to be unable to work;
4. This pain is a symptom of her neurosis;
5. She is not malingering;
6. Her injury did not cause the neurosis—the neurosis was a
   preexisting condition; and
7. Although the on-the-job injury did not 'cause' her present
   pain in a medical sense, it was the precipitating event which
   brought forth this symptom, and was therefore a legal cause
   of her resulting disability. For the foregoing reasons, this
   case is reversed and remanded to the Commission for a determination of the extent of Boyd's disability.

Defining pain and its possible deception is difficult. The standard definition
suggests that pain is a response to noxious stimuli—those which produce or
threaten to produce tissue damage. Yet, psychic pain produced by psychological
stimuli may be just as distressing as purely physical pain to affected individuals.
In many cases, there may be no difference between physical and psychological
pain in reported intensity, frequency, or duration. Both intertwine to a consider-

able extent, with depression, anxiety, and frustration increasing experienced pain, and vice versa.

The most common types of chronic pain syndromes include: (a) headaches—tension, migraine, vascular, and post-traumatic; (b) back pains—disc disease, spondylitis, osteoporosis, fractures; (c) psychologically induced pain—trauma, PTSD, etc.; and (d) others—myofascial pain, muscle spasm, and sympathetic dystrophies. These, of course, are types of disorders in which pain is the primary complaint.

In addition, headaches around the eyes can be also due to glaucoma, around the back of the neck to meningitis, and in the face to trigeminal neuralgia. Psychological pain is a common correlate of many DSM-IV conditions. These include the depressive and anxiety disorders, hypochondriasis, and hysteria, and the organic mental disorders. The International Classification of Diseases describes many pain-related diseases, including musculoskeletal disorders (e.g., osteoarthritis, Paget's disease), ischemic disorders (e.g., angina pectoris, claudication), neurological disorders (e.g., causalgia, coccydynia, scar pain), and miscellaneous categories (e.g., chronic pancreatitis, temporomandibular joint syndrome).

In sum, pain may be either the defining or an associated feature of a disorder, and may be due to either physical or psychological causes. It may be exaggerated or distorted without being totally fabricated. It may be genuine even when there is evidence of outright lying.

BIOLOGICAL/NEUROPSYCHOLOGICAL FACTORS

On a biological level, receptors to noxious stimuli are called nociceptors, which are needed for the perception of pain and are found both internally and on the surface of the skin. Together, the nociceptive and the antinociceptive pathways, which provide pain relief, constitute the beginning and end points of the body's response to physical pain.

Peripheral sites and tracts converge on the spinal cord, in particular the substantia gelatinosa, consisting of nerve cells in the dorsal horn of the spine. Pain information is sent in ascending pathways to the brain. The "gate theory" (Melzack, 1973) of pain perception suggests that a limited amount of pain signals enter the brain, and that there is a modulating influence on pain information and pathways descending from the brain. The primary modulating factor operating to reduce pain is the production of endogenous opiates. These are mainly amino acid chains (polypeptides) called *endorphins*, which emanate from CNS sites. Endorphin sites include, but are not limited to, the brain stem, especially the periaqueductal gray matter. Tolerance, withdrawal, and other morphine-like effects have been noted in regard to endorphins. In fact, much chronic pain could be due to a withdrawal reaction (due to depletion) to endogenous opioids, thus depriving the organism of relief from pain. Parker (1990) noted in this regard that pain is inversely related to pre-surgery B-endorphin levels.

The brain has few pain endings and cerebral lesions rarely cause pain. One exception is the (rare) thalamic pain syndrome, which may cause vague, difficult to localize pain. Strokes and surgery involving the thalamus create a burning sensation, contralateral from the lesioned site (Kaufman, 1985).

Dermatome analysis (Goldberg, 1987) may be relevant to the evaluation of pain deception. This involves the study of perceived pain or loss of sensation corresponding to the strip-like projection areas of individual sensory nerve roots, which are distributed over the body similarly for most humans, and then relating them to reported pain in individual cases. In general, a sensory deficit involving an extremity (rather than a specific dermatome) suggests a lesion on a sensory tract within the CNS, whereas sensory deficits along a dermatome, especially when associated with localized pain, suggests a peripheral nerve lesion (Goldberg, 1987). CNS lesions, therefore, rarely produce a correspondence between dermatomes and areas of reported pain or loss of sensation.

PSYCHOLOGICAL/AFFECTIVE FACTORS

Both physical and psychic pain pathways involve the limbic system, thus associating sensory with affective information. Parker (1990) notes some psychological features of pain:

1. At low levels of arousal, pain may serve an informative function.
2. At high levels of arousal and stress, pain is accentuated.
3. Elevated tension and anger are associated with increased acute pain; chronic anxiety (e.g., "anxiety proneness") and depression are also associated with an increased perception of pain, as well as the presence of collateral physical impairment.
4. Increased pain is associated with inability to express one's feelings.

The usual psychological consequences of chronic pain include deteriorating self-esteem, irritation, sexual dysfunction, anger, and guilt. Depression may be the key psychological correlate of chronic pain (Griffith, 1990).

SOCIAL/CULTURAL FACTORS

Pain often functions as a signal to others for help and/or attention. Flor, Kerns, and Terk (1987) reported that the best predictor of self-reported pain was the person's perception of spousal reinforcement. Patients who saw their spouses as solicitous reported higher levels of pain and lower levels of activity. Increased dependency on others as a response to pain is common. A progressive withdrawal and isolation from others is seen in some cases. This process is exacerbated by a noted tendency for family, friends, and acquaintances to avoid people in pain. One reason for this avoidance is to reduce exposure to the unpleasant displays of the affected party. Loss of work may further reduce self-esteem and increase depression, as well as destroy the financial basis for the future of the individual.

Culturally, some persons are not encouraged to show pain responses (e.g., some Oriental groups, Northern Europeans). Other groups are much more expressive (e.g., Mediterraneans, Polynesians). The evaluator needs to take communication styles into consideration when assessing an individual's complaints of pain. In some individuals apparently exaggerated complaints of pain may represent personal (e.g., histrionic) or subcultural (e.g., Mediterranean) styles of communication rather than evidence of intentional distortion.

TARGETS OF DECEPTION

Both pain and loss of sensation may be compensable losses. All chronic pain and sensation-loss syndromes can be targeted for deception. Although pain complaints are overrepresented in the lower back area (where nerves are in abundance) (Griffith, 1990), reported pain can be widely distributed over the body. Lifestyle should be adversely affected with genuine pain. Thus, the evaluator needs to be alert to many targets of deception and to assess the entire lifestyle of the assessee.

Examples of potentially malingered pain include:

Behavior: Discrete motor behaviors associated with low back pain were shown by a 25-year-old male who engaged in vigorous exercise when not posturing weakness and immobility.

Somatic/ Psychosomatic: Pseudo-seizures following an alleged painful aura-like experience were presented by a 32-year-old White brick mason in an attempt to collect workers' compensation.

Sensation: Extreme reactivity to touch and pressure was shown on two point threshold tests by an 18-year-old burn patient four years after suffering minor (first degree) burns.

Imagery: Painful images (flashbacks) of war were experienced by a 35-year-old male veteran even though it was determined that he had not been stationed in a combat area (see opening case in PTSD chapter).

Affect: Anxiety lowered, rather than raised, perceived pain in a 45-year-old female seeking compensation for an accident involving a slight fall while disembarking from a marine craft.

Cognition: "Suicide" ideation and gestures of an unrealistic nature (e.g., hitting self with fists, trying to strangle himself) were shown by a 27-year-old Puerto Rican male in an alleged attempt to escape from a painful love relationship.

Interpersonal: Interpersonal manipulation was suggested by a 59-year-old Filipino male when he required family members to wait on him after making up a history of painful heart attacks.

It is important to note genuine symptoms of pain or signs associated with pain which cannot be faked. These include (Goldberg, 1987): (a) muscle atrophy and fasciculation, the latter consisting of a sometimes painful contraction of skeletal muscles in which groups of muscle fibers innervated by the same neuron contract together and (b) visual disturbances such as the pupillary light reflex, abnormal retinal appearance, ocular divergence, and nystagmus. All of the above should be considered involuntary in nature.

Evaluators should not confuse complainers with fakers. False positives are frequent as the following case demonstrates:

> Lt. Arnold walked into the Army mental health clinic stating that he had been referred by the internist to rule out psychological factors to a reported injury. This young officer explained that no medical cause had been found for a sharp, excruciating but episodic pain in his lower back, first experienced when leading his platoon in calisthenics, and that he did not feel the examining physician believed him. Psychometric tests revealed many traits associated with hysteria including a substantial conversion "V" on the MMPI.
>
> Subsequently, the lieutenant reported that the military physician, upon receiving the psychological test results, had accused the officer of malingering and ordered him back to the field. The psychologist referred the client to an osteopath who cleared up the problem in less than 15 minutes with spinal manipulation. All complaints of pain ceased permanently.

RESPONSE STYLES

Like targets, the kinds of behaviors associated with faking some aspect of pain include any responses which may yield a successful outcome for the faker. Honesty is common when there is no reason to fake or when cross-validating data is readily available to the evaluator. Faking good sometimes occurs when the client wishes to minimize or deny a more negatively perceived problem such as sexual dysfunction. This denial covaries with cultural upbringing and with contexts where the expression of pain may be disapproved (e.g., military, sports).

Malingering pain and faking sensory numbness may be linked to a payoff for the deceiver. Mixed and fluctuating responding can be exhibited, such as when one type of pain is exaggerated (e.g., backache) and another denied (e.g., headache), with both changing in the reported level of severity over time.

Help-seeking behaviors associated with pain and injury are instructive to study. Peck, Fordyce, and Black (1978) studied a wide range of pain behavior in tort claim litigants. Only two conditions identified the possible fakers—they consulted fewer physicians and utilized more supportive devices (i.e., crutches, prosthetics) that cost more than $200. As part of this study, Peck et al. found that claimants used less prescribed pain-relieving drugs than nonlitigants for the first month of postinjury. By the sixth month, drug ingestion had dropped off sharply for both groups.

In sum, the Peck et al. (1978) study suggests that there are few differences between claimants and nonlitigants in help-seeking behaviors. If anything, those who had reason to fake seemed to avoid evaluators and treatment personnel. None of the following categories considered by these investigators should be regarded as indicative of faking: (a) number of hospital admissions, (b) length of stay in the hospital, (c) number of diagnostic procedures in the hospital, (d) help-seeking in regard to rehabilitative centers, (e) days lost from work, and (f) number of patient-physician contacts or specialists consulted.

DETECTION STRATEGIES

Most evaluators of pain use a consistency model in determining faked pain. Yet, pain may be inconstant due to habituation, change in context, psychological modification, and other factors. This argues for a multifaceted approach to evaluation, hopefully with the results pointing in the same direction.

A few methods for detecting faked pain are as follows:

1. **Anatomical inconsistencies.**
    a. Pain versus temperature: These sensations tend to coincide because they are located in the same nerve bundles. When the temperature sensation is preserved while there is a loss of pain sensation, the deficit is not considered organic in etiology. Kaufman (1985) reports that a lesion of the pain-temperature pathway (spinothalamic tract) will result in loss of pain-temperature sensation contralateral to and below the level of the lesion. This holds true whether the lesion is in the brain or in the spinal cord. Additionally, the loss of pain-temperature sensation in the right leg and loss of proprioception in the left leg suggests a single lesion on the spinal cord.
    b. Faked hemiparesis is clinically more common in the left limb than the right, perhaps because of the more frequent right-limb dominance. Often, there will be a short period of normal activity prior to the limbs "giving away" and the patient reassuming the paretic position.
    c. Fakers often have an incorrect belief about laterality of symptoms. This is exhibited when the faker describes right- or left-sided headaches in conjunction with other anomalies (e.g., hearing, sight, smell, motor deficits) on the right side. The faker is not aware that contralateral and not ipsilateral deficits are expected from the suggested injury. Multiple lesions, causing unilateral symptoms, are required to account for the reported effects.
    d. Self-inflicted pain is usually avoided when there is voluntary control. In this sense, a person will not strike himself or herself when pretending to be in a coma or paretic. Neurologists will often use a "face-hand" test assessing alleged motor impairment, pulling the hand away from the face and suddenly letting it go.
    e. Motor inconstancies are suggested when impairments disappear under hypnosis, sodium amytal, or when the faker be-

Table 7.1
Barkemeyer-Callon-Jones Malingering Detecting Scale

I.   INTERVIEW BEHAVIORS
     Instructions: For each of the behaviors described below, check those that
     occurred during your evaluation of the patient.
A. Introductory Phase: Spontaneous Comments by the Patient
_____ 1.   The patient expressed exaggerated confidence in the examiner's ability.
_____ 2.   The patient made statements or presentations that would appear in
            some way to enhance his position in society.
_____ 3.   The patient made denigrating statements about others in the immediate
            community.
B. History Taking Phase: Characteristics of the Patient's Presentation
_____ 4.   The patient focused on the severity of the reported problem.
_____ 5.   The patient focused on the impairment resulting from the reported
            problem.
_____ 6.   The patient's reasoning included no alternatives.
_____ 7.   The patient made temporal associations that are not known to repre-
            sent cause and effect relationships.
_____ 8.   The patient described an atypical or very unlikely response to treat-
            ment.
_____ 9.   The patient denied responsibility for clearly voluntary acts.
_____ 10.   The patient presented a constellation of complaints that are not con-
            sistent with a recognized abnormality of an anatomical substrata.
_____ 11.   The patient's disability was emphasized during the examination to
            the exclusion of consideration of his abilities.
_____ 12.   The patient denied the ability to learn new skills to compensate for
            those lost.
C. History-taking Phase: Manipulation Attempts
_____ 13.   The patient cited another professional who allegedly agreed there was
            a problem.
_____ 14.   The patient described the prestige of other people who allegedly found
            a pathological process.
_____ 15.   The patient quoted an authority on the subject of the suspected patho-
            logical process.
_____ 16.   The patient used an irrational analogy to justify a claim of physical
            pathology.
_____ 17.   The patient threatened harm to himself or others if relief was not
            found.
_____ 18.   The patient overstated the examiner's authority for intervening on
            the patient's behalf.
_____ 19.   The patient implied there might be legal retaliation for a missed diag-
            nosis of improper care.
D. Patient's Response to Questions
_____ 20.   The patient questioned the competence of the examiner.
_____ 21.   The patient gave an affirmative response to an inappropriate leading
            question.

(continued on next page)

Table 7.1
Barkemeyer-Callon-Jones Malingering Detecting Scale

E. Examination Phase

_____ 22. Any physical effort resulted in enhancement of the patient's presentation of symptoms.

_____ 23. The patient's responses during the examination did not support a physiological explanation.

F. Patient's Response to Disagreement

_____ 24. The patient's response to the examiner's explanation suggested a distorted meaning of the examiner's treatment.

_____ 25. The patient demanded an explanation based on inadequate data.

_____ 26. The patient questioned the examiner's motives.

II. APPARENT GOALS FOR PATIENT'S BEHAVIOR

Instructions: Rate each of the following according to the likelihood of their correctness. If the statement appears to be correct in this instance, place a check mark beside it.

_____ 27. The patient's complaints lead to the avoidance of a normal responsibility or a noxious activity.

_____ 28. The patient's complaints result in the gain of either a concrete entity or an abstract quality.

_____ 29. The patient's complaints result in the retention of either a concrete entity or an abstract quality.

Reprinted with permission of Charles A Barkemeyer, North Street Publishing Company, Baton Rouge, Louisiana. Cutoff score of 7.6 on the 29 items revealed a hit rate of 95.1% (96.7% true positives and 90% true negatives).

---

lieves he or she is unobserved. Findings from hypnosis and drug interviews, however, should be considered weak evidence unless corroborated by independent data.

   f. Alleged pain imperception or loss of sensation is difficult to fake upon repeated bilateral stimulation. This is because fakers are relying on a subjective strategy rather than responding to the strength of the stimulus. Von Frey hairs, for example, can be used to bilaterally test a faked sensory imperception.

2. **Drug response discrepancies.** Some drugs have differing chemical composition, yet are similar in terms of effect on reducing pain. Thus, two tablets of aspirin (600 mg) are reported to have the same effect as a standard dose of Darvon, codeine, or Demerol (Kaufman, 1985). Suspected faking is associated with widely divergent pain relief from expected results. This is a very weak hypothesis until confirmed by cross-validating data suggesting malingering.

3. **Clinical interview behavior**. Data are lacking on interview behavior associated with faked pain. However, systems looking at faked pain and loss of sensation are beginning to be developed. Barkemeyer, Callon, and Jones

(1989) have developed a malingering test for pain, loss of sensation, and other complaints. The full range of interviewing and evaluation behaviors are described in Table 7.1.

4. **Presence of psychometric signs.**

   a. Although the "conversion V" on the MMPI may or may not reflect a conversion based on a psychological conflict, it does suggest the clients' (a) perception of their pain, (b) their perception of affect related to their disability, and (c) degree of functional impairment (Tapp, 1990). This pattern is associated with a poorer prognosis for recovery and with the experience of acute, high-intensity pain. An hysterical overlay to exhibited pain may be present. The hysteria may not be subject to control by the assessee and should not be considered deception by the evaluator.

      Validity indices on the MMPI and other objective tests may be used to determine general response style. Indications of faking bad on the MMPI, for example, may suggest (but do not prove) that reported pain may also be exaggerated. Furthermore, pain is seldom experienced in the absence of other affective and psychological problems. These other problems should also be apparent in psychological test scores and profiles.

   b. An illness questionnaire developed in Australia by Clayer, Bookless, and Ross (1984) appears promising for the global assessment of distress. Validated on 164 male and female public utility workers, half of whom were instructed to fake a serious injury, and 82 male and female clients at a pain clinic, the questionnaire appeared effective in differentiating fakers from those experiencing distress which was neurotically determined.

      Base rates for normals and neurotics generally revealed an increasing percentage of item endorsement by the latter group. Fakers were very clearly differentiated from nonfakers (i.e, normals, neurotics) on seven of the 62 total questions. Recalculating the data, the majority of fakers (64.2%) endorsed all the following questions compared to 27% of the nonfakers, with a 25% to 50% point spread between the two groups (mean difference = 36.8%) on each question:

      1. Do you care whether or not people realize you are sick?
      2. Do you find that you get jealous of other people's good health?
      3. Do you ever have silly thoughts about your health which you can't get out of your mind, no matter how hard you try?
      4. Are you upset by the way people take your illness?
      5. Do you often worry about the possibility that you have a serious illness?
      6. Do you often think that you might suddenly fall ill?
      7. Do you get the feeling that people are not taking your illness seriously enough?

   c. The Millon Behavioral Health Inventory (MBHI) (Millon, Green, & Meagher, 1979) attempts to measure responsivity to pain treatment as well as a host of basic coping and prognostic signs. The MBHI illustrates the great difficulty of measuring variables associated with distress. The 150-item true-false questionnaire yields 20 scores and a three-item validity scale. Test construction, reliability, and validity of the measure have been vigorously challenged (Allen, 1985; Lanyon, 1985).

d. Pain Survey Check List (PSCL). The PSCL (see Appendix A) should not be considered a specific test for faking pain as no such reliable and valid measure exists. It is simply a checklist which may be useful in developing a broad data base before arriving at conclusions. It is comprehensive, covering most known parameters of the pain experience. Significant others may be asked to independently fill out the checklist in regard to the patient, thereby providing information where follow-up assessment may be needed.

e. Other methods. Previously discussed methods for detecting malingering (e.g., analysis of learning curves, regression equations, parallel testing, explicit alternative testing) may be used in pain deception analysis, if those methods measure an associated feature of reported pain (e.g., loss of sensation).

5. **Inconsistency in community versus evaluation behavior.** A detailed analysis of pain reportedly experienced outside the evaluation context is necessary for sound conclusions. This is based on two assumptions: (a) a reduced motor activity level accompanies genuine pain, and (b) the activity level shown during evaluation should be similar to that shown outside the evaluation session. Some impairment in work and in central love relationships should be reported with chronic pain. Is the claimant willing to have you talk to significant others? A refusal is suspicious. A list of specific questions that can be asked is provided in Appendix A. The same list can be given to different relatives and acquaintances to fill out independently of one another. Inconsistencies can be evaluated. A statement by significant others, for example, that nothing the claimant does changes reports of pain needs to be explored. The claimant needs to be asked what he or she does to reduce pain. The evaluator should explore statements of changes in pain in the absence of events which would explain them.

Malingered pain is suggested when behavior in the community is inconsistent with complaints of pain. For example:

> A 32-year-old mail carrier was routinely administered psychological and medical exams as part of ongoing evaluation and treatment for an alleged neck injury reportedly caused by a fall due to an attacking dog on his route several years previously. Claimed discomfort in the neck area persisted in spite of normal MMPIs and physical/neurological exams over the years. Complaints abruptly ended when a full (and permanent) medical retirement was awarded. After retirement, the party was seen frequently on the golf driving range, engaging in strenuous exercise that only a few months previously had been reported impossible to perform.

6. **Lack of response to common interventions.** Almost all clients should show some pain relief with (a) biofeedback, (b) hypnosis, (c) mild analgesics, (d) psychotherapy for anger and arousal management, (e) relaxation exercises, (f) heat and ice, and (g) mild exercise. The client should show pain relief in his limbs or lower back with transcutaneous electrical nerve stimulation (TENS). TENS involves an electric stimulus being applied

near the painful site, which has the effect of creating analgesia. Why a person with chronic pain would not show some improvement with these methods needs to be answered and integrated into evaluation findings.

INDICATIONS OF FAKED PAIN AND LOSS OF SENSATION

1. (a) Pain-free behaviors observed in community are denied during evaluation, or
    (b) Behavior in community implies sensitivity which is absent or denied during evaluation (loss of sensation complaints).
2. Admission of exaggeration or fabrication.
3. Violation of anatomical laws involving dermatomes, pain versus temperature loss, paresis, cerebral laterality, and motor functioning.
4. (a) Malingering on psychometric measures of psychopathology.
    (b) Failing tests specifically designed to assess faking.
5. Failure to show improvement when treated with typically effective interventions.

LEGAL REFERENCES

Boyd v. General Industries, 22 Ark. 103, 733 S.W.2d 750 (Ark.Ct.App. 1987)
Guidry v. J & Eads Const. Co., 11 Ark.App. 219, 669 S.W.2d 483 (1984).
Royer v. Cantrelle, 267 So.2d 601 (La.Ct.App. 3rd 1972), writ denied, 263 La. 626, 268 So.2d 680 (1972).

REFERENCES

Allen, M. (1985). Review of Millon Behavioral Health Inventory. In J. V. Mitchell (Ed.), *The ninth mental measurements yearbook* (p. 1521). Lincoln, NE: University of Nebraska Press.
Barkemeyer, C., Callon, E., & Jones, G. (1989). *Malingering detection scale manual.* Baton Rouge, LA: North Street Publishing Company.
Clayer, J., Bookless, C., & Ross, M. (1984). Neurosis and conscious symptom exaggeration: Its differentiation by the illness behavior questionnaire. *Journal of Psychosomatic Research, 28,* 237-241.
Flor, H., Kerns, R., & Terk, D. (1987). The role of spouse reinforcement, perceived pain, and activity levels of chronic pain patients. *Journal of Psychosomatic Research, 31,* 251-259.
Griffith, J. (1990). *Pain management: Learning to live with on-going pain and disability.* Presented at Hickam Air Force Base, Honolulu.
Goldberg, S. (1987). *The 4-minute neurologic exam.* Miami, FL: MedMaster.
Kaufman, D. (1985). *Clinical neurology for psychiatrists* (2nd ed.). Orlando, FL: Grune and Stratton.
Lanyan, R. (1985). Review of Millon Behavioral Health Inventory. In J. V. Mitchell (Ed.), *The ninth mental measurements yearbook* (p. 1205). Lincoln, NE: University of Nebraska Press.
Melzack, R. (1973). *The puzzle of pain.* New York: Basic Books.
Millon, T., Green, C. J., & Meagher, R. B. (1979). The MBHI: A new inventory for the psychodiagnostician in medical settings. *Professional Psychology, 10,* 529-539.
Parker, R. (1990). *Traumatic brain injury and neuropsychological impairment.* New York: Springer-Verlag.
Peck, C., Fordyce, W., & Black, R. (1978). The effect of the pendency of claims for compensation upon behavior indicative of pain. *Washington Law Review, 53,* 251-264.
Stein, J. A. (1972). *Damages and recovery—Personal injury and death actions* (Sec. 22, pp. 38-39). San Francisco, CA: Bancroft Whitney Co.
Tapp, J. (1990). A multisystems perspective on chronic pain. *Psychotherapy in Private Practice, 7,* 1-16.

8

POST-TRAUMATIC STRESS DISORDER AND DECEPTION

A 42-year-old United States Air Force veteran, determined by the Veterans' Administration (VA) to have a 50% service-connected disability for schizophrenia applied for PTSD-related VA compensation on the basis of alleged war service in Indochina. John M. claimed that he was in the Blue Berets, a special unit of the USAF trained for paramilitary and military police duties, and was stationed in the central highlands in Vietnam from 1966 to 1967. John M. reported nightmares and flashbacks, which he linked to frequent fire fights, night patrols, and venturing into neighboring Cambodia on "special assignments." His history revealed sporadic employment since the military, four marriages accompanied by spouse abuse, and chronic substance dependence. He reported multiple instances of closed head trauma due to fighting over the years.

John M. claimed that he obtained a Ph.D. in theoretical mathematics from Princeton University and an MFA from Yale University. When contacted by the evaluator, these institutions indicated that there were no records of the veteran. VA records revealed that John M. was stationed in Oregon at the time he claimed service in Vietnam. During the evaluation, he did not wish to discuss his USAF experience, stating that it brought back bad memories. Neuropsychological and psychological testing revealed no cerebral injury or psychosis, but a pronounced tendency to fake bad within a Mixed Personality Disorder. His claim was subsequently denied.

A large number of victims of post-traumatic stress disorder (PTSD) exists. They include individuals exposed to any of the overlapping categories of (a) consummated, attempted, and threatened violent crimes; (b) child and spouse abuse; (c) auto accidents involving severe injury; (d) industrial accidents; (e) civilian catastrophes; and (f) war and associated activities.

PTSD AND THE LAW

PTSD-related personal injury and wrongful death claims are yielding large awards. In a $9,250,000 verdict for the wrongful death and emotional distress related to a traffic sign falling on their car and killing the plaintiffs' three-and-a-half year old daughter (Case No. 86-6149 (CL) I; Judge Jack H. Cook presiding), PTSD-related data influenced the high award. Zarin and Weitzman (1990) stated the following in their analysis of this Palm Beach County, Florida, case.

> The treating psychiatrist testified as to the effect of the loss of a child under such sudden, unexpected, unjust, and violent circumstances. The plaintiff mother testified that every time she views her scar in the mirror or touches her scar, it causes a flashback of the vision of her daughter's face spilt [sic] in half. As of the date of trial, the plaintiff mother continued to experience multiple flashbacks on a daily basis of the vision of her daughter's face.

In a $780,000 verdict where a child was molested by a stranger inserting a finger into her vagina, the victim's PTSD and diminution in IQ were successfully asserted (*Barraza v. Jewelry Realty Corp.*, Index No. 22283/78: Judge Richard Rosenbloom, April 12, 1990). Zarin and Weitzman (1990, p. 6) state the following in their analysis of the case:

> The plaintiff's examining clinical psychologist testified that the assault caused a severe post-traumatic stress disorder which has continued to the present. The plaintiff was 19 at the time of the subject trial. The plaintiff's expert related that the plaintiff continues to experience nightmares, fear of traveling, and fear of enclosed spaces. This expert additionally related that the incident caused a flat emotional affect, rendering the plaintiff unable to express emotions normally. The plaintiff's expert educational psychologist testified that the plaintiff scored within the low/normal range upon IQ testing. The expert maintained that the plaintiff's results in various subtests differed widely and contended that such an 'inter-test score scatter' generally reflects emotional instability. The plaintiff's clinical psychologist concurred in this conclusion.

In criminal cases, PTSD is frequently asserted either as a basis for the insanity defense, as a basis for diminished capacity, or as a factor in mitigation of punishment.

BACKGROUND

PTSD has been given different names in the successive revisions of the American Psychiatric Association's Diagnostic and Statistical Manual (DSM):

DSM I   (1952) Gross Stress Reaction
DSM II   (1968) Adjustment Disorder of Adult Life
DSM III   (1980) Post-Traumatic Stress Disorder
DSM III-R   (1987) Post-Traumatic Stress Disorder
DSM IV   (1994) Post-Traumatic Stress Disorder

The introduction of PTSD in DSM-III caused considerable legal and clinical concern. An "official" mental disorder such as PTSD that is recognized by most courts and insurance companies may be misused in civil and criminal litigation. PTSD is largely subjective and may be seen as an easy (and unverifiable) mental condition to serve the vested interests of litigants seeking monetary compensation or relief from punitive action. In addition, a professional may be reluctant to diagnose faked PTSD. In the case described at the beginning of this chapter, for example, evaluation of John M. followed at least a dozen previous mental assessments subsequent to his discharge from the military. The documentation that the claimant was in Oregon when he claimed he was involved in combat was available to all examiners. Yet none questioned the genuineness of his claim.

PTSD AND ORGANIC FACTORS

Although PTSD is etiologically related to a traumatic event, recent explanations have emphasized biological factors. The search for biological anchors to PTSD is based on the notion that trauma can alter the neurochemistry of the brain. Years after a trauma, heightened states of arousal may again trigger PTSD behaviors, illustrating classical respondent conditioning in a previously traumatized person (Franklin, 1988; Kolb, 1987, 1988; Lipton & Shaffer, 1988; Van der Kolk, 1988). Affected CNS structures and functions implicated in PTSD may include the limbic system generally, projections of the septal-hippocampal complex (subserving anger control and memory), tyrosine hydroxylase production, alpha-2 inhibitory receptors (pre-synaptic), and excitatory receptors (post-synaptic).

There are also similarities between PTSD and traumatic brain injury (TBI), which feed speculations about organic components in PTSD and about delayed-stress reaction in TBI. Both involve acute signs and delayed effects. PTSD can involve symptoms similar to those stemming from cerebral insult (e.g., failing memory, difficulty in concentration, headache, vertigo), while TBI almost always involves emotional problems (e.g., elevated depression, anxiety), which are also common in PTSD. Stuss and Benson (1986) point to possible anterior brain dysfunction when a markedly diminished interest in significant activities (i.e., "emotional numbness"), a feeling of detachment or estrangement from others, and a restricted range of affect, with a depressive sense of a foreshortened future, occur.

As Wilson (1989) has stated, "(e)xtreme stress affects organismic functioning directly on four interrelated levels: physiological, psychological, social-inter-

personal, and cultural...interrelated processes which influence each other in direct and subtle ways that constitute the essence of the mind-body relationship."
Although neurochemical and neuropsychological explanations of PTSD are interesting and may stimulate fruitful lines of research, they are not necessary for
the diagnosis of PTSD.

DIAGNOSTIC CRITERIA

According to DSM-IV, PTSD requires (1) a recognizable stressor that would
evoke distress symptoms in almost everyone; (2) a re-experiencing of the trauma
in some form; (3) numbing of responsiveness or reduced involvement with the
environment starting sometime after the trauma; and (4) at least two associated
features that reflect persistent symptoms of increased arousal (e.g., exaggerated
startle responses, difficulty concentrating, sleep disturbances).

The "recognizable stressor" must lie outside the range of usual human experience and be of such an intensity as to produce distress symptoms in almost
everyone. Intensity levels are higher and PTSD more severe and long lasting if
the trauma is of human design (e.g., war), involves intrusive stimuli from the
perpetrator and helplessness on the part of the victim (e.g., torture, rape), or sets
off, or is associated with, a physical component (e.g., malnutrition, head trauma).
As Parker (1989) stated:

> Stress reactions are intense physiologically, cognitively and emotion-
> ally. *Overload leads to a variety of effects, including neuronal death*
> [emphasis added]...after stress, disturbances in both the body's im-
> mune system and in interpersonal relationships [are observed]; lead-
> ing to further vulnerability in the body's ability to handle illness and
> difficult social situations.

The traumatic event can be re-experienced by recurrent and intrusive recollections—*flashbacks*—of the event, recurrent nightmares, or suddenly behaving
as if the traumatic event was present because of a presumed association with an
environmental or mental event (e.g., dissociative states). The individual, for a
time, pays exclusive attention to the dominant reality represented by the experienced imagery, feeling state, and/or ideation. PTSD is ruled out if re-experiencing of the trauma cannot be demonstrated by relevant behaviors or be established
by diagnostically consistent self-report, observation, lab tests, or psychometric
findings.

The experience of reliving the trauma, illusions, hallucinations, dissociative
states, and intrusive recall may be organic in origin. Subsequent to a "biologically
important event...all recently active circuits may be 'printed'" (Livingston, 1985,
p. 1,270) by neurotransmitters. As Parker (1989) stated: "This creates sensitiza-
tion to dangerous stimuli, or generalizations, which are reminiscent of them,
repeating the trauma and creating new synaptic connections fixating it."

Numbing of responsiveness to, or reduced involvement with, the external
world usually begins not long after the traumatic event. An individual may show
a diminished sex drive, feel disinterested in previously enjoyed pastimes, and
complain of emotional isolation and distance from others. Affect is constricted,

meaning that the previous range of emotion shown towards others or activities is narrowed, usually in the direction of showing little emotion. In particular, tenderness and caring appear to be absent or diminished compared to premorbid behavior.

Autonomic arousal and related symptoms are experienced by the affected individual as high anxiety, depression, and guilt. There is often a lack of insight as to the reason for memory or concentration being impaired. Attempts to suppress symptoms are often revealed in substance abuse, high geographical mobility, and avoidance of activities which resemble the original trauma.

PTSD also involves difficulty falling or staying asleep, irritability, outbursts of violence with fears of losing control, difficulty concentrating, and an exaggerated startle response.

PTSD must be diagnosed differentially from other similar mental conditions (e.g., adjustment disorders) by specifying the onset and duration of the disorder. PTSD can dissipate and then be diagnosed for a later time period, especially if symptoms of the first PTSD episode persisted more than six months, the temporal cut-off point suggested by DSM-IV. There is no durational limit to PTSD; it depends upon treatment resources, individual symptoms, and severity of the original trauma(s).

A decision tree for PTSD, compatible with DSM-IV, was offered by Hall (1990) and is presented in Figure 8.1.

The following case illustrates a particularly dramatic case of PTSD in family members.

> On May 5, 1985, at around midday in his family residence, Jerry S., a single, unemployed, 23-year-old Filipino male, used a knife to destroy some family pictures and frames.
>
> This behavior followed a long series of strange and potentially violent actions, including attacking the walls, doors, and living room table with a large knife, responding to auditory hallucinations, talking to the television, and threatening family members with a knife. When his father asked him for the knife, Jerry S. started shouting as though his deceased brothers were in front of him, then attacked his father. During the next few minutes, Jerry S. attacked four family members with the knife, including his sister and his 1½-year-old nephew, fatally stabbed his mother in the heart, and attempted to run his father down with an automobile. He then went to the residence of other family members, knife in hand, covered with blood, and asked them if they wanted to die. He was apprehended the following day by police after escaping from the scene of his violence. A list of the injuries and impact on the surviving victims is provided below:
>
> 1. The father, Fred S. was stabbed or sliced multiple times in the torso, hand and shoulder. The victim was hospitalized for 10 days at Sunrise Hospital and underwent several operations for his life-threatening injuries. He was placed on psychotropic medication (Valium) upon release.

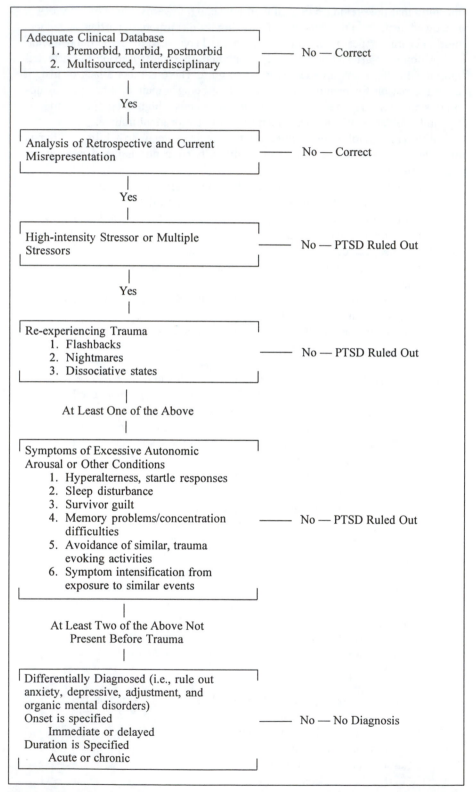

Fig. 8.1 Decision Tree for PTSD

Post-traumatic Stress Disorder (PTSD) symptoms commenced soon after the assault and included sleep problems and poor appetite. PTSD symptoms were still reported several years later.

Severe and chronic PTSD included the following:

   a. Existence of a recognizable stressor that would evoke significant symptoms of distress in almost everyone.
       This included the sustained wounds, the thought that other family members would be killed or wounded, and later finding out about the multiple assaults and his wife's death.
   b. Re-experiencing the trauma. This included frequent nightmares of the incident, vivid daytime memories of the assaults and killing of his wife, and panic attacks.
   c. Numbing of responsiveness to or reduced involvement with the external world. This included a loss of interest in usual activities, problems in trusting others, and few, if any, leisure activities. Fred attempted to remain active in the yard to a limited degree as a coping mechanism for the incident, for example, continuing to plant the favorite vegetables of his wife in the family garden even though that was seen as unnecessary by other family members. He occasionally broke down in tears.
   d. Relevant other symptoms: Including (1) difficulty falling asleep; (2) waking during the night, usually around two to three a.m. with continued wakefulness for the remainder of the day; (3) startle responses; and (4) avoidance of activities that reminded him of the incident including moving from the residence at which the violence took place.
2. Lucille L. was stabbed by her brother multiple times in the arm, back, and hand; some of her wounds were sustained when she attempted to keep the perpetrator away from her baby, Tom L. Some stab wounds were deep (e.g., right chest, three-and-a-half inch penetration; another wound two-and-a-half inches deep) with a confirmed pneumothorax (right chest) and a subsequent exploratory operation at Sunrise Hospital.
       PTSD symptoms commenced while she was at Sunrise Hospital and included insomnia and obsessive rumination about the incident. She was given Dalmane for sleep intervention at a follow-up visit with the medical observation that the patient appeared depressed. Lucille reported that, for two months after hospitalization, she could barely move. For four months after the incident, she could not engage in housework, sex, socialization with others, or take care of her son Tom. PTSD symptoms reported in 1985 continued with only mild improvement through 1990.

Inspection of pre-1985 medical records revealed that Lucille was basically a healthy person. Chronic PTSD is suggested as follows:

    a. Existence of a recognizable stressor that would evoke significant symptoms of distress in almost everyone.

       This included for Lucille the sustained wounds, fear that her wounded child would die, knowledge of the assaults on family members including the death of her mother and the stabbing of her son;

    b. Re-experiencing the trauma. This included vivid memories and flashbacks of the assaults and panic attacks where she became anxious, faint, dizzy, and behaviorally disorganized.

    c. Numbing of responsiveness to or reduced involvement with the external world. For Lucille, this meant often feeling emotionally blocked, unresponsive, and/or unable to express her feelings.

    d. Relevant other symptoms including insomnia, waking up during the night, and excessive jumpiness were present.

3. Tom L., son of Lucille L., sustained stab wounds to the left side of his forehead, left thigh, and under his chin (all about one-inch lacerations). Prolonged crying was witnessed up to and long after admission to Sunset Hospital.

    The possible onset of PTSD, shown by nightly crying (November 7, 1988) and sleep disturbances which included nightmares of a man attacking him (February 16, 1991).

4. Dolores S., sister-in-law of the perpetrator, witnessed Jerry S. walk into her house with blood on his body and a knife in his hand. He walked up to and held Dolores' daughter, Ann, age six at the time, and asked her several times if she wanted to die. He then asked Mrs. S. several times if she wanted to die, demanded that she look at the blood on his body, and informed her that he had just killed his parents and sister.

    PTSD symptoms shown by Mrs. S. appeared in 1988 and 1991 and included (a) vivid memories of the incident, (b) difficulty falling asleep, (c) difficulty concentrating, (d) waking up during the night after dreaming of the incident, (e) difficulty with her short-term memory, particularly as to whether she has flushed the toilet and washed her hands, possible indications of guilt and anxiety, (f) excessive jumpiness, and (g) avoidance of activities that remind her of the incident. She was particularly obsessed about her children's safety when they were alone at home. Work was significantly disrupted due to inquiries from others regarding the incident and when Jerry was due to leave the State Hospital. She felt that the family name had been tarnished in the small community of Maui.

5. Vicenta P., mother of Dolores, witnessed the treat towards Dolores prior to escaping from the house to get help. She believed that her daughter and granddaughter had been killed or wounded before finding out otherwise. Her PTSD symptoms included (a) vivid memories of the threatened killings, (b) panic attacks, (c) startle responses, (d) waking up early in the morning, and (e) avoidance of activities that reminded her of the incident.

6. Ann S., daughter of Dolores, whose life was threatened by the perpetrator, reported PTSD symptoms including (a) flashbacks and vivid memories of the threatened killing, (b) nightmares of the incident, (c) waking up during the night, and (d) avoidance of activities that remind her of the incident.

7. Pedro S., husband of Dolores, appeared to have suffered from secondary PTSD symptoms caused by the near death experiences of his wife and daughter, fear that the perpetrator would return prior to his apprehension, and the trauma of discovering that his mother had been killed and other relatives wounded by his brother. Symptoms included (a) vivid memories of the incident as related to him by his wife, child, and mother-in-law, and as he observed the scene prior to the arrival of the police and at the hospital where the victims were taken, (b) nightmares of the near death of his wife and daughter, (c) difficulty falling asleep with later mid-sleep cycle wakefulness, and (d) avoidance of activities that remind him of the incident.

In this case, some symptoms obviously related to the original trauma were not reported because they were not of at least moderate severity. Likewise, non-PTSD problems of a substantial severity, such as abdominal discomfort and severe headaches reported by some family members, were not reported because they are not diagnostic of PTSD.

Conservative interpretations of symptoms within the context of a comprehensive evaluation are a safeguard against overzealous diagnosis of PTSD. Not every complaint and symptom of a victim is a symptom of PTSD and not every PTSD-relevant symptom is of sufficient severity to include in the diagnosis. Feedback from the state attorney's office, which negotiated a $500,000 settlement on behalf of the victims in this case, suggested that conservative claims of post-traumatic effects are more persuasive than a laundry list of every problem experienced by the victim.

Atkinson, Henderson, Sparr, and Deale (1982) described some of the problems in diagnosing PTSD:

1. Professional bias against the diagnosis. Many clinicians believe that PTSD is not a bona fide disorder.

2. Adverse interactional styles between claimants and staff. An adversarial relationship between examining staff and clients with possible PTSD may reduce the accuracy of evalu-

ation findings. This may occur in civil cases when plaintiffs are examined by defense experts and in criminal cases where court-appointed forensic evaluators may be viewed by claimants as adversaries.

3. Lack of corroboration of data. Information from significant others, as well as supporting documentation, is critical to cross-validate a PTSD diagnosis.

4. The "silent" claimant. Avoidance of PTSD-related memories is frequent in this condition, to the point of being a cardinal diagnostic sign. Denial and minimizing are often seen in genuine PTSD and, hence, should be targets of detection and measurement.

5. Exaggeration and falsification of data. Faking bad does occur. Once PTSD is asserted, the clinician is placed in a position of refuting the existence of symptoms which may not be directly verifiable.

6. "Partial" post-traumatic stress disorder (stressors without full symptoms). Some persons exposed to substantial trauma satisfy some, but not all, of the DSM-IV criteria. In these cases, PTSD should not be diagnosed in spite of fragmentary signs in that direction. In the above case, the differentiation was made between those family members with full-blown PTSD and those having some PTSD symptoms, but not rising to the threshold of a mental disorder.

7. "Idiosyncratic" disorders (post-traumatic stress disorder symptoms without the stressors). Sometimes, persons exhibit the arousal symptoms in PTSD when no original stressor of sufficient magnitude can be uncovered. Assuming that no stressors are revealed subsequently to justify a diagnosis of PTSD, other conditions may be considered (e.g., phobias, adjustment disorder).

8. Intervening stressors. There should be a clear time frame for the onset of PTSD and a distinct set of identifiable stressors.

   Multiple events, all capable of producing PTSD, can then be distinguished in terms of their consequences. PTSD may have been triggered by a stressor unrelated to the alleged claim (e.g., intervening domestic problems or bankruptcy rather than war experiences may be responsible for the PTSD).

9. Deviant social behavior. Some behaviors are considered part of PTSD when, in fact, they are features of social deviancy (e.g., criminality, lifetime tendency to avoid or exploit others). Care must be taken to differentiate between PTSD and psychopathic behavior. Genuine PTSD-related violence, for example, has a dissociative, perseverative quality which most likely reflects a re-enactment of a previous traumatic event.

10. Either-or diagnostic judgment. PTSD may mimic other conditions or be combined with them. In fact, PTSD is often

accompanied by substance abuse disorders, depression, and organicity, if criteria for those conditions are satisfied. The combination of alcohol abuse and PTSD is a case in point.

PTSD-caused substance abuse, for example, yields an increase in flashbacks, nightmares, and other symptoms when alcohol is eliminated or reduced. In non-PTSD related alcoholism, this effect is not seen. Alcohol abuse may be used to suppress PTSD signs and to maintain a façade of normality. When alcohol consumption stops, disturbing imagery returns, whereas in non-PTSD substance abusers, nightmares usually cease as a function of abstinence.

11. Impact on examiners. "Secondary PTSD" is often encountered in examiner/therapists who have frequent contact with PTSD clients. Mental health professionals can themselves develop PTSD symptoms by listening to affected persons, all without experiencing a personal trauma.

The authors have noted the same contagious quality with family members of PTSD clients.

TARGETS

Any PTSD symptom may be targeted for deception since they are well-known in the media. Genuine but mild PTSD sufferers may exaggerate symptoms, or symptoms can be fabricated by those unaffected with the condition. Selected PTSD symptoms can be targeted for denial. Symptoms may be chosen which are unverifiable in nature (e.g., flashbacks, nightmares, suicide ideation), severe, or have a partial base in reality. As Lynn and Belza (1984) stated in reporting on seven Vietnam veterans suspected of faking PTSD in a VA hospital: "In analyzing the cases presented, one common denominator of factitious PTSD becomes apparent. Each patient had obviously acquired sufficient knowledge of PTSD to develop a tale best suited to his needs."

RESPONSE STYLES

Virtually every style of distortion is seen with PTSD. Honest responding is seen most often among fellow survivors of the original trauma and to a lesser extent with counselors or relatives. Denying and minimizing PTSD is abundant in genuine and severe cases. Faking good appears to function to maintain self-esteem and social acceptance. Faking bad is frequent, however. Mixed and fluctuating styles may occur as a function of changing motivations and goals.

In general, response styles of PTSD fakers present a varied picture and are probably not confined to war veterans. As Lynn and Belza (1984) stated:

Factitious PTSD, heretofore undocumented, is a not-uncommon entity that arose as a consequence of the Vietnam conflict. Though un-
recognized in DSM-III or DSM-IV, it probably has been in existence
as long as PTSD itself. It presents another form of a clinical deception
for which the unsuspecting clinician must develop an index or degree
of suspicion. So adept are factitious PTSD patients at their deception
that even the most experienced physicians can find themselves fooled
by the presenting complaints.

DETECTION

Measures and systems to detect faked PTSD are in a primitive stage of development. Assessment tools to gauge PTSD, therefore, include tests geared to the

Table 8.1
Psychometric Measures Sensitive to PTSD

Impact of Event Scale (IOES)	Horowitz et al. (1979)
Dissociative Experiences Scale (DES)	Bernstein et al. (1986)
Diagnostic Interview Schedule–PTSD	Helzer et al. (1987)
* Jackson Structured Interview for PTSD	Keane et al. (1985)
* PTSD Checklist	Kulka et al. (1986)
* Mississippi Scale for Combat-related PTSD	Keane et al. (1988)
Penn Inventory for PTSD	Hammarberg (1992)
* MMPI PTSD Scale	Keane et al. (1984)
Minnesota Multiphasic Personality Inventory	Fairbank et al. (1983)
	Foy et al. (1984)

* Scales marked with an asterisk are designed specifically for use
with (Vietnam) veterans but only the MMPI has built-in validity scales.

specific measurement of cumulative and acute stress, as well as to other symptoms relevant to the diagnostic criteria in DSM-III-R. Several interdisciplinary-
based PTSD measures are available and will be discussed. They typically involve
collective efforts of individuals from a variety of fields, who then create a
multisourced and interdisciplinary database. Measures reportedly sensitive to PTSD
are listed in Table 8.1; the measures developed specifically for use with (Vietnam) veterans are distinguished from more general measures of PTSD by an
asterisk.

General stress tests, such as the Social Readjustment Rating Scale (SRRS)
(Holmes & Rahe, 1967) are useful. The authors typically have the assessee complete the SRRS for (a) the present extending back one year; (b) one year before the
trauma, in order to capture an idea of premorbid functioning; (c) the time of the
trauma and the year following the trauma, reporting the worst symptoms during
this period; and (d) other times, depending on the remoteness of the original

trauma. The spouse or family members are asked to complete ratings for the same temporal periods. Differences in reporting events are often revealing.

For war veterans, a base-rate comparison of those with PTSD and those without the condition can be made. The Combat Exposure Scale provides a relevant measure for Vietnam veterans. Keane et al. (1989) built on previous efforts to develop a measure of the severity of prior combat exposure and produced a seven-item Likert-type scale with adequate reliability and discriminant validity.

Lund, Foy, Sipprelle, and Strachan (1984) offered the following advice for assessment of PTSD:

> In diagnosing and treating PTSD, it is important to ask directly about concrete events. With Vietnam veterans, asking about low-scoring, common events and proceeding to rare, more traumatic events on the Combat Exposure Scale provides a brief and systematic way of exploring war experiences.

PTSD malingerers could, of course, fabricate events associated with the scaled items. This possibility points out the necessity for a comprehensive evaluation of possible PTSD, including psychological testing and cross-validating documentation.

The importance of knowing explicit details of the alleged original stressor is illustrated in *Pard v. U. S.* (1984) involving two (unsuccessful) claims totaling $9.5 million. The plaintiff, a Vietnam veteran, asserted that the VA had failed to diagnose his combat-related PTSD, which resulted in his assaultive behavior toward the police. Sparr and Atkinson (1986) reported on events of the civil trial which culminated in a ruling that the VA was not negligent:

> At the 1984 trial, the government introduced testimony by three persons who served in Vietnam with the plaintiff: his commanding officer, a pilot, and a fellow crew chief. Their testimony made it evident that the plaintiff's helicopter was not a gunship but had been used for the administrative purposes of moving the commanding officer and his staff from place to place and for ferrying supplies. Members of the unit saw little, if any, combat. They had never been sent on missions to kill the enemy and had registered no confirmed kills. Testimony of his commanding officer demonstrated that no administratively assigned helicopter had ever been shot down during the time that the plaintiff was in Vietnam, and that no incident took place in which the plaintiff shot several children or any other Vietnamese people, civilian or military. The plaintiff had not been wounded by enemy bullets but had been injured when his own machine gun malfunctioned and a piece of the gun lodged in his arm. None of the men from the plaintiff's unit had heard of the incident in which the squad was supposed to have saved a general. Both the plaintiff's personal military record (Army 201 file) and the testimony at the trial made it plain that the plaintiff had not received the Distinguished Flying Cross or the Bronze Star.

At an earlier (February 1980) criminal trial, the jury was not aware of these facts and returned a verdict of "not guilty by reason of insanity" due to PTSD.

Neuropsychological tests should be administered if traumatic brain injury is implicated. Are neuropsychological deficits showing up on testing? The best tests to use would include those tapping PTSD-related problems such as attention, vigilance, short-term memory, judgment, planning, and execution. Nondeliberate distortion must first be ruled out. Signs of deception can be detected from those presented in Chapter 6 on malingered neuropsychological deficits.

Clinically, there is a noticeable tendency for malingerers of PTSD to avoid psychotic signs as part of their response strategy. Simulators usually do not report for any mandatory medical/psychological examinations. Often, there is a history of sporadic employment and a claimed lack of ability to work with concurrent involvement in recreation. "Soft" signs of faked PTSD include (a) bringing up the trauma early in assessment/treatment as opposed to the reluctance of genuine PTSD victims to discuss symptomatology and traumatic events, (b) indignation rather than surprise or blandness when confronted with suspicions of distortion, and (c) absence of impulse control problems, often found in the genuine PTSD client.

Resnick (1984, 1987, 1988a, b) discussed PTSD faked primarily, but not exclusively, by Vietnam veterans. His signs can be placed within the DSM-III-R

Table 8.2
Traditional Signs of Faked PTSD

A. Clinical Database
   1. Overidealization of functioning before trauma
   2. Evasiveness
   3. Uncooperativeness
   4. Understandable motive to fake PTSD
B. Stressor(s)
   1. Reporting of "incapacitating" prior injuries
   2. Emphasizing relationship of stressor(s) to symptoms
C. Re-experiencing Trauma
   1. No nightmares or an unvarying repetitive theme
   2. Grandiose dreams with power themes
D. Numbed Responsiveness/Reduced Involvement
   1. Poor work record
   2. Discrepant work and leisure activities
   3. Antisocial activities
E. Arousal Symptoms
   1. Inconsistency in symptom presentation (relevant to memory and concentration problems)
   2. No guilt over involvement or surviving the stressor
   3. Anger at authority
   4. Admission of malingering or psychometric evidence or corroborative evidence of dissimulation

criteria for PTSD, as shown in Table 8.2, but may not be relevant to all categories of PTSD-affected individuals.

One problem with these signs is the considerable overlap with genuine PTSD behavior. Resnick is to be commended, however, for his insistence on a thorough records review and interview of the subject's spouse/significant other and family. He stated in this regard (1988b, p. 94):

> The accessibility of specific DSM III-R criteria permit the re-sourceful malingerer to report the "right" symptoms. The assertion that individuals dream or think about a traumatic event should be verified by others who have heard them talk about it in situations that are not related to the litigation. In addition, the clinician must obtain a detailed history of living patterns preceding the stressor.
>
> For example, symptoms such as difficulty concentrating or in-somnia may have been present before the traumatic event.
>
> Baseline activity in a typical week before the trauma took place should be compared with reported impairment at the time of the evalu-ation. The clinician must carefully examine the reasonableness of the relationship between the symptoms and the stressor, the time elapsed between the stressor and the symptom development, and the relation-ship between any prior psychiatric symptoms and current impairment.

The Wahler Physical Symptoms Inventory (WPS) (Wahler, 1983) may be useful in evaluating physical complaints because it has a built-in decile table to examine item frequency. Overly high frequency endorsement (decile > 9) is unre-alistic unless confirmed by results from the laboratory or medical examination.

Physical symptoms most frequently faked on the WPS include, (a) severe headaches, (b) feeling hot or cold regardless of the weather, (c) difficulty sleep-ing, (d) numbness, or lack of feeling in any part of the body, (e) feeling tired, (f) dizzy spells, (g) difficulty with appetite, and (h) poor health in general. The WPS is sensitive to exaggeration of real symptoms as well as pure fabrication.

Fairbank, McCaffrey, and Keane (1985) correctly classified 90% of patients with PTSD and subjects instructed to fake PTSD on the MMPI. Specifically, both the bogus and the genuine subjects produced elevations on the F-scale and a PTSD subscale, but the genuine subjects scored significantly lower than the fakers. These two predictor variables (F-scale, PTSD subscale) combined in a discriminant func-tion to correctly classify 95.6% of the subjects who faked on PTSD. Essentially replicating this study, McCaffrey and Bellamy-Campbell (1989) found that the MMPI F-scale and PTSD subscale correctly classified 91.4% of their total sample with no fakers incorrectly classified. However, Perconte and Goreczny (1989) reported that a discriminant analysis of the F-scale and PTSD subscale correctly identified only 43.59% of the 39 subjects in their study. Their subjects consisted of Vietnam veterans being treated for PTSD, Vietnam veterans subsequently de-termined to have been malingering PTSD, Vietnam veterans without PTSD, and mental health professionals instructed to feign PTSD. Degree of combat exposure emerged as the single best predictor of PTSD in this sample.

Perr (1986) pointed out that faking subjects in the Fairbank et al. (1985) study were instructed in DSM-III symptoms. Fakers outside this context might not be so indoctrinated and may, therefore produce less deviant (and more simi-lar) scores. In rejoinder, Fairbank et al. (1986) pointed out that the F-scale cutoff and the PTSD subscale are adjuncts to be used with interviewing, other testing, and possibly psychophysiological assessment.

Dalton, Tom, Rosenblum, Garte, and Aubuchon (1989) administered the Mississippi Scale for Combat-related Post-traumatic Stress Disorder to 35 Veterans Administration patients who were instructed to fake PTSD. As a group, these pseudo-malingerers scored lower than did a group of 30 inpatients in a PTSD treatment program, but 77% of the fakers nonetheless scored above the suggested cut-off score for inferring PTSD. Similarly, Lees-Haley (1989) found between a 52% and 80% misclassification rate on the MMPI-PTSD scale among subjects instructed to fake a psychological disorder in the wake of a traumatic disorder.

Arousal measures may sometimes be useful for detecting faked PTSD. Blanchard, Kolb, Pallmeyer, and Gerardi (1982) found a 95.5% hit rate using this method. Heart rate alone yielded a hit rate of 91% in differentiating true PTSD subjects from controls. However, Gerardi, Blanchard, and Kolb (1989) examined 36 combat-experienced Vietnam veterans, half with and half without PTSD, on heart rate, blood pressure, peripheral surface temperature, forehead EMG, and skin resistance level. The PTSD group could not significantly decrease their arousal to combat stimuli when requested to do so, while non-PTSD subjects could increase their physiological responses when asked to fake arousal to the combat stimuli. There were, therefore, no significant differences between the two groups on this measure. However, discriminant analysis revealed that PTSD subjects could be distinguished from faking non-PTSD subjects by several measures. Diastolic blood pressure correctly classified 88.9 percent of all subjects (Kappa = .79) followed by heart rate (85.2%), systolic blood pressure (80.8%) and frontal EMG (70.4%).

In contrast to the Blanchard et al. (1982) finding that heart rate significantly discriminated between PTSD patients and controls, Geradi, Blanchard, and Kolb (1989) found that heart rate correctly classified only 76% of their sample. However, when heart rate difference scores from PTSD subjects were compared to non-PTSD veterans, 83% of the PTSD subjects and 89% of the non-PTSD-veterans were correctly classified by a 76 beats-per-minute cut-off score.

Only 22.2% of faking subjects were correctly identified, indicating that normals can fake PTSD-like heart rates when motivated to do so. Geradi, Keane, and Penk (1989) then took both baseline heart rate and maximum heart rate responses on any particular trial into account at the same time. They stated:

> This rule stipulates that veterans without PTSD will have baseline HR < 67 bpm or a maximum HR response < 10 bpm.... this decision rule correctly classified 16 out of 18 (89%) veterans with PTSD. For the veterans without PTSD, 6 out of the 9 (66.7%) attempting to fake PTSD, and 8 of the 9 (88%) remaining non-PTSD veterans (or 14/18 (77.8%)) are correctly classified. Altogether, 30 out of the 36 (83.3%) veterans are correctly classified as PTSD and non-PTSD by this decision rule (Kappa = .66).

The comparison of psychometric with psychophysiological measures of PTSD needs to be explored in order to revolve basic issues of accuracy and efficiency (Gerardi, Keane, & Penk, 1989). In one such investigation involving Vietnam veterans, 25 subjects with PTSD, 18 healthy subjects, and six anxious subjects completed psychometric tests, followed by measuring psychophysiological responses to combat imagery (Orr et al. 1990). Depending upon the test, 22 to 41 percent of the variance was common to both the psychometric and psychophysiological measures.

The MMPI-PTSD subscale yielded an optimal cut-off of 21, identifying 72% of the genuine PTSD subjects, 94% of the healthy subjects, and 86% of the anxious control subjects. The combined physiological measures identified 64% of the PTSD subjects, 94% of the healthy subjects, and 100% of the anxious control subjects.

The validity measures of the MMPI examined in the Orr et al. (1990) study—higher obvious than subtle item endorsement, F, F-K, and DS-R—were essentially useless because all of the factors correlated substantially with physiologic responses. There was no motive for subjects to fake in this study. Finally, the items themselves have direct relevance to PTSD (e.g., F-scale items: "I have nightmares every few nights"; "I believe my sins are unpardonable"). In sum, this study suggests that clinicians must return to observation, analysis of inconsistencies, and documented exposure to the original trauma to establish whether faking PTSD has occurred.

SUGGESTIONS OF FAKED PTSD

Malingered PTSD is suggested when any of the following occur in combination.

1. Reported PTSD symptoms conflict with (a) verified records or with (b) cross-validating sources. The reported symptoms are more pathological and similar to PTSD than those yielded from (a) and/or (b).
2. Psychometric performance reflects significant distortion in the direction of faking bad on measures reflecting PTSD symptoms.
3. Laboratory measures reflect no difference in autonomic arousal when PTSD scenes are presented to the individual.
4. Assessee admits to faking PTSD and that condition is not suggested by other evaluation results.

LEGAL REFERENCES

Pard v. U.S. 589 F. Supp. 518 (D.Ore., 1984).

REFERENCES

American Psychiatric Association. (1994). Diagnostic and statistical manual of mental disorders, (4th Ed.). Washington DC. Author.

Atkinson, R., Henderson, M., Sparr, L., & Deale, S. (1982). Assessment of Vietnam veterans for posttraumatic stress disorder in Veterans Administration disability claims. *American Journal of Psychiatry, 139,* 1118-1121.

Bernstein, E., & Putnam, T. (1986). Development, reliability and validity of a dissociation scale. *Journal of Nervous and Mental Disease, 174,* 727-735.

Blanchard, E. B., Kolb, L. C., Pallmeyer, T. P., & Gerardi, R. J. (1982). A psychophysiological study of post-traumatic stress disorder in Vietnam veterans. *Psychiatric Quarterly, 54,* 220-229.

Dalton, J., Tom, A., Rosenblum, M., Garte, S., & Aubuchon, I. (1989). Faking on the Mississippi Scale for Combat-related Posttraumatic Stress Disorder. *Psychological Assessment, 1*(1), 56-57.

Fairbank, J., Keane, T., & Malloy, P. (1983). Some preliminary data on the psychological characteristics of Vietnam Veterans with PTSD. *Journal of Consulting and Clinical Psychology, 51,* 912-919.

Fairbank, J. A., McCaffrey, R. J., & Keane, T. M. (1985). Psychometric detection of fabricated symptoms of post-traumatic stress disorder. *American Journal of Psychiatry, 142,* 501-503.

Fairbank, J. A., McCaffrey, R. J., & Keane, T. M. (1986). On simulating posttraumatic stress disorder [Letter to the editor]. *American Journal of Psychiatry, 143,* 268-269.

Foy, D., Sipprelle, R., Rueger, D., & Carroll, E. (1984). Etiology of PTSD in Vietnam Veterans: analysis of premilitary, military and combat exposure influences. *Journal of Consulting and Clinical Psychology, 52,* 79-87.

Franklin, J. (1988). *Molecules of the mind: The brave new science of molecular psychology.* New York: Dell Pub. Co.

Geradi, R., Blanchard, E., & Kolb, L. (1989). Ability of Vietnam veterans to dissimulate a psychophysiological assessment for post-traumatic stress disorder. *Behavior Therapy, 20,* 229-243.

Geradi, R., Keane, T., & Penk, W. (1989). Utility: sensitivity and specificity in developing diagnostic tests of combat-related post-traumatic stress disorder (PTSD). *Journal of Clinical Psychology, 45*(5), 691-703.

Hall, H. V. (1987). *Violence prediction: Guidelines for the forensic practitioner.* Springfield, IL: Charles C. Thomas.

Hall, H. V. (1990). *PTSD in war veterans.* Paper presented at the meeting of the Hawaii Psychological Association, Honolulu.

Hammarberg, M. (1992). Penn Inventory for Posttraumatic Stress Disorder: psychometric properties. *Psychological Assessment, 4*(1), 67-76.

Helzer, J., Robins, L., & McEvoy, L. (1987). Post-traumatic stress disorder in the general population: Findings of the epidemiological catchment area survey. *New England Journal of Medicine, 317,* 1630-1634.

Holmes, T. H., & Rahe, R. H. (1967). The social readjustment rating scale. *Journal of Psychosomatic Research, 11,* 213-218.

Horowitz, M., Wilner, N., & Alvarez, W. (1979). Impact of event scale: A measure of psychosomatic stress. *Psychosomatic Medicine, 41,* 209-218.

Keane, T., Caddell, J., & Taylor, K. (1988). Mississippi Scale for Combat-related Post-traumatic Stress Disorder: Three studies in reliability and validity. *Journal of Consulting and Clinical Psychology, 56,* 1-6.

Keane, T., Fairbank, J., Caddel, J., Zimering, R., Taylor, K., & Mora, C. (1989). Clinical evaluation of a measure to assess combat exposure. *Psychological Assessment, 1*(1), 53-55.

Keane, T., Malloy, P., & Fairbank, J. (1984). Empirical development of an MMPI subscale for the assessment of combat-related PTSD. *Journal of Consulting and Clinical Psychology, 62,* 888-891.

Kolb, L. C. (1987, August). A neuropsychological hypothesis explaining PTSD. *American Journal of Psychiatry, 144*(8), 989.

Kolb, L. C. (1988). A critical survey of hypotheses regarding post-traumatic stress disorders in light of recent research findings. *Journal of Traumatic Stress, 1*(3), 291-293.

Kulka, R., & Schlenger, W. (1986). *Report to the Office of Technology Assessment (OTA) on the Status of the National Vietnam Veterans Readjustment Study: Review of Clinical and Preclinical Studies.* Paper prepared at the Research Triangle Institute, P.O. Box 12194, Research Triangle Park, North Carolina, 27709.

Lees-Haley, P. (1989). Malingering post-traumatic stress disorder on the MMPI. *Forensic Reports, 2*(1), 89-91.

Lipton, M. I., & Shaffer, W. R. (1988, June). Physical symptoms related to PTSD in an aging population. *Military Medicine, 153*(6), 316.

Livingston, R. B. (1985). Neurophysiology. In J. B. West (Ed.), *Best and Taylor's physiological basis of medical practice* (11th ed., pp. 970-1295). Baltimore: Williams & Wilkins.

Lund, M., Foy, D., Sipprelle, C., & Strachan, A. (1984). The combat exposure scale: A systematic assessment of trauma in the Vietnam War. *Journal of Clinical Psychology, 40,* 1323-1328.

Lynn, E., & Belza, M. (1984). Factitious posttraumatic stress disorder: The veteran who never got to Vietnam. *Hospital and Community Psychiatry, 35,* 697-701.

McCaffrey, R. J., & Bellamy-Campbell, R. (1989). Psychometric detection of fabricated symptoms of combat-related posttraumatic stress disorder: A systematic replication. *Journal of Clinical Psychology, 45,* 76-79.

Orr, S. P., Claiborn, J. M., Altman, B., Forgue, D. F., de Jong, J. B., Pitman, R., & Herz, L. R. (1990). Psychometric profile of post-traumatic stress disorder, anxious, and healthy Vietnam veterans: Correlations with psychophysiologic responses. *Journal of Consulting and Clinical Psychology, 58,* 329-335.

Parker, R. S. (1989). *Traumatic brain injury and neuropsychological impairment.* New York: Springer-Verlag.

Perconte, S., & Goreczny, A. J. (1989). Failure to detect fabricated posttraumatic stress disorder with the use of the MMPI in a clinical population. *American Journal of Psychiatry, 147,* 1057-1060.

Perr, I. (1986). On simulating posttraumatic stress disorder [Letter to the editor]. *American Journal of Psychiatry, 143,* 268.

Resnick, P. J. (1984). The detection of malingered mental illness. *Behavioral Sciences and the Law, 2*(1), 21-38.

Resnick, P. J. (1987, October). *The detection of malingered mental illness.* Workshop presented at the American Academy of Psychiatry and Law, Ottawa, Canada.

Resnick, P. J. (1988a). Malingered psychosis. In R. Rogers (Ed.), *Clinical assessment of malingering and deception* (pp. 34-53). New York: Guilford Press.

Resnick, P. J. (1988b). Malingering of posttraumatic disorders. In R. Rogers (Ed.), *Clinical assessment of malingering and deception* (pp. 84-103). New York: Guilford Press.

Sparr, L., & Atkinson, R. (1986). Posttraumatic stress disorder as an insanity defense: Medicolegal quicksand. *American Journal of Psychiatry, 143,* 608-613.

Stuss, D., & Benson, D. F. (1986). *The frontal lobes.* New York: Raven Press.

Van der Kolk, B. A. (1988). The trauma spectrum: The interaction of biological and social events in the genesis of the trauma response. *Journal of Traumatic Stress, 1*(3), 273-283.

Wahler, H. J. (1983). *Wahler Physical Symptoms Inventory.* Los Angeles, CA: Western Psychological Services.

Wilson, J. (1989). The psychobiology of trauma. In J. P. Wilson (Ed.), *Trauma, transformation, and healing: An integrative approach to theory, research, and post traumatic therapy* (p. 21). New York: Mazel Publishers.

Zarin, I., & Weitzman, L. (1990). *The National Jury Verdict Review and Analysis,* 5. Newark, NJ: Jury Verdict Review Publications, Inc.

PART III

DECEPTION ANALYSIS IN CRIMINAL CONTEXTS

9

CHILDREN AND DECEPTION

The legal system is interested in two aspects of children as witnesses: 1) their competence to be a witness and 2) their credibility as a witness. The first issue is a threshold question which determines whether or not the child is even allowed to offer testimony in a legal proceeding. The second issue involves the weight to be given to the testimony of a competent child witness.

The prevailing assumption has been that the mnestic and communicative abilities of young children are too immature to allow competent testimony. However, the U. S. Supreme Court in *Wheeler v. U. S.* (1895) ruled that young children as a group cannot be declared incompetent, but each child's capacity to testify must be evaluated individually by the court. Under this rule, children are *presumed* to be incompetent to testify, but that presumption can be overcome in a particular case by evidence to the contrary. In all jurisdictions a child under the age of 10 can be allowed to testify if that child knows the difference between a truth and a lie; in some jurisdictions the child must also have the capacity to recall past incidents (Haugaard, Repucci, Laird, & Nauful, 1991). More recently, Rule 601 of the Federal Rules of Evidence has eliminated the presumption of incompetence of child witnesses and at least 13 states have adopted similar rules (Goodman & Reed, 1986). Under these new rules, children are presumed to be competent witnesses unless evidence to the contrary is offered.

Once a child has been found competent to be a witness, questions about the credibility of the witness arise. How accurate is the child's independent recollection of critical events? How susceptible are the child's recollections to influence by significant others? How resistant to leading and suggestive questioning are the child's communications about critical events? The answers to these and related questions determine the weight that a judge or jury should give to the child's testimony in deciding questions of fact.

Most American jurisdictions do not allow expert testimony on the reliability or credibility of child witnesses (McGough, 1991), because such testimony may itself be unreliable (*State of Utah v. Rimmasch,* 1989). However, a few courts have permitted such testimony (McGough, 1991) and more may be expected to do so as professional methods of credibility analysis improve. In the meantime, expert opinions on the truthfulness of children's will continue to influence law enforcement and child welfare agencies in their investigation and preparation for criminal prosecutions of sexual abusers. Experts will also continue to be influenced in their formulation of opinions on other substantive questions (e.g., parental fitness) by their personal assessments of the believability of children.

COMPETENCE OF CHILD WITNESSES

Developmental psychologists have demonstrated that children clearly have different conceptions of truth and lying than adults. In general, children define lies more broadly than do adults. Below the age of seven, children typically conceive of lies as "bad words," words which can be expected to bring negative reactions from adults. "Naughty" words, swearing, cursing, as well as deliberate untruths, are all regarded as lies. Five- to seven-year-old children begin to differentiate "bad words" from untrue statements (Peterson, Peterson, & Seeto, 1983). Inaccurate statements, whether due to ignorance, mistake, or a deliberate intent to mislead, are all categorized as lies. Not until after the age of seven do children typically consider lies as inaccurate statements intentionally designed to mislead. In general, young children employ a broader definition of lies than do older children and adults.

Children's likelihood of admitting to lying increases as a direct function of age; an inverse relationship is seen between age and viewing lying as always wrong (Peterson, Peterson, & Seeto, (1983). In terms of consequences, older children see that lying is more likely to destroy trust and create guilt, even though punishment is less apt to follow lying.

Questions about a particular child's competence to testify are questions about nondeliberate distortion. The central issues involve the *capacity* of the child to distinguish truth from lying and, in some jurisdictions, the ability of the child to recall past events. One who is incapable of recognizing a lie cannot be said to lie deliberately; one who is unable to recall the past cannot be accused of deliberate distortion. Discussion later in this chapter will maintain this distinction between a child's capacity to testify and the child's believability as a witness.

CREDIBILITY OF CHILD WITNESSES

One prevalent view holds that children rarely make up stories and, if they did, we could easily detect it. In sexual abuse cases especially, the notion is that data presented by children exceeds their capacity to fabricate. Indeed, this factor is a component of a detection method called Criteria-based Content Analysis (Raskin & Esplin, 1991a), which is described later. Groth (1980) reported that, of 147 children referred for polygraph testing from 1969 to 1974, only one child was found to have lied in regard to sexual abuse episodes.

According to this view, denial of unpleasant experiences by children is regarded as more likely than fabrication. Berliner and Barbieri (1984) stated in regard to sexual victimization: "Our clinical experience indicates that many children who report being assaulted actually underreport the amount and type of abuse; exaggeration is rare" (p. 126). Green (1986) stated in agreement that false denials are common but that false accusations are rare. False accusations may occur when the child is "brainwashed" by vindictive parents, is projecting his or her own sexual fantasy, or is seeking revenge. Green offered criteria for distinguishing false from real claims of sexual abuse (see Table 9.1).

Table 9.1 Characteristics of True and False Cases of Child Sexual Abuse	
True Cases	False Cases
Delayed, conflicted disclosure, often with retractions spontaneous	Disclosure easy and apparently rehearsed or well thought out
Disclosure usually accompanied by painful and depressive affect	Disclosure with absence of negative affect
Child uses age-appropriate sexual terminology	Child may use adult sexual terminology
Child initially reticent to discuss abuse with mother or others	Child discusses the abuse when prompted by mother–child checks with mother
Child rarely will confront father with the allegation, even with mother present	Child will often confront father with allegation in mother's presence
Child usually fearful in father's presence, congruent with ideation unless molestation was gentle and non-threatening	Discrepancy between the child's angry accusations and the apparent comfort in father's presence
Mothers often depressed; no other specific psychopathology in mothers	Prominent paranoid and hysterical psychopathology
Child usually demonstrates signs and symptoms of child sexual abuse syndrome	Child might be sexually preoccupied, but does not exhibit signs and symptoms of child sexual abuse

Reprinted with permission from Green, A. (1986). True and false allegations of sexual abuse in child custody disputes. *Journal of the American Academy of Child Psychiatry, 25*, 455.

Jones and McGraw (1987) studied 576 reports of child abuse and determined that most of the reports from children were reliable (70%) with only a small proportion being unreliable (8%). Examination of the unreliable reports suggested several commonalities: lack of emotion and detail, and the presence of coercion. In some cases, inappropriate pronouns were used ("they" instead of "I," "we" instead of "me"). Custody/visitation disputes often triggered false allegations. Parents falsely accused the other, primarily the male spouse, more often than the alleged child victim (9 parental-complaints out of 21 compared to 5 child-complaints out of 21; 7 complaints were of unknown origin). A substantial percentage of both children and adults involved in incidents of child abuse suffered from pre-existing PTSD. Jones and McGraw (1987) made the cogent point that the use of explicit detail by an alleged victim with previous PTSD cannot be used as a criterion of truth. The previous trauma may have supplied much detail which is then substituted for the instant offense. Similarly, Goodwin, Cauthorne, and Rada (1980) reported that all 10 of their adopted girl subjects who were caught lying had been physically and emotionally abused in other settings. They lied about their adoptive mothers allegedly dressing them in rags and were seen as having the "Cinderella Syndrome" by the investigators. They were essentially crying for help and, thus, were not engaging in malingering or deliberate deception.

In reviewing the relevant research on memory, Johnson and Foley (1984) found children to be credible. They argued that generally children's recall, while less developed than that of adults, does not possess many of the deficits typically imputed to children's recall (e.g., fusing fantasy with fact). Children's memories are even seen as *more* reliable than adults' on some memory tasks.

Research suggests that children may recall visual information better than verbal information (Duncan, Whitney, & Kunen, 1982). Marin, Holmes, Guth, and Kovac (1979) found that children as young as five years were no less competent than adults in their accuracy on a photo identification task. King and Yuille (1987) reported that children under the age of six were less accurate than older children in photo identification. Thus, children as young as five or six may prove to be reliable witnesses when asked to identify visually target persons.

A second view holds that children have poor recall, are uncritical, and are very suggestible. Younger children are seen as viewing lying amorally (Kohlberg, 1981). Children's motives for lying may include obtaining attention, escaping punishment, and/or receiving material rewards. Children at younger ages may create a fantasy in order to have someone else to blame.

Piaget (1929, 1959) suggested that children in late childhood may not clearly know the difference between the internal (e.g., psychic) and the external (e.g., environmental). He sees children as having difficulty recalling the origins of their knowledge. Markman (1979) found that 12-year-old children have difficulty seeing factual inconsistencies without prompting.

In spite of the accuracy of young children on photo identification tasks, Parker and Carranza (1989) found that, when children (mean age = 9 years) were given the option "none of the above" in a photo identification task, they were less likely than adults to reject all the photos.

The credibility of a child's testimony may be affected by the developmental capacities of that child. Mnestic errors in children may be attributable to a number of factors:

1. Children's capacity to store and recall information is less than that of adults (Eriksen & Collins, 1968).
2. Children are more accurate in recognition than free recall (Perlmutter, 1984).
3. Children have more difficulty than adults in retrieving long-term memory events (Brown, 1979).
4. Children are as accurate as adults in answering objective, central questions, but are less accurate than adults in an-

swering suggestive, peripheral questions (Goodman & Reed, 1986).

5. The presence of a postevent interviewer with strong preconceived notions of what happened may "lead" children to alter or supplement their recollections (Dent, 1982).

6. Leading questions in general increase the chances that memory will be distorted (Marin et al. 1979).

7. Postevent questions of any kind may distort memory (Cohen & Harnick, 1980).

8. Once a distortion occurs, it appears to be accepted as part of reality and is difficult to change in favor of a more accurate memory of the actual event (Loftus & Davis, 1984).

The discrepancies between these two views of child witnesses illustrate the complexities of the issues. While the developmental capacities of children as young as 5-years-old may permit accurate recognition of photos and accurate answers to central, objective questions, those same capacities may interfere with the accuracy of free recall and with resistance to suggestions and leading questions.

A developmental view of children as witnesses recognizes the wide variability in the cognitive, social, and moral development of children of different ages. This information must be considered in assessing a child's veracity. The most relevant findings cover distortion in such areas as intellect, memory, social interaction, achievement, sensation and perception, and speech. Indeed, Goodman (1984) recommended advanced training in child development to help evaluators detect the truth in individual cases. He presents examples of how knowledge of a child's use of words can assist in detecting perpetrators of sexual abuse when those verbalizations are understood in a developmental context.

Selected reports of developmentally related distortion from age four to adolescence are presented below. Children younger than four are generally considered unreliable because of their difficulty in telling fantasy from reality and their tendency to integrate the two in everyday experience. These thumbnail sketches are intended to illustrate the typical development of deception-related capacities in children. Individual children progress through these phases at differing rates.

AGES FOUR TO FIVE

Most children in this age group (a) show self-care; (b) can walk around the neighborhood and find their way home again; (c) draw recognizable pictures; (d) print their first names, know five capital letters, and can recognize common objects (e.g., umbrella, foot, flag, cane, arm, pocketknife, pitcher, leaf); (e) name two objects from memory and repeat a nine-word sentence, (f) complete simple analogies; and (g) correctly follow basic directions (Blau, 1986).

All capacities considered, some four-year-olds can be qualified as witnesses (Annon, 1987). According to Annon, the four-year-old is in a transition period and can be considered a competent witness if proper, nonleading questions which suggest the ability to differentiate fact from fantasy, are presented.

Relevant to deliberate distortion, various studies show that between 21 and 49% of children in this age group lie (Stouthamer-Loeber, 1986). Stouthamer-Loeber cites statistics as to the reasons for lying. Avoiding punishment is the main reason for children in this age group to lie. According to the subjects' mothers, avoidance of punishment comprised 44% of all excuses. Other reasons include confusion (15%), self-gain (14%), playing or having fun (10%) and protecting the self-esteem (6%).

AGES FIVE TO SIX

Children in this age group do not differ significantly from adults on answering simple "yes-no" questions, correctly identifying photos of confederates, or being misled by leading task instructions or questions (Marin et al.1979). In general, Marin's data revealed that eyewitness identification was poor along all age ranges, from childhood to adulthood (25 to 50% of subjects were unable to recognize a target male from six photos). The number of incorrect items (as opposed to not guessing) increased linearly with age. Marin et al. (1979) summarized the findings by stating that children are no less accurate than adults in responding to direct objective questions but are less capable in giving narrative descriptions of target events. In other words, the children in this age group said little but were accurate in their representations of events. Five- and six-year-old children are generally unable to hide their deception by controlling facial expressions, voice tone, and speech content (Morency & Kraus, 1982; Feldman & White, 1980).

AGES SIX TO SEVEN

In terms of nondeliberate distortion, Chance and Goldstein (1984) stated: "Face recognition of familiar faces under conditions that permit a clear view of the whole face is quite good, even in children as young as six years." Children of this age tend to be concrete, tending towards literal interpretations of words and phrases (Ackerman, 1981). These children can also read four or more words, add two single-digit numbers, write 10 words from memory, and spot missing parts in a picture (Blau, 1986).

Children in this age group can detect inconsistent information (Ackerman, 1983). They may contradict a person stating inconsistent information, usually when the speaker is discredited or is of low status. Children as deceivers are usually detected by untrained others, yet still have some control over their nonverbal responses. In general, children in this age group judge lies not by intent, but by whether statements invite punishment or involve forbidden actions or things (Piaget, 1965).

AGES SEVEN TO EIGHT

Developmentally, children in this age group see lies as untrue statements (Piaget, 1965). Mistakes are still labeled as lies, but dirty or obscene words are not seen as lies, as they were in earlier stages. A child in this age group can (a) keep secrets for longer than one day, (b) attend to a stimulus, (e.g., a lecture), for up to a quarter hour, (c) repeat five digits, and (d) give simple definitions (Blau, 1986).

AGES EIGHT TO NINE

Children in this age group can do all the above. They still may not see all of the conflicting information between successive statements (Markman, 1979).

AGES NINE TO 10

Children in this age range "can [successfully] fool their peers, adult strangers, and at times, their parents" (Quinn, 1988). Children from nine to 12 can fake believable neuropsychological deficits. Faust, Hart, and Guilmette (1988) found that none of 42 professional evaluators detected malingering in three children who had been instructed to fake bad. Ninety-three percent of the neuropsychologists diagnosed abnormality, with 87% stating that cortical dysfunction was indicated by test results.

AGES 10 TO 11

At this age, disguised, briefly seen, and previously unfamiliar faces can be much better recognized (Chance & Goldstein, 1984). Children younger than 10 years are largely unreliable in this ability.

There is a shift at this age to a focus on the intent of lying. Piaget (1965) noted that these children focus on intent in lying and give adult definitions of prevarication.

In a study involving 98 ten-year-olds, Braginsky (1970) investigated the effect of Machiavellianism ("Mach") on lying. He found that high Mach subjects (i.e., exploitative, manipulative) clearly gave more false information, distorted true information, concealed, presented incomplete sensory data, and acted in other misleading ways influence the target person. Gender differences emerged in that high Mach boys were best at telling lies of commission while the girls used omission to their advantage.

In terms of ability to deceive strangers, fourth and fifth graders have the ability to deceive adults if given adequate incentive (Allen & Atkinson, 1978).

AGES 11 TO 12

Social factors are an increasing focus by this age. Here, children can give an explanation as to why criminals are locked up, avoid deliberately embarrassing others, control their anger, keep secrets as long as appropriate, and practice other forms of self-control (Blau, 1986). Generally, they justify the prohibition against lying in terms of trust and fairness (Peterson, Peterson, & Seeto, 1983).

AGES 12 TO 14

In terms of nondeliberate distortion, children in this age group remembered both familiar and unfamiliar faces as well as adults (Chance & Goldstein, 1984).

Deliberate distortion is well entrenched by this age in social and achievement settings and situations. In a study of 46 boys, Mischel and Gilligan (1964) found widespread cheating in a temptation paradigm.

AGES 15-17

At this age, children see lying as a major social problem. Vidoni, Fleming, and Mintz (1983) noted that the 504 eighth graders tested ranked lying in the upper 15th percentile among social problems and viewed lying as being as serious as did teachers and clinicians. Peterson et al., (1983) see adults as more lenient than children in their moral evaluation of lying. Children of this age group are close to adults in this respect.

In another study on faking believable deficits during neuropsychological evaluation, Guilmette and Arkes (1988) found that three adolescents (15 to 17 years old) were able to fool all 60 neuropsychologists when instructed to fake brain damage. None of the evaluators detected malingering. On an even more disheartening note, the neuropsychologists appeared overconfident in their judgements.

SUMMARY

The literature suggests that conclusions regarding distortion in children should be geared toward developmental abilities and individual circumstances. It is naive to believe that a child is credible or noncredible without taking into account both group and individual information within a developmental perspective. Both unintentional distortion (i.e., developmental capacities) and deliberate misrepresentation must be considered in evaluating the credibility of child witnesses.

The combination of deliberate and nondeliberate distortion in child witnesses is difficult to untangle. Consider the accessory-to-sex syndrome where the child coerced into sex is pressured to keep quiet and to deny any sexual activity if questioned (Burgess & Holmstrom, 1985). After repeated assaults, the child tends to repress the unpleasant aspects of the activity, even if prodded by investigators. Is this deliberate or unintentional distortion? The same may be true of Munchausen syndrome by proxy (Meadow, 1982; Palmer & Yoshimura, 1984), in which a child, usually a preschooler, is ordered to remain silent about an illness or injury which is fabricated by the caretaker. Is the child's contributions to the ruse due to developmental incapacities or to intentional misrepresentation?

DETECTION

The detection of a child's incompetence to be a witness involves questions about the child's understanding of honesty and lying. The focus is not on the accuracy of particular memories, the susceptibility of the child to adult influence, or the motives of the child. Rather the focus is on the general capacity of the child to distinguish truth from lies and to subscribe to the importance of truth-telling. Table 9.2 presents some questions which the authors have found useful in assess-

---

Table 9.2
Questions for Potential Child Witness

---

1. What is a lie? Can you tell me what a lie is?
2. Why is it naughty to tell a lie?
3. Is it a lie to call someone a bad name? Is a lie to call someone a "fool"?
4. I'm going to tell you a story. There are two little boys and they each broke a cup. The first boy says it wasn't him. His mother believes him and doesn't punish him. The second boy says it wasn't him. But his mother doesn't believe him and punishes him. Are both boys equally naughty? Which boy is naughtiest?
5. I'm going to tell you another story. Two children bought some eggs for their mother, but they played on their way home and broke the eggs. The first child broke 12 eggs; the other child broke only one. When they got home, they told their mother that a big dog had jumped on them and broke the eggs. Was that telling lies? Were both the lies equally naughty? Which of these two lies is naughtiest?
6. One day a mother told her little boy, "If anyone knocks on the door, tell them I'm not home. I don't want to see anyone today." A little later, a policeman knocks on the door and asks to speak to the mother. The little boy says, "Mama isn't home. Did the boy do the right thing? Why? Was it a lie he told? (A big lie or a little lie? Should he be punished for telling the lie?)

---

ing the developmental level of a child's understanding of lying. Answers to these questions may help a court to decide if the child is legally competent to testify as a witness in a proceeding. The questions deal with the child's spontaneous definition of lying and understanding of the moral wrongness of lying. They require the child to distinguish between "bad words" and lies. They help determine whether lies are perceived as intrinsically wrong or as wrong because of their consequences. Finally, they pose a moral dilemma for the child (e.g., lying to a policeman, disobeying mother) which may be relevant to some cases in which children are asked to be witnesses. Similar questions may be constructed with facts or scenarios more similar to the cases in which child witnesses are asked to appear.

Forensic analysis of a child's credibility requires assessment of (a) the reliability of the memory and thinking skills of the child, including the ability to separate fact from fantasy; (b) the ability and inclination of the child deliberately to present falsehoods; (c) the influence of adults (including the examiner) on the child's testimony; and (d) the extent of corroborating data—if there is no corroboration of a child's allegation, there is usually no prosecution of the case.

Blau (1986) presented suggestions on enhancing the validity and completeness of later testimony by children in court. These included:

1. Know who talked to the child about the instant offense before you did.
2. Have corroborated facts separated from conjecture prior to your evaluation of the child.
3. Allow free recall without disruption.
4. Use language with which the child is familiar. Be simple and concrete.

5. Determine the child's mental age and gear questions to the appropriate level and ability.
6. Interview/test in 10- to 15-minute sessions with rest and play in between.
7. The sequence of the questions should be "what," "who," "when," and "where."

It is not enough simply to ask objective questions of children because such questions can be leading. Goodman and Reed (1986) distinguished between objective and nonleading, and objective and misleading questions. Objective and nonleading questions concern facts about time, place, appearance and actions (e.g., "Was there a TV set in the room?"). Objective and misleading questions involve incorrect facts about time, place, appearance, and actions (e.g., "How big was the TV set in the room?"). Goodman and Reed found no differences between children and adults in their responses to objective and nonleading questions, but found a significant effect for age on objective and misleading questions. Children were less likely than adults to disagree with the misleading suggestion or to answer that they did not know. Quinn (1988) presented another checklist for the evaluation of deception in children. These are geared more toward issues of developmental and mental states.

1. Does the child have the developmental capacity to deceive?
2. Is there a history of persistent lying?
3. Does a mental disorder exist which would cause distortion or deception?
4. Is there a psychosocial stressor that would cause lying?
5. Has deception guilt decreased or deception apprehension increased?
6. Is the child pursuing a nonmoral (understandable) objective like lying to remain with one parent?
7. Is an adult lying for the child or distorting the child's communication?
8. Does a complaint or symptom presented by the child agree with well-recognized criteria?
9. Have interviewing errors contributed to distortion, for example, assuming that abuse has taken place?

A clinical method (Criteria-based Content Analysis: CBCA) to assess misrepresentation in witnesses statements was presented by Raskin and Esplin (1991a). Based on the earlier work of Undeutsch (1982, 1984) in Germany, this method proposes an analysis of the content of witnesses statements obtained during a timely and noncontaminating interview. The statements are analyzed for their logical structure, their degree of organization, the quantity of details and 16 other characteristics. In a preliminary study of the method, the authors reported 100% accuracy in discriminating between "confirmed" cases of child sexual abuse and "doubtful" cases. However, Wells and Loftus (1991) raised many questions about this study's methodology and interpretation. They most importantly note that CBCA does not include age-related criteria based on developmental differences in the use of language, thus leaving the examiner without guidance in considering the age of the child-victim-witness. They decided that "strong conclusions about truth or lying based on the current, rather small amount of empirical research is premature." Raskin and Esplin (1991b) countered that "we do not advocate the use of CBCA as the basis of expert testimony that a child is or is not truthful...[P]roper interview techniques combined with CBCA and statement validity assessment analysis are best employed as investigative tools to increase the quantity of information available to decision makers, such as police investigators, caseworkers, attorneys and prosecutors."

Other commentators have cautioned that the continuous repetition of a child's story of abuse (e.g., in separate interviews with parents, social workers, investigators, psychologists, attorneys) reinforces a perceptual experience which is subsequently recalled in rich, vivid, and convincing detail (Pynoos & Eth, 1984). It is also important to consider the child-victim's conditioning history when evaluating their recollections of abuse. Past conditioning (e.g., hydrophobia) may explain parts of their reaction to an alleged crime (e.g., "freaking out" when placed into water).

Socially "disapproved" behavior is frequently seen in victims. In repeated assaults, they may enjoy some aspects of the perpetrator's behavior (e.g., prolonged clitoral stimulation, payment of "hush" money). Victims are reluctant to share these experiences which, in their thinking, adds to their contribution to the wrongdoing. An experienced clinician will try to uncover these behaviors, if they exist, for two reasons: (a) they add to the veracity of the account and (b) they are targets for later treatment.

Spontaneous corrections and additions are expected in the retelling of the true account by a victim. In contrast, a deceiver may rigidly attempt to hold on to a story and show little variation in presentation or content—that is because the deceiver's story is a product of thought and deliberation.

Psychometric evaluation is important to establish the child's functional capacities and limitations. Information on current intellectual functioning, academic achievement levels, and neuropsychological performance can provide the necessary background against which to evaluate suspicious symptoms and complaints in children. Adolescents with adequate reading skills can provide valuable self-reports of symptoms and complaints, against which to compare the results of interviews and observations. However, scales and indices of response distortions on "adult" inventories (e.g., F - K and Dissimulation Scale scores on the MMPI) have not been validated on inventories taken by adolescents and therefore should not be interpreted. Self-report scales with adolescents must be taken at face value and then compared with data from interviews, history, observation, and collateral sources.

SYNTHESIS

The assessment of a child's competence to be a witness involves the straightforward evaluation of that child's understanding of truthfulness and the necessity of telling the truth during the legal proceeding. The focus is on the child's capacity to reason about truth and deceit and willingness to answer questions honestly. Assessment of a child's credibility as a witness involves the more complex evaluation of the child's 1) capacity to recall, recognize, and communicate accurately; 2) capacity to deceive without detection; 3) resistance to the influence of others and 4) possible motives for lying. Indications of distortion may be gleaned from

(a) admissions of deception, (b) statements inconsistent with collateral information, (c) evidence of the influence of others in previous interviews, d) observation
of behavioral clues of lying, and (e) psychometric tests of current capacities. The
evaluator needs to be flexible in assessing possible deception in children, using a
variety of clinical, observational, and psychometric approaches. As always, deception is not verified until it can be corroborated and cross-validated using multiple sets of data.

REFERENCES

Ackerman, B. P. (1981). Young children's understanding of a speaker's intentional use of a false utterance.
    Developmental Psychology, 17, 472-480.
Ackerman, B. P. (1983). Speaker bias in children's evaluation of the external consistency of statements. *Jour-
    nal of Experimental Child Psychology, 35,* 111-127.
Allen, V., & Atkinson, M. (1978). Encoding of nonverbal behavior by high-achieving and low-achieving
    children. *Journal of Educational Psychology, 70,* 17-28.
Annon, J. (1987). The four-year old child as competent witness. *American Journal of Forensic Psychology, V,*
    17-21.
Berliner, L., & Barbieri, M. (1984). The testimony of the child victim of sexual assault. *Journal of Social
    Issues, 40,* 78-89.
Blau, T. (1986). *The credibility of children as witnesses.* Paper presented at the Second Annual Symposium in
    Psychology and Law of the American College of Forensic Psychology, Sanibel Island, Florida.
Braginsky, D. (1970). Machiavellianism and manipulative interpersonal behavior in children. *Journal of Ex-
    perimental Social Psychology, 6,* 77-99.
Brown, M. R. (1979). *Legal psychology.* Indianapolis: Bobbs-Merrill.
Burgess, A., & Holmstrom, L. (1985). Accessory-to-sex: Pressure, sex and secrecy. In A. Burgess, A. Groth,
    L. Holmstrom, & S. Sgroi (Eds.), *Sexual assault of children and adolescents.* Lexington, MA: Lexington
    Books.
Chance, J., & Goldstein, A. (1984). Face-recognition memory. Implications for children's eyewitness testi-
    mony. *Journal of Social Issues, 40,* 69-85.
Cohen, R. L., & Harnick, M. A. (1980). The susceptibility of child witnesses to suggestion. *Law and Human
    Behavior, 4,* 201-210.
Dent, H. R. (1982). The effects of interviewing strategies on the results of interviews with child witnesses. In
    T. A. Deventer (Ed.), *Reconstructing the past.* The Netherlands: Kluwer.
Duncan, E., Whitney, P., & Kunen, S. (1982). Integration of visual and verbal information on children's
    memories. *Child Development, 53,* 1215-1223.
Feldman, R., & White, J. (1980). Detecting deception in children, *Journal of Communication, 30,* 121-139.
Faust, D., Hart, K., & Guilmette, T. (1988). Pediatric malingering: The capacity of children to fake deficits
    on neuropsychological testing. *Journal of Consulting and Clinical Psychology, 56,* 578-582.
Goodman, G. (1984). The child witness: Conclusions and future directions for research and legal practice.
    Journal of Social Issues, 40, 157-175.
Goodman, G., & Reed, R. (1986). Age differences in eyewitness testimony. *Law and Human Behavior, 10,*
    317-332.
Goodwin, J., Cauthorne, C., & Rada, R. (1980). Cinderella syndrome: Children who simulate neglect.
    American Journal of Psychiatry, 137, 1223-1225.
Green, A. (1986). True and false allegations of sexual abuse in child custody disputes. *Journal of American
    Academy of Child Psychiatry, 25,* 449-456.
Groth, N. (1980). *The psychology of the sexual offender: Rape, incest and child molestation.* Workshop pre-
    sented by Psychological Associates, Charlotte, N. Carolina.
Guilmette, T., & Arkes, H. (1988). Neuropsychologist's capacity to detect adolescent malingerers. *Profes-
    sional Psychology: Research and Practice, 19,* 508-515.
Haugaard, J., Repucci, N., Laird, J., & Nauful, T. (1991). Children's definitions of the truth and their
    competency as witnesses in legal proceedings. *Law and Human Behavior, 15*(3), 253-271.
Johnson, M., & Foley, M. (1984). Differentiating fact from fantasy: The reliability of children's memory.
    Journal of Social Issues, 40, 76-92.
Jones, D., & McGraw, J. (1987). Reliable and fictitious accounts of sexual abuse to children. *Journal of
    Interpersonal Violence, 2,* 27-45.

King, M., & Yuille, J. (1987). Suggestibility and the child witness. In S. Ceci, D. Ross, & M. Toglia (Eds.), *Children's eyewitness memory*. New York: Springer-Verlag.

Loftus, E. F., & Davis, G. (1984). Distortions in the memory of children. *Journal of Social Science, 40*, 51-67.

Marin, B. V., Holmes, D. L., Guth, M., & Kovac, P. (1979). The potential of children as eyewitnesses. *Law and Human Behavior, 3*, 295-305.

Markman, E. (1979). Realizing that you don't understand: Elementary school children's awareness of inconsistencies. *Child Development, 50*, 643-655.

McGough, L. (1991). Commentary: Assessing the credibility of witness' statements. In J. Doris (Ed.), *The suggestibility of children's recollections* (pp. 165-167). Washington, DC: American Psychological Association.

Meadow, R. (1982). Munchausen syndrome by proxy and pseudoepilepsy [Letter to the editor]. *Archives of Disease in Childhood, 57*, 811-812.

Mischel, W., & Gilligan, C. (1964). Delay of gratification, motivation for prohibited gratification, and responses to temptation. *Journal of Abnormal & Social Psychology, 69*, 411-417.

Morency, N., & Kraus, R. (1982). The nonverbal encoding and decoding of affect in first and fifth graders. In R. Feldman (Ed.), *Development of nonverbal behavioral skills* (212-226). New York: Spring-Verlag.

Palmer, A. J., & Yoshimura, G. J. (1984). Munchausen syndrome by proxy. *Journal of the American Academy of Child Psychiatry, 23*(4), 504-508.

Parker, J., & Carranza, L. (1989). Eyewitness testimony of children in target-present and target-absent lineups. *Law and Human Behavior, 13*(2), 133-149.

Perlmutter, M. (1984). Continuities and discontinuities in early human memory paradigms, processes and performance. In R. Kail & N. Spears (Eds.), *Comparative perspectives on the development of memory*. Hillsdale, NJ: Erlbaum.

Peterson, C., Peterson, J., & Seeto, D. (1983). Developmental changes in ideas about lying. *Child Development, 54*, 1529- 1535.

Piaget, J. (1929). *The child's conception of the world*. New York: Harcourt, Brace & Co.

Piaget, J. (1959). *Judgement and reasoning in the child*. Totowa, NJ: Littlefield Adams.

Piaget, J. (1965). *The moral judgement of the child*. New York: Free Press.

Pynoos, R., & Eth, S. (1984). The child as witness to homicide. *Journal of Social Issues, 40*, 44-51.

Raskin, D., & Esplin, P. (1991a). Assessment of children's statements of sexual abuse. In J. Doris (Ed.), *The suggestibility of children's recollections* (pp. 153-164). Washington, DC: American Psychological Association.

Raskin, D., & Esplin, P. (1991b). Commentary: Response to Wells, Loftus and McGough. In J. Doris (Ed.), *The suggestibility of children's recollections* (pp. 172-176). Washington, DC: American Psychological Association.

Quinn, K. (1988). Children and deception. In R. Rogers (Ed.), *Clinical assessment of malingering and deception*. New York: Guilford Press.

Stouthamer-Loeber, M. (1986). Lying as a problem behavior in children: A review. *Clinical Psychology Review, 6*, 267-289.

Undeutsch, U. (1982). Statement reality analysis. In T. Deventer (Ed.), *Reconstructing the past*. Netherlands: Kluwer, Law & Taxation Publishers.

Undeutsch, U. (1984). *Methods in detecting assessee misrepresentation*. Presented at the European Military Psychologists' Conference, Nuremberg, Federal Republic of Germany.

Vidoni, D., Fleming, N., & Mintz, S. (1983). Behavior problems of children as perceived by teachers, mental health professionals, and children. *Psychology in the Schools, 20*, 93-98.

Wells, G., & Loftus, E. (1991). Commentary: Is this child fabricating? Reactions to a new assessment technique. In J. Doris (Ed.), *The suggestibility of children's recollections* (pp. 168-171). Washington, DC: American Psychological Association.

10

INTERVIEWING AND INTERROGATION

This chapter discusses pretrial investigation of suspects and witnesses through interviewing and observation. Extant methods are effective to varying degrees. Academic researchers frequently claim that present methods of interviewing and interrogation yield too many false positives (innocent parties labeled as perpetrators). The conclusions in this chapter are based on the writers' experiences over the years with police departments and other investigative/enforcement agencies.

The literature on word association methods and nonverbal leakage is relevant to an investigation. The evaluator should recall that interviewing is employed frequently in combination with other investigative approaches—forensic hypnosis, polygraphy, criminal profiling. All of these methods are crude, yet investigative teams persist in utilizing them. At the very least, the serious evaluator of deception should be aware of methods from other disciplines that are designed to cut through denial and fakery. Lastly, ethical and legal implications are discussed, suggesting that existing methods need to be replaced and reconceptualized so as to be congruent with the needs of society and of the interrogated individual.

REACTION TIME AS A SIGN OF DECEPTION

In a case involving a confession for the rape, sodomy, and murder of two young Asian American females and suspicion of a third murder, a 20-year-old radio repairman agreed to undergo comprehensive evaluation. For the unsolved third murder, the following methods were used and results were obtained:

> Words associated with key items and events surrounding the homicide known only to the perpetrator were completed. The victim was strangled with an orange scarf in a schoolroom, for example, so words such as "orange," "scarf," and "school" were selected. Words matched in frequency of occurrence were selected from the Lorge-Thorndike tables. A mixed list of 50

words was presented individually to the suspect, with instructions for him to associate a common word with the stimulus
word. Delay in response time and emotional indicators were
dependent variables.

The suspect presented longer latencies of response to the
critical words, evidencing facial twitching and other arousal
signs as associated features. He declined to continue after 36
words, claiming that the test made no sense and that he was
tired.

The case on the third murder was subsequently dropped
due to lack of evidence. The perpetrator was incarcerated the
first two murders. Years later, he told a cellmate that he had
killed the victim in the unsolved murder; however, he related
the information in a hypothetical manner such that he could
not be prosecuted.

Word association methods were used extensively in the early part of the century to detect deception and concealment (Goldstein, 1923; Henke & Eddy, 1909;
Leach & Washburn, 1910; Marston, 1920; Yerkes & Berry, 1909). Research was
conducted on a variety of populations including college students, criminals, and
military personnel. Despite their early promise, investigations of this sort became
less popular due to many different influences.

Goldstein (1923) summarized this early research:

The primary interest of the early workers in this field lay
in the diagnosis of the emotional complexes underlying cases
of hysteria and neurasthenia. Goldstein stated that the method
was also applied by investigators in attempts to detect crime.

In this use of the association-reaction method, the list of
words used as stimuli contains words relating to the crime. The
reaction time to these critical words was found to be lengthened
in the case of those criminals who attempted deception by avoiding responses which implicated them in the crime.

Although subject to methodological criticisms, these early investigations frequently uncovered where subjects had concealed objects. Among the findings
from this early work were:

1. Reaction words were suggested by objects in the room or by earlier words
in the series. Fakers used recent input to distort. A perseverative quality was
indicated.

2. A small subset of subjects came up with shorter reaction times (termed
"negative" subjects), which could be controlled by inclusion of neutral words
equivalent in difficulty and frequency. In some cases, a mixed pattern was observable (i.e., both negative and positive types), again detectable by a controlled comparison.

3. Fear and anger accounted for the discrepancies from expected performance.
Stress was seen to create a momentum of its own with awareness of anger or fear

generating further abnormal latencies. Fear was associated with longer latencies and anger with shorter ones.

4. Most subjects had a plan to deceive. For longer latencies, they planned to go slower and welcomed opportunities and distractions to lengthen the reaction times. This was contingent upon awareness by the faker that the method was tapping deception.

5. For shorter latencies and in anticipation of the "hamming" style of deception discussed later, Marston (1920) stated the following:

> I believe it will be commonly recognized that there are individuals among our acquaintances who can lie faster and more fluently than they can tell the truth....The behavior of the negative type subjects, as noted by the experimenter, was almost wholly calm, confident, and showed a high degree of intellectual concentration. The guilty flush was almost altogether absent and the manner of the subject was usually more convincing upon deceptive lists than upon truthful ones....In the negative type, we find the successful liar.

Interestingly, later experimentation showed that the negative types were not conscious of their deception (Goldstein, 1923). In contrast, subjects with longer latencies felt guilty and were aware when they were deceiving and relaxed when they were responding naturally. The deceivers showed more hesitation, confusion, and arousal.

NONVERBAL LEAKAGE ANALYSIS

Freud (1959) addressed nonverbal signals relating to deception when he stated, "He that has eyes to see and ears to hear may convince himself that no mortal can keep a secret. If his lips are silent, he chatters with his fingertips; betrayal oozes out of him at every pore." The literature on "body leakage," represented in part by Ekman and Friesen (1969, 1972), Ekman, Friesen, and Sherer (1976); Kraut (1978); and DePaulo (1992), reveals that a wide array of nonverbal behaviors has been associated with deception.

Knapp, Hart, and Dennis (1974), based on videotaped interviews of 140 undergraduate military veterans, found a number of significant correlates of deception: (a) uncertainty, (b) vagueness, (c) nervousness, (d) reticence (total words and probes), (e) dependence, and (f) negative affect (i.e., eye duration, group references, disparaging statements). Knapp saw these six styles as natural, common traits of all people, with liars exceeding the bounds of convention.

Knapp (1978) interpreted the "body leakage" literature as follows:

> Scholarly investigations have found a wide variety of nonverbal behaviors associated with liars rather than truthful communicators. According to these studies, liars will have high pitched voices; less gaze duration and longer adaptor duration; fewer illustrators (less enthusiastic); more hand-shrug emblems (uncertainty); more adaptors—particularly face play adaptors; and less nodding; more speech errors; slower speaking rate and less-immediate positions relative to their partners. Findings have not always been consistent, and research-

ers have used many methods of creating a deception to study. Furthermore, we don't know which, if any, of the cues just listed are used by observers when attempting to detect deception.

Table 10.1
Nonverbal Signs of Deception
1. Increased body movement 2. Gaze aversion 3. Less assertive and dominant 4. Higher voice pitch 5. Longer latency of responses, reticence 6. More speech errors and higher pitch 7. Circumstantiality, vagueness 8. Terser answers 9. Posture noncongruent with portrayed emotion 10. Self-grooming responses 11. Prolonged inappropriate smiling 12. More negative remarks 13. Distractibility 14. Greater interest in test results 15. Increase in illustrators (e.g., hand motions)

Ekman (1980, 1985); DePaulo, Stone, and Lassiter (1985) and others (Hall, 1986) suggest additional signs and some corrections. These more recent findings place a greater emphasis on the motor and verbal behavior that deceivers show (see Table 10.1).

Generally, liars are easier to detect in their fakery according to Ekman (1980, 1985) when:

1. Strong emotions are experienced by the deceiver during the interview.
2. Severe sanctions can be applied to the faker for lying.
3. The interviewer and liar share common values, culture, language, and/or are personally acquainted.
4. The interviewer has information that only the perpetrator would know.
5. An audience is present that is skeptical about the truthfulness of the deceiver.
6. The deceiver's personality predisposes him or her to fear, guilt, or "duping delight."
7. The interviewer has a reputation for being fair-minded, but difficult to deceive.

8. The interviewer is biased in the direction of believing that the deceiver is a liar or "no good," or is subject to emotion during the interrogation, although both of these increase the chances of false positives (i.e., nonliars being branded as liars).

On the other hand, Ekman (1985) stated that lie-catching is especially difficult when:

1. The deceiver's story is rehearsed.
2. Deception involves hiding the true, as opposed to presenting the false.
3. There is benefit or gain from the lie.
4. The target would ordinarily trust the judgment of the deceiver, especially if the target was successfully lied to previously by the liar.
5. The lie is authorized, and the target is a stranger.
6. The interviewer must conceal skepticism of the deceiver, as the cognitive focus may be on concealment instead of on the deceiver.
7. The liar is practiced in deception, is inventive, clever, articulate, and has good recall skills.
8. The liar consistently moves facial muscles to make conversational points.
9. The liar is self-deceived and believes in his or her lie, or is a psychopath.
10. The interviewer is the type of person who denies, avoids, and represses, expressing positive views toward most people.
11. The lie catcher receives some benefit from not exposing the deception.

Guidelines have been proffered by Ekman (1985). The face, arms/hands, and legs/feet, in that order, have the capacity to send information with a reverse pattern in actually showing the leakage. The feet/legs are considered a good source of leakage when it occurs. The face, so easily controlled for many people, serves primarily as a distractor to the evaluator. The face reveals deception from so called "microfacial" movements; however, these are often very difficult to detect. They represent the true, brief facial emotions before they are disguised.

Based on the foregoing, fakers tend to concentrate on self-control of facial movements but tend to neglect the limbs. Peripheral movement is rarely involved in positive deception; one would look for lies of omission rather than commission in the hands, for example.

Examination of verbal content may be more revealing of actual events than nonverbal behavior. This finding has implications for forensic training and practice. Reading transcripts or listening to voice tapes of defendants may yield more information than attending to available visual cues. This would partially counteract fakers who "ham," or histrionically exhibit "honest" behaviors. The criminal justice system is replete with examinees of this description. Finally, accuracy of detection seems to bear little relationship to the ability to deceive others. People are generally more consistent at successful lying than they are in detecting lies.

The following concepts have been gleaned from the literature: (a) accuracy of detecting deception is somewhat higher than chance for most people—about

10% higher (Schlenker & Weigold, 1992; Ekman & O'Sullivan, 1991); (b) skill at detection is unrelated to knowledge of the target's true affective state; (c) skill at detecting deception in women may not correlate with skill at detecting deception in men; (d) skill at detecting false negative emotional states is better than the ability to detect false positive states; (e) visual cues, such as facial movements, may actually distract examiners from the truth; (f) the presence of a person (as opposed to reading transcripts about that person) may reduce accuracy and increase judgments of dishonesty (Maier & Thurber, 1968); (g) feet and legs emit slow and limited motor patterns but are less controlled than the face; (h) the face is best controlled and has the highest chance of showing successful deceit.

CRIMINAL INVESTIGATION APPROACHES

Royal and Schutt (1976) typify an investigative approach through interviewing. Their method is based upon the assumptions that (a) induced stress in examinees is desirable because reason decreases as emotions increase; (b) polite, respectful examiner behavior can yield confessions and reduce invalid or illegal findings; and (c) the deceptive suspect will eventually trip himself or herself up. Implicit assumptions are that most people are dishonest and that almost all suspects actually committed the crime for which they are interviewed.

Table 10.2
Guidelines for Interrogating Suspects

- Suspect is isolated from all intrusions and resources.
- Suspect is kept immobile as much as possible.
- Establish dependence on the part of the suspect.
- Examiner is friendly, concerned, and firm.
- Ask open-ended questions for new information.
- Proceed from the general to the specific.
- Precise questions are asked for concrete data.
- Occasionally ask questions randomly to upset faking patterns.
- Summarize statement in sequence of events.
- Suspect verifies each part of summarized sequence material.
- Suggest excuses to crime to suspect before suspect spontaneously mentions them.
- Project indifference to criminal behavior of suspect ("Everybody does it").
- Induce stress when appropriate (e.g., initially).
- Provide relief after an admission, then induce stress again; repeat the cycle.
- Continue until a confession is obtained.

Royal, R.F., & Schutt, S.R. (1976).

Basically, their method involves detecting lies, discrediting alibis, and "pumping up" the quality of incriminating evidence. Fear of punishment, bringing shame upon the family, and other similar methods are utilized to motivate the suspect. Table 10.2 presents some of their recommended techniques used, of course, in conjunction with other forensic methods.

A structured approach to interviewing is recommended by Reid & Associates in books, articles, and seminars (1986). Many investigative agencies endorse these methods in their field work. Guidelines to truthful versus deceptive suspects are presented, with permission, in Table 10.3, followed by a sequential process recommended by Reid & Associates (1986, 1988).

Table 10.3 Differentiating Truthful From Deceptive Suspects	
Truthful	**Deceptive**
Eye contact direct and continuous	Eye contact erratic and indirect when threatened
Facial expressions vary from anger to surprise	Facial expressions vary from fear to passive/blank
Increased anger with continual accusations	Difficult to rouse to anger
More likely facial flushing	More likely blanching
Minimal body movements	More frequent and extreme body movements
Leans toward interrogator	Turns away from interrogator
Less use of barriers	More use of barriers (e.g., arms crossing chest)
Infrequent self-grooming responses	Frequent self-grooming
Responds without delay unless questions requires thought	Evasive or nonresponsive
More information about case reduces arousal	No change or increased tension with more case information
Cooperates with investigation	Noncooperation come in various forms
Prompt, with no hesitancy in delaying termination	Arrives late and desires to leave early
Task-oriented and interested in issues raised by interrogators	More likely presents physical problems, complaints, crying, etc.
Task-oriented	Emphasizes truthfulness
Some memory loss expected	Selective memory loss or too good recall
Direct	Excessive use of qualifiers
Smooth execution of words and sentences	More likely "tongue-tied" or otherwise disorganized answer
Easy to spot	Harder to determine
Denials become stronger as interrogation continues.	Denials weaken as interrogation continues

Confrontation

In this initial step, the suspect is accused of a crime (e.g., "John, evidence shows that you murdered Mrs. Jones in her house last night."). The purpose of the accusation is to increase anxiety and stress in the suspect. A transition step is often introduced here with the addition of a warm and supportive investigator.

Theme Development

The suspect's anxiety is reduced by continually plying him with rationalizations for his crime until one is workable (e.g., to suspect in wife-beating case: "Everyone pushes his wife around a little."). The idea is to prompt a confession without fear of recrimination. The seriousness of the crime is minimized, blame is projected onto the victim, and the suspect is provided with a positive image.

Rejection

Theme development continues in this stage with denials being cut off by the interrogator (e.g., "I know what you want to say, but let me share this with you...."). The interrogator meets objections by the suspect that he could not have committed the crime by character support. The suspect may state that he is a family man, for example, and could never jeopardize that status by sexually assaulting his daughter. The interrogator then supports the notion of his good character by relating it back to theme development (e.g., "Our investigation shows that you are a good and decent family man, John. I'm sure this is the only time this has occurred in your life.").

Acceptance

The defenses of the suspect begin to diminish. Cues that the suspect is tiring include muscle relaxation, slumped posture, dropping of eyes, and crying. Tears are considered a good sign because they signify that the suspect's defenses are breaking down. The interrogator is advised to press on with the attack, calling the suspect by his or her first name, touching and invading the personal space of the suspect, and using other means.

Alternatives

Two or more offense scenarios are presented to the suspect, with the option of selecting one that will inculpate him (e.g., "Your stepdaughter says that this has been going on for years. Is this true or was it a one-time thing?").

The following are alternatives presented to a therapist suspected of fraudulent billing practices by Reid and Associates (1988):

If this is something where you have built your entire practice on falsified billing statements, and that this is just one of thousands, I am going to have to spend weeks going through your records, contacting clients, and insurance companies to verify each bill. But, if this was something that just started a little while ago, you can save me a lot of time by telling me that. I'm really hoping that this was just an isolated incident, wasn't it?

CLOSURE

This involves expanding any admission to the crime into a legally acceptable format. Support of the accused with no use of leading questions is used. Follow-up questions with no note taking until details of the crime are known is encouraged.

There should be both oral and written confessions, with audio- and video-tapes of the statements. A formal statement is taken with all legal points in mind. These include (a) obtaining a witness, (b) Miranda warnings, (c) the suspect giving both a general and a detailed presentation of the offense, (d) use of exact words, (e) correction of errors being initialed by the suspect, and (f) signatures by all parties.

THE ETHICS OF INTERROGATION

The above is presented not as recommended practice by the practicing clinician, but as an illustration of commonly used interrogation techniques by investigative agencies in this country. Deception is used by the interviewers throughout these methods—the personalizing of the suspect, the minimizing of wrongdoing, the gap of time deliberately placed between signing of a waiver of rights and the interrogation, and other gimmicks and ploys.

Consider the following recommendations by Rhoads, as reported by Ditzler (1988), in setting up an interrogation room:

> Shorten the front legs of a straight chair 3/8 of an inch and keep the seat waxed. The person who comes in showing indifference is not going to talk to you. He wants to show you how cool he is by stretching out and taking up a lot of space. Normally when you sit in a chair, it leans slightly backward to support body weight.
>
> By changing the tilt, you lean slightly forward. It's really hard to stretch out and be indifferent when you're falling off the chair.
>
> People have an intimate zone of 6 to 18 inches from the body and a personal zone of 1-1/2 to 4 feet. By stepping in close to the individual to produce anxiety and backing off when you get what you want, you mentally program that person to be cooperative.
>
> Paint the room a neutral color, such as pale yellow.

The "Mutt and Jeff" technique is a classic police interrogative technique. Here, the more cynical, aggressive, and usually older officer feigns anger at the suspect while the more liberal, sympathetic, and usually younger or female officer attempts to wheedle a confession out of the suspect. Reid & Associates (1988) object to this method, not on moral grounds, but because most suspects recognize the methods and the confession may be rendered inadmissible in court.

Other methods of manipulation presented by Reid & Associates (1988) include (a) discussing the suspect in the third person, "roping" him or her in to the content in order to set up alternatives; (b) repeatedly breaking the body boundary space to induce threat and then relief; (c) presenting to the suspect aspects of the victim that can be blamed for the crime.

Reid & Associates (1988) presented the following for Borderline Personality Disorders as a sample of a recommended procedure:

> A common theory relating to the borderline personality is that these individuals suffered an early childhood loss such as the death or separation from their father. With this causality, it is not surprising that borderline individuals will easily project their behavior away from themselves.
>
> Therefore during a theme, the investigator should blame circumstances, other people, or the victim for causing the individual to commit the crime. Recommended interview strategies for other personality disorders are similarly proffered.

The above methods raise ethical concerns. First, the target's life may be in danger. Reid & Associates (1988) rightly noted that borderlines, for example, may become suicidal after being "grilled" and suggested that caution be exercised in leaving the suspect alone subsequent to the interrogation. Yet, the writers know of no investigative agency that routinely builds in deprocessing procedures and psychiatric safeguards following interrogation. The investigators appear to be playing junior psychologist or psychiatrist—diagnosing the suspect, but having no skill in intervening if the person becomes destabilized. Suspects remain a part of the community until they are convicted and they are entitled to fair treatment. A final concern is that the suspect's view of the legal process may be tarnished forever and an increased alienation from police may be the result.

The second harmful effect is the corrosive influence these techniques have on police officers in particular. Police become overly suspicious of the citizens they have sworn to protect, thus predisposing them to make false positive errors in spite of their experience with crime. Cynicism and hostility abound with the belief by officers that most people would commit crimes if they could "get away with it" (Bartol, 1983, p. 59). Later, the cynicism expands from the public to the police system and its failings, and eventually becomes directed against life itself (Niederhoffer, 1967). Niederhoffer found that cynicism among police increases in proportion to the length of service. As response, police officers withdraw from the public, forming cliques of drinking buddies, becoming more distant, cold, angry, and authoritarian, and developing a dogmatic attitude toward life. There are increases in substance abuse, depression, family problems, and difficulties with authority figures.

The third harmful effect is felt by the community itself. The many interviews that end in confessions through dubious practices may not alter the overall effect of crime; however, an increasing alienation of the community may result, as shown by the King case in Los Angeles in 1991. Recall that most encounters between police and citizens are initiated by citizens, rather than by police. A ratio of six to one was found by Black (1971). This fact alone suggests that community acceptance of the police is imperative.

A reconceptualization is in order. The central issue is detecting deception while preserving the integrity of both the suspect and the police. To do this, the authors recommend abandoning lies and manipulation, and instead, practicing the following:

1. Psychologically screen police applicants not only to avoid the misfits, but also to obtain officers who are warm, compassionate, and flexible thinkers.
2. Rotate shifts and duties so that interrogators will have to perform patrol duty and other routine police assignments.
3. Introduce mandatory psychotherapy for all officers and teach them the skills to reduce stress in themselves and in one another. Every department should have a psychologist on the staff.
4. Use noninvasive deception methods that only the perpetrator can respond to (e.g., word association tests, forced choice testing). Eliminate methods and techniques that are unreliable or which violate the integrity of the suspect.
5. Develop the attitude that not all cases involving deception can be solved. The short-term gain in obtaining a confession may not outweigh the long-term harm to police officers and the community.

REFERENCES

Bartol, C. R. (1983). *Psychology and American law*. Belmont, CA: Wadsworth Publishing Co.

Black, D. (1971). The social organization of arrest. *Stanford Law Review, 23*, 1087-1111.

DePaulo, B. (1992). Nonverbal behavior and self-presentation. *Psychological Bulletin, 111*(2), 203-243.

DePaulo, B., Stone, J., & Lassiter, G. (1985). Deceiving and detecting deceit. In B. Schlenker (Ed.), *The self and social life* (pp. 323-370). New York: McGraw-Hill.

Ekman, P. (1980, August). Asymmetry in facial expression. *Science, 209*, 833-836.

Ekman, P. (1985). *Telling lies: Clues to deceit in the marketplace, politics, and marriage*. New York: W. W. Norton.

Ekman, P., & Friesen, W. V. (1969, February). Nonverbal leakage and clues to deception. *Psychiatry, 32*(1), 88-106.

Ekman, P., & Friesen, W. (1972). Hand movements. *Journal of Communication, 22*, 353-374.

Ekman, P., Friesen, W. V., & Scherer, K. R. (1976). Body movement and voice pitch in deceptive interaction. *Semiotica, 16*(1) 23-27.

Ekman, P., & O'Sullivan, M. (1991). Who can catch a liar? *American Psychologist, 46*(9), 913-920.

Freud, S. (1959). Fragment of an analysis of a case of hysteria (1905). In *Collected Papers* (Vol. 3) (pp. 329-331). New York: Basic Books.

Goldstein, E. R. (1923). Reaction times and the consciousness of deception. *The American Journal of Psychology, 34*(4), 562-581.

Hall, H. V. (1986). The forensic distortion analysis: Proposed decision tree and report format. *American Journal of Forensic Psychology, 4*(3), 31-59.

Henke, F. G., & Eddy, M. W. (1909, September). Mental diagnosis by the association reaction method. *The Psychological Review, 16*(5), 399-409.

Knapp, M. (1978). *Nonverbal communication in human interaction* (2nd ed.). New York: Holt, Rinehart and Winston.

Knapp, M. L., Hart, R. P., & Dennis, H. S. (1974, Fall). An exploration of deception as a communication construct. *Human Communication Research, 1*(1), 15-29.

Kraut, R. E. (1978). Verbal and nonverbal cues in the perception of lying. *Journal of Personality and Social Psychology, 36*(4), 380-391.

Leach, H. M., & Washburn, M. F. (1910). Some tests by the association reaction method of mental diagno-sis. *The American Journal of Psychology, 21*(1), 162-167.

Maier, N. R. F., & Thurber, J. A. (1968). Accuracy of judgments of deception when an interview is watched, heard, and read. *Personnel Psychology, 21,* 23-30.

Marston, W. M. (1920). Reaction-time symptoms of deception. *Journal of Experimental Psychology, 3,* 72-87.

Niederhoffer, A. (1967). *Behind the shield: The police in urban society.* New York: Doubleday.

Reid, J. E., & Associates, Inc. (1986). 1986 seminar schedule, *The Reid technique of interviewing and interro-gation.* Based on over 200,000 successful interviews and interrogations by Reid & Associates, Inc.

Reid, J. E., & Associates, Inc. (1988, Spring). *The Investigator, 4*(2). Chicago, IL: Author.

Royal, R. F., & Schutt, S. R. (1976). *The gentle art of interviewing and interrogation: A professional manual and guide.* Englewood Cliffs, NJ: Prentice-Hall, Inc.

Schlenker, B., & Weigold, M. (1992). Interpersonal processes involving impression regulation and manage-ment. *Annual Review of Psychology, 43,* 133-168.

Yerkes, R. M., & Berry, C. S. (1909). The association reaction method of mental diagnosis. *The American Journal of Psychology, 20,* 22-37.

CRIMINAL PROFILING

Forensic professionals have been increasingly involved in crime profiling in the last few decades (Brussel, 1968; Hazelwood & Douglas, 1980; Leyton, 1983; Ressler, Burgess, & Douglass, 1988; Rider, 1980). Profiling involves the analysis of crime scene characteristics in order to narrow the search for a perpetrator. These characteristics of the crime scene may yield information about the general traits or characteristics of the perpetrator of the crime. An organized crime scene, for example, may suggest that the perpetrator has an organized lifestyle, is meticulous, careful, intelligent, and given to planning.

The use of information about a crime scene and about a victim to describe probable characteristics of the perpetrator illustrates the wealth of information contained in *base rates* and its usefulness in understanding typical criminal behavior. Such information is not only practically useful in narrowing the range of potential suspects, but also forms a "background" against which distortion analysis may be performed. Is this suspect typical of others charged with the same offense? If not, what are the differences? Is the suspect genuinely atypical or is there substantial distortion in his self-presentation? The general methods of criminal profiling are therefore useful in formulating hypotheses about a suspect during evaluation, in "raising suspicions" regarding distortions by the suspect, and in assessing the genuineness of a particular suspect's behavior during evaluation.

Criminal profiling is most helpful in (a) sex-related assaults and homicides; (b) unique homicides, such as those involving torture, mutilation, evisceration, and ritualistic violence; (c) assassination; (d) child molestation and abduction; (e) fire-setting, arson, and bombing; and (f) extortion. Terroristic threats can also be analyzed through the psycholinguistic aspects of notes or recorded conversations (Miron & Goldstein, 1979; Miron & Pasquale, 1978).

Bizarre crimes lend themselves to profiling because of the distinct patterns that emerge, thus narrowing the pool of potential suspects to manageable proportions. In general, the behavior of the perpetrator in any given crime determines whether or not profiling can be used.

The FBI's Behavioral Science Unit has a computerized profiling system, the results of which are available to local police departments on request (Ressler et al., 1988). Douglass, Burgess, Burgess, and Ressler (1992) have described sub-types of murders, arsons, and sexual assaults based on this system. Characteristics of several hundred rapists and rape murderers are shown in Tables 11.1 and 11.2.

Generally, the process of crime profiling focuses on (a) primary profiling inputs, from evaluation of the criminal act, crime scene, victim, and significant/ knowledgeable others; (b) secondary inputs involving suppositions on time, location, acceleration, and other factors; (c) crime assessment in terms of the overall

---

Table 11.1
FBI Base Rates for Serial Rapists

Stable employment	54%
Married at least once	71%
Served in military	51%
Above average on intelligence tests	52%
Average or better SES	54%
Sexual abuse as child	76%
Physical abuse as child	38%
Collected pornography as child	36%
Witnessed sexual violence by others	25%
Compulsive masturbation	54%
History of voyeurism	68%
History of fetishism	41%
History of cross-dressing	23%
History of obscene phone calls	38%
History of sexual bondage	26%
Selected victim because of availability	98%
Selected victim because of gender	95%
Selected victim because of age	66%
Selected victim because of location	66%
Selected victim because of race	63%
Victim a targeted stranger	80-88%
Victim raped at home	45-52%
Mean number of rape convictions	7.6
Mean number of actual rapes consummated	27.8

Adapted from Hazelwood and Warren (1989).

---

reconstruction and dynamics of the crime; (d) development of a profile (see Pinizzotto & Finkel, 1990, for one of the few empirical studies of the process of developing criminal profiles); (e) investigation and comparison of characteristics to a suspect pool; and (f) possible apprehension. Some crimes are solved by this process (Ressler et al., 1988; Ressler, 1990); many others are resolved by "dumb luck," involving the victim escaping or the perpetrator being arrested on another charge.

Table 11.2
FBI Base Rates for Serial Rape Murderers (up to 1990)

Male	100%
White	92%
Poor high school grades	60%
Average or better intelligence	80%
Stable SES of parents	86%
Poor relationship with male caretakers	72%
Pornography exposure as child	81%
Intact family as child	85%
First rape fantasies, CA 12-14	50%
Assaultive to adults (adolescent)	86%
Stealing (adolescent)	81%
Isolation as child/adolescent	71%
Chronic lying as child/adolescent	71%
Enuresis as child/adolescent	68%
Fire-setting as child/adolescent	56%
As adult, 1-6 sexual assaults not resulting in apprehension	57%
As adult, >25 unapprehended assaults	21%
As adult, acquittals for previous sex offenses	35%
Behaviors/Events during escalation stage	
Stress increase before killing	100%
Preoccupation with murder	100%
Fantasy intensifies	100%
Increase in hostility and anger	46%
Increase in frustration	50%
Increase in agitation	43%
Increase in excitement	41%
Common suspected or actual work problems	65%
Plans killing	50%
Open to opportunities for killing	34%
Drinks prior to violence	49%
Takes drugs prior to violence	35%
Conflict with a woman	59%
Conflict with parents	53%
Financial problems	48%
After the murder	
Follows investigations in media	46%
Introjects self in investigation	20%
Disposes of body, conceals	58%
Exposes body of victim at disposal site	42%
Victim nude or partially clothed	72%
Obtains souvenirs from victim	27%
Has sex with victim after death	42%
Returns to crime scene	27%
Returns to crime scene to relive the fantasy	26%
Returns to crime scene to gauge progress of police	19%

Adapted from Ressler, Burgess, & Douglas (1988).

The process is similar to that used by forensically oriented clinicians to diagnose and treat offenders. Collected data is scrutinized, reconstruction of behavioral patterns and lifestyle is conducted, and hypotheses are formulated. Priorities for treatment are established, and intervention is implemented, all in a feedback loop with ongoing and continual assessment.

Another way to analyze the process of profiling is by following a traditional scientific method. This includes (a) identification of the problem and collection of facts, (b) creation of preliminary hypotheses, (c) the collection of additional facts, (d) formulating the investigative hypotheses, (e) deducing further consequences, (f) testing the consequences, and (g) application. An illustration follows.

DEFINING THE FORENSIC PROBLEM

The forensic problem is often framed in the referral question and has, as its basis, a group of facts which do not have a ready or acceptable explanation without analysis and synthesis. An illustration is chosen that utilizes a forensic task (criminal profiling) and a means to assess the utility of the sequence (narrowing the range of possible perpetrators). The illustration starts with a letter of referral received several months after the instant offenses:

> As we discussed on the telephone today, our office wishes to retain your consultation services in relationship to an unsolved murder-rape-kidnapping that occurred on October 8, 1991 in Port Hueneme, California (see enclosed police reports). Briefly, the victim, Tanya B. Reynolds, a 24-year-old, white seamstress for a local firm, was abducted at a bus stop at Main and Roan Streets and was dragged into a nearby hillock area, where she was raped and murdered.
>
> We can establish a foot trail from the bus stop to the hillock, but the perpetrator's footprints are indistinct due to poor soil conditions. Witnesses on several buses observed only one party near the victim at the approximate time of the instant offenses, with descriptions centering on either a white or Chicano male wearing military fatigues, being of a height between 5'6" and 5'11", weighing between 130 and 160 pounds, and appearing to be in his late teens or early 20s. It should be added that there are approximately 40,000 military personnel stationed in this area at any one time, representing all branches of the military.
>
> Evidence shows that the victim's throat was cut with a broken wine bottle, possibly occurring after both anal and vaginal penetration by the perpetrator (no semen was found).
>
> The trail of blood extends from the hillock into a small ravine 20 to 30 feet away, where the victim's head and upper chest were crushed by a 50-pound boulder being dropped or possibly thrown from a vertical position. As far as we can tell, no money was taken, but the victim's photographic identification was missing.

Please let us know if you would consider involvement in this case. If you are able to go to the crime scene, we can make arrangements for the police evidence specialist to be there. All the physical evidence, minus the victim's body, can be returned to the crime scene to reenact the appropriate elements. We can then process the case with the investigation team.

Thank you very much, and I look forward to hearing from you.

Sincerely,

Chief Detective
Oxnard Police Department

PRELIMINARY HYPOTHESES

The key consideration at this phase is to suspend judgment until a great deal of data has been obtained. In particular, the evaluator should steer clear of assumptions of psychopathology because of the bizarreness of the violence. The evaluator may otherwise go down a blind alley early in the evaluation process.

Yet, some opinions must be formulated before the forensic evaluation can proceed. In this case, the assumptions were made that:

1. The instant offenses were crimes.
2. Similar crimes have yielded apprehension of some criminals who were eventually detected.
3. Criminals are of different personality types depending on previous criminality, developmental history, intelligence, employment and educational factors, and a host of other variables.
4. Personality types and background features of criminals can be measured and assigned to distinct profile types. In this regard, Megargee and Bohn (1979) have such a system of classifying criminals on the basis of their Minnesota Multiphasic Personality Inventory (MMPI) responses. To date, thousands of criminal offenders have been measured, with 95% of the criminal population assigned to one of the 10 discrete types.

   The Megargee taxonomy is important because it has been determined to be reliable and valid (e.g., Edinger, 1979). Of considerable interest for forensic evaluators are the associated background characteristics that come with each profile type.
5. The perpetrator in this case left suggestions at the crime scene and/or from observation that could be used to formulate a tentative profile.

6. The tentative profile type can yield descriptive traits or leads for investigation, ultimately reducing the number in any suspect pool.

COLLECTING ADDITIONAL FACTS

The forensic evaluator collects as much data as possible in regards to the perpetrator, victim, and crime scene to describe the interaction of the three that was operative at the time of the crime. Data may be historical in nature (e.g., developmental history of the victim), instant offense-related (e.g., physical evidence at the crime scene), molar in scope (e.g., assumed perpetrator traits), or molecular in focus (e.g., specific autopsy results), as long as the crime is better described. These additional facts may lead to new hypotheses, which must be investigated, if only to rule them out as competing explanations.

Relevant to the victim in our criminal profiling case, data was collected on her background, lifestyle, and physical characteristics. Generally, she was quite ordinary and conservative in nature, with no criminal record, a high school education, and one year of technical education in textiles. This 24-year-old woman was unmarried, with a long-term boyfriend whose movements were accounted for during the period of the crime. She was living at home with her parents and was waiting at the bus stop, on her way home, when the attack occurred. There were no distinguishing features to her appearance, with a medium build (5'5", 130 pounds) and plain looks, as described by friends and family. Her clothing consisted of a grey dress and black jacket. The principal themes which emerged about the victim included unobtrusiveness, conservativeness, and high conventionality.

Relevant to the crime context, the location was a bus stop at a busy intersection next to a vacant lot with a hillock in its center, approximately 30 yards away from the bus stop. The time of the crime was estimated at 8:30 a.m., plus or minus 15 minutes. Trees hid from view the hillock and the adjacent small ravine where the victim was dragged.

Relevant to the possible perpetrator, general characteristics were available from the investigation reports. Extrapolating from crime scene and victim data, a probable profile type was constructed. First, this perpetrator was seen as an hostile, insensitive man (possible MMPI elevations on Scales 4 and 6), with poor social skills, who was probably clumsy around people (MMPI profiles elevation on Scale 0). He traversed a good distance from the bus stop to consummate the deed and, therefore, may be manic or hyperactive under stress (high Scale 9). Perhaps the perpetrator was not concerned about disease from the victim, or cleanliness (low on Scales 1, 2, and 3). Some stress can be assumed due to the time of the day, the busy intersection, no similar crimes before in the area, and the disorganized manner of the crime (high F and 8).

A list of approximately 300 suspects was compiled by investigators riding the bus route and questioning riders around the time of the offense. The assumption was made that the suspect rode the bus and that the crime scene was possibly located between his residence and job site.

FORMULATING THE HYPOTHESIS

All facts or assumed facts needed to solve the problem may not be available at this stage, yet a synthesis of the data must be performed. What is needed is a hypothesis that will account for all data and will lead to further inquiry.

Putting all speculations together, the possible perpetrator fits the profile of a disorganized psychopath, an individual of average or lower intelligence who is not psychotic, yet who is deeply antisocial and passive in coping with stress, and whose interpersonal skills are intact but who lacks reciprocity towards others and is immature. Previous criminality was probably not extensive, as it would have been detected during the military screening process. Also, the instant offense was "sloppy" in its commission, requiring both a throat cut and a crushing blow with a boulder to "finish the victim off." Triggering stimuli included possible alcohol consumption, but since the incident occurred in the morning, the abuse was possibly chronic or, at least, episodic in pattern. Other stress could be anticipated, the most likely (and most common) explanation being that there may have been problems in this individual's central love relationship. Most likely, therefore, the possible perpetrator was married or had a girlfriend with whom he was in conflict. The profile the possible perpetrator most likely fits (Megargee's Group How), included a person from the rural as opposed to the city area, second or later born as opposed to first born or the only child in the family, a high school education or less, a strong possibility of substance abuse tendencies, and eventual problems and resentment against authority.

In short, the final hypothesis involved the profile of a chronically sociopathic, nonpsychotic, but somewhat passive individual. Alcohol and relationship triggers may have been operative. He picked out a target of opportunity to aggress upon. He didn't care about consequences to the victim, or the busy crime context; thus we must remove those two primary factors as contributing to the violence that occurred. Most likely, the victim's behavior represented a displaced target of aggression, and the victim was, therefore, probably not known to him previously.

Other characteristics of the disorganized type included: (a) lives/works near the crime scene and (b) has a minimal change in lifestyle (Ressler et al., 1988). Based on these factors, the perpetrator could be expected to have remained in the area of the rape-murder.

DEDUCING FURTHER CONSEQUENCES

The hypothesis must be checked for degree of predictiveness. It should point beyond known data to new areas where confirmatory information can be obtained regarding its accuracy. The new facts help confirm, deny, or render moot the final hypothesis.

The possible perpetrator in the instant case was hypothesized to be in a state of high stress, with displaced aggression toward the victim. This meant that other violence within the same geographic area may have functioned in the same way as the instant offense, although perhaps not resulting in homicide. Unprovoked and unexplained stranger violence towards females was sought with the sexual motive seen as secondary. Police files were checked, and one such event which fit this picture emerged. A 35-year-old, White woman was walking along a park trail not far from the site of the present murder. A lone perpetrator with a description closely fitting that of the possible perpetrator in the instant case passed her. He then turned around, walked back, and punched her in the mouth for no apparent reason. Additional data, as gleaned from that victim, included the perpetrator's height (5'10"), weight (140-150 pounds), race (Caucasian), and enlisted military clothing, with no recall of identifying marks or insignia.

The 300-person suspect pool was scrutinized in terms of the above characteristics. These included height, weight, race, previous criminality, place of origin, ordinal position, enlisted status, and other factors which could be verified. The list of 300 was narrowed down to 10 males who fit the pattern.

TESTING THE CONSEQUENCES

The deductions or inferences from the hypothesized type require some means of verification; in other words, there must be a way to see if the deductions that can be derived from any hypothesis can be affirmed. Observation and oral interview can be used for this stage.

In the instant case, all 10 individuals were staked out by investigators. The identification card of the victim was found in the garbage bin of the apartment complex in which one of the suspects lived. All 10 individuals were brought in and questioned, followed by a polygraph examination. One suspect, the one who lived in the apartment complex where the identification card was found, failed the polygraph. Five-point fingerprint identification was found on the broken wine bottle and matched this perpetrator's prints. When confronted with this evidence, the individual confessed to the crime.

APPLICATION

This stage of the process involves the application of the hypothesis for the original purpose. In this case, the perpetrator was brought to trial, charged with rape and murder, and subsequently released on technicalities. He was suspected in at least one other similar crime some years prior to this, but there was insufficient proof to charge him in that matter. The case was dismissed when it was determined that the police had not properly informed him of his rights, and, therefore, that his confession was not admissible. The other evidence was all circumstantial.

GENERALIZATION

Regardless of the ultimate outcome, all forensic evaluations must follow a sequence of stages. This applies to most problems in forensic psychology, from criminal profiling to insanity evaluations to violence predictions. A problem is defined, and the evaluator works toward a hypothesis and application of that hypothesis.

Several caveats apply. First, to apply the procedure, the investigator must be free from bias and moral values that would contaminate the accuracy of the data collection efforts. But is that ever possible? Often, this requires that the forensic evaluator undergo a rigorous self-examination.

In pure form, the above procedure can be used for focal problems (e.g., criminal profiling), but when most forensic issues involve value-laden opinions relevant to risk, criminal responsibility, or some other global type of issue, the task becomes less specific and more subject to moral bias. Evaluators are typically biased in the direction of suspiciousness. Falsely accepting that there is no difference between the suspect and the universe of confirmed perpetrators is a cardinal error.

PROFILING ORGANIZED RAPE-MURDERERS

This section focuses on traits associated with rape-murderers of the organized type. All traits stem from the writers' experience, the FBI system, and the clinical-forensic literature. Keep in mind the above considerations for profiling in general. For organized rape-murderers (almost all male) in particular, the number of victims (usually, but not always, female) often runs into the double figures. Serial murderers do not "burn out" of their own accord; in this sense, their assaults are self-generated. "Clumping" occurs in that there is usually a spree of killing followed by long durations between series. Much self-control and premeditation is shown.

Based upon several serial cases, and FBI data, the authors propose the following traits associated with organized rape-murderers:

DEVELOPMENTAL TRAITS (BIRTH TO APPROXIMATELY 18 YEARS OF AGE)

The developmental history of the organized serial rape-murderer can be characterized by family instability, poor bonding with significant others, emotional isolation from others, underachievement, and the emergence of violent sexual fantasies and behaviors.

Family:
    (a) White or high status racial/ethnic group membership in area
    (b) Lower-middle socioeconomic status
    (c) Family moves frequently in early years; minimal attachment to the community
    (d) Mental illness or history of criminality in at least one parent; alcohol abuse very common
    (e) Family is intact (two-parent) in early years
    (f) Inconsistent parental discipline
    (g) Sexually repressed environment with possible covert sex abuse of offspring by father
    (h) Frequent arguments in home

Father:
- (i) Uninvolved with perpetrator; perpetrator feels emotional coldness toward father
- (j) Unskilled, blue-collar, but steadily employed
- (k) Moderate likelihood of father leaving family unit before perpetrator grows up

Mother:
- (l) Dominant and hostile parent
- (m) Perpetrator experiences most physical and psychological abuse from mother
- (n) Strong dislike toward mother, coupled with ambivalent feelings of tolerance and hate

Siblings:
- (o) Compete with each other for rewards in an emotionally deficient environment; perpetrator often given responsibility for care of siblings

Animals:
- (p) Animal cruelty, including mutilation and torture
- (q) Perpetrator has developing interest in firearms and activities (e.g., hunting) which provide opportunity for safe aggression

Perpetrator:
- (r) Unknown prenatal problems
- (s) First or second born, or oldest son
- (t) School problems in pattern of underachievement (low grades, discontinuation of school with above-average intelligence)
- (u) Turns mentally inward where he can gain control
- (v) Isolates self from others, weak attachments to other family members and peers
- (w) Not physically unattractive, no distinguishing physical handicaps/defects which set him apart
- (x) Emergence of violent/sadistic fantasies which become functionally autonomous (i.e., independent of initial need to go inward to gain control from overwhelming stress
- (y) Preference for autoerotic sex
- (z) Heterosexual sex on low frequency with developing interest in degradation of females

ADULT TRAITS (AFTER APPROXIMATELY 18 YEARS OF AGE TO LATE MIDDLE AGE)

The adult period is characterized by a continuation of many of the above behavioral patterns and violent fantasies, eventually crystallizing into a set of fixed attitudes.

1. **Devaluation of people.** He remains emotionally distant from others, self-centered in thinking, and perceives others as objects rather than as unique, positive, and important.
2. **World viewed as unjust.** Projection of blame for misdeeds and shortcomings can be expected, as others have primarily caused his problems. He perceives himself as having

been "ripped off" and exploited in his early years and believes that others do not acknowledge his assets in adulthood. He has learned to cover this attitude (and the others) and may, in fact, verbalize self-blame when deemed congruent with vested interests. Social skills can be described as superficial, and he is often viewed by others as friendly and unobtrusive but distant.

3. **Authority and life viewed as inconsistent.** He does not trust authority figures. Male figures are especially distrusted and disliked. The ambivalence, interspersed with hate, continues towards females, especially those in a position to influence or control his behavior.

4. **Autoerotic preference.** Preferred isolated sex experiences include interest in pornography, compulsive masturbation, fetishism, and voyeurism, alone or in combination. Isolated sex is usually interspersed with heterosexual intercourse, and the perpetrator is usually living with a partner.

5. **Obsession and dominance through aggression.** Violence-related fantasies and sexual activities become increasingly frequent, especially during periods of interpersonal stress, but also continue during periods of low conflict with others. At this point, the fantasies are internally generated, controlled, and concealed from others in their expression. The mate usually is the recipient of requests to engage in violent or potentially violent sexual activities (e.g., bondage, slapping), but is rarely the target of the consummated homicide, primarily because the acts are under the control of the perpetrator and the chances of apprehension are high.

6. **Fantasy is reality.** The perpetrator equates his inner world with his outer world, although he is rarely psychotic. A decision is made to act out on the violent sex fantasies, and may be followed by a lag period of several years to several decades.
   Opportunity variables achieve importance at that time.

Family:

(a) May be married or have a girlfriend. The female is the nondominant member of the dyad and may be many years younger than the perpetrator.

(b) Poverty is not a significant factor, but a pattern of underachievement continues.

(c) Family moves frequently.

(d) Mental illness may be in family, but criminality is low grade in terms of arrests, or is undetected. May not be known to police, especially if family moves frequently. Mental health treatment is rarely sought.

(e) Sadistic impulses may be shown toward mate in less than lethal fashion (e.g., requests or acts relating to bondage, anal sex, physical violence to mate during sex). Bizarre sex (hanging mate upside down on hook while she fellates him) and power themes emerge, with perpetrator in dominant role.

Peers/Work:

(f) Adequate social skills.

(g) Often seen as personable, friendly, socially competent, but distant.

(h) Passive-aggressive in interpersonal style.

1) not seen as demanding

2) reluctant to express negative/angry feelings

3) denies and is uncomfortable with anger

4) distortion by omission if possible rather than proactive lying

(i) Has few close male friends; a socially adept loner.

(j) Thrives on omnipotence and power usually achieved by indirect means. He prides himself on his intelligence and ability to manip-late others.

(k) Seen as helpful towards others.

(l) A steady job at one location is unlikely.

1) usually absent or poor military history

2) skilled work preferred

Perpetrator Traits:

(m) Psychometrics show distinct strengths and problems.

1) IQ is above average and may be superior.

2) Projectives (e.g., Rorschach, TAT) suggest much suppressed vio-lence.

3) Objective testing (e.g., MMPI) shows elevated distress scores (e.g., high F) and social alienation patterns (e.g., high O).

4) Signs do not show brain damage or psychosis; some symptoms of depression and inferiority and inadequacy.

5) Above-noted psychopathology usually not picked up during clini-cal interviewing as opposed to psychometric testing.

(n) Pleasant general appearance.

(o) Height and weight within normal limits.

(p) Energies funneled into fantasies of aggression and mastery over others.

(q) In mid-20s or early 30s at time of first series of murders.

PERPETRATOR'S ASSAULT CYCLE

An individual's typical assault cycle for particular crimes is the behavioral equivalent of recurring physical evidence, although not as easily measurable. That is, cognitive, affective, behavioral, and interactional themes emerge which re-main remarkably constant across particular types of crimes. They may differ from each other primarily in terms of environmental circumstances, such as triggering stimuli and opportunity factors.

A standard assault cycle is presented in Figure 11.1. The cycle consists of a baseline period of (a) adult traits and circumstances, (b) an escalation or trigger-ing phase, (c) the actual violence, (d) a recovery phase, and (e) a return to baseline. The assault cycle is strengthened and modified by previous assaults, usually mak-ing future violence more likely, easy, and rewarding for the perpetrator.

The typical assault cycle for serial rape-homicides is unique. The baseline period (1) is represented by the adult traits and events listed in the previous section.

The triggering or escalation stage (2) consists of the following:

a. Stress is experienced due to conflict or disappointment with the perpetrator's mate, work situation, or other factors, (e.g., financial problems).

b. Anniversary triggers reflecting negative events may fuel the accelerating process (e.g., death of a close family member, divorce from previous wife).

c. The perpetrator feels inferior more than usual as a result.

d. Violent fantasies increase; he sees violence as a means to regain self-esteem, mastery, and enjoyment. Yet, self-control is high; there are no sudden explosions of rage. If the perpetrator resists his compulsion during this stage, high tension and other arousal symptoms (e.g., headaches, gastrointestinal tract upset) may occur.

e. He begins to abuse alcohol or, to a much lesser extent, drugs. Arguments increase with his mate, and he begins to engage in escapist activities, such as taking walks or drives.

f. He has a vehicle in good working order.

g. Planning and rehearsal for the violence preoccupies much of his time. Enactment of fantasies is also rehearsed, which includes the fate of the victim. The rape-murder is calculated and preplanned. The intent is to abuse and torture the victim, thereby gratifying himself.

h. Cruising or stalking victims in various areas, usually not too far from his home or work site, takes place. Many victims are considered, but only a few are chosen, since the perpetrator has particular tastes. Vulnerability of the victims is important.

The first victim in a series, for example, may be physically more vulnerable than the others due to size, weight, or other factors.

As the perpetrator recognizes his own strength, this becomes less important as the series progresses. Hence, a considerable amount of time may be devoted to the escalation and search process.

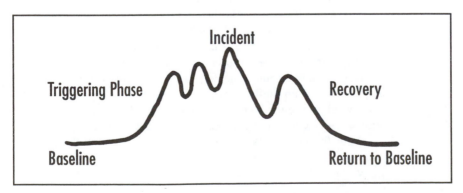

Figure 11.1 Standard assault cycle.

The first victim in a series may be of a different race than later victims in the series. The first victim's race usually matches the perpetrator's race.

i.   He becomes more secretive, concealing, and provides excuses for his whereabouts to others.

j.   A rape-murder kit is assembled, consisting usually of a weapon, and a means of binding or immobilizing the victim.

Gagging and blindfold material and instruments of torture are sometimes part of the rape-murder kit. Precautions are taken against discovery of the assembled kit.

k.   Clothing that would not intimidate and may even win the confidence of the victim (e.g., work uniform, business suit, casual clothes) is chosen. The perpetrator may impersonate vocations of others in his dressing.

l.   Just prior to the violence, a victim who meets the perpetrator's requirements and is within his staked out or patrolled area is finally selected.

m. He almost always engages in verbal interaction. His demeanor is not suspicious.

n.   There is an attempt to establish a pseudo-relationship, which may include offering the victim a ride or otherwise assisting her.

o.   After the pseudo-relationship is established and the opportunity to aggress with concealment is available, the rape-murder kit weapon is brandished.

p.   The weapon is usually not used initially, if at all, and the victim is often promised no harm if she cooperates.

q.   The victim is immobilized through binding, fear, or some other means. Control is now firmly in the hands of the perpetrator.

The actual violence portion of the assault cycle (stage 3 of the cycle) is characterized by high self-control, mounting excitement, sadism, and the victim's death. The victim is bound or immobilized at this point. The eroticized aggression can take place now without fear of discovery. The death of the victim is prolonged as the perpetrator feeds off the pain cues of the victim taking place often over a period of hours or even days if the opportunity allows.

1.   This is a sadistic rape, as opposed to a power or anger rape. Sadistic rapes constitute less than 5% of the three main types of rapists (i.e., see Groth, 1979).

2.   Initially, the mood of the perpetrator is controlled.

Mounting excitement is seen, especially when the victim resists in any manner. The perpetrator may continue to degrade the victim until she resists, as this provides pain cues which are rewarding to the perpetrator. He may be without an erection until the victim's resistance begins.

Look for suggestions of biting, burning, whipping, slapping, or strangulation. Slow strangulation is possible, with some perpetrators reviving the victim to prolong the ordeal.

3. Sexual areas (breasts, buttocks, genitalia, anus) are specific foci of abuse. He may use a stick or other implement to penetrate the victim's orifices, possibly masturbating at the same time. The perpetrator may vaginally penetrate the victim with his penis while strangling or striking the victim.

4. Ritualistic or bizarre acts are frequent. The perpetrator may clip the hair of the victim, wash her body, force her to dress in some way, or demand any variety of "kinky" sex.

5. Finally, the perpetrator works himself into a frenzy of rage and lust, fueled by the pain cues of the victim. The actual killing of the victim is the ultimate orgasm, and the perpetrator attempts to conjoin the two. Repeated rape-murders perfect the unison of these two behaviors.

The next stage of the assault cycle for the serial murderer is the recovery phase (stage 4). The perpetrator now has a dead body on his hands. He is late for work, home, or some other activity, and must cover his tracks. Precautions are taken against discovery, such as insuring that the weapon from the rape-murder is not left at the crime scene. The site of the rape-murder is often tidied up—blood and fingerprints from the victim being a first priority for removal. The victim may be totally or partially redressed.

Remembrances of the victim are collected and set aside for later enjoyment or as a gift to "loved" females (e.g., his mother, girlfriend). The perpetrator almost always disposes of the body at a location other than the crime scene, but again in his own "turf"—that is, in the general proximity of home/work sites. The best "dumping" sites are those that are isolated (unpopulated areas), corrosive (e.g., fresh, but especially salt water; shallow graves allowing for body decomposition), or consuming (e.g., fire, acid pits), the latter infrequently chosen due to availability factors. The symbolic significance of certain dumping sites (e.g., water points), signifying possible guilt, redemption, or some other despairing motive, are usually weak and unhelpful hypotheses.

The return to the baseline portion of the assault cycle (stage 5) is characterized by a lack of remorse for the rape-murder, prodigious efforts at concealment, and resurgence of fantasy, now fueled by the memorabilia of the victim coupled with masturbation. These are hidden in his special place but can be easily retrieved. Newspaper accounts of the crime are read avidly and often clipped out for retention. Almost always, he is aware that he will kill again. The acted upon rape-murder fantasy now providing a sense of purpose and fulfillment. Within a series of rape-murders, fantasies of his previous homicides contribute to subsequent killings. He thinks of means to perfect the phases of the assault cycle. Other events during this stage include:

1. Repetitive sadistic attacks toward female strangers may be interspersed with consenting encounters.

2. He may contact the police to assist in their search of the perpetrator or victims. All this is rehearsed mentally and provides more excitement to the perpetrator as well as helping him learn the status of the investigation or alter its outcome. He also believes that if he does not contact the

police, he may be selected as the logical final suspect, due to many factors.

3. If questioned by the police, he will more likely than not deny the crimes. He may have elaborate excuses for each bit of evidence. Remember that he is manipulative of others and is accomplished at deception. He also considers himself superior to the interrogator(s).

   a. He may show distress or depression when questioned about the instant offenses within a context of ostensible cooperation. Look for body leakage, especially upper arm and hand movements associated with lying, as compared to known data (e.g., see Ekman, 1985, for target illustrators, emblems, manipulators, and other clues to deceit). These signs can be used to gather hypotheses about unknown data, for example, where to search for his rape-murder kit. The forced-choice methodology can be used to demonstrate statistically his involvement in the killing.

   b. He may have an erection during the portion of the interview which triggers recollections of the rape-murders. Consider interviewing where the full body of the perpetrator can be observed.

   c. These perpetrators often relate better to male interviewers, than female interviewers, toward whom they feel hatred.

   d. There is a tendency to ramble on when allowed. Often, there is a subtle quality of omnipotence during the interview, as if he were comfortable in knowing that no one knew of the rape-murders except himself and that he had the ability to explain away the evidence.

   e. If psychiatrically hospitalized during the general time of the interview, he will not exhibit signs of a mental disorder. Suggestions of low psychological disorganization will emerge upon interviewing and observation.

4. The perpetrator often leaves town or changes his job after a series of rape-murders.

In returning to baseline, the perpetrator assumes all prior traits (see Adult Trait section) with an enhanced chance of committing another series. Intervals of many years between series are well known, contrasted to the relatively close temporal period of the homicides within a series. Look within a series to determine whether each assault cycle for each victim was well formulated—that is, with no evidence of learning new methods of procuring, attacking, and disposing of a victim. If not, there is a possibility that a previous series was committed, perhaps in another jurisdiction.

Table 11.3
Sexual Homicides: Perpetrators and Crime Scene Characteristics

Organized	Disorganized
Average or higher intelligence	Average or lower intelligence
Socially skilled	Socially immature
Adequate work history	Poor work history
Sexually competent	Sexually incompetent
First born or eldest son	Minimal birth order status
Father's work stable	Father's work unstable
Inconsistent discipline in childhood	Harsh discipline in childhood
Lives with intimate other	Lives alone
Lives/works away from crime scene	Lives/works near crime scene
Keen interest in news media	Minimal interest in news media
Changes lifestyle to avoid detection	Minimal change in lifestyle
Heavy use of alcohol	Minimal use of alcohol
Significant stress triggers violence	Minimal situational stress
Weapon brought and taken from scene	Weapon found and left at scene
Victim a targeted stranger	Victim or location of crime known
Controlled conversation	Minimal conversation
Controlled mood during crime	Anxious mood during attack and kills quickly
Use of ruse or con to lure victim into vulnerable position	More likely direct attack and kills quickly
Scene reflects planning and overall control	Scene reflects impulsivity and disarray
Ritualistic and planned quality	Symbolic and spontaneous quality
Victim patterning, shares common traits with others	Victim attached in her routine activities
Specific areas of body damaged and cause death	Specific areas of body targeted for mutilation after death
Sexual torture before death	Sexual mutilation after death
Sexual acts before death	Sexual acts after death
Restraints likely with demands for submission	Restraints not likely
Crime control reflective of obsessive-compulsive lifestyle	Crime disorganization reflective of lifestyle
Controlled perseveration likely (e.g., continuous choking of victim to prolong sexual assault)	Uncontrolled perseverative responses likely (e.g., continuous slashing/stabbing, bite marks)
Death scene and crime scene are separate	Death scene and crime scene are same
Less likely destruction of face	Destruction of face more likely
Hides body	No attempt to conceal body
Alters crime scene, conceals/destroys evidence	More likely leaves crime scene intact

(Continued on next page)

RAPE-MURDER BASE RATES

The preceding sections should make it clear that rape-murderers have certain characteristics, and that these can be differentiated on the basis of primary factors. The organized versus disorganized crime scene differentiation is the primary split. Culling together all sources, but especially from Ressler, Burgess and Douglass (1988), the differences between organized and disorganized perpetrators and crime scene characteristics are shown in Table 11.3.

In sum, the crime profiling process—essentially a base rate comparison approach—describes a sequence of clinical-forensic activities used to uncover concealment of offenses. The state of the art is rudimentary, yet cues have been provided leading to the identification of perpetrators. The process of crime profiling illustrates the wealth of information contained in statistical base rates and the value of such information in forming "empirical stereotypes" of offenders against which to compare individual suspects. Such empirical stereotypes could also prove useful in describing typical cases of mental disorders and in evaluating the self-presentations of individual clients.

Table 11.3
Sexual Homicides: Perpetrators and Crime Scene Characteristics
(continued from previous page)

Organized	Disorganized
Fingerprints/footprints not likely	Fingerprints/footprints likely
Less likely insertion of items into victim's orifices	Inserts items into victim's orifices
Body dumped at another site	Body left at scene
Relies on own or victim's vehicle	Relies on public transportation
Does not take souvenir, article, or clothing	Takes souvenirs, article, or clothing
Blood smearing or other unusual acts less likely	Blood smearing, cannibalism, anthropophagy more likely
Less likely to return victim's items to grave site	May return souvenir to grave site

Adapted from Ressler, Burgess and Douglass (1988) and other sources.

REFERENCES

Brussel, J. A. (1968). *Casebook of a crime psychiatrist.* New York: Dell.

Douglas, J., Burgess, A., Burgess, A., & Ressler, R. (1992). *Crime classification manual.* New York: Lexington Books.

Edinger, J. (1979). Cross-validation of the Megargee MMPI typology for prisoners. *Journal of Consulting and Clinical Psychology, 47*(2), 234-242.

Ekman, P. (1985). *Telling lies.* New York: W. W. Norton & Co.

Groth, A. (1979). *Men who rape: The psychology of the offender.* New York: Plenum Press.

Hazelwood, R. R., & Douglas, J. E. (1980, April). The lust murderer. *FBI Law Enforcement Bulletin*. 61-68.

Hazelwood, R., & Warren, J. (1989). The serial rapist: His characteristics and victims, Part I: Conclusion. *FBI Law Enforcement Bulletin, 1*, 10-25.

Leyton, E. (1983). A social profile of sexual mass murderers. In T. Fleming & L. A. Visano (Eds.), *Deviant designations: Crime, law, and deviance in Canada*. Toronto: Butterworths.

Megargee, E., & Bohn, M. (1979). *Classifying criminal offenders: A new system based on the MMPI*. California: Sage Publications.

Miron, M., & Goldstein, A. (1979). *Hostage*. New York: Pergamon Press.

Miron, M., & Pasquale, A. (1978). Psycholinguistic analysis of coercion. *Journal of Psycholinguistic Research, 7*, 95-120.

Pinizzotto, A., & Finkel, N. (1990). Criminal personality profiling. *Law and Human Behavior, 14*(3), 215-233.

Ressler, R. (1990). *Crime profiling*. Workshop presented by FBI at Hickam USAF Base, Honolulu, HI.

Ressler, R., Burgess, A., & Douglass, J. (1988). *Sexual homicide: Patterns and motives*. Lexington, MA: Lexington Books.

Rider, A. (1980). The firesetter: A psychological profile. *FBI Law Enforcement Bulletin*, 1-23.

12

FORENSIC HYPNOSIS

Authorities generally agree that there are no reliable physiological determinants that unequivocally differentiate between the hypnotic and normal waking states (Barber, 1965c; Diamond, 1980; Gorten, 1949; Hilgard, 1965a). It was therefore necessary for researchers in the field of hypnosis to define the state of hypnosis in terms of particular displayed behaviors, given a specified set of conditions (i.e., procedures used, induction techniques employed, etc.). For example, researchers (Hilgard, 1965a; Weitzenhoffer, 1963) have contended that some evidence for the hypnotic state exists when individual suggestibility is increased. It is in this light that certain types of behavior (e.g., catalepsy), ideosensory activities (e.g., hallucinations), ideomotor activities (e.g., arm levitation), automatic writing, dissociation, age-regression, anesthesia, and posthypnotic suggestion have been considered to be hallmarks of the hypnotic trance (Erickson, 1944; Kroger, 1963; Weitzenhoffer, 1963). Usually included in this category of hypnotic markers is hypnotically induced amnesia (Clemes, 1964; Hammer, 1954; Scott, 1930; Weitzenhoffer, 1963; Williamsen, Johnson, & Ericksen, 1965). Despite the accumulated evidence supporting the contention that amnesia is a reliable index of hypnosis, however, laboratory research (Barber & Calverly, 1966) casts doubt on the typicality of memory distortions attributed to hypnosis. In essence, it is questioned whether the hypnotic state is either necessary or sufficient to elicit mnestic distortions. Moreover, most of the early studies have been attacked on methodological grounds, contending that when proper controls are absent (e.g., including a waking condition in the design and isolating the role of motivating instructions to the subjects), no valid inferences concerning hypnotic phenomena can be made (Barber, 1965a, 1965b; Parker & Barber, 1964).

As prototypic investigations, Hall (1969) and Thorne and Hall (1969) found that amnesia was elicited as easily in the waking state as under hypnosis. In their studies, the Harvard Group Scale of Hypnotic Susceptibility (HGSHS) was administered to 667 undergraduate students. Out of this original group, 120 subjects of high and low hypnotic susceptibility were asked to participate in the experimental procedures. Each subject was randomly assigned to one of six treatments, which varied in terms of the type of amnesia suggestion given (authoritarian or permissive), and the kind of motivational procedure employed (hypnotic and waking motivation, and waking nonmotivation). Each procedure started with instructions to learn a list of paired associates well. Later and in conjunction with one of three motivational procedures, the subjects were given a suggestion to forget what they had previously been instructed to learn. A partially related Word Association Test (WAT) was presented to test the relative effectiveness of the memory suggestion and analyzed in terms of word response (WR) and reaction time (RT) scores. Statistical analysis of the data suggested: (1) Association responses were differentially affected by susceptibility level. High susceptibility subjects tended to forget more in terms of WR scores than low susceptibility subjects; (2) Task motivation to forget the paired words was more effective in terms of WR scores than instructions to forget without task motivation. Within the task motivated procedures, there was no difference in amnesia performance between the hypnotic and waking groups; (3) Type of suggestion did not differentially affect association responses. All except the second finding conformed to popular hypnotic theories. In general, it would not be predicted that hypnotic-like behavior can be produced as readily in the waking compared to the "trance" state.

Since hypnosis is inferred from its manifestations and since these manifestations may also be produced in nontrance states, the question of deception by subjects during hypnotic recall is important to consider. Can subjects successfully feign a hypnotic trance and its manifestations (e.g., amnesia)? Investigators have found differences between faking and genuine subjects in tasks tapping memory skills (Orne, Sheehan, & Evans, 1968; Spanos, Radtke, Bertrand, Addie, & Drummond, 1982; Worthington, 1979). The Orne et al. (1968) study, for example, found that subjects given posthypnotic instructions ran their hands through their hair when they were cued with the word "experiment." Fake subjects responded only to the experimenter; genuine subjects responded to a secretary outside the research room, thus showing response generalization to hypnotic stimuli.

Faking amnesia during recall may create unusual features, which the evaluator can note. Spanos et al. (1982) found that recall is not disorganized in genuine hypnosis. The large majority of subjects who faked loss of the target words organized their recall in a manner detectable by the experimenter.

In sum, hypnosis appears to create mnestic changes (e.g., amnesia, enhanced recall), but so do other methods that merely require focusing and concentration. All behaviors elicited in hypnosis, including amnesia and enhanced recall, can be replicated in the waking state. Some means of detecting faked hypnosis have been proffered, which occasionally have been replicated in other studies. Some suggested signs of faked hypnosis are presented in Table 12.1.

EVIDENTIARY PROBLEMS

It should come as no surprise that the pretrial use of hypnosis has substantial problems. Diamond (1980) presents critical questions pertaining to the hypnotist, the subject, and hypnosis itself. Is the hypnotist trained, experienced, and certified in practicing hypnosis? Can he or she detect faked hypnosis, avoid planting suggestions in the subject's mind, and distinguish fact from fiction after the trance state? Is it possible to have confidence in presented opinions beyond a reasonable degree of scientific certainty?

Table 12.1
Traditional Signs of Simulation in Hypnosis

More likely faking if:	Example
1. Susceptibility scale scores change upon repeated testing.	Genuine subjects' Harvard or Stanford scale scores remain stable over time.
2. Increased arousal creates variable performance.	Genuine subjects show steady improvement in performance from stupor to arousal.
3. Distress tolerance decreased.	Prolonged arm levitation without tiring is unusual.
4. Atypical ocular movements.	Genuine subject moves eyes and head; faker tracks moving objects with fixed head.
5. Increased arousal state (unless suggested by hypnotist).	Elevated pulse and respiration rate.
6. Suggested acts are discontinued when hypnotist leaves.	Toe-tapping to music in fakers ceases after experimenter creates sham interruption.
7. Negative hallucinations create atypical behavior in forced choice situations.	Stumbles or stops in front of "invisible" chair; genuine subjects will walk around it.
8. Logical thinking guides responses to hypnotist.	Fakers will not affirm feeling in hand suggested to be numb despite later contrary instructions.

Questions also arise concerning the subject. Can a hypnotizable person ever be free of heightened suggestibility and, if not, can even waking memories be free from their projections and fantasies? Does the richness of hypnotic recall indicate truthfulness, or must memories be verified by corroborating data? After the hypnotic trance, do subjects continue to distort information and do they believe in their own hypnotically produced fabrications?

Lastly, Diamond (1980) suggests we ask whether or not hypnosis can ever be truly recorded or observed, because it is largely an internal event. In the final analysis, with all of its flaws, is hypnosis any better than more acceptable techniques such as interviewing and interrogation?

CASE LAW

The consensus of modern legal opinion is that hypnotically induced testimony is unreliable and, therefore, inadmissible (Spiegel & Spiegel, 1987). The basic problem is that hypnosis is both a procedure and a state which relies on suggestion. The suggestion may create pseudomemories, which may confuse the trier-of-fact in the determination of a case. In questioning experts, courts are aware that there is no extant method to determine which is faked versus genuine hypnosis (*State v. Mack*, 1980).

A number of states have set out rules that differentiate between memories produced (a) prior to hypnosis, (b) within the hypnotic trance administered during pretrial investigation, and (c) during hypnosis administered as therapy to victims, witnesses, or a defendant. These rules are important to consider because they may affect the use of other focusing, suggestive, or relaxation techniques in forensic settings and situations.

In spite of trends, some states have ruled that hypnotically produced memory is admissible under certain conditions (*Harding v. State of Maryland*, 1968; *Kline v. Ford Motor Co, 1975*; *State of New Jersey v. Hurd*, 1981; *United States v. Adams*, 1978; *United States v. Miller*, 1969). Generally, these courts have held that cross-examination enables a jury to evaluate hypnosis in terms of its affect on the credibility of the witness (see Table 12.2).

In *State of New Jersey v. Hurd* (1981), a variant rule was adopted making hypnosis admissible provided that very stringent criteria were met. In doing so, the court was appalled that, among other events, the witness in question was hypnotized in the presence of a third party (a police officer) who even asked questions during the trance state. The court noted that hypnosis renders subjects vulnerable to suggestion, creates loss of critical judgement, and has a tendency to confound genuine with hypnotic memories.

State of New Jersey v. Hurd (1981) lays out the requirements for hypnotically-induced evidence to be considered admissible. At a minimum, Orne (1979) standards should be met: (1) The hypnotist should be a psychiatrist or psychologist trained in hypnosis; (2) the hypnotist should be independent of the defense or prosecution; (3) all transactions between hypnotist and subject, as well as between referring party and hypnotist, must be recorded; (4) a prehypnotic interview covering the instant offense or tort event must take place; and (5) only the hypnotist should be present prior to, during, and after the hypnosis.

Other requirements set forth in *State of New Jersey v. Hurd* (1981) include determining whether hypnosis is appropriate, based on expert testimony, and the "amenability of the subject to hypnosis." Finally, the burden of establishing admissibility by clear and convincing evidence should be on the party who tenders the hypnotically influenced testimony.

Some courts have permitted witnesses to testify as to facts occurring prior to the induction of hypnosis (*People v. Hughes*, 1983; *Commonwealth v. Kater*, 1983; *State of Arizona v. Collins*, 1982). In *Hughes*, for example, the New York Court of Appeals held that, although the victim's posthypnotic recollections were inadmissible at a rape trial, she would not necessarily be precluded from testifying about events recalled before the induction of hypnosis. However, the prosecution was admonished for failure to give the defendant pretrial notice of its intention to

---

Table 12.2
Cases on Forensic Hypnosis

Harding v. State (1968)	Testimony based on hypnosis admissible, with weight for trier of facts (since overruled).
United States v. Miller (1969)	Defendant entitled to new trial due to nondisclosure to defense of hypnosis; jury must be aware of hypnosis.
United States v. Adams (1978)	Hypnosis process should be considered in terms of weight, as opposed to admissibility.
State of New Jersey v. Hurd (1981)	Testimony based on hypnosis permissible if stringent criteria set by court are met.
State of Arizona v. Mena (1981)	Hypnosis so unreliable that hypnotically induced testimony should be excluded until Frye test requirements met.
People v. Shirley (1982)	Hypnosis renders witnesses incompetent to testify on any matters covered during hypnosis.
State of Arizona v. Collins (1982)	Witnesses can testify as to facts recalled from hypnosis.
State of Wisconsin v. Armstrong (1983)	Hypnosis did not render inadmissible subsequent identification of defendant or in-court testimony of events covered during trance state.
Commonwealth of Mass. v. Kater (1983)	Hypnosis fails the Frye test. The proposed standards are not workable.
People v. Hughes (1983)	Witnesses can testify as to facts recalled prior to hypnosis.

---

call a witness who had previously been hypnotized in connection with the case. The state was seen as having the burden of proving that the hypnotized witnesses would be reliable.

Viewing hypnosis as a hopeless contaminant of memory, other courts have invoked a bright line rule that witnesses are incompetent to testify on any matters covered in hypnosis (*Polk v. State of Maryland*, 1981; *State of Arizona v. Mena*, 1981; *People v. Shirley*, 1982). The Shirley court disallowed testimony even when the recall was recorded on other sources. This view holds that hypnosis simply does not meet the basic requirement set forth in *Frye v. United States* (1923), because hypnosis is not generally accepted as reliable in the scientific community.

People v. Shirley (1982) would abolish hypnosis in the courtroom even if strict procedural safeguards are built into the evaluation of hypnosis. The court noted that the stringent *State of New Jersey v. Hurd* (1981) requirements are geared toward preventing the hypnotist from exploiting subject hypersuggestibility in hypnosis and do not prevent (a) hypnotically related loss of critical judgement, (b) false confidence in memory, and (c) confusion of real and confabulated memories.

In an ironic twist, *People v. Shirley* (1982) would allow for the investigative use of hypnosis (e.g., recalling a license plate number), but not for the fruits of that inquiry if the hypnotic trance were successful. Likewise, treatment of posttrauma reactions by hypnosis would eliminate victims from testifying in court on instant matters. Justice Klaus, in a concurring and dissenting opinion, notes that the defendant would be prevented from testifying if hypnotized for forensic evaluation or treatment.

Klaus stated that "it is a mistake to adopt a sweeping 'per se' rule that the majority proposes—excluding virtually all testimony of a witness who had undergone pretrial hypnosis" without further investigation into the merits and demerits of the method. Finally, he makes the cogent argument that other forms of memory evaluation (e.g., eyewitness testimony) in general, have similar problems in reliability and validity.

In sum, hypnosis is not currently viewed favorably by the courts. Perhaps another quarter century or so of research and clinical application will yield a different legal attitude. In the meantime, the forensic evaluator is encouraged to utilize other memory enhancing methods—general relaxation, motivation to do well, instruction in focusing—which may equal hypnosis in recalling past experiences but do not carry its stigma of creating the distortion it is attempting to uncover.

LEGAL REFERENCES

Commonwealth v. Kater, 388 Mass. 519, 447 N.E.2d 1190 (1983).
Frye v. United States, 293 F.1013 (D.C.Cir. 1923).
Harding v. State of Maryland, 5 Md.App. 230, 246 A.2d 302 (1968).
Kline v. Ford Motor Co., 523 F.2d 1067 (9th Cir. 1975).
People v. Hughes, 59 N.Y.2d 523, 453 N.E.2d 484, 466 N.Y.S.2d 255 (Ct. App. 1983).
People v. Shirley, 31 Cal.3d 18, 181 Cal.Rptr. 243, 641 P.2d 775 (1982).
Polk v. State of Maryland, 48 Md.App. 382 427 A.2d 1041 (Md. 1981).
State of Wisconsin v. Armstrong, 110 Wis.2d 555, 329 N.W.2d 386 (1983).
State of Arizona v. Collins, 132 Ariz. 180, 644 P.2d 1266 (1982).
State of New Jersey v. Hurd, 432 A.2d 86 (N.J. 1981).
State of Arizona v. Mena, 128 Ariz. 226, 624 P.2d 1274 (1981).
United States v. Adams, 581 F.2d 193 (9th Cir. 1978).
United States v. Miller, 411 F.2d 825 (2nd Cir. 1969).

References

Barber, T. X. (1965a). The effects of "hypnosis" on learning and recall. *Journal of Clinical Psychology, 21,* 19-25.

Barber, T. X. (1965b). Experimental analysis of "hypnotic" behavior: A review of recent empirical findings. *Journal of Abnormal Psychology, 70,* 132-154.

Barber, T. X. (1965c). Physiological effects of "hypnotic suggestions": A critical review of recent research (1960-1964). *Psychological Bulletin, 63,* 201-222.

Barber, T. X., & Calverly, D. S. (1966). Toward a theory of "hypnotic" behavior: Experimental analysis of suggested amnesia. *Journal of Abnormal Psychology, 71,* 95-107.

Clemes, S. R. (1964). Repression and hypnotic amnesia. *Journal of Abnormal and Social Psychology, 69,* 62-69.

Diamond, B. (1980). Inherent problems in the use of pre-trial hypnosis on a prospective witness. *California Law Review, 68,* 313.

Erickson, M. R. (1944). An experimental investigation of the hypnotic subject's apparent ability to become unaware of stimuli. *Journal of General Psychology, 31,* 191-212.

Gorten, B. E. (1949). The physiology of hypnosis. *Psychiatric Quarterly, 16,* 317-343; 547-585.

Hall, H. V. (1969). *Hypnosis and memory: The comparable effects of various suggestions, procedures, and susceptibility variables.* Unpublished master's thesis, Brigham Young University, Provo, UT.

Hammer, E. F. (1954). Post-hypnotic suggestion and test performance. *Journal of Clinical and Experimental Hypnosis, 2,* 178-185.

Hilgard, E. R. (1965a). Hypnosis. In P. R. Farnsworth (Ed.), *Annual review of psychology.* Palo Alto, CA: Annual Review.

Hilgard, E. R. (1965b). *Hypnotic susceptibility.* New York: Harcourt, Brace, and World, Inc.

Kroger, W. S. (1963). *Clinical and experimental hypnosis in medicine, dentistry and psychology.* Philadelphia: J. B. Lippincott Co.

Orne, M. T. (1979). The uses and misuses of hypnosis in court. *International Journal of Clinical and Experimental Hypnosis, 27,* 311-341.

Orne, M. T., Sheehan, P. W., & Evans, F. J. (1968). Occurrence of posthypnotic behavior outside the experimental setting. *Journal of Personality and Social Psychology, 9,* 189-196.

Parker, P. D., & Barber, T. X. (1964). Hypnosis, task motivating instructions, and learning performance. *Journal of Abnormal and Social Psychology, 69,* 499-504.

Scott, H. D. (1930). Hypnosis and the conditioned reflex. *Journal of General Psychology, 4,* 113-130.

Spanos, N. P., Radtke, H. L., Bertrand, L. D., Addie, D. L., & Drummond, J. (1982). Disorganized recall, hypnotic amnesia, and subjects' faking: More discomfirmatory evidence. *Psychological Reports, 50,* 383-389.

Spiegel, D., & Spiegel, H. (1987). Forensic uses of hypnosis. In I. Weiner & A. Hess (Eds.), *Handbook of forensic psychology* (pp. 490-507). New York: J. Wiley & Sons.

Thorne, D. E., & Hall, H. V. (1969, November). *Hypnosis and memory: The comparable effects of various suggestions, procedures and susceptibility variables.* Paper presented at a meeting of the International Conference on Hypnosis, Palo Alto, CA.

Weitzenhoffer, A. M. (1963). The nature of hypnosis: Part I. *American Journal of Clinical Hypnosis, 5,* 295-321.

Williamsen, J. A., Johnson, J. G., & Eriksen, C. W. (1965). Some characteristics of posthypnotic amnesia. *Journal of Abnormal Psychology, 70,* 123-131.

Worthington, T. S. (1979). The use in court of hypnotically enhanced testimony. *International Journal of Clinical and Experimental Hypnosis, 27,* 402-416.

13

COMPETENCY TO PROCEED AND DECEPTION

The legal requirement of competency to stand trial is an extension of the general rule that no one should be tried for a crime in his or her absence. If a defendant must be physically present to defend against criminal charges, that defendant must also be "mentally present." Disorders which interfere with the psychological participation of a defendant at trial render that defendant incompetent to stand trial and require that the proceedings be postponed until effective participation can be assured.

Reviews of the forensic literature or clinical applications which discuss competency to proceed may be found in Blau (1984); Curran, McGarry, and Shah (1986); Ewing (1985); Gutheil and Appelbaum (1982); Melton, Petrila, Poythress, and Slobogin (1987); Shapiro (1984); Weiner and Hess (1987); and Ziskin and Faust (1988). Works devoted exclusively to competency to stand trial include those of Grisso (1986, 1988); McGarry (1973); and Roesch and Golding (1980).

Most jurisdictions use a variation of the rule to define competency to stand trial outlined by the U. S. Supreme Court in *Dusky v. United States* (1960). *Dusky* requires that a defendant have the ability to (a) understand rationally and factually the legal proceedings and (b) cooperate with one's attorney in one's defense. A disorder which interferes with either of these capacities is sufficient to render the defendant incompetent to stand trial. However, incompetency to stand trial is not to be equated with the mere presence of mental illness (*Feguer v. U. S,* 1962; *U. S. v. Adams,* 1969), of amnesia (*U. S. v. Wilson,* 1966), or of a need for treatment. The claimed disorder must be of the kind and severity which impairs the functional capacities outlined in *Dusky.*

Usually the question of competency to stand trial is raised by the defense attorney, who has the most frequent contact with the defendant and who has the professional and legal obligation to raise the question in appropriate cases. However, case law suggests that the question *must* be raised, even by the prosecution or the court itself, whenever a "bona fide doubt" exists regarding the defendant's capacity to mount a defense (*see Drope v. Missouri*, 1975; *Pate v. Robinson* [1966]). The question of a defendant's competency to proceed may be raised at any time from the defendant's first appearance in court to the time of sentencing.

In actual practice, the majority of incompetent defendants are easily identified by participants in the criminal process. Actively psychotic, demented, and severely mentally retarded persons are usually recognized by arresting officers, jail personnel, or defense attorneys and transferred to treatment facilities prior to any court appearances. However, defendants charged with particularly notorious crimes and defendants who decompensate while awaiting trial often require professional evaluation before criminal proceedings are postponed. In addition, defense attorneys sometimes raise questions of competency to stand trial for their apparently competent clients to secure a court-ordered professional evaluation of their clients which would otherwise be unavailable. These evaluations may produce evidence relevant to an insanity plea, to the question of diminished capacity, or to mitigating factors which may be considered at the time of sentencing.

The majority of court-ordered referrals for evaluation of competency to stand trial are clearly and obviously competent. The defendant usually readily admits that the evaluation was requested by the attorney, typically cooperates with all assessment tasks, and presents no claims of mental disorder. Everyone understands that the evaluation is really a "fishing expedition" for evidence on questions other than competency to stand trial.

The question of competency to stand trial involves three separate questions: 1) does the defendant have a genuine mental disorder sufficiently severe to justify a finding of incompetency (diagnosis); 2) is the defendant unable (a) to understand rationally and factually the legal proceedings or (b) to assist counsel in defense (incapacity); and 3) is this incapacity caused by the mental disorder (causation). The answers to these three questions lead to several possible scenarios (Drob, Berger, & Weinstein, 1987): 1) a genuine mental disorder causes a defendant to be incapacitated and 2) a genuine mental disorder does not cause a defendant to be incapacitated. Defendants may have a genuine condition which causes an insufficient incapacity to stand trial (e.g., circumscribed delusions about the "facts" of the alleged crime, but no impairment in trial capacity). Defendants may have a genuine mental disorder whose impaired capacity to stand trial is due to fabrication or exaggeration (e.g., malingering in the context of a genuine disorder). Lastly, defendants may have a genuine mental disorder and are incapable of standing trial, but the mental disorder is not severe enough to justify a finding of incompetency (e.g., a depressed defendant whose guilt over the alleged crime leads to disinterest or lack of cooperation in putting on a defense).

TARGETS OF DECEPTION

The frequency of faking incompetency to stand trial is unknown. Cornell and Hawk (1989) reported that 8% of 314 consecutive admissions to the Michigan Center for Forensic Psychiatry for pretrial evaluation were diagnosed by staff as malingering. These results suggest that malingering incompetency among criminal defendants may occur considerably less often than suggested by popular stereotypes—a suggestion also supported by the authors' experiences in the criminal justice system.

Virtually any target discussed in this book may be faked in an attempt to obtain a better judicial outcome. Two types of faking may be selected (Grisso, 1988): (a) those behaviors directed towards mental conditions and (b) those aimed at specific competency abilities. The targeting of mental conditions is illustrated as follows:

> Defendant Smith, a 28-year-old white male charged with several counts of bank robbery, presented with a florid psychosis upon evaluation. There was no history of mental history but a confirmed history of prior arrests, including several for bank robbery. Validity scales on the MMPI and behavioral observations indicated a pronounced tendency to fake bad. During the evaluation, he appeared genuinely ignorant of the competency criteria in spite of his demonstrated understanding of legal proceedings and defense strategies. The accused stated his belief that a psychotic condition would render him incompetent to proceed.

Contrast this with the following case:

> Defendant Arder, a 45-year-old woman charged with the fatal shooting of her husband during a quarrel, exhibited a logical and coherent stream of thought during evaluation. She went over the instant offense in minute detail. No mental conditions were proffered except for mild stress due to the legal proceedings. Her attorney suggested to the court that her recollections of the instant offense were vague and consisted only of her feelings at the time. Ms. Arder was found competent to proceed with the trial. Eventually, she successfully plea bargained for manslaughter.

Thus, targets of distortion can consist of deficits representing a mental condition or the specific ingredients of trial competency. Both approaches have met with success in obtaining long-range goals. With competency issues, the courts traditionally bend over backwards to give the accused "a break." This usually results in a finding of incompetency with a recommendation for continued observation and treatment.

RESPONSE STYLES

HONESTY

Honest responding is the norm among defendants referred for evaluation of their competency to stand trial. The vast majority of defendants, even those with extensive criminal backgrounds, are cooperative with the evaluator and try neither to exaggerate nor minimize psychopathology. Many of these honest responders, especially those new to the criminal system, show signs of anxiety and depression. However, these symptoms are rarely so incapacitating that the defendant is found incompetent to stand trial. In addition, many criminal defendants—even those with prior experience in the courts—are ignorant of legal procedures and options (Grisso, 1988). However, this ignorance is not grounds for a finding of incompetency to stand trial, unless it is due to an *incapacity* to understand the proceedings when properly explained by the defense attorney.

FAKING GOOD

This style is seen when the defendant desires to go forward with the proceedings, but believes a mental deficit or condition may thwart that goal. It is relatively rare and occurs most frequently among paranoid defendants who are suspicious of the criminal proceedings. These rare instances of blatant faking good must be distinguished from the more common tendency of defendants to minimize or deny wrongdoing. Minimization of psychopathology is relevant to the question of competency to stand trial only when it interferes with the defendant's capacity to understand rationally and factually the criminal proceedings or cooperate with defense counsel.

INVALIDATING

This response style occurs when an accused tries to invalidate either the entire competency evaluation or a particular evaluation procedure. The most common example of invalidation is uncooperativeness. When a defendant refuses to be interviewed or tested, the examiner is left wondering whether the refusal signifies an intent to distort the evaluation or an underlying incapacity. Is the lack of cooperation due to fear of being detected as faking bad or is it a symptom of genuine paranoia and delusional thinking? One defendant, accused of murdering a female acquaintance and her mother with a machete, refused to be interviewed about the alleged offense. Although he later agreed to complete a self-report measure of psychopathology, he consistently failed to answer the questions. His responses to interview questions which did not involve the alleged crime were all coherent and generally rational. Only review of an interrogation by police shortly after his arrest and a social history given by his parents revealed a long history of paranoid schizophrenia and a delusional justification for the killings. When the evaluator informed the defendant that the court would be informed of his incompetency to stand trial, the defendant unleashed a torrent of threats against the examiner. In such cases the evaluator can only rely on historical records, personal observations, and the observations of others to discern the meaning of the uncooperativeness.

Mixed Styles

Mixed styles involve elements of faking good, faking bad, honest respond-ing, and/or invalidation in the same competency evaluation. Certain test patterns may suggest a tendency to exaggerate, while interviews suggest honest respond-ing. Historical records may reveal past problems, which are denied or minimized by the defendant during interviews. A defendant may initially be cooperative with the examiner, only to refuse further participation later in the evaluation. In general, the interpretation of these mixed signals is made easier if the examiner distinguishes between the defendant's *capacity* and the defendant's *willingness*. In spite of exaggeration, minimization, or uncooperativeness, is the defendant capable of understanding the legal proceedings and capable of cooperating with defense counsel?

Fluctuating Styles

Fluctuating response styles are most frequently seen when the defendant's goals change. The accused may, for example, fake bad to gain a trial delay, but then switch to honesty, or even faking good, to have the trial proceed. In one case, a defendant who presented a mixed picture of competency to proceed was kept at the hospital for treatment. A few days later, he asked to be sent back to court and acknowledged that he had not been honest during the evaluation.

Detection Methods

Any of the methods presented elsewhere in this book may be utilized for the detection of distorted competency skills. In terms of faked mental conditions or deficits, the following are relevant with sources for the detection methods listed in the right hand column:

Syndromes/Symptoms	Chapters
1. Primary disturbance of thought	16, 17
2. Primary disturbance of communication	6, 16
3. Secondary disturbance of communication	6, 16, 17
4. Delusional processes	6, 16
5. Hallucinations	17
6. Unmanageable or disturbing behavior	9, 19
7. Affective disturbances	7, 8, 19
8. Disturbances of consciousness/orientation	6, 7, 8, 15
9. Disturbances of memory/amnesia	15
10. Severe mental retardation	6, 9
11. General impairment of judgment/insight	6, 18

A defendant may choose to distort specific trial competencies rather than psychopathology. These competencies include the capacity to (1) know the exact charges; (2) disclose elements of the instant offense(s); (3) understand the roles of the court actors; (4) know the nature and process of the court proceedings; (5) appreciate the possible consequences of the various legal options; (6) cooperate with one's attorney; and (7) present oneself appropriately in court. The examiner must be prepared to probe each of these areas within a comprehensive evaluation.

Several competency questionnaires are available for use in evaluating trial competencies: the Competency Assessment Instrument (CAI) (Grisso, 1986, 1988), the Interdisciplinary Fitness Interview (IFI) (Golding, Roesch & Schreiber, 1984), and the Competency Screening Test (CST) (McGarry, 1973). The forensic evaluator should utilize these methods within a broadbanded assessment approach which also assesses present psychopathology and response styles.

KEY LEGAL CASES

Drope v. Missouri, 420 U.S. 162 (1975).
Dusky v. United States, 362 U.S. 402 (1960).
Estelle v. Smith, 451 U.S. 454 (1981).
Feguer v. U.S., 302 F.2d 214 (1962).
Jackson v. Indiana, 406 U.S. 715 (1972).
Lyles v. U. S., 254 F.2d 725 (1957).
Pate v. Robinson, 383 U.S. 375 (1966).
U. S. v. Adams, 297 F. Supp. 596 (1969).
U. S. v. Wilson, 391 F.2d 460 (1966).

REFERENCES

Blau, T. (1984). *The psychologist as expert witness*. New York: Wiley.
Cornell, D., & Hawk, G. (1989). Clinical presentation of malingerers diagnosed by experienced forensic psychologists. *Law and Human Behavior, 13*(4), 375-383.
Curran, W., McGarry, A., & Shah, S. (Eds.). (1986). *Forensic psychiatry and psychology: Perspectives and standards for interdisciplinary practice*. Philadelphia: F. A. Davis.
Drob, S., Berger, R., & Weinstein, H. (1987). Competency to stand trial: A conceptual model for its proper assessment. *Bulletin of the American Academy of Psychiatry and Law, 15*(1), 85-94.
Ewing, C. (Ed.). (1985). *Psychology, psychiatry, and the law: A clinical and forensic handbook*. Sarasota, FL: Professional Resource Exchange, Inc.
Golding, S., Roesch, R., & Schreiber, J. (1984). Assessment and conceptualization of competency to stand trial: Preliminary data on the interdisciplinary fitness interview. *Law and Human Behavior, 9*, 321-334.
Grisso, T. (1986). *Evaluating competencies: Forensic assessments and instruments*. New York: Plenum.
Grisso, T. (1988). *Competency to stand trial: Evaluations*. Sarasota, FL: Professional Resource Exchange, Inc.
Gutheil, T., & Appelbaum, P. (1982). *Clinical handbook of psychiatry and the law*. New York: McGraw-Hill.
McGarry, A. (1973). *Competency to stand trial and mental illness* (DHEW Publication No. ADM. 77-103). Rockville, MD: Department of Health, Education and Welfare.
Melton, G., Petrila, R., Poythress, N., & Slobogin, C. (1987). *Psychological evaluations for the courts: A handbook for mental health professionals and lawyers*. New York: Guilford.

Roesch, R., & Golding, S. (1980). *Competency to stand trial.* Urbana-Champaign, IL: University of Illinois Press.

Shapiro, D. (1984). *Psychological evaluation and expert testimony.* New York: Van Nostrand Reinhold.

Weiner, I., & Hess, A. (1987). *Handbook of forensic psychology.* New York: Wiley.

Ziskin, J., & Faust, D. (1988). *Coping with psychiatric and psychological testimony* (4th. ed.). Los Angeles: Law and Psychology Press.

14

CRIMINAL RESPONSIBILITY AND DECEPTION

The insanity defense has undergone substantial changes in recent years. Based on the mistaken arguments that the insanity defense is easily "faked" and that many guilty criminals are unjustly spared from punishment by use of the insanity defense, several state legislatures have abolished the defense. Other states and the U. S. Congress have severely curtailed their definitions of legal insanity and still others have introduced an alternate verdict ("Guilty but Mentally Ill") in hopes of persuading courts to find fewer defendants legally insane.

Among those jurisdictions which still retain the insanity defense, there are varying definitions of legal insanity. Some jurisdictions will excuse criminal behavior if it is the product of a mental disorder; others require that the perpetrator, at the time of the offense, was so mentally impaired that he could not appreciate the criminality of his conduct or could not conform his conduct to the requirements of law; a few require that the accused could not tell the difference between right and wrong in regard to the criminal act; at least one states that a person's criminal behavior will be excused only if it was the result of a "delusional compulsion" which overpowered the will of the perpetrator.

This chapter focuses on distortions during evaluations of criminal responsibility rather than on the insanity defense per se. Specific techniques for evaluating deception are described throughout this book. In this chapter, the fundamental importance of self-control and choice at the time of the instant offense is highlighted. Demonstrating self-regulation—if it exists during the alleged offense—has three important by-products: (1) the defendant's mental condition is clarified in terms of severity (hence its impact on responsibility for the crime); (2) self-reports by the defendant become less relevant than the abilities and skills evidenced by the defendant during the commission of the crime; and (3) the impact of information about self-control on the trier of fact is maximal, since judges and juries typically respond favorably to a description of the defendant's acts which are behaviorally anchored and cross-validated.

PREVIOUS ATTEMPTS TO STANDARDIZE CRIMINAL RESPONSIBILITY EVALUATIONS AND MALINGERING

Various forensic investigators have attempted to standardize criminal responsibility evaluations. Rogers and his colleagues analyzed malingering along the decision path of the evaluator (Rogers, 1984; Rogers, Seman & Wasyliw, 1983). In offering the Rogers Criminal Responsibility Assessment Scales (R-CRAS), Rogers (1984, p. 24) stated the following in the test manual:

> Malingering. The authenticity of the symptoms presented by the patient-defendant in the retrospective account of the time of the crime forms a necessary prerequisite to subsequent psycholegal decisions. Although rare, the forensic examiner must consider the possibility that the patient-defendant is both malingering and had a bona fide mental disorder at the time of the crime.

The R-CRAS asks the examiner to judge the severity of malingering on a five-part Likert scale:

1. Reliability of patient's self-report under his/her voluntary control.
   (0) No information.
   (1) Highly reliable self-report; examiner is impressed by the patient's openness and honesty which may include volunteering potentially self-damaging information.
   (2) Reliable self-report; the patient reports in a factual, sincere manner. The accused may not volunteer potentially self-damaging information and may gloss over a few incidental details.
   (3) Self-report with limited reliability; the patient answers most of the questions with a fair degree of accuracy (volunteers little or nothing and distorts or evades a few specific areas).
   (4) Self-report without reliability; the patient, through guardedness, exaggeration, or denial of symptoms, convinces the examiner that the patient's responses are inaccurate. There may be suspected malingering.
   (5) Definite malingering.

The evaluator is then asked to integrate the reliability of self-reports with other information and to compare the total information with the applicable legal definition of insanity. As an illustration, the R-CRAS sequentially analyzes (1) malingering, (2) organicity, (3) mental disorder(s), (4) loss of cognitive control, (5) loss of behavioral control, (6) whether the loss of cognitive and/or behavioral control resulted directly from organicity or from a mental disorder, and (7) conclusions regarding "insanity" using the American Law Institute (ALI) and M'Naughton definitions of insanity.

Decisions using R-CRAS have shown high agreement with actual court outcomes (Rogers, 1984). Rogers' system is data-based, flexible in terms of definition of insanity, and represents a clear advancement in assessment of criminal responsibility. It is therefore puzzling that the R-CRAS has received mixed reviews in the courtroom.

Possible reasons for the lack of acceptance include the reluctance of criminal courts to have anyone but themselves define "insanity" (in accordance with the relevant statutes). Moreover, there is a general judicial resistance to accepting criterion-based or statistical approaches in favor of the qualitative analysis of each criminal case (Hall, 1982, 1985, 1987).

The R-CRAS is confined to malingering (faking bad). Yet, other response styles need also be considered, as this book discusses. The R-CRAS procedure considers malingering as a preclusion to criminal responsibility. Even though there is a provision in the R-CRAS for mentally ill defendants who malinger, many evaluators may not seriously consider that defendants who blatantly malinger can still be genuinely mentally ill. In the authors' experience, and in the literature cited elsewhere in this book, the most disturbed defendants are sometimes the ones most likely to malinger. Generation of false negatives (i.e., those falsely considered to be sane or responsible) is a possible outcome of the R-CRAS and needs to be researched.

A RECOMMENDED PROCESS APPROACH TO CRIMINAL RESPONSIBILITY

A heuristic model for criminal responsibility evaluations is presented by Hall (1985, 1987). This involves the sequential and post hoc analysis of the (1) forensic database; (2) type of distortion and/or deception shown by the accused; (3) defendant's reconstruction of the instant offense; (4) long-term (i.e., historical) versus instant crime behavior; (5) mental disorder of the accused in terms of whether it is causally connected to the instant offense and sufficiently severe; (6) self-determination and choice of crime-related behaviors; and (7) conclusions regarding criminal responsibility.

STEP 1: ADEQUATE FORENSIC DATABASE

The first step involves the creation of a reliable and valid database, multisourced and interdisciplinary in nature, that forms the basis for all opinions regarding criminal responsibility. The content of the database is provided by looking at the perpetrator, victim, context of the crime, and other data relevant to the accused's current and past circumstances.

The most important part of the forensic analysis may be the database upon which the eventual conclusions rely. Criteria for including data in the database are that they are multisourced and interdisciplinary, based on information drawn from sources other than the client for purposes of cross-validation. Criteria for excluding data from the database include bias, unreliability, and intentional distortion (Hall, 1985, 1987). It is especially important to gather data from sources the defendant wishes to conceal, because of the likelihood of finding unfavorable information (e.g., juvenile records, so-called "expunged" records which may be available in unmodified form at government archive centers, interviews with ex-

spouses and mates, military performance reports, information from other states
or countries). It is helpful, for the credibility of the examiner, to base the forensic
evaluation on as many database sources as possible.

A strong note of caution needs to be sounded regarding use of an interview
with the defendant as the principal source of data. Empirical research indicates
that the clinical interview is so poor that forensic examiners are frequently unable
to repeat their own performances. In this regard, Ziskin and Faust (1988) stated,
"The clinical interview is a completely unreliable data gathering process." Ziskin
and Faust (1988) go on to state:

> The more than 80 references cited in [this] chapter...shows that be-
> cause of examiner and situation effects which are almost invariably
> present in forensic matters, but incapable of segregation or measure-
> ment, the data—that is, the raw data—the clinical examinations are
> worthless for legal purposes. Thus the process commences with worth-
> less data.

STEP 2: ANALYSIS OF DISTORTION AND DECEPTION

The next step in the decision process consists of ruling out or accounting for
nondeliberate distortion within (a) the reporting person and (b) the reported event.
Nondeliberate distortion due to anxiety, fatigue, or other factors may largely explain both evaluation and crime behavior and is, therefore, considered first.

Deliberate distortion, the next step in the evaluation process, should be ruled
in, by a positive and replicable demonstration of misrepresentation. Deliberate
distortion may be shown by the examiner, the client, and all cross-validating
sources. Examiners can, and do, deliberately distort for various reasons. The authors know of some forensic examiners who appear to thrive on the drama and
publicity of court work and whose judgment and decisions are clearly influenced
by a personal desire to "stir up controversy." It is not inappropriate to look at the
evaluator's track record for particular types of forensic assessments (e.g., percentage of time for which he or she testifies for the defense versus for the prosecution), rate of court agreement with rendered opinions, and whether or not proffered findings can be replicated by equally competent examiners.

The evaluation of the defendant's self-reports should be scrutinized for misrepresentation by examining third party reports and material evidence of the crime.
Psychometric testing is very appropriate for assessing distortion in victims and
other parties. Data derived from the input of significant or knowledgeable others
which indicate bias or a given motivational set (e.g., desire for revenge, to rejoin
defendant) should be excluded from the data pool or placed into proper perspective by being compared with other known data.

STEP 3: DEFENDANT RECONSTRUCTION OF THE INSTANT OFFENSE

A defendant's recollection of an alleged crime is usually helpful in inferring
the defendant's state of mind. Even when the defendant does not testify or when
state law shifts the burden of proving sanity to the government after the defendant has raised the possibility of insanity, the defendant's state of mind at the

time of the crime is critical to the successful application of the insanity defense. Although state of mind can often be inferred from eyewitness accounts, material evidence, and reports of third parties regarding events before and after the crime, the defendant's own description of events is helpful as one source of data.

Before eliciting a defendant's version of the alleged offense, however, it is critical that the examiner determine the legal admissibility of the defendant's statements. In some jurisdictions, a defendant's statements to an examining professional may be admitted not only as evidence of state of mind (i.e., legal insanity), but also as evidence that the defendant committed the crime (i.e., a confession). In such jurisdictions, the examiner is ethically obliged to inform the defendant of the potential uses of the statements (American Psychological Association Division 41, 1991) and, under some circumstances, is legally obligated to do so (*Estelle v. Smith*, 1981).

STEP 4: ANALYSIS OF HISTORICAL VERSUS CRIME BEHAVIOR

The next step involves an historical analysis of past criminal behavior versus that shown during the instant offense. The goal is to determine whether the instant offense is typical or atypical for the defendant. Rare events are most likely triggered by high stress or an unusual combination of environmental or internal events. Common events suggest a habitual pattern and are considered more inculpatory.

STEP 5: MENTAL DIAGNOSIS

A diagnosis of the defendant's mental state at the time of the crime usually requires evidence in support of a DSM IV mental condition. The diagnosis requires evidence that the condition existed at the time of the crime, regardless of whether or not it also existed prior to or after the crime. Evidence of a chronic mental disorder (e.g., schizophrenia, mental retardation, organic personality disorder) in existence before the instant offense increases the likelihood that the disorder also existed at the time of the crime, but is not sufficient by itself. Some chronic mental disorders can be in remission or partial remission or can be controlled with psychotropic medications. Evidence of prior episodic explosive episodes is relevant to diagnosis at the time of the instant offense only if the instant offense was also explosive and insufficiently provoked. Evidence of a mental disorder (e.g., depression, anxiety disorder) which arose after the instant crime is irrelevant to a diagnosis at the time of the offense. Most jurisdictions exclude (from their definitions of legal insanity) certain mental disorders (e.g., voluntary substance intoxication, antisocial personality disorder).

STEP 6: ANALYSIS OF SELF-REGULATION

The existence of a mental disorder at the time of the instant offense may not shed any light on the (legal) blameworthiness of the defendant. The severity of the disorder and its impairment of critical faculties at the time mediate its exculpatory effect. The analysis of self-control and choice by the accused is central to the determination of criminal responsibility. Intact self-control and choice for the time of the alleged crime often lead to a finding of criminal responsibility. Conversely, impaired self-control frequently results in exculpation or mitigation of responsibility for the instant offense.

Appendix C presents a detailed checklist of discrete behaviors for the times before, during, and after the instant offense. Examiners are encouraged to utilize this checklist (and/or give it to referring attorneys to fill out and return). It has been refined after application to several cases of evaluation for criminal responsibility.

The following report section presents a self-control analysis of a 25-year-old, White male who was subsequently found guilty of hammering his homosexual lover to death:

> Factors suggesting intact self-control for the time of the instant offense included the following:
>
> (a) No reported hyperactivity except during the commission of the homicide; that motor activity was necessary to complete the assault on the victim;
>
> (b) No reported rapid, pressured, perseverative, or incoherent speech;
>
> (c) No reported mental confusion or disorganization of behaviors;
>
> (d) No amnesia for alleged crime-related events;
>
> (e) No other alleged uncontrollable/impulsive behavior aside from the instant offenses; the accused showed a wide range of appropriate and controlled behavior for the week previous to the alleged crimes;
>
> (f) No substance intoxication, although he did ingest some cocaine and several beers on the night prior to the offense;
>
> (g) No heightened anxiety of maladaptive proportions or of such a nature as would create immobilization; the accused reported anxiety over whether the victim would wake up just prior to the homicide; this elevated anxiety did not prevent the attack;
>
> (h) Intact gross and fine motor skills, suggested by the physical activity engaged in by the accused prior to, during, and after the homicide;
>
> (i) Intact recall of alleged crime events, as shown by later recollection of specific events (e.g., during interrogation) and by reliance on recall in order to carry out the instant offenses;
>
> (j) Intact ability to interact verbally with the victim and to utilize auditory feedback, even though his responses may have been maladaptive (i.e., violent);
>
> (k) The ability to delay gratification of anger impulses by waiting until the victim returned to sleep and by starting the sequence of assaultive behaviors (i.e., raising his arm) only to interrupt the chain of behaviors by setting the hammer down for a period of time when the victim moved;

(l) A specific focus on the killing, with a particular victim, a particular weapon which could easily be lethal, a particular method of attack (striking blows to the head) in a manner likely to produce death. Crime photos show the victim's skull caved in on both sides—on the left side, primarily in the temporal lobe area, and on the right side, extending from the prefrontal area back to parietal-occipital sites;

(m) The perceptual-motor skills required to ambulate to a point beside the victim, to aim at a vital spot, and to strike that spot multiple times, killing the victim in the process. Discrete victim behavior was recalled, such as him turning on his side after the first blow;

(n) Increasing the severity of the hammer attack after the victim opened his eyes following the first blow;

(o) The ability to monitor and tactilely recall the results of the hammer attack (e.g., stating that the victim's head felt like "broken glass" after the attack);

(p) Intact recall, scanning, and other skills required to search the apartment and successfully locate and retrieve valuable items belonging to the victim;

(q) Attempting to avoid apprehension, represented by hiding the murder weapon, leaving the alleged crime scene, traveling away from the crime scene, lying to friends regarding how he acquired the van, eventually hiding the van, and throwing the keys in the bushes. He specifically recalled that he left his blood-stained yellow/blue striped underpants in the apartment of the victim. Each of these self-controlling behaviors was confirmed by cross-validating data.

STEP 7: PROFFERING CONCLUSIONS

The last step in the retrospective decision process consists of offering conclusions in regard to criminal responsibility. Adequacy of the database, degree of self-control exhibited, and criminal responsibility are all issues that must be addressed. The report format should conform to the retrospective decision path. Appendix D presents a mental capacity report format that has been developed and refined by the authors. At the very least, use of the format sequence and content factors will communicate to the court that the evaluator has been thorough in his or her assessment of issues relating to insanity.

SYNTHESIS

A heuristic model of seven discrete steps is proposed for evaluating criminal responsibility. The model explicitly integrates distortion analysis into the evaluation. The concept of self-control rather than diagnosis is the center point of the evaluation. A self-control checklist (Appendix C) and an Insanity Report Format (Appendix D) are offered. Appendix E contains an analysis of a criminal case from the perspective of self-control.

LEGAL REFERENCES

Estelle v. Smith, 451 U.S. 454 (1981).

REFERENCES

American Psychological Association Division 41. (1991). *Specialty guidelines for forensic psychologists*. Washington, DC: Author.

Hall, H. V. (1982). Dangerous predictions and the maligned forensic professional: Suggestions for detecting distortion of true basal violence. *Criminal Justice and Behavior, 9*, 3-12.

Hall, H. V. (1985). Cognitive and volitional capacity assessment: A proposed decision tree. *American Journal of Forensic Psychology, 3*, 3-17.

Hall, H. V. (1987). *Violence prediction: Guidelines for the forensic practitioner*. Springfield, IL: Charles C. Thomas.

Rogers, R. (1984). *R-CRAS: Rogers Criminal Responsibility Assessment Scales*. Odessa, FL: Psychological Assessment Resources, Inc.

Rogers, R., Seman, W., & Wasyliw, O. (1983). The R-CRAS and legal insanity: A cross-validation study. *Journal of Clinical Psychology, 39*, 554-559.

Ziskin, J., & Faust, D. (1988). *Coping with psychological and psychiatric testimony* (4th ed.). Los Angeles: Law and Psychology Press.

15

FAKED AMNESIA AND RECALL SKILLS

Memory deficits are found in everyday life and in pathological conditions. They span chronological ages from childhood to old age. They are transient and permanent, specific and global, functional and organic, normal and pathognomonic. And of course, because they are largely private events, they are fakeable.

Memory problems can arise from dysfunctions at any stage of information-processing: registration, short-term storage, consolidation, long-term storage, or retrieval (McCarthy & Warrington, 1990). Failure of registration, for example, may be due to limits in the span of apprehension (e.g., children may apprehend three items of information, while adults may apprehend seven items) or to deficits in "chunking" or categorizing information. Problems in short-term storage may be due to deficits in the durability of the memory trace or to attentional deficits. Problems in retrieval may be due to a heightened sensitivity to interference or to a failure of consolidation.

These various deficits may have diverse origins. Impaired memory performance per se has no value for differential diagnosis of pathological conditions. Table 15.1 presents examples of conditions which may be associated with mnestic difficulties.

FORENSICS ISSUES

Claimed memory problems are frequent in civil cases involving both tort claims and eligibility claims. Motor vehicle accidents, assaults, industrial accidents, and sporting accidents are leading causes of head injuries which frequently find their way into civil suits for negligence, Social Security Disability claims, and Workman's Compensation claims. Mnestic deficits are the most prevalent residual symptoms of head injuries and, therefore, figure prominently in civil claims. "In extreme cases, the injured person is forever bound to an extended present, with recollections of the past and anticipation of the future only fleetingly within awareness. In milder cases, where performance on experimental psychometric memory tasks fall within premorbid expectations, attention, and memory difficulties may show as periodic absent-mindedness, especially when dealing with tasks that place a strain on these functions and that rarely can be simulated by conventional assessment procedures" (Grimm & Bleiberg, 1986, p. 500).

Table 15.1
Etiologies of Mnestic Problems

Condition/Event	Mnestic problem may be due to:
1. Neuropsychological	
Organic Brain Syndrome	Traumatic brain injury, epilepsy, tumor, stroke, dementia
Toxic states	Intoxication, poisoning, neuroleptic syndrome
2. Psychosis	
Schizophrenia	Florid states
Affective disorders	Agitated or depressed periods
3. Psychogenic	
Repression	Intense stress
Dissociation	Hysteria, fugue, Multiple Personality Disorder
Depression	Slowing of cognitive processes
Adjustment disorders	Acute stress
4. Pure malingering	Prevarication not associated with mental disorder or condition
5. Combinations	Malingering associated with genuine deficits/conditions

---

Memory problems in cases of closed head injury involve both anterograde and retrograde amnesia. Anterograde amnesia (sometimes called posttraumatic amnesia) refers to memory deficits during the period after a head injury and includes the time of any coma, the time of any confusional period after consciousness is regained and, in severe cases, a time of varying length thereafter. Retrograde amnesia refers to deficits in the retrieval of memories already consolidated prior to the head injury. In the natural course of recovery from head injury, "anterograde posttraumatic amnesia gradually improves, after which the duration of the retrograde amnesia commonly shows a progressive shrinking to within a few minutes or seconds of the accident" (Cummings & Benson, 1983). This process of salvaging old memories and consolidating new memories is quite variable, depending on the severity of the injury and age of the patient, and may range from a few seconds to years.

Even in cases of mild closed head injury, with no loss of consciousness and normal radiological and neurological test results, memory deficits may be apparent in everyday functioning. As Corthell and Tooman (1985) stated:

> After even the mildest of injuries, *incidental* memory, i.e., the ability to recall information not specifically attended to, may be severely impaired. For example, misplaced keys, charge cards, packages, and shoes are common; appointments and commitments are instantly forgotten if not written down, despite every good intention and motivation to carry through. Standard intellectual examinations tend to test familiar, previously learned information and skills.
>
> Very little new learning or extended memory may be required on standard psychological examination. Head trauma clients often score in the "average" range or above on standard mental ability (IQ) tests, and yet can be severely impaired in their capacities for new learning and memory. (p. 15)

In general, there is a positive correlation between the severity of a head injury (as measured, for example, by length of coma) and the severity and duration of both anterograde and retrograde amnesia. There is also a positive correlation between the severity/duration of anterograde amnesia and the severity/duration of retrograde amnesia, although retrograde amnesias tend to be brief. Furthermore, there is a positive correlation between the duration of anterograde amnesia and everyday functioning. "Within broad limits it may be predicted that a patient with a[n anterograde amnesia] of less than an hour will usually return to work within a month, with a[n anterograde amnesia] of less than a day within two months, and with a[n anterograde amnesia] of less than a week within four months. [Anterograde amnesias] exceeding a week will often be followed by invalidism extending over the greater part of a year." (Lishman, 1987, p. 145). Therefore, the severity of a closed head injury and the duration of anterograde amnesia can provide a rough clue as to the genuineness of claimed memory deficits. If a head injury was mild, residual memory deficits should be mild and should be more apparent in incidental memory than in psychometric memory. A patient presenting with a history of mild head injury and complaints of severe mnestic deficits would appear suspicious. If the closed head injury was severe, longer lasting and more severe anterograde amnesia can be expected. A patient presenting with a history of severe head injury and complaints of mnestic difficulties even years after the injury is more plausible.

When the head injury is caused by penetrating or crushing forces (e.g., a gunshot wound), the duration of anterograde amnesia is a less reliable guide to severity and prognosis. "With penetrating injuries due to missiles or with depressed skull fractures,...Concussion and amnesia may then be brief or absent, yet focal cognitive deficits can be severe especially if hemorrhage or infection have occurred." (Lishman, 1987, p. 157). These focal deficits include specific amnesias, (e.g., auditory-verbal, visual mnestic deficits) rather than global amnesia. Depending on the severity of the specific deficits, the degree of everyday impairment may vary from mild to incapacitating. In such clinical cases, there is no "natural course" of recovery against which to assess the genuineness of a patient's complaints.[1]

Similarly the residual effects of anoxia or exposure to neurochemicals (including prescription medications) are highly variable, depending on such factors as the extent and duration of the anoxia and the toxicity and dosage of the neurochemical and on patient variables (e.g., age, sensitivity). In drowning cases, the extent of central nervous system damage, for example, is mediated by the victim's core body temperature during the period of anoxia. In cases of heavy metal poisoning (e.g., lead, mercury, manganese) and solvent inhalation (e.g., "glue sniffing") the cumulative dosage level is determinative of any residual effects of exposure. Dosage, individual sensitivity and length of exposure to phenothiazines (e.g., Haldol) are all critical in producing Parkinsonism, akathisia, and tardive dyskinesia.

In criminal cases, claimed memory problems are most likely to involve substance intoxication or psychiatric disorders. Guttmacher (1955) and Bradford and Smith (1979) reported that amnesia occurred in 30 to 55% of homicide cases. Amnesia associated with violence was generally a short-term, partial, and recoverable phenomenon. Bradford and Smith found that 37% of their sample of 30 defendants arrested for homicide reported amnesia for a period of less than 30 minutes, with 60% claiming some sort of amnesia for less than 24 hours. They also found 44% of the subjects reporting partial (patchy) amnesia, with sudden onset and cessation. This was the largest group, followed by those who claimed no amnesia (37%). Only 3% (one subject) reported a complete amnestic blackout for the entire time period. Likewise, only one subject showed lack of complete recovery. Bradford and Smith (1979) concluded that malingered amnesia is most likely to be 30 minutes or less in duration.

Taylor and Kopelman (1984) reported no cases of amnesia associated with nonviolent crimes in a sample of 212 men in custody for a variety of offenses. All of their amnesia cases had psychiatric disturbances with substance abuse and depression most frequent.

Almost one-half (41 out of 98) of young military male patients studied by Kiersch (1962) admitted that they had faked memory problems. These individuals were amnestic for a period of intoxication, but exaggerated the duration of the amnesia into times when they were sober. Psychogenic patients with exaggeration were also found.

In a study of 105 males being held on murder charges, Parwatikar, Holcomb, and Menninger (1985) reported that those who faked amnesia may have been more sophisticated in terms of knowing the criminal justice system and having been arrested previously. Those murderers who admitted responsibility and also claimed amnesia, tended to be substance intoxicated at the time of the instant offense, and/or exhibited higher levels of hysteria, depression, and hypochondriasis on the MMPI.

---

[1] An exception would be penetrating wounds to the hippocampal or parahippocampal areas, directly affecting the recall abilities of the wounded individual. In these cases, virtually no improvement subsequent to the trauma may take place.

In a review article, Schacter (1986) suggested that genuine versus faked recall in criminal cases can be distinguished by examining the accused's behavior in general. For example, was the offense well-prepared or impulsive? Secondly the amnesia claim itself may help to identify malingered amnesia. Limited recall during the crime with a sharply defined onset and termination is suggestive of faked or exaggerated amnesia. A suspect's feeling of knowing may also be used as a detection method. According to Schacter, a feeling of knowing is a "subjective conviction that one could retrieve or recognize an unrecalled item, event, or fact if one were given some useful hints or cues." The examiner asks possible fakers to rate their feeling of knowing that they could recall or recognize crime events if given assistance. Fakers tend to discount the chance that their recall would improve.

Thus, feigning memory problems is a fundamental concern for forensic professionals in both civil and criminal cases. The essentially private nature of the complaint of amnesia and the possible motive to malinger in legal situations encourage some persons to hide their intentional deception behind the variability and complexity of genuine amnesia. Distinguishing genuine from faked memory problems calls upon the best of psychological, neuropsychological and forensic skills.

EVERYDAY ASSUMPTIONS ABOUT MEMORY

Faked recall almost always involves assumptions about the way memory normally functions. These assumptions may conform to a common sense or layman's view of memory, but rarely encompass empirical facts about memory processes. The typical person is unlikely to distinguish recognition and recall processes, primacy and recency effects, learning curves and forgetting curves (e.g., Wiggins & Brandt, 1988).

Evaluation of erroneous assumptions made by deceivers should be studied for clues to deception. Herrmann (1982) noted that:

1. People know their memory only to a moderate degree. Fakers may wrongly think, for example, that they can recall their answers to a particular test, yet are unable to repeat their performance when retested.

2. Some types of memory are more stable over time than others; for example, visual experiences involving places (visual memory) are generally recalled more reliably than conversations (auditory-verbal memory). The faker may not know this and perform differentially on various sensory tasks. Information that even true amnesiacs generally don't forget over time also includes word completion. Graf, Squire, and Mandler (1984) found that word completion (cued recall) in amnesic patients declined at a normal rate when subjects were presented with the first three letters of each word presented earlier. They

also cite literature which shows that amnesic patients perform normally when (1) given degraded versions of previously presented words, (2) reading words from a mirror-reversed display and (3) completing puzzles.

3. In most people, recognition appears better than free recall. This is true in normals, those experiencing post-hypnotic amnesia, and the brain damaged (Iverson, Franzen, & McCracken, 1991; Brandt, Rubinsky, & Lassen, 1985). In this latter study, subjects feigning amnesia (N = 10) performed worse on free recall compared to normals (N = 12), those with Huntington's Disease (N = 14), and those with head trauma (N = 5). Recognition performance was above chance levels for both normals and head trauma subjects. Of the 14 subjects with Huntington's Disease, eight performed better than chance, and the rest at chance levels. All of the malingerers performed at chance (N = 7) or below chance (N = 3).

Wiggins and Brandt (1988) presented critical questions for which the probability of obtaining wrong answers by both nonsimulating controls and amnesiacs with bona fide organic conditions approaches zero (see Table 15.2). Incorrect answers to these questions should be expected only among those with clinically severe retrograde amnesia and, even in those cases, performance may be improved by cuing, prompting, or presenting choices (McCarthy & Warrington, 1990, pp. 307-313).

Table 15.2
Suspicious Memory Deficits If Wrong or Implausible Answers are Presented

1. "What is your...
   a. name?"
   b. age?"
   c. birth date?"
   d. telephone number?"
   e. address?"
   f. mother's first name?"
   g. mother's maiden name?"
   h. brother's name and/or sister's name?"

2. "What did you have for breakfast this morning?"

3. Recognizes examiner's name from four choices on Day 2 of evaluation if failed to recall it.

From Wiggins, E. C. & Brandt, J. (1988).

TARGETS

Any mnestic deficit can be faked. This includes immediate, short-term, and long-term recall problems. Any event that occurred in a person's life can be denied; recollection can be patchy and variable as memory returns.

Fakers tend to distort signs relevant to intended symptoms only on certain tests. Further, mild to moderate deficits appear to be faked more often than severe memory problems (e.g., dementia, global amnesia). Most likely, these types of deficits are selected because of their difficulty in detection. Faking recall should be suspected if (a) there is a loss of crystallized knowledge of skills, which almost never happens; (b) recognition is worse than recall, for example, for lists of words; (c) the person is exhibiting inconsistent organic or psychiatric signs (e.g., DSM-IV conditions).

RESPONSE STYLES

Most fakers show longer latencies in responding to recall questions (Resnick, 1984). This may be because they are simultaneously performing two mental operations—stopping a correct response and presenting another. Many of the faking-bad response styles, which depend on memory tasks, may be utilized by the malingerer (see previous chapter). Faking partial deficits may include the following strategies: (a) fractional effort, (b) approximate answers, (c) distributing errors among correct answers, and (d) overall attempt to control error percentage. Fakers often make intentional mistakes early in the evaluation and may change style (Pankratz, 1988; Hall, 1990).

DETECTION STRATEGIES

Herrmann (1982), in his review, discusses a wide variety of commonly used memory questionnaires. Yet, these tests correlate only moderately with actual recall abilities. A further problem is they have no built-in deception scales, and are predicated on the notion that the subject will give his or her best performance. At best, they can be used in parallel fashion if test-retest improvement is taken into consideration. The faker may have difficulty repeating his or her own first (inferior) performance.

Rey (1964) devised a 15-item visual memory test specifically designed to detect feigned memory difficulties. The task consists of five rows of patterned stimuli (e.g., ABC, 123, abc) which give the impression of task complexity (15 items) but which are easily "clustered" into just five memory units. Lezak (1983) and Goldberg and Miller (1986) suggested a cut-off score of nine recalled items was optimal for detecting suspicious mnestic performances. Bernard and Fowler (1990) suggested a cut-off score of eight and Lee, Loring, and Martin (1992) suggested a cut-off score of seven. Clearly the optimal cut-off score for detecting malingering will vary from population to population (e.g., demented patients, retarded patients) (Schretlen, 1991).

The Wechsler Memory Scale-Revised (WMS-R) (Wechsler, 1987) and the Memory Assessment Scale (Williams, 1991) are multifaceted measures of memory functioning. They can be used for adolescents and adults, and include tests for verbal and figural stimuli, meaningful and abstract material, and delayed as well as immediate recall. Olfactory and tactile recall, autobiographical memory, and recall of learned skills (e.g., operating a machine) are not tested with these measures.

Deception on the WMS-R can be assessed by (a) comparing test scores between retests; (b) comparing WMS-R subscale scores with those of other tests with the same task (e.g., digit span on WMS-R with WAIS-R, visual reproduction scores with performance on Bender-Gestalt); (c) comparing test performance with cross-validating sources (e.g., significant others); (d) comparing the Wiggins and Brandt's (1988) list to responses on the information and orientation questions since there is considerable overlap; (e) comparing easy versus difficult item scores on the verbal paired associates tasks; and (f) observing behavior during testing (see p. 12 of WMS-R manual) and noting attitude toward testing, motivation, reaction to success or failure, and work habits.

FORCED CHOICE TESTING

Explicit Alternative Testing (EAT) is a promising forensic neuropsychological tool that attempts to measure faked sensory and recall deficits (Grosz & Zimmerman, 1965; Pankratz, 1979, 1983, 1988; Pankratz, Fausti, & Peed, 1975; Theodor & Mandelcorn, 1973). Also known as *forced choice, two alternative*, or *symptom validity testing*, EAT involves the presentation of stimuli, which the client denies or affirms that he or she can perceive/remember. Almost no one should miss presented items unless a genuine impairment exists, in which case one's performance should approximate chance responding (one-half of the items in two-choice formats). Deviation from chance is defined as a total percentage-correct which falls significantly below 50% as defined by the binomial probability distribution (e.g., 1.96 standard deviations below 50% correct). For example, the (one-tailed) probability of obtaining fewer than 40 correct responses in 100 trials of a two-choice task is less than 2%. Obtaining less than 36 correct answers in the 100 trials would occur by chance less than two times in 1,000. Subjects intent on faking typically make an initial assumption that they must respond correctly less than 50% of the time to demonstrate mnestic difficulties (Haughton, Lewsley, Wilson, & Williams, 1979; Pankratz, 1988).

Hall and Shooter (1989) achieved a positive hit rate of 84.6% in identifying 52 subjects instructed to fake bad on a forced-choice memory recognition task. Shooter and Hall (1990) boosted the positive hit rate to almost 95% (N = 19) on the same task. A third study addressed the question of whether 50 or 100 trials are required for successful detection of faking in EAT. Thirty-five subjects (males = 16, females = 19; mean age = 29.37, SD = 10.46; mixed ethnicity; mixed occupations) were randomly assigned to one of two groups: (1) those administered 100 trials (N = 10) or (2) those administered 50 trials (N = 25). There were two (20%) successful fakers in the 100-item group and six (24%) in the 50-item group. Chi-square analysis comparing the successful and unsuccessful fakers for the 100- versus 50-trial group showed no significant differences.

As one would suspect, deception strategies differed between the successful versus unsuccessful fakers. The most popular strategy used by the unsuccessful fakers was consistently choosing the incorrect response, accounting for 41% of the strategies named. The second most common strategy used by the unsuccessful fakers was giving occasional correct or incorrect responses (accounting for 20% of the strategies used), with attempts to forget being the third most common strategy. It was not uncommon for those employing a shift in strategy to switch from consistently choosing the incorrect answer to giving an occasional correct response.

The successful group employed random responding most frequently (accounting for 28%). The second most frequent strategy was consistently using the same response (19%), which necessarily resulted in a total-%-correct of 50%. The third most frequent strategy was consistently choosing the incorrect response (16%), which necessarily involved a strategy shift at some point in order to produce a total-%-correct greater than 40%. Among those subjects who identified a shift in strategy during the test, 29% named adhering to one response as their first strategy, while 21% reported using random responding as their first strategy. Random responding was named 40% of the time as the second strategy.

Pritchard (1992) has developed a computerized version of EAT, which employs a 72-trial memory recognition task divided into three subsets of 24-trials each. The subject is presented on each trial with a 5-digit number ("target") for five seconds, followed by a 3 to 5 second delay and then a pair of 5-digit numbers from which to select the "target" previously shown. A %-correct score is calculated for each subset of 24 trials and for the total 72 trials. Pritchard and Moses (1992) demonstrated that this task was 100% accurate (negative hit rate) in identifying a sample of severely impaired psychiatric and brain-injured patients and was 66% accurate (positive hit rate) in identifying a sample of subjects instructed to fake bad without being detected.

Results from EAT studies suggest that:

1. Forced-choice methodology is indeed promising. The hit rates of EAT studies far exceed other deception-detecting strategies, even when distinguishing "fakers" from severely impaired patients. Individuals with a high vested interest in faking—such as defendants facing prison terms or plaintiffs standing to gain monetary compensation for damages—may be even more strongly motivated than volunteer subjects to fake successfully. This would then increase the power of the EAT technique when applied to clinical cases. Indeed, anecdotal examples from the authors' experiences confirm the success of EAT with actual clinical cases.

   Case #1. A 45-year-old Filipino male charged with the murder of his wife claimed amnesia for the instant offense. No history of neurological problems was apparent. He presented with severe short-term visual and auditory recall deficits on the Wechsler Memory Scale-Revised and other testing. He obtained about 20% accurate responses on EAT and later admitted to exaggerating his recall deficits when confronted with the results. He maintained amnesia for the homicide and was eventually found guilty of manslaughter.

Case #2. A White, right-handed, 23-year-old female ex-stripper at a go-go club was stabbed in the neck by her boyfriend, creating a through and through puncture wound of the jugular vein and carotid artery. Residual signs included the Brown-Sequard syndrome, a right Horner's pupil, and an ataxic gait favoring the left. Neuropsychological testing several months after the trauma revealed normal functioning except on tasks requiring motor speed, coordination of upper extremities, manual dexterity, and sensitivity to stimulation. Recall abilities were above average for both short- and long-term memory. The victim later sued the nightclub for failure to protect her, claiming pervasive mental deficits stemming from the stabbing. Neuropsychological testing on the same battery two years afterwards revealed uniformly poor scores with an impairment index of 1.0, meaning 100% of her scores were in the impaired range. This was in striking contrast to her normal clinical appearance and lack of any event since the stabbing which would explain this deterioration. MMPI testing revealed a pronounced tendency to fake bad. On the EAT, 15% of her responses were accurate, strongly suggesting that she was feigning a visual memory deficit.

She did not admit to faking, but was eventually awarded a reduced settlement upon negotiation with the (civil) defendant.

2. Results suggest that as few as three sets of 24 trials or even 50 total trials of EAT can be utilized with no loss of detection accuracy. Thus, EAT can be designed to be both accurate and economical.

3. The use of successive sets of EAT trials, rather than just a total accuracy score based on all trials, appears to make EAT sensitive to fluctuating deception strategies. Fakers may perform poorly in the beginning of EAT testing and switch to honest responding after it is too late to hide their deception. Or subjects may attempt to fake bad after they have adapted to the test and decided on a strategy for deception.

4. EAT may be uniquely adapted to detect deception in individual cases. For criminal cases, this might involve information about an offense that only a perpetrator would know. As suggested by Hall and Shooter (1989), data bits—such as type of weapon utilized, injuries sustained by the victim, and clothing characteristics—could be presented to the suspect with instructions to affirm or deny recognition of them. A suspect with no knowledge of the instant crime should perform at approximately chance levels, while the perpetrator may be (statistically) placed at the scene of the crime.

Summary and Conclusions

Feigned memory deficits are essentially private events, which require sensitive psychological and neuropsychological skill to detect. By way of summary of the current state-of-the-art in detecting faked memory problems, Table 15.3 presents a summary of the best signs for the detection of faked memory.

Table 15.3
Suspicious Signs for Faked Memory Across Detection Methods

Consider faking of recall if any of the following occur in combination:

1. Loss of crystallized memory with intact anterograde recall.
2. Recognition worse than recall.
3. Forced choice worse or better than chance on skill for which the assessee claims total impairment.
4. "Feeling of knowing" confidence low.
5. Misses on critical autobiographical items.
6. Increased in latency of verbal response to memory-related queries.
7. Memory skill levels significantly change upon parallel or repeat testing.
8. Confession of faked recall with recaptured memory.
9. Third-parties report subject previously discussed the now "lost" memories.
10. Faking response style identified and can be reproduced upon retesting.

REFERENCES

Bernard, L., & Fowler, W. (1990). Assessing the validity of memory complaints: Performance of brain-damaged and normal individuals on Rey's task to detect malingering. *Journal of Clinical Psychology, 46,* 432-436.

Bradford, J. W., & Smith, S. M. (1979). Amnesia and homicide: The Padola case and a study of thirty cases. *Bulletin of the American Academy of Psychiatry and the Law, 7,* 219-231.

Brandt, J., Rubinsky, E., & Lassen, G. (1985). Uncovering malingered amnesia. *Annals of the New York Academy of Sciences, 44,* 502-503.

Corthell, D., & Tooman, M. (1985). *Rehabilitation of TBI (Traumatic Brain Injury).* Menomonie, WI: Stout Vocational Rehabilitation Institute.

Cummings, J., & Benson, D. (1983). *Dementia: A clinical approach.* Boston: Butterworths.

Goldberg, J., & Miller, H. (1986). Performance of psychiatric inpatients and intellectually deficient individuals on a task that assesses the validity of memory complaints. *Journal of Clinical Psychology, 42,* 792-795.

Graf, P., Squire, L. R., & Mandler, G. (1984). The information that amnesic patients do not forget. *Journal of Experimental Psychology: Learning, Memory, and Cognition, 10,* 164-178.

Grimm, B., & Bleiberg, J. (1986). Psychological rehabilitation in traumatic brain injury. In S. Filskov & T. Boll (Eds.), *Handbook of clinical neuropsychology: Volume 2* (pp. 495-560). New York: J. Wiley & Sons.

Grosz, H., & Zimmerman, J. (1965). Experimental analysis of hysterical blindness: A follow-up report and new experiment data. *Archives of General Psychiatry, 13,* 255-260.

Guttmacher, M. S. (1955). *Psychiatry and the law.* New York: Grune and Stratton.

Hall, H. V., & Shooter, E. (1989). Explicit alternative testing for feigned memory deficits. *Forensic Reports, 2,* 277-286.

Haughton, P. M., Lewsley, A., Wilson, M., & Williams, R. G. (1979). A forced-choice procedure to detect feigned or exaggerated hearing loss. *British Journal of Audiology, 13,* 135-138.

Herrmann, D. (1982). Know thy memory: The use of questionnaires to assess and study memory. *Psychological Bulletin, 92,* 434-452.

Iverson, G., Franzen, M., & McCracken, L. (1991). Evaluation of an objective assessment technique for the detection of malingered memory deficits. *Law and Human Behavior, 15*(6), 667-676.

Kiersch, T. A. (1962). Amnesia: A clinical study of ninety-eight cases. *American Journal of Psychiatry, 119,* 57-60.

Lee, G., Loring, D., & Martin, R. (1992). Rey's 15-item visual memory test for the detection of malingering: Normative observations on patients with neurological disorders. *Psychological Assessment, 4,* 1, 43-46.

Lezak, M. (1983). *Neuropsychological assessment* (2nd ed.). New York: Oxford University Press.

Lishman, W. (1987). *Organic psychiatry.* London: Blackwell Scientific Publications.

McCarthy, R., & Warrington, E. (1990). *Cognitive neuropsychology: A clinical introduction.* New York: Academic Press.

Pankratz, L. (1979). Symptom validity testing and symptom retraining: Procedures for the assessment and treatment of functional sensory deficits. *Journal of Consulting and Clinical Psychology, 47,* 409-410.

Pankratz, L. (1983). A new technique for the assessment and modification of feigned memory deficit. *Perceptual and Motor Skills, 57,* 367-372.

Pankratz, L. (1988). Malingering on intellectual and neuropsychological measures. In R. Rogers (Ed.), *Clinical assessment of malingering and deception* (pp. 169-192). New York: The Guilford Press.

Pankratz, L., Fausti, S., & Peed, S. (1975). A forced-choice technique to evaluate deafness in the hysterical or malingering patient. *Journal of Consulting and Clinical Psychology, 43,* 421-422.

Parwatikar, S. D., Holcomb, W. R., & Menninger, K. A. (1985). The detection of malingered amnesia in accused murderers. *Bulletin of the American Academy of Psychiatry and Law, 13,* 97-103.

Pritchard, D. A. (1992). *Tests of neuropsychological malingering.* Winter Park, FL: GR Press, Inc.

Pritchard, D., & Moses, J. (1992). Tests of neuropsychological malingering. *Forensic Reports, 5,* 287-290.

Resnick, P. J. (1984). The detection of malingered mental illness. *Behavioral Sciences and the Law, 2*(1), 21-38.

Rey, A. (1964). *L'examen clinique en psychologie* (The clinical examination in psychology). Paris: Presses Universitaires de France.

Schretlen, D., Brandt, J., & Kraft, L. (1991). Some caveats in using the Rey 15-item memory test to detect malingered amnesia. *Psychological Assesssment, 3*(4), 667-672.

Schacter, D. L. (1986). Amnesia and crime: How much do we really know? *American Psychologist, 41,* 286-295.

Shooter, E., & Hall, H. V. (1990). Explicit alternative testing for deliberate distortion: Toward an abbreviated format. *Forensic Reports, 3*(2), 115-119.

Taylor, P., & Kopelman, M. (1984). Amnesia for criminal offenses. *Psychological Medicine, 14,* 581-588.

Theodor, L. H., & Mandelcorn, M. S. (1973). Hysterical blindness: A case report and study using a modern psychophysical technique. *Journal of Abnormal Psychology, 82*(3), 552-553.

Wechsler, D. (1987). *Wechsler Memory Scale - Revised Manual.* New York: Psychological Corporation.

Wiggins, E., & Brandt, J. (1988). The detection of simulated amnesia. *Law and Human Behavior, 12,* 57-78.

Williams, J. (1991). *Memory Assessment Scales Professional Manual.* Odessa, FL: Psychological Assessment Resources.

PSYCHOSIS AND DECEPTION

For as muche as sometyme some personnes beinge accused of hyghe treasons, haue after they haue beene examined before the kinges miesties counsayle, confessed theyr offences of hyghe treason, and yet neuer the lesse after the dynge of theyr treasons, and examinations and confessions thereof, as is afore saide, haue falled to madness or lunacye, wherby the condygne punyshemente of theyr treasons, were they neuer soo notable and detestable, hath ben deferred spared and delayed, and whether theyr madness or lunacye by them outwardly shewed, were of trouth or falsely contriued and counterfayted, it is a thing almost impossible certainely to judge or try

33 Henry VIII, c.xx

Since feedback is rarely obtained on successfully faked psychosis, we know little about its true prevalence or how to detect it in specific cases. The above quote by Diamond (1956), from 1542, during the reign of Henry VII, suggests that the problem is not new and continues to be vexing.

Most probably, malingered psychosis (a) varies according to context—faked psychosis may be more frequent in criminal cases, but low in civil settings; (b) varies in degree within the same individual in his or her attempts to be consistent or inconsistent; (c) is more frequently engaged in by those who are already maladjusted and (d) is encouraged by widespread dissemination of information on genuine psychosis, the attempts by deinstitutionalized people to return to the state hospitals, and the increasing mood of the judiciary to imprison felons.

Diverse circumstances and mental conditions are associated with faked psychoses. Ritson and Forrest (1970), in common with others, suggested that the malingering of psychosis is more serious than the faked condition, meaning that faking psychosis can be considered an illness in itself. Their patients had a number of reasons for faking, including (a) not wishing to leave the hospital, (b) being criminally charged, (c) financial problems or seeking a new residence, (d) manipulating unsympathetic doctors; and (e) escaping from an intolerable domestic situation. They proposed we go beyond the unconscious versus conscious dichotomy, in the fashion of Freud and the neodynamically oriented, and focus on the communication or message that the faked behavior represents. The real problem may be the outrage and the indignation shown by the clinician. In the Ritson and Forrest study, most of the 12 fakers originally had personality disorders (or features thereof), but later showed schizophrenic symptoms, a finding cross-validated by Pope, Jonas, and Jones (1982) in their study of factitious psychosis among hospitalized patients. Like Ritson and Forrest (1970), Pope et al. (1982) found that their fakers of psychosis had a poor prognosis. Almost one-half of their malingering patients were hospitalized four to seven years later.

TARGETS

The long-range goals of the faker of psychosis may include a desire to avoid the unpleasant (e.g., imprisonment, combat duty) and/or to obtain rewards (e.g., financial compensation in Veterans Administration litigation; drugs; transfer within institutional settings, such as protective custody or the medical unit; admission to agencies for food and lodging).

Feigned behaviors chosen at the time of evaluation include alternations in speech, motor changes, the presentation of unexpected behavior, and the withholding of expected responses. As with all faked conditions, the faker of psychosis selects targets designed to accomplish a particular goal. Responses that the faker chooses should leave him or her blameless or, at least, point to uncontrollable forces beyond his or her ability to initiate, modulate, or stop.

To assist the evaluator, the faker of psychosis often calls attention to faked symptoms. This does not necessarily imply consistency of responding or a desire to be detected. Rather, the examiner must be aware of psychotic symptoms in order to respond to them.

The faker of psychosis may present faked symptoms in writing, only to repudiate the symptoms when questioned orally. Presumably, the stress of verbal inquiry may be greater than in the written form. The evaluator should be prepared for both the presentation of moving targets and a wide variation in response styles.

Targets of faked psychosis, with examples, are presented in Table 16.1.

Research on forensic subjects may yield important guidelines for the detection of disingenuous psychosis. A unifying theme of these investigations is that, given motivation to fake, malingerers of psychosis appear to exhibit patterned responses and can be detected by conformance to an inner logic (Bash, 1978; Bash & Alpert, 1980). These investigators determined that increased specificity of response style is associated with less involvement of the faker's own personality. Conversely, the more adaptive and widespread the malingering is to a variety of situations, the greater the likelihood that the faker's own enduring personality traits and lifestyle come into play. As discussed later, this finding has important implications for the assessment of deception.

Table 16.1
Targets of Faked Psychosis

Targets	Examples
1. Behavior	Bizarre motor behavior Audible self-talk
2. Somatic	Internal body changes Physical disease processes
3. Sensation	Vivid hallucinations Strange illusions
4. Imagery	Terrifying nightmares Uncontrollable flashbacks
5. Affect	Immobilizing fear Suicidal depression
6. Cognition	Delusions of persecution, grandiosity; Looseness of thought
7. Interpersonal	Inability to respond: mutism Sexually inappropriate questions

RESPONSE STYLES

The focus of this chapter is on variations of faking the presence or severity of psychosis. However, malingering is often combined with defensiveness, for example, when the faker denies symptoms before military service and asserts severe symptoms during or after military service. The evaluator must be aware that clients may deny genuine psychosis for various motives, for example, to preserve the ego. Diamond (1956) speculates that simulating sanity occurs very frequently. He encourages the clinician to investigate simulated sanity actively instead of waiting for the client inadvertently to reveal psychosis.

Even severely maladjusted persons can fake bad or good, depending on their vested interests and opportunities for deception. Braginsky and Braginsky (1967) showed, in a study of 30 long-term schizophrenics, that subjects could present themselves as "sick" or "healthy," depending on their goals. The former response set was presented when the subjects were faced with discharge, while "healthy" behaviors were shown when their open ward status was challenged. Three staff psychiatrists who blindly reviewed tapes of interviews with patients were erroneously convinced by the patients' impressions. Later work by the Braginskys (Mozer, 1978) substantiated the notion that psychiatrists performed poorly in describing the severity of mental illness in bogus patients. Instead, the ratings of mental illness increased substantially (i.e., patients were more likely to be diagnosed as psychotic) when the "patient" criticized mental health professionals. A later study, where only praise was used by "patients," found a reduction in the level of diagnosed mental illness and subjects were generally seen as reasonable and rational.

The importance of assessing for all response styles, even among persons with well-documented histories of psychopathology, is thus strongly indicated.

DETECTION STRATEGIES

Hollender and Hirsch (1964) presented five criteria for the detection of "hysterical" psychosis involving schizophrenic symptoms: (a) sudden, dramatic onset; (b) temporally linked to trauma; (c) schizophrenic symptoms in the absence of psychosis or a gross mood disorder; (d) no residual symptoms; and (e) premorbid hysterical personality traits.

Hollender and Hirsch (1964) concluded by suggesting the following criteria for distinguishing faked from genuine psychosis: (a) delusions or hallucinations as the main symptoms; (b) no derailment of thought or blunted affect; (c) presence of identifiable causative factors, such as a linkage between critical events and symptom onset, or of secondary gain in terms of avoiding punishment or receiving a reward; (d) presence of two of the following symptoms: visual hallucinations, amnesia, sexual problems, pains, or other body distress suggesting loss or change in function, and a histrionic or antisocial personality disorder; and (e) no evidence of brain damage, schizophrenia, or a psychotic affective disorder.

Resnick (1984, 1988) presented clinical signs for detecting faked psychosis, which are presented in Table 16.2.

Rogers (1984, 1988) presented a structured interviewing approach to the problem of malingered psychosis. He analyzed the Schedule of Affective Disorders and Schizophrenia (SADS), (Spitzer & Endicott, 1978), stemming from a 1978 study on depression but which measures a wide variety of psychiatric symptomatology (Endicott & Spitzer, 1978). He next developed the Structured Interview of Reported Symptoms (SIRS), (Rogers, 1986), which is intended for the identification of unreliable or inconsistent presentations during clinical interviews.

The discriminating ability of the SIRS is shown by the frequent and significant differences between malingerers and genuine patients. Symptom combinations are endorsed on Form A of the SIRS by only 2.4% of the patient population, but was endorsed by 28.9% of malingerers (Form B, 6.8% and 18.8% respectively). Symptom combinations on the SADS which were rare (all endorsed by less than 10% of genuine patients) included reporting (a) an adequate appetite together with current feelings of inadequacy, discouragement, distrust, and anger; (b) agitation together with anxiety or discouragement; and (c) persecutory delusions together with worrying, discouragement, insomnia, and anger.

Table 16.2
Clinical Signs for Detecting Faked Psychosis

Sign of Simulation	Relevant Factor for Client
1. Overplaying psychotic role	Attempts to behave congruently with idiosyncratic view of psychosis.
2. Calling attention to symptoms	Rare psychotic conditions.
3. Difficulty in imitation of form and style of psychosis	Often focuses on content of psychosis.
4. May fit no diagnostic	Unaware of DSM-IV inclusionary and exclusionary criteria.
5. Sudden onset and termination	Unaware that delusions usually develop and remit over time.
6. Unlikely to conform to delusional content	Discrepancy between delusional content and behavior may not occur to client.
7. Far-fetched story	Often seen in naive simulators.
8. Contradictions in crime account more likely	Misrepresentation involves remembering and making up a wide range of information.

Rogers (1988) suggested a number of criteria for detecting malingering which formed the basis for the development of the SIRS. The criteria which are empirically validated included the following:

Descriptor	Malingerers Endorse
1. Symptom subtlety	More blatant than subtle symptoms
2. Severity of symptoms	Items reflecting extreme or unbearable severity
3. Rare symptoms	Infrequent symptoms
4. Improbable or absurd	Items of fantastic or symptoms preposterous quality
5. Symptom combinations	Symptoms unlikely to coexist
6. Consistency of symptoms	Inconsistent items when repeated
7. Nonselective endorsement	More nonselective in choosing psychiatric symptoms

However, even rare items sometimes are seen in psychotics. These include symptoms such as (a) thought withdrawal, (b) delusions of guilt, (c) somatic delusions, (d) loosening of associations, (e) incoherence during the past week, and (f) neologisms (Rogers, 1988). As Rogers noted, contradictory symptoms are seen in cyclothymic or bipolar disorders such as (a) depressed and elevated mood, (b) worthlessness and grandiosity, (c) insomnia and hypersomnia, (d) decreased and increased energy, (e) decreased and increased appetite, (f) decreased and increased interests, and (g) psychomotor retardation and agitation.

In sum, Rogers' (1988) approach to structured interviewing appears promising. The SADS is an established approach to assessing psychiatric problems, but the SIRS is not yet fully developed for clinical use. At this point, a compelling case for the incremental validity of the SIRS and SADS (compared, for example, to psychometric approaches to the assessment of malingering) has not yet been presented. They both, however, represent improvements over unstructured interviewing.

PSYCHOMETRIC APPROACHES TO FAKED PSYCHOSIS

M TEST

A short test for measuring malingering in schizophrenic persons has been developed by Beaber, Marston, Michelli, and Mills (1985). The "M" Test consisted of three scales: (a) Confusion (C) Scale where subjects were expected to respond in a particular way (e.g., "I believe that cancer is a horrible disease."); (b) Schizophrenia (S) Scale where items reflect known associated features of schizophrenia (e.g., "Periodically, I am bothered by hearing voices that no one else hears."); and (c) Malingering (M) Scale or indicators of malingered schizophrenia.

The M scale showed the largest absolute mean difference between normals (x = .36; SD = .83), schizophrenics (x = 2.07; SD = 2.83), and fakers (x = 8.07; SD = 4.94). The M scale consists of items that cannot be true because they are comprised of nonexistent entities (e.g., "I believe that God has appointed me to teach the Zolan beliefs to all people that I meet."). Atypical hallucinations, even for genuine experiences, are presented in this scale (e.g., "Sometimes after waking up in the morning, I am bothered by seeing colored triangles in my field of vision."). Items reflecting extreme severity not characteristic of schizophrenia are also included (e.g., "Sometimes my need to be alone and my fear of people are so powerful that I will spend hours in a closed closet by myself."). Other items reflect atypical delusions (e.g., "There have been times when I have found myself thinking that as a teenager, I was the chairman of the board of a major corporation."). The "M" Test identified 87.3% of 65 schizophrenics (true negatives) and 78.2% of 104 normal persons who were in fact malingering (true positives).

Smith (1990) attempted to cross-validate the "M" Test on 23 malingerers and 62 inmates referred for a forensic evaluation, but was able to detect only 69.6% of the malingerers. Rogers, Bagby, and Gillis (1992) were able to identify only 40% of suspected malingerers with the "M" Test and, therefore, proposed a revised "M" Test, which has yet to be cross-validated.

MMPI

A large field of literature on the MMPI shows that normals who fake psychosis, and psychotics who feign normality or exaggerate their disorder, can be detected with some degree of accuracy. Throughout this literature, however, it is important to distinguish the specific contrasting groups used to support the detection of distorted responding. MMPI scores and indices are better at discriminating between normal MMPI profiles and those of normal subjects instructed to feign psychopathology (normal pseudo-malingerers) than they are at discriminating between genuine patients and normal pseudo-malingerers (Berry, Baer, & Harris, 1991; Schretlen, 1988). MMPI indices of malingering are even less accurate in distinguishing genuine, honest patients from genuine, exaggerating patients. Furthermore, some indices of distortion on the MMPI are consistently more effective than others. For example, Berry et al. (1991) concluded that "the largest mean effect size [for discriminating genuine from malingered MMPI profiles] was T-scaled F...followed by raw F...the original dissimulation scale...F minus K...obvious item scales...obvious minus subtle scales...subtle item scales...and the revised dissimulation scale" (p. 593). Finally, Berry et al. (1991) noted that the search for a universal cut-off score for distinguishing genuine from faked MMPIs on any of these indices is ill-advised. Cut-off scores must be locally determined according to the base rate of malingering in the population of interest and according to the costs of classification errors. For example, to achieve a given level of false positive errors, cut-off scores would need to be higher when discriminating exaggerating patients from genuine patients than when discriminating malingering normals from genuine normals.

The MMPI-2 was introduced in 1989. Shooter and Hall (1989) compared the various validity indicators available on the MMPI and the MMPI-2 (Table 16.3) based upon extant information (Anderson, K., personal communication, 1989; Butcher, 1990).

The clinician should use the original MMPI to detect faked psychosis until explicit studies on deception detection with the MMPI-2 have been conducted. However, available research suggests that the original MMPI is less useful in discriminating malingering from genuine psychopathology than in discriminating malingering from normalcy (Berry, et al. 1991). Since the MMPI-2 is so similar in content and function to the original MMPI, it would not be surprising to discover that the MMPI-2 is similarly less sensitive to feigned psychopathology.

PSYCHOLOGICAL TESTING BATTERIES

Bash and Alpert (1980) tested four groups of 30 subjects each—(a) suspected malingerers, (b) schizophrenics who reported auditory hallucinations, (c) nonhallucinatory schizophrenics, and (d) nonpsychotic subjects with no history of auditory hallucinations. All subjects were tested in two sessions on a variety of neuropsychological and personality measures.

To assess faking on the WAIS, a malingering score based on approximate answers, each scored plus one, was developed (see Table 16.4). The total number of approximate answers for each subtest was transformed into a standard score

Table 16.3
MMPI and MMPI-2 Validity Indicators

Validity Indicators	MMPI	MMPI-2
1. Item omissions	a. Present	a. Present
2. Consistency	b. Test-Retest (TR) index	b.& c. Replaced with 2 new scales based on the same rationales: Variable Response
	c. Carelessness (CLS) scale	Inconsistency (VRIN) 49 pairs of items True Response Inconsistency (TRIN) 20 pairs of items indicating a true or a false set
	d. Sum of TR and CLS	d. Eliminated and replaced by above scales
	e. Weiner and Harmon obvious and subtle scales	e. Present
	f. Gough Dissimulation Scale-Rev.	f. Information not available
	g. Lochar and Wrobel Critical Items	g. Present with minor revision (4-5 items)
	h. F Scale	h. Present
	i. Absent	i. F(B) or Back-page F scale. Designed to assess the validity of responses to the latter part of the MMPI (e.g., random responding after tiring)
	j. Positive malingering	j. Present
	k. L and K scales	k. Present
	l. F-K	l. Present
	m. Individual item endorsement vs. cross-validated historical behavior	m. Present

Table 16.4
WAIS Approximate Answers and Malingering

Subtest	Criterion
Arithmetic	Answer is +1 from correct answer
Block design	Answer is correct except for one block, placed 90 degrees or less off
Digit span	Digits reported one above or below correct number
Picture arrangement	All pictures are correct except for 1, placed as first or last in series
Information	Total score of "don't know" answers to items 1, 2, 3, 4, 5, 6, 8, 11
Picture completion	"Nothing is missing" response to more than three consecutive items

Constructed from data presented by Bash & Alpert (1980).

based on the distribution of all subjects, and was then summed for each individual. The average score of malingerers was 358, with all other groups ranging from 279 to 283.

Although malingerers obtained the lowest scores on every WAIS subtest, they differed significantly from other groups only on Information, Comprehension, Arithmetic, Picture Completion, Verbal, and Full Scale scores. The authors speculated that nonsignificant differences were due to fakers (correctly) believing that schizophrenics would score worse on those subtests.

The Bender-Gestalt visual-motor test successfully discriminated between malingerers and other subjects. The criteria are shown in Table 16.5. The mean score for known malingerers was 39; the other groups ranged from 11.6 to 12.6.

The Sheehan 1967 form of the Betts test was used to successfully detect fakers. Bash and Alpert (1980) used this test on the assumption that fakers would exaggerate the intensity of their imagery. They also assumed that there should not be substantial differences in intensity across modalities for individual fakers. Using transformed scores based upon the original Sheehan distributions for normal subjects, the mean total score for fakers was 1888, with the other groups ranging from 1388 to 1583. Table 16.6 presents the Betts test items.

Table 16.5
Malingering Criteria on the Bender-Gestalt

Targets	Characteristics	Examples
1. Figures	Small and inhibited	Figures all in one corner of page
2. Performance	Uneven quality	Mature mixed with regressed drawings
3. Patterns	Remain unchanged	Squares do not become loops
4. Relationship/ direction of parts/ details	Remain unchanged	Diamond shape reproduced accurately
5. Symbols	Simplification	Line for series of dots
6. Complexity	Added	Triangle added to Figure A
7. Recall	Low number recalled	0 to 3 figures recalled

Table 16.6
Betts Test

Modality	Examples of requested imagery
1. Vision	Body image, manner of walking, color of clothing for a known person
2. Hearing	Whistle of a train
3. Touch	Feel of sand, linen, fur
4. Body movement	Running upstairs
5. Taste	Salt in mouth
6. Smell	Fresh paint, cooking cabbage, new leather
7. Body sensations	Hunger, fatigue, sore throat

Adapted from Bash and Alpert (1980). Vividness of items rated on following scale: 1 = perfectly clear; 2 = very clear; 3 = moderately clear; 4 = not clear, but recognizable; 5 = vague and dim; 6 = very vague and dim; 7 = no image present.

Table 16.7
Perceptual Characteristics Questionnaire (PCQ)
and Faked Hallucinations

1. Duration of hallucination (three years or more).
2. Aggressive and hostile messages.
3. Occur more than four times per day.
4. Visual hallucinations.
5. Nonvocal sounds in addition to voices.
6. Source localized outside of reporter.
7. More frequent with isolation.
8. More frequent with emotional arousal.
9. More frequent with decreased light.
10. Medication does not reduce frequency.

Adapted from Bash & Alpert (1980). Items scored +1 if present, zero if absent.

The Perceptual Characteristics Questionnaire (PCQ) (Table 16.7) was also utilized by Bash and Alpert (1980). Malingerers obtained a mean score of 900, compared to a mean score of 1161 for genuine schizophrenic hallucinators.

In sum, six of seven tests used by these investigators discriminated fakers from nonfakers (a structured clinical interview failed to discriminate between the two groups). As a general decision rule, subjects who scored in the range of malingering on at least three of the six (valid) tests could tentatively be classified as malingerers. Subjects were considered nonmalingerers if they scored in the range of malingering on less than three of the tests. A phi correlation of .8872 between diagnosis and performance on three or more tests was reported.

It should be noted that the battery used by Bash and Alpert (1980) has not been used in a cross-validation study and the criteria for malingering specified for the component tests of the battery have not been individually cross-validated. Consequently, these results should point the way to additional research rather than be adopted for immediate clinical use.

Schretlen, Wilkins, Van Gorp, and Bobholz (1992) developed and cross-validated a three-test battery on samples of prison inmates and alcoholic inpatients instructed to fake bad and samples of prison inmates, alcoholic inpatients, and psychiatric inpatients who took the tests under standard instructions. The three tests were the MMPI, a specially scored Bender-Gestalt and a specially developed Malingering Scale (Table 16.8). A discriminant function of three scores from these tests correctly classified 80% of the "fakers" with no false positive errors among their original subjects and 95% of the "fakers" with no false positive er-

---

[1] The discriminant equation was $(2.5 + (.06 \ast (\text{MMPI F}_{(\text{raw})} - \text{K}_{(\text{raw})}) - (.17 \ast (\text{VOCABULARY}_{(\text{Malingering Scale})}) + .11 \ast \text{Bender Gestalt score}))$. Scores greater than 1 have a 100% probability of faking, while scores less than 1 have a 92% probability of not faking.

Table 16.8
Malingering Scale

Name _____ Age _____

VOCABULARY

Circle the word that means the same thing as the word in CAPITAL letters.

Sample: LAW   book   rule
   1. PENNY   money   candy
   2. STEP   write   walk
   3. STREET   road   path
   4. SAUCER   spoon   dish
   5. COUCH   sofa   glass
   6. FABRIC   cloth   shirt
   7. ENORMOUS   huge   gentle
   8. FIDDLE   story   violin
   9. REMEMBER   recall   number
  10. EVIDENT   separate   obvious
  11. HAT   coat   cap
  12. DONKEY   dreadful   mule
  13. THIEF   robber   driver
  14. REPAIR   fix   rest
  15. TUMBLE   dress   fall
  16. FURIOUS   angry   noisy
  17. SHIP   jump   boat
  18. MANY   several   coins
  19. FRY   cook   eat
  20. APPLE   fruit   berry
  21. PARDON   divide   forgive
  22. IMMUNE   diseased   protected
  23. TALK   speak   sleep
  24. GAMBLE   join   bet
  25. DIAMOND   follow   jewel
  26. LIKE   new   same

(Continued on next page)

Table 16.8
Malingering Scale
(continued from previous page)

ABSTRACTION

Circle the answer that should go in the blank (_____) space.

1.	ABC _____	D	R
2.	1234 _____	5	4
3.	Scape Cape Ape _____	Ca	Pe
4.	North South East _____	Winter	West
5.	A AB ABC _____	DEF	ABCD
6.	56/65 24/42 73/ _____	37	10
7.	Mouth/Eat Eye/See Hand/_____	Smell	Touch
8.	AB AC AD _____	AE	BC
9.	Over/Under In/Out Above/_____	Below	Behind
10.	A1 B2 C3 _____	D4	E5
11.	White/Black Fast/Slow Up/_____	Side	Down
12.	Bus Car Ship _____	Truck	Table
13.	2 4 6 _____	5	8
14.	Red Blue Green _____	Yellow	Chair
15.	Monday Friday Sunday _____	March	Tuesday
16.	5 10 15 _____	50	20
17.	Candy/Bar In/Side Light/_____	Bulb	Ball
18.	Dog Bird Cat _____	Tree	Horse
19.	Bread Fruit Meat _____	Cheese	Fork
20.	* ** *** _____	****	*

(Continued on next page)

Table 16.8
Malingering Scale
(continued from previous page)

ARITHMETIC

1. How much is 6 divided by 2?
2. A woman has 2 pairs of shoes. How many shoes does she have alto-gether?
3. How much does 19 minus 5 equal?
4. How much is 50 cents plus 1 dollar?
5. If you have 3 books and give 1 away, how many will you have left?
6. How much does 1 plus 1 plus 3 equal?
7. If you have 19 dollars and spend 7 dollars and 50 cents, how much will you have left?
8. How much is 20 cents plus 5 cents?
9. How much does 6 divided by 3 equal?
10. A boy had 12 newspapers, and he sold 5 of them. How many did he have left?
11. How much is 4 dollars plus 5 dollars?
12. How much does 1 times 8 equal?
13. If I cut an apple in half, how many pieces will I have?
14. Raffle tickets cost 25 cents each. How much will 6 tickets cost?
15. How much does 3 times 9 equal?
16. If you buy 6 dollars worth of gasoline and pay for it with a 10 dollar bill, how much change should you get back?
17. How much does 7 plus 4 equal?
18. How many hours will it take for a person to walk 24 miles at the rate of 3 miles per hour?
19. A girl had 1 dollar in change. She lost 50 cents. How much did she have left?
20. How much does 10 minus 5 equal?

(Continued on next page)

```
┌─────────────────────────────────────────────────────────────────┐
│                         Table 16.8                               │
│                      Malingering Scale                           │
│                 (continued from previous page)                   │
├─────────────────────────────────────────────────────────────────┤
```

INFORMATION

1. What are the colors of the American flag?
2. How many months are there in a year?
3. How many things make a dozen?
4. What must you do to make water boil?
5. Who discovered America?
6. How many pennies make a nickel?
7. From what animal do we get bacon?
8. Why does oil float on water?
9. What is the capital of Italy?
10. What is a thermometer?
11. How many days make a week?
12. Where does the sun rise?
13. Name the two countries that border the United States.
14. Who wrote Hamlet?
15. Name the four seasons of the year.
16. Who invented the electric light bulb?
17. Name the month that comes next after March.
18. What does the stomach do?
19. What is the shape of a ball?
20. In what direction would you travel if you went from Chicago to Panama?
21. How many weeks are there in a year?
22. Who runs a courtroom?
23. Who was president of the United States during the Civil War?
24. How many legs does a dog have?

Vocabulary ____ Abstraction ____ Arithmetic ____ Information ____ Total ____
Score +1 for each correct answer on each of the four subtests.

rors among their cross-validation subjects.[1] These results were substantially higher than those obtained from any of the three tests used singly.

In an interesting application of explicit alternative testing (EAT); (*see* Chapter 6), Schretlen et al. (1992) used a two-alternative, forced-choice format for their Vocabulary and Abstraction subtests of their Malingering Scale. This permitted them to examine how many of their subjects scored significantly below chance based on the binomial distribution. Since scoring correctly on less than 18 of the 46 items on these two subtests would occur by chance with $p < .05$, they examined how many of their faking and nonfaking subjects scored below this cutoff. Twenty-six percent of the faking subjects scored below 18 and 100% of the nonfaking subjects scored above 18. Thus, this paper-and-pencil application of EAT showed results comparable to other applications of EAT: when a person performs below chance level, one can be confident that they are faking, but few genuine fakers do so.

PROJECTIVE TESTING AND DETECTION OF MALINGERING

The Rorschach test will be discussed only because faking on other projective tests has rarely been investigated systematically. In early studies, the Rorschach test was presented as an instrument that could not be faked at all (Fosberg, 1938, 1941). Features of this test supposedly lent themselves to detection of malingering (Benton, 1945). Later studies showed that the Rorschach could be faked partially (Carp & Shavzin, 1950; Easton & Feigenbaum, 1967). Belief in the Rorschach's supposed resistance to faking persists today (Exner, 1978; M. Ackland, personal communication, 1990), in spite of studies showing the inability of experts to detect malingering on this test.

One such investigation found that Fellows of the Society for Personality Assessment, supposedly representing high competency in Rorschach assessment, were unable to detect malingering of psychosis by normal subjects who were not sophisticated about psychosis (Albert, Fox, & Kahn, 1980). The confidence expressed by these experts in their judgments did not differ between faked and nonfaked protocols. Each protocol was (blindly) judged by six to nine experts. In general, very little malingering was detected, even when malingering was explicitly presented to the judges as an alternative.

In this often-cited study, the ability to fake psychosis was directly related to the information subjects possessed about this mental condition. More psychotic disturbance was shown by fakers to whom a taped description of schizophrenia was presented. These subjects were not, however, told how to fake on the Rorschach.

A rather disturbing finding involved false positives and false negatives from the two control groups not concerned with faking. Twenty-four percent of the normals were seen as psychotic and only 48% of the psychotics were correctly identified. These results suggest that use of expert judgments of Rorschach protocols is of dubious value not only in detecting malingering, but also in distinguishing normal from psychotic protocols.

Mittman (1983) essentially replicated these findings when 60 clinicians were generally unable to detect faked schizophrenia on the Rorschach. The clinicians did detect uninformed more often than informed fakers, but only a small percentage of the protocols were diagnosed as malingered, in spite of the judges possessing formally scored and summarized protocols.

The lack of specific criteria for malingering on the Rorschach continues to plague this test (Perry & Kinder, 1990). Experienced clinicians persist in their false belief that they can detect faking on the Rorschach even when they do not utilize objective, shareable, teachable criteria. To overcome this problem, M. Bennett, personal communication, (1988) stated the following in regard to the Exner scoring system and malingering:

> Schizophrenics who are attempting to simulate nonschizophrenia are generally not able to produce records that would be judged as "normal." You would still want to analyze the patient's level of cooperation and test-taking attitude, the number of popular responses, the X + %, the X - %, and the special scores. The uninformed schizophrenic would have a difficult time not producing special scores such as malignant FABCOMs or CONTAMs, which would indicate the presence of disordered thinking.
>
> Conversely, most nonschizophrenic patients cannot produce a schizophrenic record, but there are exceptions.
>
> Analysis of the same variables of test-taking approach, X + %, X - %, and the special scores will show better reality testing, better form quality, and fewer malignant special scores in a record that "appears" bizarre and detached from the inkblot stimulus. Very long responses and overelaboration are suggestive of deception. Average response is 15 words, and if the patient responds with about 35 words or more per response, this is often a sign of malingering.

In spite of the lack of a rationale for these criteria, they are at least explicit and testable in properly designed studies.

Seamons, Howell, Carlisle, and Roe (1981) used the Exner system to judge protocols of 48 subjects (36 schizophrenics) who were asked to take the Rorschach twice—assuming first that they were mentally ill and then as normal individuals. This study clearly showed that the instructions affected the content of responses, but not ratios, percentages, or deviations. More dramatic and bizarre responses were associated with faking, particularly those involving sex, blood, mutilation, and fighting. Seamons et al. stated:

> Caution should be exercised by the clinician when response simulation is suspected in a forensic or prison population.
>
> For example, if the protocol contains an excessively high number of popular responses, the subject may be attempting to "fake" normal. On the other hand, when X+%, F+%, and L variables are within the normal range, and a high number of dramatic, blood, texture, shading, vista, nonhuman movement, or inappropriate combination responses are observed, it may be indicative of an attempt to appear mentally ill. Finally, it should be noted that the different diagnostic groups accounted for many more significant findings than did the varied instructions, reaffirming the discriminative ability of the Rorschach irrespective of instructions.

The simulation of psychosis was also detected on a multiple choice group Rorschach (Pettigrew, Tuma, Pickering, & Whelton, 1983). In this study of 75 students and 50 schizophrenics who selected one of four choices to each of the (miniature) Rorschach inkblots, the 62 student-fakers chose responses with significantly more good form with bizarre wording than did the schizophrenics. Thus, fakers were exposed by their own perceptual accuracy.

In spite of the limitations of the Rorschach test in assessment of malingering of psychosis, several criteria are worth further investigation (Stermac, 1988). Good form with dramatic/bizarre wording or dramatic content by itself may indicate faking bad. For faking good, Stermac (1988) suggested that no good Rorschach indicators have been presented.

SYNTHESIS

Available research suggests that the following may indicate manufactured or exaggerated psychosis:

1. Production of psychotic symptoms is apparently under voluntary control and is understandable in terms of payoff and environmental circumstances.
2. Psychotic symptoms worsen when being observed or when being interviewed, are bizarre for the circumstances, involve quick shifts to nonpsychotic behavior when not being observed, or symptoms cease under mild environmental stimulation.
3. Patient has a history of faked mental problems.
4. Patient admits to faking psychosis and his or her behavior can be explained in terms of environmental events.
5. Patient uses an alias, is unwilling to allow access to old records, displays evidence of a severe personality disorder, has a history of substance abuse, to include possession of paraphernalia, etc., which explain psychotic symptoms.
6. Laboratory testing suggests malingering (e.g., as in factitious disorders).
7. Psychological tests suggest deception in regard to psychosis.
8. Patient has rapid remission of symptoms.
9. Crime is associated with accomplices; crime fits into history of defendant's criminality; defendant has nonpsychotic motives for the crime.

REFERENCES

Albert, S., Fox, H. M., & Kahn, M. W. (1980). Faking psychosis on a Rorschach: Can expert judges detect malingering? *Journal of Personality Assessment, 44*, 115-119.

Bash, I. (1978). *Malingering: A study designed to differentiate between schizophrenic offenders and malingerers.* Unpublished doctoral dissertation. New York University, New York.

Bash, I., & Alpert, M. (1980). The determination of malingering. *Annals of the New York Academy of Science, 347*, 86-98.

Beaber, R., Marston, A., Michelli, J., & Mills, M. (1985). A brief test for measuring malingering in schizophrenic individuals. *American Journal of Psychiatry, 142*, 1478-1481.

Bender, L. (1938). *A visual motor Gestalt Test and its clinical use.* New York: The Orthopsychiatric Association.

Bennett, M. (1988). Personal communication.

Benton, A. L. (1945). Rorschach performances of suspected malingerers. *The Journal of Abnormal and Social Psychology, 40*, 94-96.

Berry, D., Baer, R., & Harris, M. (1991). Detection of malingering on the MMPI: A meta-analysis. *Clinical Psychology Review, 11*, 585-598.

Braginsky, B. M., & Braginsky, D. D. (1967). Schizophrenic patients in the psychiatric interview: An experimental study of their effectiveness at manipulation. *Journal of Consulting Psychology, 31*, 543-547.

Butcher, J. N. (1990). *User's guide to the Minnesota clinical interpretive report for MMPI-2.* Minneapolis, MN: University of Minnesota Press.

Carp, A. L., & Shavzin, A. R. (1950). The susceptibility to falsification of the Rorschach psychodiagnostic technique. *Journal of Consulting Psychology, 14*, 230-233.

Diamond, B. (1956). The simulation of insanity. *Journal of Social Therapy, 2*, 158-165.

Easton, K., & Feigenbaum, K. (1967). An examination of an experimental set to fake the Rorschach test. *Perceptual and Motor Skills, 24*, 871-874.

Endicott, J., & Spitzer, R. L. (1978). A diagnostic interview: The schedule of affective disorders and schizophrenia. *Archives of General Psychiatry, 35*, 837-844.

Exner, J. E. (1978). *The Rorschach: A comprehensive system. Vol. II: Current research and advanced interpretation.* New York: John Wiley & Sons.

Fosberg, I. A. (1938). Rorschach reactions under varied instructions. *Rorschach Research Exchange, 3*, 12-30.

Fosberg, I. A. (1941). An experimental study of the reliability of the Rorschach psychodiagnostic technique. *Rorschach Research Exchange, 5*, 72-84.

Gillis, J., Rogers, R., & Bagby, R. (1992). Validity of the M test: simulation design and natural group approaches. *Journal of Personality Assessment, 57*(1), 130-140.

Hollender, M. H., & Hirsch, S. J. (1964). Hysterical psychosis. *The American Journal of Psychiatry, 120*, 1066-1074.

Mittman, B. L. (1983). Judges' ability to diagnose schizophrenia on the Rorschach: The effect of malingering. *Dissertation Abstracts International, 44*(4), 2148-B.

Perry, G., & Kinder, B. (1990). The susceptibility of the Rorschach to malingering: A critical review. *Journal of Personality Assessment, 54*, 1-2, 47-57.

Pettigrew, C. G., Tuma, J. M., Pickering, J. W., & Whelton, J. (1983). Simulation of psychosis on a multiple-choice projective test. *Perceptual and Motor Skills, 57*, 463-469.

Pope, H. G., Jonas, J. M., & Jones, B. (1982). Factitious psychosis: Phenomenology, family history, and long-term outcome of nine patients. *The American Journal of Psychiatry, 139*(11), 1480-1483.

Resnick, P. J. (1984). The detection of malingered mental illness. *Behavioral Sciences and the Law, 2*(1), 21-38.

Resnick, P. J. (1988). Malingering of posttraumatic disorders. In R. Rogers (Ed.), *Clinical assessment of malingering and deception* (pp. 84-103). New York: The Guilford Press.

Ritson, B., & Forrest, A. (1970). The simulation of psychosis: A contemporary presentation. *British Journal of Medical Psychology, 43*, 31-37.

Rogers, R. (1984). Towards an empirical model of malingering and deception. *Behavioral Sciences and the Law, 2*, 93-112.

Rogers, R. (1986). *Structured interview of reported symptoms (SIRS).* Toronto: Clark Institute of Psychiatry. Unpublished scale.

Rogers, R. (Ed.) (1988). *Clinical assessment of malingering and deception.* New York: The Guilford Press.

Rogers, R., Bagby, M., & Gillis, R. (1992). Improvements in the M test as a screening measure for malingering. *Bulletin of the American Academy Psychiatry and Law, 20*(1), 101-104.

Seamons, D. T., Howell, R. J., Carlisle, A. L., & Roe, A. V. (1981). Rorschach simulation of mental illness and normality by psychotic and nonpsychotic legal offenders. *Journal of Personality Assessment, 45*, 130-135.

Schretlen, D. (1988). The use of psychological tests to identify malingered symptoms of mental disorder. *Clinical Psychology Review, 8*(5), 451-476.

Shretlen, D., Wilkins, S., Van Gorp, W., & Bobholz, J. (1992). Cross-validation of a psychological test battery to detect faked insanity. *Psychological Assessment, 4*(1), 77-83.

Shooter, E., & Hall, H. V. (1989). Distortion analysis on the MMPI and MMPI-2. *Bulletin of the American Academy of Forensic Psychology, 10*, 9.

Smith, G. (1990). *Detection of malingering of schizophrenia in male prisoners.* Unpublished paper, University of Missouri at St. Louis (cited in Rogers, Bagby, & Gillis (1992), op.cit.)

Spitzer, R. L., & Endicott, J. (1978). *Schedule of affective disorders and schizophrenia.* New York: Biometric Research.

Stermac, L. (1988). Projective testing and dissimulation. In R. Rogers (Ed.), *Clinical assessment of malingering and deception.* New York: Guilford Press.

17

Hallucinations and Deception

This chapter suggests three basic methods for assessing misrepresentation in regard to faked hallucinations. These involve assessing (a) violation of base-rate expectancies, (b) degree of complex and self-controlled behavior shown by the client, and (c) the details of hallucinatory experiences via a structured questionnaire.

The Ubiquity of Hallucinatory Experiences

Hallucinations are typically defined as false sensory impressions. The "false" part of this definition refers to the lack of an external set of referents which, to the assessor, would explain and support the assessee's description of the event. Dreaming is considered by some to be a common example of a hallucinatory experience, surrounded at the onset of sleep in some people by hypnogogic hallucinations and waking up with hypnopompic hallucinations (Kaplan & Sadock, 1985; American Psychiatric Association, APA, 1987).

Approximately 12% of the normal population has experienced hallucinations while awake (Parish, 1914; Coleman, 1984). In nonpsychiatric populations, hallucinations have been known to be caused by (a) exhaustion, as in the last stage of the General Adaptation Syndrome (Selye, 1980-1983); (b) sleep deprivation; (c) social isolation, as in the "long eye" syndrome caused by rejection by working peers (Coleman et al., 1984); (d) severe reactive depression; (e) amputation of limbs, as in the phantom limb experience; (f) heart conditions, secondary to cardiovascular medication or to atropine or its derivatives in hypersensitive persons (Kaplan & Sadock, 1985); and (g) secondary to intoxication by the hallucinogenics, particularly LSD, mescaline, psilocybin, and other drugs such as morphine, heroin, and cocaine.

In the organic brain syndromes, hallucinations may be caused by a variety of events (see reviews by Lezak, 1983; Strub & Black, 1981) including (a) delirium, (b) tumors associated with increasing intracranial pressure, (c) temporal lobe lesions, (d) seizures of several types, (e) alcohol-related encephalopathy, (f) head injury, as in postcoma experiences and disorientation, and (g) irritation of various sensory pathways, such as the visual pathways transversing the temporal lobes causing Lilliputian hallucinations, or the olfactory pathways causing distinctive odors such as burnt rubber.

Not all organic brain-induced hallucinations involve the perception of a separate reality. In organic hallucinosis, for example, the (usually auditory) hallucinations may arise within a full state of alertness and orientation. In Lilliputian hallucinations, the affected person knows the small figures are not real; they are not associated with delusions.

The major psychotic disorders are often associated with hallucinations (APA, 1987). Vivid hallucinations can be seen in all the schizophrenic subtypes. Within the affective disorders, hallucinations are encountered. In major depression, for example, the examiner using DSM-IV is asked to determine whether or not reported hallucinations are mood congruent or mood incongruent. Schizoaffective psychosis, a combination of thought disorder and affective psychosis, often has hallucinations as an associated feature.

Early work suggesting that different mental conditions involve different types of hallucinations is illustrated by Alpert and Silvers (1970). Eighty adult hallucinating inpatients who were either alcoholics or schizophrenics were studied. Table 17.1 reveals the differences in hallucinations between the two groups.

Table 17.1 Auditory Hallucinations in Schizophrenia and Acute Alcoholic Psychoses		
	Alcoholics	Schizophrenics
Onset of illness	Early	Later
Temporality	Continuous or frequent	Episodic, separated by hours, days, or weeks
Type of sound	Nonverbal noises or unintelligible voices	Voices, usually clear
Source	Outside body	Within body
Effect of patterned visual stimulation	Decrease in frequency	No change in frequency
Effect of arousal	Increase in frequency	No change in frequency
Willingness to discuss hallucinations	Eager	Withdrawal response
Insight	Better	Worse
Delusions	Less frequent	More frequent

From Alpert and Silvers (1970)

The experience of hallucinations is so common that some believe that an endogenous hallucinogen will be found; that is, a chemical synthesized within the body due to stress, which in turn creates an hallucination. Hallucinations may represent an attempt to restructure reality or at least to perceive the stress in a more adaptive fashion.

As a further common feature, most hallucinations can be set off by multiple or indirect combining conditions. Tactile (haptic) hallucinations can be secondary to schizophrenia, withdrawal from alcohol, or drug intoxication. Olfactory hallucinations, the false perception of smell, and gustatory hallucinations, the false perception of taste, are often experienced together in such conditions as temporal lobe epilepsy and schizophrenia. Reflex hallucinations involve irritation in one sense creating an hallucination in another, for example, a toothache setting off an auditory hallucination in a schizophrenic. Lastly, kinesthetic hallucinations involve the sensation of altered states in body organs where no receptor apparatus could explain the experience. This is found in psychotic patients but also among organic patients (e.g., a burning sensation in the brain caused by schizophrenia or a major depression with psychotic features).

In sum, hallucinations are found in a wide variety of unimpaired and impaired individuals. Evaluators of possible deception are thus cautioned to consider hallucinations separately from psychosis. Linking hallucinations to one or two mental conditions neglects the ubiquity of the phenomenon.

TARGETS

Any sensory system can be targeted for hallucinations. These include the chemical sensory (i.e., smell, taste), mechanical (i.e., touch, hearing, vestibular—head movement and orientation, joint-position and movement, muscle), photic (i.e., seeing), and thermal (i.e., cold and warmth) systems.

The faker may choose a hallucination for a certain time and circumstance (e.g., previous to, during, or after a crime; at the time of an evaluation). Targets may be chosen with distinctive qualities in terms of duration, intensity, form, and frequency. Some aspects are particularly difficult to fake without prior experience or knowledge of hallucinations. These include one's expected response to bona fide hallucinations, the "origin" of the hallucinations, and the normal sequence of prodromal and residual symptoms. The faker often finds himself or herself in a position of having to generate information when questioned and of hoping to maintain consistency. Targets are chosen in the service of a long-range goal, such as exculpation or mitigation in a criminal proceeding.

Hallucinations falsely superimposed on mental disorders such as schizophrenia are most difficult to detect. When a person has a history of genuine hallucinations, but fabricates one for the relevant situation, it is difficult to detect. The best lie is the partial truth, and this applies to faked hallucinations as well.

The evaluator should keep in mind that some distortion in falsely describing hallucinations may be nondeliberate. Junginger and Frame (1985) reported a negative relationship between clarity and location. Hallucinations most clearly heard originated inside the head, yet a bimodal distribution was seen in ascribing origination of voices.

RESPONSE STYLES

Various forms of distorting hallucinations are seen as follows:

Style	Example
Responding Honesty	An organic shares his or her hallucinations with accuracy
Faking Good	A schizophrenic denies hallucinations (e.g., to get out of hospital)
Faking Bad	A psychopath makes up hallucinations to avoid imprisonment
Invalidating	No conclusions can be drawn; the faker may have unsuccessfully attempted to fake good or bad
Mixed Responding	Admits to hallucinations but denies schizophrenia.
Fluctuating	Admits to hallucinations and then changes story as vested interests change when re-evaluated

DETECTION METHODS

THE BASE RATE APPROACH

The use of base rate information to detect feigned hallucinations is discussed by Resnick (1984, 1988) and involves the assumption that fakers may not be aware of the true nature and quality of hallucinations. For example, they may not know that hallucinations are usually (a) related to some psychic purpose; (b) associated with delusions; (c) eliminated or reduced when the individual is involved in activity; (d) perceived as emanating from outside the head—many schizophrenics affirm that the voices could have been due to their imagination; (e) female and/or male voices with clear and not vague messages. Talking back to voices and perceiving the voices as accusatory occur a minority of the time; schizophrenics usually perceive voices speaking directly to them; (f) with no prodromata; (g) perceived as unpleasant in odor (olfactory hallucinations); (h) of normal-size people and are in color; (i) seen in acute schizophrenia by an onset of peculiar tastes (gustatory hallucinations); and (j) composed of vivid figures often discussing the person in the third person (alcoholism). The alcoholic's actions are rarely the result of command hallucinations and seem motivated by a desire to avoid threat or disgrace.

A base-rate approach is suggested from Resnick's work and his review of the literature. He cogently states: "Detailed knowledge about actual hallucinations is the clinician's greatest asset in recognizing simulated hallucinations" (1988, p. 37). This material is presented in Table 17.2.

Thus, characteristics of reported hallucinations are compared to their overall base-rate percentage. Rare responses would thus be the focus of detailed probing by the evaluator, all within a comprehensive assessment to determine possible deception.

Table 17.2
Base Rates of Hallucinations

		Percentage
1.	Overall incidence of psychotic and acute schizophrenia	76%
2.	Auditory in schizophrenia	66%
3.	Visual in psychotics	27%
4.	Associated with delusions	88%
5.	"Yes" to "Could voices have been due to your imagination?" [schizophrenia]	56%
6.	Both male and female voices	75%
7.	Vague voices heard	7%
8.	Voices are accusatory	33%
9a.	Originated outside head (all psychotics and schizophrenics)	88%
9b.	Originated outside head (schizophrenics only)	50%
10.	Talking back to voices	45%
11a.	Voices associated with commands (all patients)	38%
11b.	Voices associated with commands (schizophrenics only)	47%
12.	Overall incidence in hospital alcoholics (75% auditory; 70% visual)	84%
13a.	Command hallucinations in alcoholics	35%
13b.	Command hallucinations in affective disorders	46%
14.	Content of command hallucinations (all patients)	
	a. Suicide	52%
	b. Nonlethal injury	12%
	c. Nonviolent acts	14%
	d. Unspecified	17%

Adapted from Resnick (1988).

Much is owed to Resnick for his base-rate approach. He suggests a "Threshold Model" in regard to whether faking psychotic hallucinations may have occurred (1988). Faking hallucinations is suspected if any of the following occur:

1. Continuous rather than intermittent hallucinations
2. Vague or inaudible hallucinations
3. Hallucinations not associated with delusions
4. Stilted language reported in hallucinations
5. Inability to state strategies to diminish voices
6. Self-report that all command hallucinations were obeyed (p.47)

The last item (#6) is especially helpful to evaluators because, as Resnick (1988) points out, command hallucinations are often ignored. Further, they can be actively made to temporarily disappear altogether by interpersonal contact, motor activity (e.g., working, exercising), taking psychotropic medication, and even passive activities such as watching TV and lying down.

Some caution is needed with Resnick's approach, however. Hallucinations can occur in the absence of delusions, particularly in organic states and substance intoxication (#3). Stilted language is occasionally used to describe actual hallucinations (#4), especially if there is psychotic recall of the hallucinations and the person is reporting a nonverbal event with familiar verbal labels. Likewise, the inability to state strategies to diminish voices (#5) may be a function of the severity of a mental condition, poor verbal skills, or resistance towards the evaluation.

Congruent with Resnick's (1988) findings, instructions to aggress within a hallucinatory experience probably do not contribute to dangerousness (Hellerstein, Frosch, & Koenigsberg, 1987). Contrary to clinical lore, these investigators' study of 789 sequentially admitted inpatients showed no significant differences between patients with command hallucinations and patients without command hallucinations on such variables as assaultiveness, suicidal behavior (or ideation), time in seclusion, use of restraints, and length of hospitalization.

In this important study, Hellerstein et al. (1987) found that about 19% of the patients reported auditory hallucinations with about 7% of the total sample (58 of 789 patients) experiencing command auditory hallucinations. About 38% of the patients with hallucinations experienced such commands.

Interestingly, in all cases of Borderline Personality Disorder, command hallucinations were experienced. Of the schizophrenic subjects, those with command hallucinations (N = 29) had significantly shorter (less than 15-day) hospitalizations than those with noncommand hallucinations. Hellerstein et al. (1987) opine that command hallucinations may be a risk factor only when superimposed upon a previous history of violence. This last point is dangerousness supported by the literature (e.g., Hall, 1987).

COMPLEX BEHAVIOR AND HALLUCINATIONS

A clear distinction should be made between alleged hallucinations at the time of the evaluation versus some other relevant time (e.g., the instant offense). Hallucinations can bear upon competency to proceed if they adversely affect (a) the ability to cooperate with one's attorney, (b) knowing the nature and quality of the legal proceedings, and (c) knowing the possible punitive consequences to oneself. The faker may portray incompetence by presenting hallucinations for the time of evaluation. Feigning hallucinations for the past is more congruent with attempting to escape criminal responsibility rather than with incompetency.

Genuine hallucinations in the present do not imply that previously reported hallucinations were genuine. The two time periods (e.g., offense, evaluation) must be considered separately. One can fake for the present and still have had genuine hallucinations at the time of the alleged crime. Perhaps the accused (now stabilized and not experiencing hallucinations) feels the need to remain consistent with previous behaviors. In sum, both current and previous time periods can involve fake or genuine hallucinations.

For criminal responsibility, the most relevant period is in the past. Questions to be asked for past events include the following:

A. According to the victim or witnesses, did the accused
   1. state that he or she was experiencing hallucinations?
   2. act in a manner congruent with hallucinations (e.g., turn in direction of "voices," continually scratch his or her skin for tactile hallucinations, stare at one spot)?
B. Did the accused exhibit purposeful and self-controlled motor behavior?

Complex, effective, self-controlled performance is antithetical to disorganized behavior typically caused by hallucinations.

Occurring during the violence sequence, effective performance reflects the notion that the accused may simultaneously observe and change his or her behavior in response to a fluctuating environment, all in accordance with the goal or desired object of the action sequence. Hypothesis testing is the highest form of effective performance, as when the accused changes his or her own behavior (e.g., threatens victim, puts key in lock) in order to see the reaction (e.g., victim acquiescence, door becomes unlocked) and then changes his or her own behavior accordingly (e.g., proceeds to rape victim, goes through door to bedroom). In essence, this skill taps the ability to show a concordance between intentions/plans and actions.

Some of these complex behaviors and abilities suggest that hallucinations were not operative:

1. Demonstrates a variety of acts (flexible behavior such as using several weapons)
2. Displays multiple sets of simultaneous motor behaviors
3. Orchestrates multistep, multitask scheme (e.g., long-connected chains of behaviors)
4. Shows change in principle (e.g., from robbery to rape)
5. Shows self-controlled somatic responses (e.g., sex with ejaculation, eating, drinking; all within violence sequence)
6. Delays responses
7. Monitors and self-correct ongoing behavior
8. Shows hypothesis testing, as illustrated above
9. Shows awareness of wrongdoing during violence (e.g., from statements to victim)
10. Stops violence (e.g., response cessation with no perseveration)
11. Shows ability to regulate tempo, intensity, and duration of behaviors
12. Demonstrates systematic obliteration or destruction of evidence during instant violence

In sum, the evaluator determines whether there was a rational motive to the crime, (e.g., planning or rehearsal); self-controlled, effective behavior; or attempts to hide or minimize the offense. If so, hallucinations may be absent, low in intensity, or irrelevant to the analysis of criminal responsibility.

CHECKLIST SPECIFICALLY FOR HALLUCINATIONS

The evaluator may want to probe particular aspects of hallucinations. The checklist, presented in Appendix C may be administered (a) at several points in time to assess consistency of the client's response; (b) for a particular time (e.g., before the crime, after it occurred); (c) to significant/knowledgeable others to complete about the accused, returning it directly to the evaluator. Significant/knowledgeable others may also fill it out for different times; and (d) in both verbal and written form, as some persons affirm in writing what they will not orally, and vice versa.

The evaluator must review the answers with the assessee to insure accuracy and completeness. The assessee may be confronted with contradictions and inconsistencies, which then become part of the database material (*see* Chapter 3 for confrontation methods).

SIGNS OF FAKED HALLUCINATIONS

1. The person admits to faking or is inconsistent in symptom presentation, along with confirming evidence (e.g., *see* Checklist of Sensory Experiences in Appendix C).
2. The hallucination cannot be explained by any known condition or event, along with the ability of the examiner to show faking in testing or observation.
3. Knowledgeable/significant others or the evaluator report complex, purposeful behavior while the accused is allegedly subject to hallucinations.
4. Alleged command hallucinations occurred when behavior can be explained by secondary gain or an identifiable goal.

REFERENCES

Alpert, M., & Silvers, K. (1970). Perceptual characteristics distinguishing auditory hallucinations in schizophrenia and acute alcoholic psychoses. *American Journal of Psychiatry, 127,* 298-302.

American Psychiatric Association. (1987). *Diagnostic and statistical manual* (3rd ed., rev.). Washington, DC: Author.

Coleman, J., Butcher, J., & Carson, R. (1984). *Abnormal psychology and modern life* (7th ed.). Glenview, IL: Scott, Foresman & Co.

Hall, H. V. (1987). *Violence prediction: Guidelines for the forensic professional.* Springfield, IL: Charles C. Thomas.

Hellerstein, D., Frosch, W., & Koenigsberg, H. (1987). The clinical significance of command hallucinations. *American Journal of Psychiatry, 144,* 219-221.

Junginger, J., & Frame, C. (1985). Self-report of the frequency and phenomenology of verbal hallucinations. *Journal of Nervous and Mental Diseases, 173,* 149-155.

Kaplan, H., & Sadock, B. (1985). *Comprehensive textbook of psychiatry* (4th ed.). Baltimore: Williams & Wilkins.

Lezak, M. (1983). *Neuropsychological assessment* (2nd ed.). New York: Oxford Press.

Parish, E. (1914). *Hallucinations and illusions.* London: Walter Scott.

Resnick, P. (1984). The detection of malingered mental illness. *Behavioral Sciences and the Law, 2,* 21-38.

Resnick, P. (1988). Malingered psychosis. In R. Rogers (Ed.), *Clinical assessment of malingering and deception* (pp.34-53). New York: Guilford Press.

Selye, H. (Ed.). (1980-1983). *Selye's guide to stress research* (Vols. 1-3). New York: Van Nostrand Reinhold.

Strub, R., & Black, F. (1981). *Organic brain syndromes.* Philadelphia, PA: F. A. Davis Company.

18

DENYING SUBSTANCE ABUSE

A vast literature exists on the causes, associated features, and effects of substance intoxication, abuse, and dependence (e.g., see Armor, Polich, & Stanbul, 1976; Bailey, 1961; Bean, 1981; Blane, 1968; Jellinek, 1952, 1980; Mulhaney & Trippett, 1979; Nace, 1982, 1987).

In spite of its deleterious medical and psychological effects, incapacitating self-induced ethanol or drug intoxication at the time of an alleged criminal act is not considered a valid argument for claiming an impairment. Mitigation can be claimed if substance intoxication removed the criminal intent—mens rea—necessary for the offense to have occurred. Information relevant to substance abuse that is to a defendant's advantage can also be presented in regard to sentencing options or dangerousness. The argument is usually that previous violence was a function of substance dependence, a medical condition that is not the entire fault of the defendant. If the substance abuse is controlled through treatment, the argument goes, the future risk of violence is reduced. Prosecutors aim to show that substance use was an independent phenomenon or even operated to make the crime easier, as in building up false courage or lowering the fear to commit burglary, robbery, or rape. In most criminal settings, however, denial of substance use is typical. The defendant may wish to avoid the appearance that the instant offense was contributed to by substance use.

Within the civil arena, the existence of substance use by plaintiff or defendant may affect whether damages are awarded and, if so, how much. Denial is very common by both parties. In most cases, the faker attempts to simulate a nonintoxicated state, or hide symptoms, for some relevant time. A history of substance addiction is typically kept from view.

TARGETS

The DSM-IV diagnostic criteria for substance intoxication are known by the lay community. Drug and alcohol intoxication is commonly understood to be characterized as (a) a recent ingestion of a particular substance; (b) maladaptive behavioral changes, such as poor judgment, labile behavior, or physical or sexual aggression, without which it would not matter from a legal viewpoint whether the person was intoxicated, and (c) critical physical and psychological signs which will vary according to the substance.

The deceiver may try to hide these symptoms in an attempt to foil an investigation (e.g., field testing, urinalysis). Typically, noncooperation with police when alcohol intoxication takes the form of belligerence and aggressiveness. The range of reactions with drugs other than alcohol is wide, ranging from aggressiveness to almost catatonic immobility.

The person who has a vested interest in denying or minimizing substance use may selectively hide symptoms. Symptoms chosen for denial depend on the faker's understanding as to what constitutes a substance problem. Any of the following for Psychoactive Substance Dependence, Polysubstance Dependence, (American Psychiatric Association, APA, 1994), or Psychoactive Substance Dependence NOS may be targeted for denial:

1. Substances ingested in larger amounts or over a longer period than the person intended
2. At least one unsuccessful effort to cut down or control substance use, or continuing desire to quit
3. Much time devoted to procuring, actually ingesting the substance (e.g., frequent smoking of "ice"), or recovering from the substance
4. Interference with work, school, or home obligations when intoxicated or in withdrawal, or when intoxication is imminently dangerous (e.g., while driving)
5. Substance use leading to decreased involvement in work, play, or social activities
6. Continued use with awareness of a medical or other problem that is created because of it (e.g., alcohol use with cirrhosis, "ice" use with heart problems)
7. Substantial tolerance with at least a 50 percent increase to attain the same high, or a decrease in positive effects as experienced by the individual over time
8. Withdrawal symptoms with discontinued use
9. Withdrawal symptoms are avoided on purpose by reuse of substance.

RESPONSE PATTERNS

Faking good is the dominant response style. Exaggeration of substance use occurs in some cases. Mixed styles are fairly common—the faker may deny substance use for drugs but admit to depression, marital problems, and alcohol use. Usually the substance abuse is justified by blaming outside problems or other people.

Fluctuating response styles are also seen. The faker may deny substance use problems during a criminal trial to reduce culpability, but admit or even exaggerate the problems to obtain a sentence to a community treatment setting rather than prison.

DETECTION METHODS

The traditional method for establishing substance use involves the gathering of cross-validating material. This involves a search for substance-related behaviors and events from significant others, neighbors, bartenders, friends, and family. Supporting material should be collected if available (e.g., DUI arrest reports, mental health treatment records). The evaluator should always review the material before questioning the person. The alternative is to conduct a second session to ask pinpoint questions about the civil or criminal event.

Critical events which should raise the suspicion that alcohol (or other substance) abuse has occurred are reported by Nace (1987) and Paolino and McCrady (1977):

1. *Any person with a history of substance abuse.*
2. *Referrals from corporations or industry secondary to job-related problems.* Nace (1987) cites base rates which suggest that about one-half of job-related problems are alcohol related. Drugs are often interchangeable with alcohol, as some abusers seek different intoxicants after alcoholism has been identified as a problem.
3. *Hospital and emergency room consultations.* The high rate of substance abuse in hospital populations is well known. Nace (1987) states that about 40% of the persons in emergency rooms in urban settings have recent detectable alcohol use, and this is in a setting which generally underdiagnoses substance use.
4. *DUI or DWI history.* Scrutinizing the actual police reports will often reveal more information relevant to the pattern of abuse.
5. *Persons with a history of divorce, especially multiple divorces.* Substance abuse generally deteriorates social relationships of all sorts. Separation and divorce occur seven times more frequently among alcoholics than normals (Paolino & McCrady, 1977).
6. *Persons who express even minimal concern that they may be substance abusers.* In light of the pervasive problem of denial, any admission of substance use should be the springboard for further inquiry.

Chronic alcoholic behaviors can serve as signals (Jellinek, 1952, 1980). The more easily verified ones include (a) frequently drinking alcohol, (b) multiple benders, (c) loss of tolerance, (d) tremors, (e) psychomotor inhibition, (f) verbally admitting defeat, (g) impairment of cognition, (h) alcoholic psychosis, and (i) continual drinking after a medical problem has been identified.

Laboratory methods and results can be utilized to indicate substance intoxication. Blood, breath, and urine analysis have long been used to detect substances in the body, despite controversy on their efficacy and intrusiveness. Generally, the tests have high accuracy rates and are carefully controlled. Urine specimens are typically evaluated, for example, by booking facilities in American cities as follows (O'Neil, Wish, & Visher, 1990):

> Urine specimens are analyzed by EMIT for 10 drugs: cocaine, opiates, marijuana, PCP, methadone, benzodiazepine (Valium), methaqualone, propoxyphene (Darvon), barbiturates, and amphetamines. Positive results for amphetamines are confirmed by gas chromatography to eliminate positives that may be caused by over-the-counter drugs. For most drugs, the urine test can detect use in the prior 2 to 3 days. Exceptions are marijuana and PCP, which can sometimes be detected several weeks after use. (p. 2)

BASE-RATE APPROACH

One means to assess denial is to compare self-reports to the results of urinalysis. The National Institute of Justice (see O'Neil, et al., 1990) has done exactly that for many metropolitan areas (see table 18.1). They confirmed and extended the results of an earlier study in Washington, DC, and New York in 1984 where self-reports were generally found to have underestimated recent drug use by about one-half.

Table 18.1
Drug Use by Self-report and Urinalysis

1. More than 70% of the male and female arrestees in San Diego, New York, Philadelphia, and Washington, DC, tested positive for one or more drugs. San Antonio and Indianapolis had the lowest rates of drug use.
2. More arrestees tested positive for multiple drug use in San Diego than any other city. Arrestees there tended to use cocaine, marijuana, and methamphetamines.
3. PCP is found in about one-quarter of arrestees in Washington, DC. The only other city where PCP is prevalent is St. Louis, where 20% of females arrestees tested positive for the drug.
4. The highest rates of cocaine use—above 60%—were found in Washington, DC, New York, and Philadelphia.
5. There is no evidence of an increase in heroin use in male arrestees. In every city, opiates were found in fewer than 20% of tested males. Opiates were more common in females, especially in Washington, DC, Portland, Oregon, and San Antonio.

National Institute of Justice data (O'Neil, Wish, & Visher, 1990).

Further findings from O'Neil, et al. (1990) included the following:

1. Drug use from arrestee self-report as compared to urinaly-
    sis was underreported and different for particular drugs—
    marijuana, cocaine, and opiates.
2. The differences between self-report and urinalysis occurred
    for marijuana and the opiates, with many geographical ar-
    eas having identical or nearly identical percentages for the
    two methods.
3. Cocaine was grossly underreported, generally one-third to
    one-half less than what was indicated by urine tests. In
    Dallas, for example, 14% of arrestees reported cocaine use,
    but 50% tested positive for the drug. Clearly, without urine
    testing, recent cocaine use would have been greatly unde-
    tected.
4. Cocaine was more frequently detected in the urine than the
    other two drugs, with opiates coming in last. The worst
    cities involving cocaine use as indicated by urinalysis were
    New York (76% of arrestees) and Philadelphia (74%). In
    the latter city, males and females had almost equal percent-
    ages.
    The cities with least cocaine use were Indianapolis, Indi-
    ana (26%), and San Antonio, Texas (24%).

Results suggest an anchoring strategy as a first estimate that given substances
were ingested. Conclusions should not be generalized beyond people arrested for
crimes involving substance abuse in reported geographical areas. Additional information can sharpen the speculation that substance intoxication took place by a
particular individual.

The above general findings are augmented by data relevant to youthful offenders. Urine tests and self-reports were collected for 201 male and female youths
tested twice (Dembo, Williams, Wish, & Schmeidler, 1990). In terms of denial,
only about one-quarter of the youths who tested positive for cocaine reported
using it in the prior two to three days. Racial differences emerged, with Blacks
underreporting cocaine use substantially more than Whites.

A limitation of the self-report data is that these NIJ (1990) statistics were
collected under confidential research conditions. In the adversarial system of criminal justice, arrestees may be even less likely to report illicit drug use, for example,
when the evaluator is conducting a forensic evaluation.

In the final analysis, base rates are lacking for many critical groups and,
hence, limit the detection strategies we may employ. Most clients will not have
the above characteristics (i.e., arrestees in given areas within certain time periods). In this case, the base rates should not be utilized as a first estimate of substance abuse. The general minimization of drug usage can be noted, however.

Relying on the spoken word of the assessee is hazardous because of the denial phenomenon. In substance abuse, particularly alcoholism, moreover, the
assessee may not be consciously denying because of (a) blackouts; (b) repression,
including the need to protect ego esteem and to stave off hopelessness and de-
spair; and (c) the tendency for euphoric recall (Bean, 1981, Nace, 1987). Com-

mentators point out that piercing denial appears to come in stages, from recognizing that substances have created havoc in one's life to recognizing the need for substances to cope, and, lastly, to allowing oneself to experience the guilt not expressed during the active part of the abuse. Finally, there is some evidence that memories are better produced in a similar physical condition. Termed "state-dependent learning," this means that recall of a previous episode of intoxication may be possible only when the person is in a similar state. Thus, not reporting on previous intoxication may not be denial, rather an inability.

EVALUATING SIGNIFICANT OTHERS

In a study of schizophrenics, about one-half of whom were alcoholic, as shown on the Self-Administered Alcoholism Screening Test (Smith and Pristach, 1990) found that interviews with significant others and chart reviews were extremely helpful. Only one-half of the alcoholics admitted to their substance abuse problems. The authors conclude that schizophrenic alcoholics show more denial than nonschizophrenic alcoholics when compared to findings of earlier studies.

Case managers' ratings, which used reports from collaterals as well as longitudinal observations, were found to be superior to formal clinical evaluations, which frequently missed alcohol problems due to denial (Drake et al., 1990). Interestingly, case managers' ratings were also more accurate than structured research interviews, although the two measures were highly correlated. Drake et al. (1990) point out that a reliable and valid alcohol assessment instrument has not yet been developed, at least for schizophrenics, primarily because these people underreport the extent of their substance abuse.

A closer correspondence between the reports of alcoholics and significant others in nonpsychotic samples is quite possible. Loethen and Khavari (1990) found that there were no significant differences between patients' self-reports compared to reports from collaterals. Further, patients' self-reports showed a direct relationship with both the Self-Administered Alcoholism Screening Test and the Khavari Alcohol Test (KAT).

The evaluator can assess family, friends, acquaintances, and others for information regarding substance use of the assessee. The authors have found this to be the best source of data for a specific individual. The questions in Table 18.2 are adapted from the Michigan Alcoholism Screening Test (MAST) (Selzer, 1971) and are intended for use with significant others.

The evaluator should probe all positive answers. The original cut-off score for the MAST (> 5 endorsed items indicating alcoholism) cannot be used with this modified questionnaire because of deletions and adaptations and because items are answered by parties other than the client. However, giving the original MAST to the suspected substance abuser and then comparing answers with those produced by significant others may be instructive. The suspected abuser can then be questioned about discrepancies.

Table 18.2 Questions for Significant Others	Don't Know	Yes	No	Describe
1. Is _____ a (Name) normal drinker in your opinion?	———	———	———	———
2. Has s/he reported or acted in a way where part of the previous evening could not be remembered?	———	———	———	———
3. Do you worry or complain about his or her substance use?	———	———	———	———
4. Once s/he starts using substances, can it be easily stopped?	———	———	———	———
5. Does s/he express guilt or remorse about the substance abuse?	———	———	———	———
6. Does s/he try to limit the substances to certain times of the day or to certain places?	———	———	———	———
7. Has s/he ever attended a meeting of AA, NA, or the like?	———	———	———	———
8. Has s/he ever gotten a DUI, DWI, or any arrest related to substances?	———	———	———	———
9. Has s/he gotten into physical fights when using substances?	———	———	———	———
10. Does s/he mix substances (e.g., drink and smoke marijuana)?	———	———	———	———
11. Has his/her substance habits ever created a problem for you?	———	———	———	———
12. Have you ever sought help from his/her substance problems?	———	———	———	———
13. Has s/he lost friends or turned people off because of substance abuse?	———	———	———	———
14. Has s/he gotten into trouble at work because of substance use?	———	———	———	———
15. Has s/he ever lost a job because of the same reason?	———	———	———	———

(Continued on next page)

	Don't Know	Yes	No	Describe
16. Has s/he ever neglected the family or work obligations for two days or more because of substance use?	_____	_____	_____	_____
17. Does s/he take substances by noon?	_____	_____	_____	_____
18. Has s/he ever had physical problems because of substances (e.g., liver, rashes, DTs)?	_____	_____	_____	_____
19. Has s/he ever been in a general hospital or psychiatric hospital because of substance use?	_____	_____	_____	_____
20. Has s/he ever seen a doctor or a counselor on an outpatient basis for substance problems?	_____	_____	_____	_____
21. Was s/he ever put on medication for his/her substance problems?	_____	_____	_____	_____

Table 18.2
Questions for Significant Others
(continued from previous page)

Adapted from Michigan Alcoholism Screening Test, Selzer, 1971.

PSYCHOLOGICAL TESTING

Few psychometric devices exist which are directly relevant to the detection of the denial of substance abuse. An exception is the Denial Rating Scale (DRS) reported by Goldsmith and Green (1988). This preliminary test is designed to determine whether alcoholism as a condition is denied, or whether particular aspects within the condition, (e.g., loss of control once drinking starts), are denied. Promising interrater reliability and construct and predictive validity are reported.

Denial of substance abuse on testing has sometimes been associated with relatively positive traits. Rohsenow, Erickson, and O'Leary (1978) found that lower levels of psychopathology were related to the use of denial and intellectualization as ego defenses on the Defense Mechanism Inventory (DMI). Reviewing the locus of control research, Rohsenow and O'Leary (1978) found that internality was related to better social functioning and the defenses of denial, intellectualization, and repression. Lastly, Pekarik, Jones, and Blodgett (1986) found that denial scores on the MMPI were positively correlated with intelligence, but only for completers of an alcohol treatment program.

The MMPI MacAndrew Alcoholism (MAC) Scale (MacAndrew, 1965) has been traditionally considered an index of substance abuse tendencies. However, in a comprehensive review of the empirical literature, Gottesman and Prescott (1989), concluded that the scale makes so many false positive errors that use of the scale should be suspended. They reviewed 74 studies on the MAC published between 1976 and 1987. They calculated that the positive hit rate (percent of positive scorers who are actually alcoholic) in the general population is only 15% and that 85% of persons called alcoholic by the test are, in fact, not alcoholic.

In a study of 63 White, male forensic patients, Wasyliw, Grossman, Haywood, and Cavanaugh (1990) stated the following:

> While the MacAndrew Alcoholism Scale is the most widely used MMPI measure of vulnerability to alcohol abuse, its accuracy has not been studied in patients intrinsically motivated to exaggerate or minimize psychopathology. We examined the accuracy of the MAC in forensic patients with high rates of response-bias. Results indicated:
>
> (1) MAC scores were correlated positively with exaggeration and negatively with minimization for subjects with histories of alcohol abuse.
> (2) MAC scores were related to exaggeration or minimization of psychopathology rather than to admission or denial of alcohol abuse.
> (3) MAC scores were only moderately more accurate in valid than in exaggerated or minimized MMPI protocols.
> (4) Validity scale cut-off scores generated by discriminant function analyses were effective in identifying MAC misclassifications. Results suggest that the MAC should be used cautiously, particularly when motivation to minimize psychopathology is suspected.

Davis, Offord, Colligan, and Morse (1991) have recently reported the development of a new MMPI scale for alcoholism designed to detect alcoholism among medical inpatients. Using a construction sample of 736 medical inpatients with a diagnosis of alcoholism, a cross-validation sample of 485 medical patients with alcoholism and three nonalcoholic samples totaling 13,120 individuals, the new scale yielded a (cross-validated) valid positive rate of 90% and a valid negative rate between 90% and 96%. This promising scale needs to be investigated further for the possible effects of malingering and denial and for its applicability to nonmedical populations (e.g., psychiatric inpatients/outpatients, criminal offenders).

SUMMARY OF CRITICAL POINTS

The following criteria should be used for a diagnosis of substance abuse or dependence:

1. A history of maladaptive behavior and substance abuse as suggested by DSM-IV criteria, and evidenced by cross-validating sources to include:
   a. significant/knowledgeable others
   b. medical/psychological records of evaluation and/or treatment
   c. criminal history data involving maladaptive behavior associated with substance abuse
2. Psychological test scales if accompanied by a, b, or c
3. Admission of substance use if accompanied by a, b, or c
4. Withdrawal symptoms if accompanied by #1 or #2.

REFERENCES

American Psychiatric Association. (1994). *Diagnostic and statistical manual IV*. Washington, DC: Author.

Armor, D. J., Polich, J. M., & Stanbul, H. B. (1976, June). *Alcoholism and treatment*. Santa Monica, CA: Rand Corporation.

Bailey, M. B. (1961). Alcoholism and marriage: A review of research and professional literature. *Quarterly Journal of Studies of Alcohol, 22*, 81-97.

Bean, M. H. (1981). Denial and the psychological complications of alcoholism. In M. H. Bean & N. E. Zinberg (Eds.), *Dynamic approaches to the understanding and treatment of alcoholism* (pp. 55-96). New York: The Free Press.

Blane, H. J. (1968). *The personality of the alcoholic: Guises of dependency*. New York: Harper and Row.

Davis, L., Offord, K., Colligan, R., & Morse, R. (1991). The CAL: An MMPI alcoholism scale for general medical patients. *Journal of Clinical Psychology, 47*(5), 632-646.

Dembo, R., Williams, L., Wish, E., & Schmeidler, J. (1990, May). *Urine testing of detained juveniles to identify high-risk youth*. Rockville, MD: National Institute of Justice.

Drake, R. E., Osher, F. C., Noordsy, D. L., Hurlbut, S. C., Teague, G. B., & Beaudett, M. S. (1990). Diagnosis of alcohol use disorders in schizophrenia. *Schizophrenia Bulletin, 16*, 57-67.

Goldsmith, R. J., & Green, B. L. (1988). A rating scale for alcoholic denial. *Journal of Nervous Mental Disorders, 176*, 614-620.

Gottesman, I., & Prescott, C. (1989). Abuses of the MacAndrew MMPI Alcoholism scale: A critical review. *Clinical Psychology Review, 9*, 223-242.

Jellinek, E. M. (1952). Phases of alcohol addiction. *Quarterly Journal of Studies of Alcohol, 13*, 673-684.

Jellinek, E. M. (1980). *The disease concept of alcoholism*. New Haven: College and University Press.

Loethen, G. J., & Khavari, K. A. (1990). Comparison of the self-administered Alcoholism Screening Test (SAAST) and the Khavari Alcohol Test (KAT): Results from an alcoholic population and their collaterals. *Alcohol: Clinical and Experimental Research, 14*, 756-760.

MacAndrew, C. (1965). The differentiation of male alcoholic outpatients from nonalcoholic psychiatric outpatients by means of the MMPI. *Quarterly Journal of Studies on Alcohol, 26*, 238-246.

Mulhaney, J. A., & Trippett, C. J. (1979). Alcohol dependence and phobias: Clinical description and relevance. *British Journal of Psychiatry, 135*, 565-573.

Nace, E. P. (1982). The role of craving in the treatment of alcoholism. *National Association of Private Psychiatric Hospitals Journal, 13*(1), 27-31.

Nace, E. P. (1984). Epidemiology of alcoholism and prospects for treatment. *Annual Review of Medicine, 35*, 293-309.

Nace, E. (1987). *The treatment of alcoholism*. New York: Brunner-Mazel.

O'Neil, J., Wish, E., & Visher, C. (1990, March). *Drug use forecasting: July to September 1989*. Rockville, MD: National Institute of Justice.

Paolino, T., & McCrady, B. (1977). *The alcoholic marriage: Alternative perspectives.* New York: Grune & Stratton.

Pekarik, G., Jones, D. L., & Blodgett, C. (1986). Personality and demographic characteristics of dropouts and completers in a nonhospital residential alcohol treatment program. *International Journal of Addiction, 21,* 131-137.

Rohsenow, D. J., Erickson, R. C., & O'Leary, M. R. (1978). The Defense Mechanism Inventory and alcoholics. *International Journal of Addiction, 13,* 403-414.

Rohsenow, D. J., & O'Leary, M. R. (1978). Locus of control research on alcoholic populations: A review. *International Journal of Addiction, 13,* 231-236.

Selzer, M. L. (1971). The Michigan Alcoholism Screening Test: The quest for a new diagnostic instrument. *American Journal of Psychiatry, 127,* 89-94.

Smith, C. M., & Pristach, C. A. (1990). Utility of the Self-Administered Alcoholism Screening Test (SAAST) in schizophrenic patients. *Alcohol: Clinical and Experimental Research, 14,* 690-694.

Wasyliw, O., Grossman, L., Haywood, T., & Cavanaugh, J. (1990). *Is the MacAndrew Alcoholism Scale related to response-bias: A forensic study.* Presented at the American Psychological Association, Boston, Massachusetts.

Wish, E., & O'Neil, J (1989). *Drug Use Forecasting (DUF).* Research update. National Institute of Justice, Rockville, Maryland.

19

DANGEROUSNESS EVALUATION AND DECEPTION

Dangerousness may be defined as to the likelihood of threatened, attempted, or consummated physical harm to others, self, or property within a certain time period. Typically, a person with a history of violence, the best predictor of future violence, will downplay previous aggression and project blame for acknowledged violence onto victims and contexts. Minimizing and denying dangerousness is a pervasive phenomenon (Hall, 1987; Kutash, Kutash, Schlesinger & Associates, 1978; Monahan, 1981).

TARGETS

A history of violence, situational and dispositional triggers to violence, and opportunities for violence are the three main factors associated with violence and are commonly the targets of denial and minimization by suspects (Hall, 1982, 1984, 1987). Any of the variables associated with violence may be targeted for denial or minimization.

Dispositional and situational influences on violence may encourage violence in individual cases and are often denied. These include the subcultural acceptance of violence as a solution to interpersonal problems, perceiving one's self as dangerous, believing that certain types of violence will go undetected or unpunished, violent fantasies, violent friends, substance abuse or dependence, psychiatric conditions, and hostility.

Triggering stimuli, short-term in duration and intense in impact, which set the violence into motion, are often distorted by clients. Short-term events include, as the two most frequently mentioned triggering events, substance abuse and the breakup of a central love relationship (e.g., Bandura, 1973). Other examples are insults to self-esteem (Toch, 1969) and invasion of body space (Kinzel, 1970).

The presence of opportunity factors which allow the occurrence of violence or expand the various ways it can be expressed may also be minimized or denied. Opportunity factors expand the possible severity of exhibited violence or allow its expression. Examples in the former category include availability of a firearm (Berkowitz & Le Page, 1967), presence of a physically weaker potential victim (Bandura, 1973), and elevation to positions of authority where violence towards others is institutionally sanctioned (Fromm, 1973; Milgram, 1963). Variables which allow the expression of violence include release from incarceration into the community (Kelly, 1976) and cessation of taking tranquilizing medication (Stone, 1975).

Table 19.1 presents features of violence which are commonly minimized or denied by clients.

Table 19.1
Targets of Violence-related Features Frequently Denied or Minimized

Past multiple violence
Previous "big four" crime (rape, robbery, aggravated assault, homicide)
Recency within last several years
History of reinforcing results from aggression
Pain cues from victim maintained/intensified perpetrator aggression
Institutional conduct involving threats or violence
Assaults or threats to authority figures
Arrests and hospitalizations for violence
Felony arrest before 15th birthday
Dangerous weapon used in offenses
Possession or recent purchase of firearm
Paraphernalia of weapons or substances
Cessation of stabilizing medication
Activities associated with substance abuse
Violent or substance-abusing peers
Self-reinforcement for aggression
Insults to the self-esteem leading to violence
Job loss or problems due to aggression
High hostility, low frustration tolerance
Chronic anger towards targeted others
Self-perception as dangerous
Belief that certain types of violence will go unpunished
Violent fantasies and dreams

Some associated features of violence are typically affirmed by clients. These include easily verifiable associations of violence such as convictions, prison incarcerations, and body tattoos with violent theme. Other associations that are usually affirmed include a preference for violent films (TV, movies), books, etc., release from incarceration, and physical prowess in relationship to the (potential) victim. Some factors are blamed on others or are regarded as irrelevant to violence and hence not denied. These include physical abuse as a child, praise or reward by parents for aggression, a violent model in the home, substance abuse by the same-sex parents, and a history of reinforcing outcomes for violence.

Inhibitory variables which lower the chances that violence will occur typically are affirmed by clients. These variables fall into the lower range of frequency, intensity, severity, or duration of any quantifiable factor which is positively associated with violence. A minimal history of violence may be regarded by a client as a sign of dispositional nonviolence, for example, and many subjects will therefore claim a nonviolent basal history. Stabilizing psychotropic medication generally acts as an inhibitor to violence, and most patients will assert compliance with medication.

Dispositional factors associated with a lower propensity to aggress include high socioeconomic status and high educational level (Kelly, 1976; Monahan, 1981) and clients may, therefore, distort reports of occupational and educational achievement. The opportunity for violence may eliminate or reduce the probability of aggression and subjects may claim, for example, a lack of transportation or a physical disability.

Contextual stimuli include such variables as location of the crime scene and the presence of third parties (Steadman, 1981), architectural features (Atlas, 1982), availability of a weapon at the scene (Boyanowky & Griffith, 1982), and noxious environmental stimuli (Berkowitz, 1983; Horowitz & Willging, 1984). Some subjects may therefore emphasize the improbability of violence given eyewitnesses, bright lighting, or other physical "barriers" to violence.

RESPONSE STYLES

Forensic information is often distorted by clients who have a vested interest in a desired legal outcome. However, assuming that clients only hide violence (i.e., fake good) to escape conviction or punishment can, and does, lead to serious data misinterpretation. Honest responding, invalidation, faking bad, and fluctuating styles are also possibilities (see Hall, 1982, 1985, 1986; Rogers, 1984). The person may employ these strategies differentially for questions relevant to past violence and to present condition. Thus, there are at least 36 distinct distortion strategies possible, corresponding to six response strategies (faking good, faking bad, honesty, invalidation, mixed styles, fluctuating styles) for two time intervals (past, present). The point is that distortion by a client does not always conform to the strategy which is most obvious to, or suspected by, the clinician (i.e., faking good).

A defendant may attempt to portray past, but no current, dangerousness. The defendant may be saying that he or she was a dangerous person in the past but is not a risk presently. The message communicated may be that it is appropriate to trust this individual or at least to perceive change in a positive direction. The implication for a lesser sentence, release from a state hospital, placement in a witness protection program, etc., may represent the desired outcome. Faking good for both the past and present may occur when the crime was minor and the defendant does not desire to have psychological intervention. If it serves the interests of the defendant, honest responding may be shown, as evidenced by verification from independent facts and sources, and other factors. Faking bad for the present with faking good for the past may be associated with a plea for help, as when the individual has been typically harmless, but is now dangerous due to unusual and highly stressful outside events.

Hall (1987) requested over 1,000 enlistees, dependents, and civilian workers to fabricate acts of violence as well as to relate their genuine accounts of experienced violence. Themes of faked violence fell into four distinct categories:

1. *Unlikely behaviors.* This included females attacking males, calmness in the face of lethal attack, and smooth execution of behaviors when highly stressed.
2. *Symbolic significance of the violence.* For example, in the faked accounts, a rapist is struck in the groin with a hat pin, and a "P" (for "prick") is carved on the forehead of a vanquished enemy.
3. *Bragging and exaggeration.* There appears to be a component of self-esteem to even faked violence. Both of a victim's legs are shot off by the perpetrator in one account.

   Every bone in the victim's hand is broken by another, and the richest person in the area is kidnapped for ransom.
4. *Revenge scenes were common, perhaps as a means to justify the violence.* They were accompanied by a large number of acts of self-defense, again, possibly to provide a rationale for the aggression. Because of this, the majority of faked accounts involved the use of weapons not designed for attack. A 37-year-old, White female reported the following in her false account:

   > I was walking downtown one night, on a very busy road with many people around. Nevertheless, I could not feel relaxed.
   >
   > I was very conscious of my environment when I left the crowded area to go to a streetcar stop, I felt it almost physically that somebody followed me. I heard footsteps picking up my speed and the heavy breathing of a man behind me. My heartbeat became faster, as my hands formed a fist.
   >
   > I felt cold sweat on my head, but my conscience and rationality froze up. I was not going to allow this individual to hurt me or even touch me. Without any sign of nervousness, I reached in my purse to get out a letter-opener which I always had in there—just in case! It had a wooden handle with a sharp blade. I was also thankful that I had high heels with a metal part. I slowly lifted my knee up to swing my foot back in speed. I heard a moan and felt hands on my hips. That did it! I turned and stared in the face of a man whose face expressed anger and hate. Without hesitation I raised my arm and ran the blade in him. At the same time I kicked him hard with my knee against his abdomen, while my hands scratched his face and slapped him. I did not stop till he was on the ground—motionless. I had done it and felt no regret.

Response style analysis is in a rudimentary stage of development. Different response styles, conceptualized separately for past and for present violence, appear to represent a fruitful area of study. Knowing how people distort their past violence and their present potential for violence will likely increase the accuracy of predictions of dangerousness.

DETECTION METHODS

Accurate prediction of dangerousness in individual cases requires (a) obtaining a multisourced, interdisciplinary forensic database upon which to draw conclusions; (b) analysis of retrospective and current distortion; (c) determining the characteristics of basal violence (frequency, intensity, severity of past dangerousness); (d) determining the presence of triggering stimuli (especially substance intoxication, breakup of a central love relationship, and work conflict) and (e) examination of opportunity factors (Hall, 1987).

The instant violence can be represented in a description of the assault cycle of the incident. The typical assault cycle consists of a baseline (past or basal violence), a triggering phase, an escalation phase (where arousal mounts and the perpetrator becomes more threatening), a crisis phase (where the actual violence occurs), and a recovery phase. An assault cycle is illustrated in Chapter 11 on criminal profiling.

COMMON ERRORS

Under some circumstances, failure to warn a defendant that information regarding dangerousness may be presented to the court for purposes of sentencing may constitute a violation of the defendant's constitutional rights (*Barefoot v. Estelle*, 463 U.S. 880, 1983; *Estelle v. Smith*, 451 U.S. 454, 1981; *Powell v. Texas*, 57 U.S.L.W. 3857, 1989). "A criminal defendant, who neither initiates a psychiatric examination nor attempts to introduce any psychiatric evidence, may not be compelled to respond to a psychiatrist if his statements can be used against him at a capital sentencing proceeding" (*United States v. Byers*, 740 F.2d 1104, D.C. Cir. 1984 *certiorari denied* 104 S.Ct. 717., p. 465). It is ethically, and sometimes legally, incumbent on examiners to inform defendants how the information obtained during an evaluation will be used.

Other common errors in the assessment of dangerousness include (a) the lack of an adequate forensic database; (b) the failure to account for retrospective and current distortion; (c) the prediction of future dangerousness in the absence of previous dangerousness; (d) the reliance on illusory correlations of dangerousness; (e) the prediction of dangerousness solely from clinical diagnosis; (f) the failure to consider triggering stimuli; (g) the failure to take into account opportunity variables; (h) the failure to evaluate inhibitory factors; (i) ignoring relevant base rates; and (j) the failure to formulate circumscribed conclusions.

The FBI's recidivism data for 1972 showed that 64% of individuals convicted for homicide, 77% of those convicted for robbery, 73% of those convicted for rape, and 70% of those convicted for aggravated assault committed new offenses within four years of release from prison. The PROMIS research project (Institute for Law and Social Research, 1977) showed that with five or more arrests for violent crimes, the probability of similar future arrests approaches certainty. Wolfgang (1977) reported that the probability of future arrest varied directly with the number of previous arrests (e.g., 80% probability with four prior arrests).

In general, there should be compelling reasons for ignoring or disagreeing with the base rate of violence relevant to individuals. Individual predictions of future dangerousness should be "anchored" (Shapiro, 1977) by relevant base rates before adding client-specific data to individualize the prediction. The initial use of baserates also helps avoid the error of overplaying current events and downplaying the violence history.

REFERENCES

Atlas, R. (1982). Crime site selection for assaults in four Florida prisons. *Man-Environment Systems, 12,* 59-66.

Bandura, A. (1973). *Aggression: A social learning analysis.* Englewood Cliffs, NJ: Prentice Hall.

Berkowitz, L. (1983). Aversively stimulated aggression: Some parallels and differences in research with animals and humans. *American Psychologist, 38,* 1135-1144.

Berkowitz, L., & Le Page, A. (1967). Weapons as aggression-eliciting stimuli. *Journal of Personality and Social Psychology,* 202-207.

Boyanowky, E., & Griffith, C. (1982). Weapons and eye contact as instigators or inhibitors of aggressive arousal in police-citizen interaction. *Journal of Applied Social Contact, 12,* 398-407.

Fromm, E. (1973). *The anatomy of human destructiveness.* New York: Holt, Rinehart, & Winston.

Grisso, T., & Appelbaum, P. (1992). Is it unethical to offer predictions of future violence? *Law and Human Behavior.*

Guze, S. (1976). *Criminality and psychiatric disorders.* New York: Oxford University Press.

Hall, H. V. (1982). Dangerousness predictions and the maligned forensic professional: Suggestions for detecting distortion of true basal violence. *Criminal Justice and Behavior, 9,* 3-12.

Hall, H. V. (1984). Predicting dangerousness for the courts. *American Journal of Forensic Psychology, 4,* 5-25.

Hall, H. V. (1985). Cognitive and volitional capacity assessment: A proposed decision tree. *American Journal of Forensic Psychology, 3,* 3-17.

Hall, H. V. (1986). The forensic distortion analysis: A proposed decision tree and report format. *American Journal of Forensic Psychology, 4,* 31-59.

Hall, H. V. (1987). *Violence prediction: Guidelines for the forensic practitioner.* Springfield, IL: Charles C. Thomas.

Horowitz, I., & Willging, T. (1984). *The psychology of law.* Boston, MA: Little, Brown, & Company.

Institute for Law and Social Research. (1977). *PROMIS research project: Highlights of interim findings and implications.* Washington, DC: Author.

Kelly, C. (1976). *Crime in the United States: Uniform crime reports.* Washington, DC: U. S. Government Printing Office.

Kinzel, A. (1970). Body-buffer zones in violent prisoners. *American Journal of Psychiatry, 127,* 59-64.

Kutash, Kutash, Schlesinger & Associates. (1978). *Violence: Perspective on murder and aggression.* San Francisco: Jossey-Bass.

Milgram, S. (1963). Behavioral study of obedience. *Journal of Abnormal and Social Psychology, 67,* 371-378.

Monahan, J. (1981). *The clinical prediction of violent behavior* (National Institute of Mental Health, DHHS Publication No. ADM 81-92). Washington, DC: U. S. Government Printing Office.

Petersilia, J., Greenwood, P., & Lavin, M. (1977). *Criminal careers of habitual felons.* Santa Monica, CA: Rand.

Rogers, R. (1984). Towards an empirical model of malingering and deception. *Behavioral Sciences and the Law, 2,* 93-111.

Shapiro, A. (1977). The evaluation of clinical prediction: A method and initial application. *New England Journal of Medicine, 296,* 1509-1514.

Steadman, H. (1981). A situational approach to violence. *International Journal of Law and Psychiatry, 5,* 171-186.

Stone, A. (1975). *Mental health and the law: A system in transition* (National Institute of Mental Health, DHEW Publication No. ADM 76-176). Washington, DC: U. S. Government Printing Office.

Toch, H. (1969). *Violent man.* Chicago, IL: Aldine.

Wolfgang, M. (1977). *From boy to man—From delinquency to crime. Serious juvenile offender.* National symposium, Minneapolis, MN.

Wolfgang, M. (1978). *An overview of research into violent behavior.* Testimony before the U. S. House of Representatives Committee on Science and Technology.

20

CONCLUSIONS AND EXPERT TESTIMONY

The wealth of studies reviewed in previous chapters can easily lead to myopia. The FDA model can lead to a preoccupation with distortions at the expense of sound clinical diagnosis and assessment. To counter this constrictive view, this chapter focuses on broader questions than are reviewed in preceding chapters. In particular, the chapter discusses 1) when a distortion analysis is necessary, 2) what methods should be used in such an analysis, 3) what conclusions are justified from such an analysis, and 4) when the clinician should become an expert witness. Finally, the chapter discusses some issues involved in assuming the role of expert witness.

WHEN IS FDA NECESSARY?

Distortion analysis is the process of evaluating the effects of intentional and unintentional distortions on the information received from clients during psychological assessment. It always requires an expenditure of time and resources over and beyond that required for the assessment itself. It is therefore appropriate to ask when such expenditures are proper and necessary.

In general, distortion analysis is proper whenever the cost of conducting the analysis is less than the cost of making an assessment error and the likelihood of an assessment error is high. If, during intake at a private practice or a mental health clinic, it is routine to collect background information, an MMPI and a sentence completion test, it would not be justifiable to spend an additional two hours assessing the "genuineness" of answers to these instruments. However, if a particular applicant's answers are suggestive of distortion (i.e., the likelihood of an assessment error is increased), then additional testing for distortions may be justified. During psychological screening of police applicants, routine distortion analysis may be justified on the basis that most applicants will "put on their best faces" (i.e., the likelihood of missing psychopathology is increased) and that the cost of recommending poor risks for hire outweighs the cost of the additional testing.

However, whenever the cost of an assessment error is greater than the cost of conducting a distortion analysis and the resulting decision is *irreversible*, then distortion analysis is *necessary*. In most clinical situations, assessment decisions lead to treatment decisions which are subsequently revised based on feedback on the effectiveness of the treatment. Treatment decisions are usually reversible if it appears that the original assessment was in error. In fact, response to treatment is sometimes used as a clinical criterion against which to judge the accuracy of the initial assessment. In addition, most errors in assigning clients to inappropriate psychological and psychiatric treatments are reversible without permanent cost to the client. Switching a patient from one psychotropic medication to another rarely results in serious or irreversible consequences for the patient; substituting behavior therapy for insight-oriented psychotherapy rarely causes a loss to the client. In other situations, however, the decision resulting from the initial assessment is irreversible. In nearly all forensic situations, for example, a psychological assessment results in an irrevocable report (written or testimonial) which cannot be "taken back." The report becomes a permanent (though not necessarily determinative) factor upon which the judge, jury, hearing officer, appeals panel, or other legal decision maker relies. There is no opportunity for the forensic expert to recall and revise the original assessment, conclusions, or decisions based on new information[1]. In addition, most forensic evaluations involve an increased risk of assessment errors because of the motivation of the client to influence the outcome in one way or another. In such situations of *irreversible* decisions with increased risk of assessment errors, an analysis of the distortions which may have affected the assessment is not merely proper, but is necessary.

WHAT METHODS SHOULD BE USED IN DISTORTION ANALYSIS?

The preceding chapters have reviewed numerous signs, scales, patterns, and other indicators of distortion. The accuracies of these proposed indicators for particular types of distortion (e.g., for detecting denial of substance abuse, or exaggeration of memory dysfunction) vary considerably. At one extreme, indicators are merely suggestive of distortion (e.g., indicators of malingered pain), while at the other extreme, indicators are highly probative of distortion (e.g., explicit alternative testing of neuropsychological complaints). Which indicators of distortion are appropriate for use in individual cases depends on the type of decision being made. If the purpose of the original assessment leads to a reversible decision, then less accurate indicators would be acceptable than if the decision is irreversible. Correlatively, if the cost of an assessment error is tolerable, then less accurate indicators may be used than if such costs are intolerable. In clinical situations, it would be acceptable to note indicators which suggest denial, mini-

---

[1] It is legally permissible for an expert witness to repudiate a previously submitted written report during oral testimony at a deposition or trial. However, it requires a special hearing to recant previous testimony once the expert has been dismissed as a witness.

mization, exaggeration, or fabrication, because subsequent treatments can be modified with little cost to the client. In forensic situations, however, the most accurate indicators available should be employed and suggestive indicators should be avoided, both because of the irreversibility of the resulting decision and the costs associated with assessment errors.

Replicated indicators of distortion must be distinguished from experimental indicators of distortion. Both replicated and experimental indicators are associated with rates of error; no prediction is error-free. However, replicated indicators are those which have been shown in multiple studies to distinguish between "malingerers" and other comparison groups relevant to the use for which the indicator was developed. For example, if an indicator has been developed to distinguish between "malingered psychosis" and "genuine psychosis" among criminal defendants, then the indicator would be replicated if there were multiple studies which showed that the indicator distinguished between groups of "psychotic defendants" and groups of "nonpsychotic defendants instructed to feign psychosis"; the indicator would be experimental if there was only one study showing such discrimination or if there were only studies showing that the indicator distinguished between other groups (e.g., psychotic defendants vs. normal subjects instructed to feign psychosis). Replicated indicators are distinguished from experimental indicators on the basis of their repeatability and their "ecological validity."

This distinction between replicated and experimental indicators does not preclude the possibility that an indicator may be accurate in many different situations. The F - K index on the MMPI, for example, may be accurate in identifying distortions among psychiatric outpatients, medical inpatients, and prison inmates. However, the question is an empirical one. It cannot be assumed that, because an indicator reliably distinguishes between two conditions (e.g., genuine vs. exaggerated back pain) or two groups (e.g., honest vs. malingering parolees), it will also reliably distinguish between other conditions (e.g., headaches) and groups (inpatients).

Multiple indicators are needed in individual cases to assure that the result of any single indicator is generalizable. Given that all indicators are subject to some error—no matter how small, it is possible that a single indicator of distortion is not truly representative of either the client's condition or intention. However, a finding of distortion on multiple indicators increases the confidence that one can place in the final decision that distortion is occurring. The most convincing case occurs when the results of tests are supported by direct observation during the assessment process or in the "real world." For example, one young defendant awaiting trial on multiple charges of breaking and entering and theft 1) refused to be tested by two different forensic psychologists (experimental indicator), 2) answered their questions about the alleged crimes in a tangential, evasive manner while answering other questions responsively (experimental indicator), and 3) failed an explicit alternative test administered by a third psychologist (replicated indicator). The probability that this combination of indicators arose by chance is far less than the probability that any one of the indicators arose by chance and, therefore, is more convincing.

But, if multiple indicators of distortion are needed, how are they to be combined into a single decision regarding distortion? And what if the indicators are conflicting? There does not appear to be any research on these important questions, but guidelines for the practicing clinician may be taken from the existing literature on clinical versus statistical prediction. Sawyer (1966) distinguished eight types of decision procedures involving types of data collection (judgemental, mechanical, both, either/both) and types of data combination (clinical, statistical). Of particular interest here are the procedure of clinical synthesis and the procedure of mechanical synthesis. In clinical synthesis, judgmental and/or mechanical (e.g., psychometric, physiological) information is input into an actuarial system which combines the information and makes a decision; this statistical decision, together with the original input information, is then given to a clinician who can 1) ignore the actuarial decision and make a clinical decision, 2) adopt the actuarial decision, or 3) modify the clinical decision in accord with the actuarial decision. Which choice is made presumably depends on unique features of each case which are known only by the clinician (i.e., not used as input to the actuarial system). In mechanical synthesis, judgmental and/or mechanical information is given to the clinician, who in turn makes a clinical prediction. This clinical prediction is then placed, together with the original input data, into an actuarial system which makes the final decision. The actuary can either ignore the clinician's decision entirely, agree with the clinician's decision, or adapt its own decision in accord with the clinical decision. Research suggests that the procedure of mechanical synthesis is more accurate than the procedure of clinical synthesis (Sawyer, 1966; Wiggins, 1973).

The problem is that no actuarial system for predicting distortions from multiple inputs yet exists. Therefore, the practicing clinician is left with the method of clinical synthesis for dealing with multiple indicators of distortion. In the final analysis, the clinician must use personal judgment in weighting, combining, and using multiple indicators of distortion. However, the clinician would be well-advised to give greater weight to mechanical than to judgmental information and to replicated than to experimental indicators. If indicators of distortion are conflicting, then the more accurate, more mechanical, and more replicated input should prevail. Kleinmuntz (1990) presented many ideas for improving the accuracy of clinical synthesis of assessment data. His suggestions, in combination with the development of new procedures for detecting deception, may contribute significantly to the accurate detection of deception by clinicians in the future.

WHAT CONCLUSIONS ARE JUSTIFIED?

In clinical situations, decisions regarding distortions are intended for professional use. In-house treating professionals or referring treating professionals are assumed to be the intended audiences for conclusions regarding distortions in a client's self-presentation during assessment. These professionals will presumably use the information to guide their initial treatment plans. However, it cannot be assumed that these intended professionals or future unknown professionals will necessarily be aware of the complexities of distortion analysis. Therefore, clarity in communicating conclusions regarding distortion is necessary and summary labels should be avoided.

Concluding that a client is "malingering" or "in denial" tells nothing about the scope of the client's distortion (Which targets are being distorted? Which response style is being used?) or the accuracy of the distortion assessment (Which indicators of distortion were used to arrive at the conclusion?). The diagnostic label "malingering," for example, does not distinguish between conscious exaggeration of a genuine problem and total fabrication of the problem; it does not distinguish between honest reporting of one problem and distorted reporting of another problem; it does not distinguish between honest reporting of a problem on one instrument and distorted reporting of the same problem on a different instrument; it does not distinguish between accurate, replicated indicators of distortion and inaccurate, experimental indicators. It is therefore preferable to avoid summary labels in clinical communications and to use succinct descriptive statements instead.

For example, to state:

> Although his wife expressed concern about his drinking and police records indicate two arrests for driving under the influence, Mr. Jones denied any problems with alcohol both during interview and on self-report measures

is clearer than to state:

> Mr. Jones appears to be denying his alcohol problems.

Similarly, to state:

> Mr. Jones complained of memory failures which interfered with on-the-job performance. However, explicit alternative testing suggested a gross exaggeration of memory dysfunction and a test of serial learning did not show the pattern of results expected among amnestic patients

is preferable to stating:

> Mr. Jones' test results suggest malingering.

In forensic situations, the intended audience of communications regarding distortions includes the case attorneys and fact-finders (judge, jury, hearing officer). This audience has an even greater need for detailed explanations of procedures and findings than do professional colleagues. Whereas colleagues will use the information to build a tentative treatment plan, attorneys will use the information to support or undermine legal arguments in the case. Fact-finders will use the information as one justification for their verdict in the case. In general, suggestions of distortions should be avoided unless they are based on accurate, replicated indicators. Courts require that an expert's opinions be based on a "professional certainty," which refers to the expert's degree of confidence in the opinion (Black, 1988). Professional standards require that such confidence be empirically based on the accuracy of the techniques used and not merely on the subjective appraisal of the expert. The courtroom is no place to spin hypothetical yarns about what might be happening in a case. If only experimental indicators of distortion exist in a case, the question of distortion should not be addressed at all by the examiner. When questioned about the issue by attorneys, the examiner should then admit the possibility of distortion affecting the examination, but state that no acceptable (accurate, replicated) methods currently exist for detecting distortion in this type of case. While hypotheses and hunches may assist treating professionals in clinical cases, such speculative statements in forensic cases can result in misleading and irreversible outcomes.

WHEN SHOULD AN EXPERT BECOME AN EXPERT WITNESS?

There are two kinds of witnesses in law: material witnesses and expert witnesses. Material witnesses are allowed to testify as to personal knowledge which is relevant to the legal questions at hand. For example, eyewitnesses to a crime may testify as to what they saw or heard at the time of the crime; police officers may relate what they discovered in their investigation of a crime; participants in a situation may explain what transpired in their presence. However, material witnesses are not allowed to express opinions regarding causes, effects, intentionality, responsibility, or other matters outside their personal experience. Expert witnesses, in comparison, are allowed to testify to professional opinions on questions which are related to the legal questions at hand, but which are beyond the understanding of the lay person. For example, questions about firearms, fingerprints, genetic profiles, accounting procedures, medical diagnoses/treatment, and psychological assessment/treatment generally require information beyond that possessed by the ordinary person. When a legal case involves technical or scientific questions, the court may allow expert witnesses to testify as to their opinions regarding those questions.

In clinical practice, mental health professionals do not generally anticipate being called as an expert witness in a legal case involving one of their clients. The assessments, treatments, reports, and correspondence which are generated in the course of providing clinical services to clients are not necessarily the best basis for answering technical or scientific questions in a courtroom. As mentioned previously, clinical communications may include hypotheses and speculations intended to frame tentative and revisable treatment plans. Such communications, if offered as the basis for a professional opinion in the courtroom, could be misleading and inaccurate in a situation where they cannot be revised. In addition, the clinical professional has an ethical and legal responsibility to protect the client's best interests, which may conflict with the ethical and legal responsibility to testify truthfully in court.

The best way to protect the flexibility and commitment to the client which are required for clinical practice is simply to refuse to become an expert witness in any legal case involving a former or current clinical client. Although the professional may be subpoenaed to testify as a material witness regarding, for example, questions about dates of treatment, types of treatment, diagnoses, etc., the professional cannot be compelled to render a professional opinion regarding any fact in dispute in the case and should not volunteer to do so (American Psychological Association [APA], 1992). For example, if a client currently in treatment is involved in an automobile accident, the treating professional may be called to testify that the client was receiving treatment at the time of the accident, that the focus of treatment was social anxiety and that the client was making satisfactory progress after seven sessions of treatment. However, the professional should not answer questions regarding the impact of the automobile accident on the client's current functioning, regarding the role of the preexisting social anxiety in causing the accident, or regarding the prognosis for the client.

A professional can be compelled to be a lay witness in a trial, just as can any other person, but a professional cannot be compelled to be an expert witness. We strongly advise that professionals refuse to become an expert witness in any case involving former or current clients, even if the client approves it, and that testimony in such cases be limited to the material facts of the professional relationship. "Psychologists avoid accepting an assignment as an expert consultant or witness for a party when they have had a prior professional relationship with an adverse party to the proceedings" (APA, 1992). Such a position precludes the development of dual relationships, avoids the appearance of biased testimony, and safeguards the therapeutic relationship from injurious statements made under oath.

In forensic cases, however, the professional is specifically employed to evaluate a case and render an expert opinion regarding technical/scientific/professional questions. From the very beginning, the professional's responsibilities are clear to the client, the attorneys, and the fact-finder. The forensic expert's job includes conducting a professionally acceptable evaluation, forming expert opinions regarding technical/scientific/professional questions in dispute, and communicating those opinions and their factual bases to the fact-finder.

Whereas material witnesses are allowed to testify if they have personal knowledge of facts-in-question, the expert witness must first be accepted as an expert by the court. Courts have wide latitude in defining who is an expert, but the *sine qua non* is that the witness possess professional/scientific/technical knowledge or skill as a result of experience, training or education. In mental health matters, the expert witness is usually a psychiatrist, neurologist or psychologist, but some courts have qualified general physicians, social workers, bachelor-level "psychologists," and even laymen as experts on mental health questions. In other cases, competent psychologists have been excluded as expert witnesses and not allowed to testify.

Faust and Ziskin (1988; Ziskin & Faust, 1991) have argued that the testimony of mental health professionals should not be admitted on questions of diagnosis, prediction of future dangerousness, and malingering Brodsky (1989), Hoge and Grisso (1992), and Matarazzo (1990, 1991) have countered that such testimony is based on reliable and valid methods and is helpful to fact-finders. McCloskey and Egeth (1983; Egeth & McCloskey, 1984) have argued that expert testimony on the credibility of witnesses is not based on a body of replicable, relevant, and valid facts and therefore should not be admitted in court; Loftus (1983, 1984) and Wells (1984) have argued the contrary. In spite of this professional controversy, courts continue to admit psychological and psychiatric testimony "for whatever it may be worth."

In this respect, legal standards for admissibility of expert testimony are far less demanding than professional standards for clinical practice. While professional standards require, for example, that assessment techniques meet certain standards of reliability and validity in order to assure an acceptable level of accuracy, legal standards of admissibility do not necessarily focus on the accuracy of those assessments (Black, 1988). The empirical accuracy of procedures used by professionals is, in the eyes of the law, a question of how much weight the fact-finder should give to the expert's findings and opinions, not a question of the admissibility of the expert's testimony.

Once a professional has formed professional opinions based on a "professional certainty," has been accepted as an expert by the court, and has communicated those opinions and their bases, the trier-of-fact (judge, jury, hearing officer) must determine how much weight to give the opinions in disposing of the case. A professional's opinions are never determinative of the ultimate legal questions in a case, but are merely one more piece of evidence to be considered by the fact-finder. The fact-finder may ignore the opinions completely, may give them partial weight or may endorse them entirely.

THE ROLE OF EXPERT WITNESS

Poythress (1979), Rigling and Russo (1990), and Rosen (1983) have highlighted the need for special training in forensics for mental health professionals who become expert witnesses. Attorneys have access to training material to determine the credibility of a witness (e.g., *see* Aron, Duffy, & Rosner [1990], who give clear examples of differentiating between nondeliberate distortion and deception on the part of witnesses). Law schools offer courses in handling experts. Temple University in Philadelphia and Southern Methodist University (SMU) in Dallas offer law courses to prepare law students to work with experts. SMU's program involves the highly regarded author Shuman and his text, *Psychiatric and Psychological Evidence* (1986). The Association of Trial Lawyers of America offers training in handling expert witnesses. Finally, the well-known texts by Ziskin and Faust (1988) and Faust, Ziskin, and Hiers (1991) present attorneys with well-documented lines of attack on mental health professionals in the role of expert witness. In the face of this increasing sophistication by attorneys, clinical training by itself does not properly prepare clinicians to become effective expert witnesses.

The following sections briefly introduce the clinician to selected aspects of the expert role. Brown (1987) and Wellman (1986) discuss cross-examination of witnesses from an attorney's point of view; Singer and Nievod (1987) and Brodsky (1991) discuss the role of expert witness from a psychologist's point of view.

HEARSAY

Hearsay is a verbal out-of-court statement made by a person with no personal knowledge of the facts, but offered as evidence to prove the truth of an asserted matter. For example, when a professional quotes another professional about the results of a consultation, the quoted material is hearsay. Such third-party information is frequently used by mental health professionals in assessing clinical cases. But hearsay is generally inadmissible as evidence in trials and hearing, because the third-party is unavailable for direct examination and the reported material is subject to distortion by the witness. Lay witnesses can testify only to the personal information they possess.

However, expert witnesses are frequently allowed to base their opinions on hearsay under certain exceptions to the general inadmissibility of hearsay. One such exception allows a witness to rely on records kept in the course of the normal conduct of the business. Consultation reports prepared about a client by another professional would be an example of a routine record prepared in the normal course of clinical assessment. A psychiatrist testifying as an expert witness could rely on a report prepared by a psychologist or a psychologist could rely on a report prepared by a neurologist. Another exception is reliance on the work of an agent of the witness such as a nurse or psychometrician. If it is generally accepted practice for the professional to employ a technician to administer tests, the professional may rely on the results of those tests even though they were prepared by a third-party. Finally, if it is customary for the professional to interview or test third parties (e.g., relatives, arresting officers), then the professional may rely on the results in forming an expert opinion. In assessing victim credibility, for example, the authors often evaluate significant/knowledgeable others in order to determine if the "victim" is exaggerating or fabricating symptoms.

Although hearsay may be legally admissible as the basis for an expert opinion, professionals should be aware of the limitations of such data. The *Specialty Guidelines for Forensic Psychologists* (Committee on Ethical Guidelines for Forensic Psychologists, 1991) state that "when hearsay or otherwise inadmissible evidence forms the basis of their opinion, evidence, or professional conduct, [forensic psychologists] seek to minimize sole reliance upon such evidence. Where circumstances reasonably permit, forensic psychologists seek to obtain independent and personal verification of data relied upon as part of their professional services to the court or to a party to a legal proceeding.... When using hearsay data that have not been corroborated, but are nevertheless utilized, forensic psychologists have an affirmative responsibility to acknowledge the uncorroborated status of those data and the reasons for relying upon such data" (p. 662).].

DISCOVERY

Discovery is the pretrial process by which opposing parties exchange information which they believe is supportive to their cases. Courts have developed detailed rules governing the timing and scope of the discovery process. However, in all jurisdictions, attorneys must declare their intention to call particular experts as witnesses, must make those witnesses available for pre-trial deposition, and must share with opposing counsel all documents upon which the expert will rely in testifying.

During a pretrial deposition, the expert may be asked to state all professional opinions relevant to the case and to describe the factual bases for those opinions. The facts supporting the professional opinions would include personal observations, responses to interview questions, results of psychological and medical tests, reports by consultants, observations of ward personnel, and any other information upon which the expert actually relied in formulating the professional opinions. If the evaluation was audio- or videotaped, as recommended by the American Bar Association for certain criminal cases (American Bar Association [ABA],

1989, p. 100), copies of such tapes should be produced by the expert. Personal notes of the expert, which may include speculations and hypotheses about the client, are not subject to discovery.

One problem which may arise during discovery is the request for copies of raw data from psychological tests. In general, raw test data should not be released directly to attorneys or to courts, but may be released to another psychologist who agrees not to further release the data. This procedure should satisfy the psychologist's ethical responsibility to "provide appropriate interpretations when test score information is released to...legal representatives" (American Educational Research Association et al., 1985, p. 84), to "establish procedures for insuring the adequacy of...explanations [of test results]...[provided by others] (APA, 1989a) and to "ensure that the receiving party is informed that raw scores must be interpreted by a qualified professional in order to provide reliable and valid information" (Committee on Ethical Guidelines for Forensic Psychologists, 1991, p. 664).

Another problem is the request for any self-incriminating statements made during the evaluation by a defendant in a criminal case. In most jurisdictions, statements made by a defendant in the course of a forensic examination are admissible as evidence only on the question of the mental condition of the defendant. They cannot be used as evidence that the defendant actually committed the crime charged. However, in other jurisdictions (e.g., Georgia), statements made by a defendant during a forensic examination can by used as a "confession" to the alleged crime. Therefore, it is imperative that the professional examiner be aware of the rules prevailing in their local jurisdiction. Otherwise the professional may unwittingly elicit a "confession" from a defendant and be compelled to testify to that confession. It is essential that the professional advise the defendant of the purpose of the evaluation, of the potential uses of the results and, where appropriate, of the defendant's right to remain silent and to have an attorney present during the evaluation (ABA, 1989; Committee on Ethical Guidelines for Forensic Psychologists, 1991). It should be noted that, in all jurisdictions, defendants must be given a warning of their "Miranda rights" prior to a forensic evaluation, if the defendant has not raised questions of mental capacity but has been ordered by a court to submit to a pretrial mental evaluation and if the results of the evaluation may used in the sentencing phase of a capital case (*Estelle v. Smith*, 451 U.S 454, 1981; *Barefoot v. Estelle*, 463 U.S. 880, 1983).

FORENSIC REPORTS

The American Bar Association (1989, p. 109-110) has offered guidelines for preparation of written forensic reports in criminal cases. With appropriate modifications, these guidelines are applicable to noncriminal proceedings as well:

(a) Requirement of written report. Promptly upon concluding the evaluation, the mental health or mental retardation professional should prepare a complete, written report. However, at the specific request of the defense attorney, a professional who conducted an evaluation initiated by the defense attorney may make only an oral report.

(b) Contents of written report.
  (i) The written evaluation report should ordinarily:
    (A) identify the specific matters referred for evaluation;
    (B) describe the procedures, tests, and techniques used by the evaluator;
    (C) state the evaluator's clinical findings and opinions on each matter referred for evaluation and indicate specifically those questions, if any, that could not be answered.
    (D) identify the sources of information and present the factual basis for the evaluator's clinical findings and opinions; and
    (E) present the reasoning by which the evaluator utilized the information to reach the clinical findings and opinions. The evaluator should express an opinion on a specific legal criterion or standard only if the opinion is within the scope of the evaluator's specialized knowledge.
  (ii) Except as limited by standard 7-3.8(a), the evaluator should include in the written report any statements or information that serve as necessary factual predicates for the clinical findings or opinions, even if the statements or information are of a personal or potentially incriminating nature.
(c) Clarification of written report. The attorney who requested the evaluation should not edit, modify, revise, or otherwise compromise the integrity of the report. However, after the report has been completed and submitted, the attorney may correspond in writing with the mental health or mental retardation professional to clarify the meaning or implications of the evaluator's findings or opinions. The report and any clarifying correspondence between the attorney and the evaluator should be disclosed at the time established for discovery of written reports.

Standard 7-3.8 of the ABA Standards states, *inter alia*, that "the evaluator should prepare a separate report on [the issue of present mental competency] even if other issues have also been referred for evaluation" (ABA, 1989, p. 112).

Once a defendant has proceeded to the trial stage, and all pretrial mental health issues such as competency have been resolved, forensic psychologists may include in their reports or testimony any statements made by the defendant that are directly relevant to supporting their expert evidence, providing that the defendant has 'introduced' mental state evidence or testimony within the meaning of Federal Rule of Procedure 12.2(c), or its state equivalent (Committee on Ethical Guidelines for Forensic Psychologists, 1991).

The evaluator's written report is usually not admitted as evidence in court, unless opposing attorneys stipulate to its content. The written report cannot be cross-examined and the examining professional is, therefore, usually required to testify personally. If the expert who prepared the report is unavailable for testimony, the opposing attorneys typically conduct a pretrial deposition which is then read into evidence at the trial. Otherwise, the written report is used by trial attorneys to frame their line of questioning and, if possible, to impeach the credibility of the testifying witness. Thus, an expert's testimony should not differ in substance from the facts and opinions expressed in the written report or in a pretrial deposition.

Although most state and federal jurisdictions allow for the introduction of testimony regarding the reliability and validity of data obtained during a forensic evaluation, distortion-related data may be attacked on the grounds that it impugns the credibility of other witnesses and therefore invades the province of the jury to determine the credibility of witnesses.

When the primary focus of the entire examination is itself a question of distortion, (e.g., a victim's credibility in a sexual assault case), the examiner may use a two-step process. This would include (a) commenting on any distortion affecting each source of data and (b) offering a separate opinion regarding the subject's deception about the alleged crime. Findings should be circumspect, with descriptors tied to base rates as much as possible. The evaluator is advised to define words which have dissimilar psychological and legal meanings—"credibility," "reliability," "validity." Inflammatory words should be avoided in one's reports—"faking," "deceitful," "lying,"—so as to reduce the impression of bias. Lastly, ultimate issues should be avoided, if possible. An expert testifying on credibility should not conclude with an opinion on the presence or absence of the (legal) facts. These always involve moral or social value judgements which are reserved for the court or jury. Appendix E contains a sample report of an evaluation of a violent offender and his victim. Nondeliberate and deliberate distortion emerged as central referral and assessment issues in this case.

Legal Guidelines for Determining Credibility

Triers of fact have their own criteria for assessing the credibility of witnesses, including expert witnesses. Thus, it is instructive for forensic mental health professionals to understand what jurors and judges employ as factors in determining the believability of witnesses. In one jurisdiction (California), jurors are instructed to consider the following: (a) whether the witness had the opportunity to see, hear, smell, touch, or otherwise become aware of the matter about which the witness has testified; (b) the ability of the witness to remember or communicate the content of events; (c) the general character and quality of the testimony; (d) the demeanor and manner of the witness while testifying; (e) whether the witness has a bias, vested interest in a given outcome, or other relevant motive; (f) whether matters testified to can be or have been corroborated by other evidence; (g) the attitude of the witness toward what he or she has testified to and toward the giving of the testimony itself; (h) inconsistency or consistency of previous statements made by the witness; and (i) the witness' prior conviction of a felony. The trier of fact may apply some of these criteria to the expert witness as well. The lesson for the expert witness is to try to anchor testimony to concrete, observable behavior and then abstract to patterns and attitudes of the subject.

TESTIMONY

A few useful rules based on numerous court appearances by the authors may assist the beginning expert witness. First, the chances of a court hearing proceeding as scheduled is not very likely in most jurisdictions due to an overcrowded calendar, delaying tactics by attorneys, and other factors. The evaluator may want to take a book or laptop computer for the waiting, which is sure to follow. Second, even if called to testify, the evaluator may not ever make it to the witness chair for a variety of reasons; this should be accepted with equanimity. Third, if and when the evaluator testifies, the chances of him or her being cross-examined and attacked approach certainty. The American system is adversarial in nature.

Generally, the expert, as with any other witness, is subject to cross-examination. The attack will generally come in one or more of four areas:

1. **Credibility.** The opposing party attempts to diminish the expert's credibility. Thus, the evaluator's training, experience, personal ethics, and anything the evaluator has done or failed to do professionally may be scrutinized.
2. **Database.** The opposing party tries to demonstrate that it is limited, replete with biased input sources, invalid, or deficient in some other way. The evaluator may have to show that familiarity with the instant offense or other relevant event.
3. **Basis for Conclusions.** The decision path which the evaluator used to arrive at conclusions may be scrutinized.
4. **Conclusions.** Ultimate conclusions will most likely be attacked by the opposing party.

Usually, the lead expert for one side takes the "heavy hit" and is on the stand for the longest time. The middle expert plays a supporting role and may focus on one aspect of the case. The last expert is the "clean-up batter" and must integrate all previous material and, in general, leave the trier of fact with a favorable impression. No cross-examination or a few questions indicates that the other side does not want to interact with the expert witness either because the evaluator's points are too solid or they consider the input irrelevant. A lengthy attack is directed at vulnerable experts or conducted by desperate cross-examiners. Redirect and recross-examinations may prolong the proceedings, but they focus only on issues covered in the previous interaction with the expert.

Four general factors may ease the distress associated with testifying:

1. **Data preparation for court.** All data relevant to a case should be reviewed. There should be a broad database, and the decision path used to come to decisions should be identified. All data to be used in court should be broken into areas of presentation and anticipated attack. Audio-visual aids should be ready for display.
2. **Nonverbal and psychological preparation.** Casual dress should not be worn to court. Calmness before and during

the proceedings should be developed by the evaluator. The witness should assume the role of a teacher, even though this is an adversarial system. This helps put attacks into perspective. It involves a fundamental belief that the evaluator has something to offer the court from a behavioral science perspective.

3. **Credibility factors.** The expert witnesses' backgrounds and qualifications (i.e., affiliation with academic, professional, and power organizations, such as the police or the state) and the use of the passive tense (e.g., "My system has been accepted in federal jurisdictions.") may be the two most potent determinants of courtroom credibility. Based on courtroom segments of expert testimony, Hurwitz, Miron, and Johnson (1990) stated that the use of the passive tense may create an impression of objectivity.

   Other factors which correlate positively with enhanced expert credibility included the use of words associated with (a) suffering and distress (e.g., "depressed," "pain," "emotional," "trauma," "loss"), suggesting empathy on the part of the evaluator; (b) evaluation, as in performing an assessment; (c) certainty (e.g., "correct," "really," "right," "know"); (d) caution (e.g., "some," "generally," "about," "only"); and (e) causes of damage or harm (e.g., "condition," "develop," "change," "start").

4. **Flexibility of response during the proceedings is important.** The evaluator may be directed, on purpose, to widely disparate areas of inquiry during questioning. Shifting of conceptual gears may be required in order to address legal issues.

   After testifying, the expert should leave and not return to the courtroom, unless invited, as this gives the impression of bias. Feedback on how well the evaluator performed can be obtained from the retaining attorney.

Table 20.1 presents a summary of cross-examination tactics, with special regard to the expert's role in commenting on deception. The readership is encouraged to role-play an expert witness (e.g., with "mock trials") in order to enhance the prospects of a favorable outcome in court.

	Table 20.1		
	Summary of Cross-examination Tactics		
Method	Rationale	Example(s)	Counteraction
1. Attack expert's integrity.	Expert may be for sale if he/she (a) charges large fees, (b) spends much time in court, (c) testifies too much for one side.	"Aren't you a hired gun?" "How much do you charge?"	Keep list of court involvements and outcomes.
2. Show controversy in expert's field.	Expert's opinion on faking may be one amongst many.	"Isn't there much controversy concerning how alleged malingering should be measured?"	Use as opportunity to educate on recent developments.
3. Show expert ignored literature.	Expert opinion may be personally biased.	"Cite some research literature of deception which support what you just said."	Read and apply literature in area of expertise to specific cases.
4. Impeach with authority.	Expert may be wrong if disagrees with "giant" in the field.	"Do you accept *The Encyclopedia of Psychology* as authoritative?"	Caution: Don't accept any treatise as authoritative unless you wish to take responsibility for its contents.
5. Compare expert unfavorably to peers.	Expert's impact diluted when he/she disagrees with peer.	"Do you concede that the other expert is well respected?" "Why should we not believe him (her)?"	Refer to wide database and decision rules used in cases.
6. Attack credentials.	Lack of "medical" training may preclude proper commentary.	"Do I call you Mister, Doctor, or what?"	Emphasize areas of competence leading to degrees in qualification.
7. Attack expert's training or experience.	Always highlight areas of incompleteness that can be probed.	"Are you an expert in psychology of just in the particular field of deception analysis?"	See above; use as basis for educating cross-examiner.
8. Show that expert's training was irrelevant.	Relevant training on deception may be limited or nonexistent.	"Why are your observations on 'response style' even relevant? Is this something you made up?"	Show how apparently irrelevant areas illuminate forensic issues.
9. Attack methods and tools.	Invalid measuring devices render conclusions meaningless.	"Why should we believe the results of your faking tests?"	Have reliability and validity data on methods.

(Continued on next page)

Table 20.1
Summary of Cross-examination Tactics
(continued from previous page)

Method	Rationale	Example(s)	Counteraction
10. Suggest demand characteristics were not taken into account.	Poor assessment conditions may render conclusions meaningless.	"Wouldn't you try to put your best foot forward if tested in jail by the prosecution?"	Assess over multiple and varied circumstances.
11. Suggest expert is biased due to language or cultural differences.	Relying on stereotypes reduces expert's accuracy.	"Have you ever before assessed a Western Samoan for believability?"	Demonstrated use of safeguards (e.g., use of interpreter, cross-cultural norm base).
12. Attack second-order conclusions.	Experts who rely on investigations of others are vulnerable.	"Did you know that a witness you interviewed was convicted for perjury in 1988?"	Directly assess litigants and other parties for deception.
13. Show that DSM-IV was not designed to illuminate forensic issues.	Weakening the foundation of a diagnosis weakens subsequent conclusions.	"Are you aware of the specific disclaimer in DSM-IV for forensic work?"	Agree but add that possible deception is a separate and testable issue.
14. Argue that experience/training not connected to accuracy of diagnosis/prediction.	Relegates qualification period to waste of time for trier of fact.	"Isn't there a body of literature that suggests experts don't know when they are fooled by defendants?"	Have available your percent of true positives and negatives for deception cases.
15. Vary the hypothesis.	Reveals the sometimes flawed decision path of expert.	"How would it change your conclusions if you found out the accused concealed past violence?"	Know the criteria at each point of your decision path.
16. Make expert your witness.	Create an ally if there is a strong case for causation.	"You say he told a lie?"	Anticipate and amplify on leading words/questions of cross-examiner.
17. Show inconsistency across trials.	Expert may be making up decision rules during questioning.	"Aren't you contradicting what you said about deception in *State v. Jones*?"	Use identical decision rules unless change is warranted by data.
18. Show database sources are biased.	Opinions resting on flawed database sources are flawed.	"Describe the tests with results inconsistent with your conclusions on validity."	Advance disconfirming hypotheses in report and in direct examination.

REFERENCES

American Bar Association. (1989). *ABA Criminal Justice Mental Health Standards*. Washington, DC: Author.

American Educational Research Association, American Psychological Association, & National Council on Measurement in Education. (1985). *Standards for Educational and Psychological Testing*. Washington, DC: American Psychological Association.

American Psychological Association. (1989a). *Ethical Principles of Psychologists*. Washington, DC: Author.

American Psychological Association. (1989b). Practice directorate: Expert testimony in mental health useful in courtrooms, Newman argues. *Psychological Practitioner, 3*, 12.

American Psychological Association. (1992). Ethics code. *APA Monitor, 23*(5), 38-42.

Aron, R., Duffy, K., & Rosner, J. (1990). *Cross-examination of witnesses: The litigators puzzle*. Colorado Springs: Shepard's McGraw-Hill.

Black, B. (1988). Evolving legal standards for the admissibility of scientific evidence. *Science, 239*, 1508-1512.

Brodsky, S. (1989). Advocacy in the guise of scientific advocacy: An examination of Ziskin and Faust. *Computers in Human Behavior, 5*, 261-264.

Brodsky, S. (1991). *Testifying in court: Guidelines and maxims for the expert witness*. Washington, DC: American Psychological Association.

Brown, P. (1987). *The art of questioning: Thirty maxims of cross-examination*. New York: MacMillan Publishing Co.

Egeth, H., & McCloskey, M. (1984). Expert testimony about eyewitness behavior: Is it safe and effective. In G. Wells & E. Loftus (Eds.), *Eyewitness testimony* (pp. 283-303). Cambridge, MA: Cambridge University Press.

Committee on Ethical Guidelines for Forensic Psychologists. (1991). Specialty guidelines for forensic psychologists. *Law and Human Behavior, 15*, 655-666.

Faust, E., & Ziskin, J. (1988). The expert witness in psychology and science. *Science, 241*, 31-35.

Faust, D., Ziskin, J., & Hiers, J. (1991). *Brain damage claims: Coping with neuropsychological evidence* (Vols. I-II). Los Angeles, CA: Law and Psychology Press.

Hoge, S., & Grisso, T. (1992). Accuracy and expert testimony. *Bulletin of the American Academy of Psychiatry and Law, 20*(1), 67-76.

Hurwitz, S., Miron, M., & Johnson, B. (1990, August). *Source credibility and the language of expert testimony*. Presented at the 98th Annual Convention of the American Psychological Association, Boston, MA.

Iacono, W., & Patrick, C. (1987). What psychologists should know about lie detection. In I. Weiner & A. Hess (Eds.), *Handbook of forensic psychology* (pp. 460-489). New York: J. Wiley & Sons.

Kleinmuntz, B. (1990). Why we still use our heads instead of formulas: Toward an integrative approach. *Psychological Bulletin, 107*(3), 296-310.

Loftus, E. (1983). Silence is not golden. *American Psychologist, 38*, 564-572.

Loftus, E. (1984). Expert testimony on the eyewitness. In G. Wells & E. Loftus (Eds.), *Eyewitness testimony* (pp. 273-282). Cambridge, MA: Cambridge University Press.

Lykken, D. (1981). *A tremor in the blood: Uses and abuses of the lie detector*. New York: McGraw-Hill.

Matarazzo, J. (1990). Psychological assessment versus psychological testing. *American Psychologist, 45*(9), 999-1017.

Matarazzo, J. (1991). Psychological assessment is reliable and valid: Reply to Ziskin and Faust. *American Psychologist, 46*(8), 882-884.

McCloskey, M., & Egeth, H. (1983). What can a psychologist tell a jury? *American Psychologist, 38*, 550-563.

Poythress, N. G. (1979). A proposal for training in forensic psychology. *American Psychologist, 34*, 612-621.

Rigling, C., & Russo, M. (1990). *Psychologists' attitude survey: Courtroom experience and perceived competence in the court system*. Presented at the 98th Annual Convention of American Psychological Association, Boston, MA.

Rosen, R. H. (1983). The need for training in forensic child psychology. *Professional Psychology: Research and Practice, 14*(4), 481-489.

Sawyer, J. (1966). Measurement and prediction, clinical and statistical. *Psychological Bulletin, 66*, 178-200.

Shuman, D. (1986). *Psychiatric and psychological evidence*. Colorado Springs: Shepard's McGraw Hill.

Singer, M., & Nievod, A. (1987). Consulting and testifying in court. In I. Weiner & A. Hess (Eds.), *Handbook of forensic psychology* (pp. 529-556). New York: J. Wiley & Sons.

Wellman, F. (1986). *The art of cross-examination* (4th ed.). New York: Dorset Press.

Wells, G. (1984). A reanalysis of the expert testimony issue. In G. Wells & E. Loftus (Eds.), *Eyewitness testimony* (pp. 304-314). Cambridge, MA: Cambridge University Press.

Wiggins, J. (1973). *Personality and prediction: Principles of personality assessment.* Reading, MA: Addison-Wesley.

Ziskin, J., & Faust, D. (1988). *Coping with psychiatric and psychological testimony* (Vols. I-III) (4th ed.). Los Angeles, CA: Law and Psychology Press.

Ziskin, J., & Faust, D. (1991). Reply to Matarazzo. *American Psychologist, 46*(8), 881-882.

APPENDICES

APPENDIX A

PAIN SURVEY CHECK LIST (PSCL)

Full name: _____

Date: _____

Other names used: _____

Birth date: _____

Reason for referral: _____

Soc. Sec. No.: _____

Referral source: _____

In state since: _____

Place of birth: _____

Sex: _____

Educational level and last school attended: _____

Race/ethnic group: _____

Occupation: _____

Employer's name, address and phone no.: _____

Your residential address and phone no.: _____

Attorney's name, address and phone no. (for pending legal cases or Workers' Compensation):

_____

_____

_____

Physical Questions

1. Height _____

2. Weight _____

3. Blood type _____

4. List all disorders or diseases you have had in the past: _____

    _____

5. List all significant injuries you have had in the past: _____

    _____

6. List all present medical or psychological conditions you have now:

    _____

7. List operations and dates: _____

    _____

8. List hospitalizations and dates: _____

    _____

9. Who is your primary physician? _____

Address: _____   Phone: _____

Date of last physical exam. _____

10. What other doctor(s) are you seeing? _____

11. Have you been treated for a psychological concern? What, when, and by
    whom?

    _____

    _____

12. Is there a family history of similar pain problems? Please explain.

    _____

    _____

13. Have you been treated for this pain condition in the past? Explain.

_____

_____

14. What is your overall physical condition?_____

Pain Questions

1. When did your present pain start?_____

_____

    Where was the location of the accident?_____

_____

    Who was there at the time besides yourself?_____

_____

    What were you doing?_____

_____

    What did you do about the pain?_____

_____

    In your opinion, what do you think was the cause of the pain?_____

_____

2. Did your pain start gradually? _____ suddenly? _____
   Did it spread? _____

    Explain any details_____

_____

_____

3. What is the most frustrating thing about your pain?

_____

_____

4. Can you work? _____ Have you changed jobs? _____

5. What do your relatives or acquaintances do when you show pain?

_____

6. What factors seem to bring on or are associated with the pain?

_____

_____

7. Where do you feel your pain now?_____

_____

_____

8. Is your pain with you all the time? Or does it change during the day? Please
    explain.

_____

_____

9. Does your pain spread?_____

_____

10. Does your pain have a pattern (e.g., continuous, periodic, brief)?

_____

11. How long does it take for the worst pain to develop?_____

_____

12. How long does your pain usually last?_____

_____

13. How many times during a typical day do thoughts of pain cross your mind?

_____

14. How would your future change if your pain went away for good?

_____

When I experience the following:

My Pain Is:

	Better	Worse	Same	Comment
Coughing or sneezing	_____	_____	_____	_____
Alcohol drinking	_____	_____	_____	_____
Riding in a car	_____	_____	_____	_____
Waking up in the morning	_____	_____	_____	_____
Tension	_____	_____	_____	_____
Cold	_____	_____	_____	_____
Dampness	_____	_____	_____	_____
Middle of night	_____	_____	_____	_____
Lying on my back	_____	_____	_____	_____
Urinating	_____	_____	_____	_____
Defecating	_____	_____	_____	_____
Having sex	_____	_____	_____	_____
Sitting (straight chair)	_____	_____	_____	_____
Sitting (soft chair)	_____	_____	_____	_____
Being massaged	_____	_____	_____	_____
Talking with people	_____	_____	_____	_____
In whirlpool/jacuzzi	_____	_____	_____	_____
Brushing teeth	_____	_____	_____	_____
Sleeping or napping	_____	_____	_____	_____
Standing	_____	_____	_____	_____
Distracted (T.V., etc.)	_____	_____	_____	_____
Hearing loud noises	_____	_____	_____	_____
Middle of the day	_____	_____	_____	_____
Lying on side with knees bent	_____	_____	_____	_____
Doing housework	_____	_____	_____	_____
Exercising	_____	_____	_____	_____
Seeing bright lights	_____	_____	_____	_____
Feeling tired	_____	_____	_____	_____
Weather changes	_____	_____	_____	_____
Drinking coffee or tea	_____	_____	_____	_____
Eating a meal	_____	_____	_____	_____
Swimming	_____	_____	_____	_____
Working at my job	_____	_____	_____	_____
Standing after sitting	_____	_____	_____	_____
Lifting	_____	_____	_____	_____
Walking	_____	_____	_____	_____
Running	_____	_____	_____	_____
Leaning over	_____	_____	_____	_____
Swallowing	_____	_____	_____	_____
Elevated blood pressure	_____	_____	_____	_____
Certain foods	_____	_____	_____	_____
Boredom	_____	_____	_____	_____
Being alone	_____	_____	_____	_____

1.   What medication did you take, for any reason, before the injury or pain started?

Medication/Purpose   How long did you take it?   How effective was it?

_____   _____   _____
_____   _____   _____
_____   _____   _____
_____   _____   _____

2.   What medication have you taken specifically for the pain?
     a. _____ dosage: _____ times a day: _____
     b. _____ dosage: _____ times a day: _____
     c. _____ dosage: _____ times a day: _____
     d. _____ dosage: _____ times a day: _____

3.   How well does the medication work?_____

_____

_____

4.   What other medication do you take currently?
     a. _____ dosage: _____ times a day: _____
     b. _____ dosage: _____ times a day: _____
     c. _____ dosage: _____ times a day: _____
     d. _____ dosage: _____ times a day: _____

5.   What do you do, besides taking pain medication, to relieve pain?

_____

_____

6.   How much alcohol do you drink on the average during the week?

_____

_____

7.   What kind of alcohol?

_____

8.   Do you mix alcohol with medication (i.e., take at the same time)?

_____

9.   What kind of over-the-counter medication do you take?_____

_____

10. Do you take any illicit drugs? Which kind?_____

_____

_____

11. Have you ever received a traffic citation for alcohol- or drug-related behavior (e.g., DUI)?

What	When	Where	Disposition
_____	_____	_____	_____
_____	_____	_____	_____
_____	_____	_____	_____
_____	_____	_____	_____

12. What other arrests, if any, have you had since 18 years of age?

What	When	Where	Disposition
_____	_____	_____	_____
_____	_____	_____	_____
_____	_____	_____	_____
_____	_____	_____	_____

13. Have you ever received treatment for a drug/alcohol problem?

What	When	Where	Disposition
_____	_____	_____	_____
_____	_____	_____	_____
_____	_____	_____	_____
_____	_____	_____	_____

14. Does drinking coffee or tea bring on or affect the pain?

_____

15. What other factors associated with eating food or drinking liquid affect your pain?

_____

_____

_____

Signs Which Accompany My Pain
(Mark all which apply)

	Before Pain	During Pain	After Pain
A. Dull ache	_____	_____	_____
B. Sharp pain	_____	_____	_____
C. Burning	_____	_____	_____
D. Steady pain	_____	_____	_____
E. Throbbing pain	_____	_____	_____
F. Deep pain	_____	_____	_____
G. Shooting pain	_____	_____	_____
H. Tingling	_____	_____	_____
I. Pins and needles	_____	_____	_____
J. Tender to touch	_____	_____	_____
K. Vomiting	_____	_____	_____
L. Feeling sick	_____	_____	_____
M. Fear	_____	_____	_____
N. Stress	_____	_____	_____
O. Rapid breathing	_____	_____	_____
P. Dizziness	_____	_____	_____
Q. Heart beating fast	_____	_____	_____
R. Flushed	_____	_____	_____
S. Blurred vision	_____	_____	_____
T. Sweating	_____	_____	_____
U. Fainting	_____	_____	_____
V. Bleeding	_____	_____	_____
W. Skin color change	_____	_____	_____
X. Epileptic seizures	_____	_____	_____
Y. Falling down	_____	_____	_____
Z. Others (specify)	_____	_____	_____

Please give your comments on anything which would help us understand your pain better.

_____

_____

_____

_____

_____

_____

List several people who can be reached for additional information.

Name	Relationship	Address	Phone no.
_____	_____	_____	_____
_____	_____	_____	_____
_____	_____	_____	_____
_____	_____	_____	_____

Pain Chart

1. Please mark all the locations of pain and numbness on your body. Use two different colors of markers, one for pain and the other for numbness.

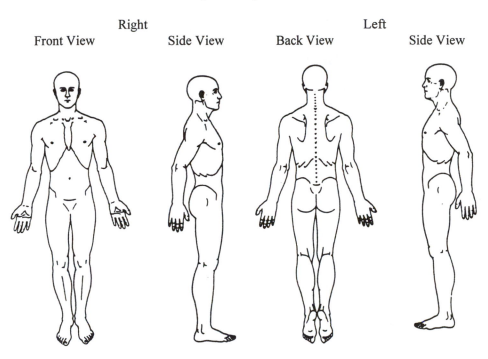

Right   Left
Front View   Side View   Back View   Side View

My color code for the above drawing:
The _____ color stands for pain.
The _____ color stands for numbness.

2. Now, just for the pain locations, please put letters inside the marked areas to indicate any of the following:
   - Write A to indicate a dull ache.
   - Write B to indicate a sharp pain.
   - Write C to indicate a burning pain.
   - Write D to indicate a steady pain.
   - Write E to indicate a throbbing pain.

- Write F to indicate a deep pain.
- Write G to indicate a shooting pain.
- Write H to indicate a tingling pain.
- Write I to indicate pins and needles.

3. For traveling pain, draw a line from where it starts to where it ends.

4. For pain you feel right now, show where the pain is with the color marker.

APPENDIX B

SELF-CONTROL AND INSTANT OFFENSE BEHAVIORS: CHECKLIST OF DEFENDANT COMPETENCIES

Please complete this checklist as carefully as you can before drawing conclusions in regards to a particular criminal case. This checklist may be helpful to the forensic professional in assessing different levels of self-control before, during, and after alleged criminal behavior.

In several of the sections, you will be asked to think about the sequence of the alleged behaviors in addition to a number of content factors. The ultimate purpose of this checklist is to illuminate the decision path of the evaluator. Please try to go along with this new perspective because, in doing so, you may be able to gain additional insight into the ability of the defendant to choose and self-regulate instant offense behaviors.

Evaluator's Name: _____

Agency: _____

Part A: Demographic and Background Factors

Present Date _____

Accused's Full Name _____

Address _____

Contact parties	Relationship to accused	phone number(s)

_____

_____

Aliases _____

Social Security No. _____

Reason for Referral _____

Criminal No. _____

Referral Source _____

Charges _____

Date of Birth _____

Place of Birth _____

In State Since _____

Sex _____

Marital Status _____

Race/Ethnic Group _____

Languages Spoken _____

Educational Level _____

Occupation _____

Hand Dominance _____

Accused's
    Height _____ Weight _____# Blood Type_____

Victim's
    Height _____ Weight _____# Blood Type_____

BACKGROUND FACTORS

• History of alcohol abuse or dependence? Specify._____

_____

• History of drug abuse or dependence? Specify._____

_____

• Psychiatric/Psychological History

Date of Diagnosis	Diagnosis	Agency	Therapist

Specify if there is a history of critical conditions/events not presented on previous page (e.g., psychosis, retardation, brain damage, homicidal/suicidal behaviors)

_____

_____

_____

• Juvenile Arrest History

Offense	Date of Offense	Disposition	Date of Disposition

- Adult Arrest History

	Date		Date of
Offense	of Offense	Disposition	Disposition

_____

_____

_____

- Physical/mental deterioration for one week before alleged offense? Specify.

_____

- Physical/mental deterioration for 90 days before alleged offense? Specify.

_____

- Physical/mental deterioration for one year before alleged offense? Specify.

_____

- Anticipated stressors at time of instant offenses? Specify.

_____

- Employment in the three months before evaluation:
  _____ None   _____ Part-time   _____ Full-time

Where and what?

_____

- Estimated income from employment in last year $_____/year

CURRENT FACTORS

1. Is accused fit to legally proceed (if no, why not)?_____

_____

2. Accused's present status?
   _____ Incarcerated   _____ Outpatient   _____ Inpatient

3. Present medications

_____

4. Present alcohol abuse or dependence? ____ Yes ____ No

_____

5. Present drug abuse or dependence? ____ Yes ____ No

_____

6. Significant current psychiatric deficits or problems

_____

7. Relevant medical problems

_____

_____

_____

_____

8. Relevant other current information

_____

_____

_____

_____

_____

_____

Part B: Basal Violence Analysis

Previous violence to others is scrutinized to determine whether instant violence is part of a habit pattern or an isolated event. Since attaining adulthood, indicate whether each act of significant violence had the associated feature listed on the left. Threats to do significant violence to another are considered violence and are rated as such. First, threats create psychological trauma in victims. Second, some threats are arrestable behaviors (e.g., robbery, terroristic threatening).

Look at the entire basal history of violence to see if trends emerge. Determine whether these trends are operative in the instant violence and the degree to which they were the result of choice and self-control factors.

Associated Features of Previous Violence	# Violent Acts to Others						
	1	2	3	4	5	6	7
1. Date of violence or serious threat	—	—	—	—	—	—	—
2. Description of violence or threat (e.g., assault in the third degree)	—	—	—	—	—	—	—
3. Injury to victim (one or more of following for each act:)							
a) Verbal or physical intimidation of victim	—	—	—	—	—	—	—
b) Intimidation by weapon	—	—	—	—	—	—	—
c) Minor harm	—	—	—	—	—	—	—
d) Treated and discharged	—	—	—	—	—	—	—
e) Hospitalized	—	—	—	—	—	—	—
f) Killed	—	—	—	—	—	—	—
4. Forced sex act	—	—	—	—	—	—	—
5. Relationship to victim							
a) Stranger	—	—	—	—	—	—	—
b) Acquaintance	—	—	—	—	—	—	—
c) Family	—	—	—	—	—	—	—
d) Institutional (e.g., police, military)	—	—	—	—	—	—	—
6. Accomplice present	—	—	—	—	—	—	—
7. Instructions to aggress (e.g., military police, contract murder)	—	—	—	—	—	—	—
8. Weapons (one or more of following):							
a) Firearms	—	—	—	—	—	—	—
b) Knife	—	—	—	—	—	—	—
c) Other weapon (e.g., hammer, rope)	—	—	—	—	—	—	—
d) Weapon found at scene	—	—	—	—	—	—	—
e) Use of protected body part (e.g., victim kicked with boots)	—	—	—	—	—	—	—
f) Use of unprotected body part (e.g., hands)	—	—	—	—	—	—	—
g) Use of primitive weapons (e.g., bites or clubs victim with head)	—	—	—	—	—	—	—

9. Substance intoxication
    a) Alcohol intoxication   __ __ __ __ __ __ __
    b) Drug intoxication   __ __ __ __ __ __ __
    c) Pathological
    intoxication   __ __ __ __ __ __ __
    d) Cessation of prescribed
    medication   __ __ __ __ __ __ __
10. Pain cues from victim
    which enhanced violence __ __ __ __ __ __ __
11. Positive consequences
    for violence (e.g.,
    money, praise,
    no incarceration)   __ __ __ __ __ __ __
12. Disrupted central love
    relationship (e.g., from
    intimate other)   __ __ __ __ __ __ __
13. Work-related violence   __ __ __ __ __ __ __
14. Characteristics of victims
    a) Female gender   __ __ __ __ __ __ __
    b) Weighs less than
    accused   __ __ __ __ __ __ __
    c) Shorter than accused __ __ __ __ __ __ __
    d) Alone before violence __ __ __ __ __ __ __
    e) Victim displayed
    weapon   __ __ __ __ __ __ __
    f) Physical infirmity   __ __ __ __ __ __ __
15. Violence context
    characteristics
    a) Night-time occurrence __ __ __ __ __ __ __
    b) Weekend occurrence   __ __ __ __ __ __ __
    c) Private residence   __ __ __ __ __ __ __
    d) Public building   __ __ __ __ __ __ __
    e) Roadway or trans-
    portation system   __ __ __ __ __ __ __
    f) Property aggression
    involved   __ __ __ __ __ __ __
16. Acknowledgement of
    violence (e.g.,
    spontaneous statements,
    written confession)   __ __ __ __ __ __ __
17. Apologizes for violence __ __ __ __ __ __ __
18. Suicidal/self-mutilative
    gestures in response to
    violence   __ __ __ __ __ __ __

Synthesis: Examine the above tables after completion for behavioral themes. Look for themes that are common both to previous violence and the instant case. Place the common descriptors on the assault cycle.

Estimate of Self-control by Temporal Period

	Before	During	After
Substantial	—	—	—
Considerable	—	—	—
Moderate	—	—	—
Mild	—	—	—
Minimal	—	—	—
Negligible	—	—	—

Before   During   After
Instant Violence

Combining all events within a time period, present the overall degree of self-control for BEFORE, DURING, and AFTER the instant violence on the above histogram.

(Date, time, & day of week)

Event	Defendant Time	Specify Behavior	Victim Time	Specify Behavior
1. Significant events the night before	_____		_____	
2. Intoxicating substances ingested before instant violence occurred	_____		_____	
3. Procurement of weapons	_____		_____	
4. Presence of other people	_____		_____	

5. Arrival at instant
   violence scene   _____   _____
6. First sighting of
   victim (accused)   _____   _____
7. Verbal interaction with
   victim (accused)   _____   _____
8. Time of instant
   violence   _____   _____
9. Time left scene   _____   _____
10. Destination   _____   _____

PERPETRATOR AND VICTIM CHARACTERISTICS AT THE TIME OF THE INSTANT OFFENSE

Please check as many as apply. Fill in the blanks when indicated.
P = Perpetrator   V = Victim

P	V	SEX	P	V	BUILD
___	___	Male	___	___	Skinny
___	___	Female	___	___	Slim
___	___	Unknown	___	___	Medium/Average
			___	___	Heavy
___	___	KNOWN AGE	___	___	Husky
			___	___	Muscular
		ESTIMATED AGE	___	___	Fat
___	___	Below 15 years	___	___	Unknown
___	___	15 yrs. to 19 yrs.			
___	___	20 yrs. to 24 yrs.			POSTURE
___	___	25 yrs. to 29 yrs.	___	___	Stooped
___	___	30 yrs. to 39 yrs.	___	___	Bowed Legs
___	___	40 yrs. to 49 yrs.	___	___	Bent to One Side
___	___	50 yrs. to 65 yrs.	___	___	Normal/Erect
___	___	Over 65 yrs.	___	___	Stiff
			___	___	Unknown
		HEIGHT			
___	___	Under 5'0"			GAIT
___	___	5'0" to 5'1"	___	___	Slow
___	___	5'2" to 5'3"	___	___	Shuffle
___	___	5'4" to 5'5"	___	___	Limp
___	___	5'6" to 5'7"	___	___	Walks with Cane
___	___	5'8" to 5'9"	___	___	Normal
___	___	5'10" to 5'11"	___	___	Fast
___	___	6'0" to 6'1"	___	___	Runs
___	___	6'2" to 6'3"	___	___	Unknown
___	___	6'4" to 6'6"			
___	___	Over 6'6"			

P	V	WEIGHT	P	V	
___	___	Under 100 lbs.			
___	___	100 lbs. to 119 lbs.			ACCENT
___	___	120 lbs. to 139 lbs.	___	___	Specify
___	___	140 lbs. to 159 lbs.	_____		Specify
___	___	160 lbs. to 179 lbs.	___	___	Unknown
___	___	180 lbs. to 199 lbs.			
___	___	200 lbs. to 219 lbs.			INJURIES
___	___	220 lbs. to 239 lbs.	___	___	Specify
___	___	240 lbs. to 260 lbs.	_____		Specify
___	___	Over 260 lbs.	___	___	Unknown
		ETHNICITY			TATTOOS
___	___	Black	___	___	Arm, Left
___	___	White	___	___	Arm, Right
___	___	Hispanic	___	___	Back
___	___	Chinese	___	___	Chest
___	___	Filipino	___	___	Fingers, Left
___	___	Hawaiian	___	___	Fingers, Right
___	___	Japanese	___	___	Hand, Left
___	___	Polynesian	___	___	Hand, Right
___	___	Portuguese	___	___	Leg, Left
___	___	Samoan	___	___	Leg, Right
___	___	Mixed/Combo	___	___	Elsewhere
___	___	_____	___	___	Unknown
___	___	Unknown			
					HEAD HAIR — Length
		BODY SCARS	___	___	Bald
___	___	Abdomen, Left	___	___	Crew Cut
___	___	Abdomen, Right	___	___	Neck Length
___	___	Arm, Left	___	___	Shoulder Length
___	___	Arm, Right	___	___	Long
___	___	Back	___	___	Unknown
___	___	Chest			
___	___	Hand, Left			FACIAL HAIR — Type
___	___	Hand, Right	___	___	Mustache
___	___	Leg, Left	___	___	Goatee
___	___	Leg, Right	___	___	Beard
___	___	Wrist, Left	___	___	Sideburns
___	___	Wrist, Right	___	___	Unknown
___	___	_____			
___	___	Unknown			

P   V   P   V

FACIAL SCARS   FACIAL HAIR—Color

_____   _____   Cheek, left   _____   _____   Black
_____   _____   Cheek, right   _____   _____   Brown
_____   _____   Chin   _____   _____   Blond
_____   _____   Eyebrow, left   _____   _____   Red
_____   _____   Eyebrow, right   _____   _____   Gray
_____   _____   Forehead   _____   _____   White
_____   _____   Harelip   _____   _____   Mixed
_____   _____   Lip, lower   _____   _____   Unknown
_____   _____   Lip, upper
_____   _____   Nose   EYES — Color
_____   _____   Ears, pierced   _____   _____   Black
_____   _____   Other   _____   _____   Brown
                                     _____   _____   Blue
                JEWELRY   _____   _____   Gray
                                     _____   _____   Green
_____   _____   _____
_____   _____   _____   _____
_____   _____   _____   _____   _____   Unknown

                HEAD HAIR — Color   EYES — Glasses

_____   _____   Black   _____   _____   Bifocals
_____   _____   Brown   _____   _____   Other Prescription
_____   _____   Blond   _____   _____   Contact Lenses
_____   _____   Dirty Blond   _____   _____   Sunglasses
_____   _____   Red   _____   _____   Reflective
_____   _____   Gray
_____   _____   White   _____
_____   _____   _____   _____   _____   Unknown
_____   _____   Unknown
                                                     EYES — FRAMES
                HEAD HAIR — Style   _____   _____   Wire
_____   _____   Straight   _____   _____   Plastic
_____   _____   Curly   _____   _____   Rimless
_____   _____   Wavy   _____   _____   Clear
_____   _____   Afro   _____   _____   _____
_____   _____   Tied Back   _____   _____   Unknown

                                                     EYES — Traits
                                     _____   _____   Crossed
                                     _____   _____   Squinted
                                     _____   _____   Bloodshot
                                     _____   _____   Dilated/Constricted
                                                     Pupils

P   V   P   V

_____   _____   Braided   _____   _____   Lazy Eye
_____   _____   Neat   _____   _____   Wide
_____   _____   Flat Top   _____   _____   Missing, Left
_____   _____   Wig   _____   _____   Missing, Right
_____   _____   Unknown   _____   _____   _____
                                               _____   _____   Unknown

                  COMPLEXION   CLOTHING—Top
_____   _____   Pale   _____   _____   T-Shirt
_____   _____   Fair   _____   _____   Pull Over
_____   _____   Medium   _____   _____   Sport Shirt
_____   _____   Ruddy   _____   _____   Dress Shirt
_____   _____   Tanned   _____   _____   Blouse
_____   _____   Brown   _____   _____   None
_____   _____   Black   _____   _____   Unknown
_____   _____   Clear   _____   _____   _____
_____   _____   Moles   _____   _____   Sleeve Length
_____   _____   Freckles   _____   _____   Unknown
_____   _____   Blackheads   _____   _____   Markings
_____   _____   Acne/Pimples
                                                                 CLOTHING—Trousers
_____   _____   Pock-marked   _____   _____   Jeans
_____   _____   Birthmark(s)   _____   _____   Dress Slacks
_____   _____   _____   _____   _____   Shorts
_____   _____   Unknown   _____   _____   None
                                               _____   _____   Casual
                  TEETH   _____   _____   Corduroy
                                               _____   _____   _____
_____   _____   Yellow   _____   _____   Unknown
_____   _____   White   _____   _____   Length
_____   _____   Normal   _____   _____   Markings
_____   _____   False
_____   _____   Broken   CLOTHING—Shoes
_____   _____   Braces   _____   _____   Barefoot
_____   _____   Missing   _____   _____   Slippers
_____   _____   Stained   _____   _____   Dress Shoes
_____   _____   Filled   _____   _____   Work Shoes
_____   _____   _____   _____   _____   Boots
_____   _____   Unknown   _____   _____   Athletic Shoes

                  MOUTH
_____   _____   Stink Breath
_____   _____   Alcohol Smell
_____   _____   Saliva
_____   _____   Normal
_____   _____   Unusual Lips

P	V		P	V	
_____	_____	Mouth Concealed	_____	_____	Sandals
_____	_____	_____	_____	_____	_____
_____	_____	Unknown	_____	_____	Unknown
			_____	_____	Color
		HANDS			_____
_____	_____	Small	_____	_____	Material
_____	_____	Stubby			_____
_____	_____	Large			
_____	_____	Spotted			CLOTHING — Dress
_____	_____	Normal	_____	_____	Formal
_____	_____	Hairy	_____	_____	Casual
_____	_____	Injured	_____	_____	Work
_____	_____	_____	_____	_____	Unknown
			_____	_____	Color
		CLOTHING — Hat	_____	_____	Length
_____	_____	Baseball Cap	_____	_____	Markings
_____	_____	Business			
_____	_____	Military			VEHICLE
_____	_____	None	_____	_____	Automobile
_____	_____	_____	_____	_____	Bicycle
_____	_____	Color	_____	_____	Motorcycle
_____	_____	_____	_____	_____	Truck
_____	_____	Designs	_____	_____	_____
			_____	_____	Unknown
_____	_____	Unknown	_____	_____	Make
					_____
		TYPE OF	_____	_____	Color _____
		WEAPON	_____	_____	Year_____
_____	_____	Arson	_____	_____	Unusual Features
		Ax	(e.g., damage)		_____
		Blunt Instrument			
		Firearm	_____	_____	Decals_____
		Handgun ____ Cal.	_____	_____	Tag#_____
		Shotgun ____ Cal.	_____	_____	State _____
		Rifle ____ Cal.			
					CRIMINAL
					OCCUPATION
			_____	_____	Arson
			_____	_____	Burglary
			_____	_____	Fraud
			_____	_____	Gambling
			_____	_____	Homicide
			_____	_____	Larceny
			_____	_____	Motorcycle Gang

P   V

P	V	
___	___	Machine Gun ___ Cal.
___	___	Garrotte/Ligature
___	___	Hatchet
___	___	Knife, Large (> 6")
___	___	Knife, Small (< 6")
___	___	Odd/Unusual Weapon
___	___	Physical Force
___	___	Sharp Instrument (other than knife)
___	___	Vehicle
___	___	Tire Tool
___	___	_____
___	___	Unknown
___	___	Color_____
___	___	Composition_____
___	___	Container_____

FIRST SEEN BY OTHERS

P	V	
___	___	Car
___	___	Club/Disco
___	___	Date First Seen____
___	___	Estimated Time____
___	___	Health Club
___	___	Hitchhiking
___	___	House/Apartment
___	___	Playground or Parks/ Yards
___	___	Public Conveyance
___	___	School
___	___	Shopping
___	___	Walking
___	___	Work
___	___	City/State
___	___	_____
___	___	Unknown

LAST SEEN BY OTHERS

P	V	
___	___	Car
___	___	Club/Disco
___	___	Date Last Seen_____
___	___	Estimated Time_____
___	___	Health Club
___	___	Hitchhiking
___	___	House/Apartment
___	___	Playground or Parks/Yards

P   V

P	V	
___	___	Narcotics
		Organized Crime
___	___	Pornography
		Prostitution
___	___	Robbery
		_____
___	___	Unknown

LIFESTYLE

P	V	
		Bisexual
___	___	Day Person-in early
		Heterosexual
___	___	Homosexual
___	___	Involved/Outgoing
___	___	Narcotics User
___	___	Night Person- stays out late
___	___	Socializes Frequently
___	___	Socializes Seldom
___	___	Withdrawn/Shy
___	___	_____
___	___	Unknown

OCCUPATION

P	V	
___	___	Gas Station Attendant
___	___	Business/ Professional
___	___	Homemaker
___	___	Laborer/Services
___	___	Street Person
___	___	Student
___	___	None
___	___	Realtor
___	___	Priest/Minister
___	___	Convenience Store Clerk
___	___	_____
___	___	Unknown

P   V

_____   _____   Public Conveyance
_____   _____   School
_____   _____   Shopping
_____   _____   Walking
_____   _____   Work
_____   _____   City/State

_____   _____   _____
_____   _____   Unknown

CRIME CONTEXT AND MODUS OPERANDI:

Location Where Occurred   Modus Operandi
_____   Apartment/House   _____   False Pretense
_____   Building   _____   Hitchhiker
_____   Construction Site   _____   Impersonates Doctor
_____   Field   _____   Impersonates Police
_____   Hotel/Motel   _____   Newspaper Ad
_____   Interstate or Highway   _____   Random
_____   Rural   _____   Robbery/Burglary
_____   Street/Alley   _____   Stalker
_____   City/State_____   _____   Stranger
_____   River/Lake   _____   Victim Knew Suspect
_____   Woods   _____   Arms Self at Scene
_____   Other_____   _____   Disables Lights/Electricity
                                        _____   Disables Telephone
                                        _____   Disables Security System
                                        _____   Disables Victim's Car
                                        _____   Fingerprints Removed
PLACEMENT/POSITION OF VICTIM _____   Ransacks
_____   Buried   _____   Suspect Clean up Scene
_____   Concealed   _____   Suspect Injured at Scene
_____   Displayed   _____   Suspect Returns to Scene
_____   Dumped   _____   Takes Souvenirs
_____   Face Down   _____   Wears Disguises/Gloves
_____   Face Up   _____   Suspect Takes Victim's Vehicle
_____   Fetal Position
_____   In Receptacle   VULNERABILITY ANALYSIS
_____   In Water   Lighting_____
_____   Moved After Injury or Death
_____   Nude   Security_____
_____   Partially Nude
_____   Propped-up Sitting   Presence of Others_____
_____   Fully Clothed
_____   _____   Exits_____

TREATMENT OF VICTIM   Locking System_____
_____   Bound
_____   Body Covered   Visibility_____
_____   Burned

_____ Face Covered	Noise_____
_____ Gagged	
_____ Handcuffed	Temperature_____
_____ Kidnapped	
_____ Raped	History of Violence_____
_____ Sodomized	
_____ Tortured	Architecture_____
_____ Duct Tape Used To Bind	
_____ Rope/String Used To Bind	Concealment_____
_____ Clothes Used To Bind	
_____ Surgical Tape Used To Bind	
_____ Other Tape/Material Used To Bind	
_____ _____	

HOMICIDE CASES:

CAUSE OF DEATH
- _____ Asphyxiation
- _____ Bludgeoning
- _____ Burning
- _____ Drowning
- _____ Drug Overdose
- _____ Electrocution
- _____ Poisoning
- _____ Scalding
- _____ Shooting
- _____ Slashing
- _____ Stabbing
- _____ Strangling
- _____ Unknown
- _____ _____

SECONDARY WOUNDS
- _____ Asphyxiation
- _____ Bite Marks
- _____ Bludgeoning
- _____ Burning
- _____ Drowning
- _____ Drug Overdose
- _____ Electrocution
- _____ Multiple Wounds
- _____ Poisoning
- _____ Scalding

TECHNICAL/PHYSICAL EVIDENCE
- _____ Body X-rays Available
- _____ Casting Available
- _____ Composite Available
- _____ Dental X-rays Available
- _____ Fibers
- _____ Fingerprints Available
- _____ Fingernail Scrapings
- _____ Fluids
- _____ Footprints Available
- _____ Hair
- _____ Multiple Perpetrators
- _____ Semen
- _____ Tire Impressions Taken
- _____ Weapon Found at Scene
- _____ _____
- _____ Written Evidence

ARTICLES LEFT ON BODY
- _____ Clothing
- _____ Jewelry
- _____ _____

MEDICAL INFORMATION (DESCRIBE)
- _____ Broken Bones _____
- _____ Blood Type_____

_____ Shooting   _____ Pregnancy_____
_____ Slashing
_____ Stabbing   _____ _____
_____ Strangling
_____ Unknown
_____ Other_____

CONDITION OF BODY WHEN FOUND
_____ Mutilated
_____ Necrophilia
_____ Objects in Throat/Mouth
_____ Objects in Penis
_____ Objects in Rectum
_____ Objects in Vagina
_____ Objects or Symbols Placed on Body
_____ Penile/Anal Penetration
_____ Penile/Oral Penetration
_____ Penile/Vaginal Penetration
_____ Possible Sexual Contact
_____ Decomposed/Skeletal
_____ Other_____

PART D: SELF-CONTROL DURING THE INSTANT OFFENSE SEQUENCE

Please complete items based upon the various data base sources relevant to the day of the instant violence.

PHYSICAL AND MENTAL ACTIVITIES

These refer to rudimentary skills and/or homeostatic activities of the defendant. They create the foundation for all self-control behaviors exhibited before, during, or subsequent to instant violence by the accused. Check the appropriate space and present comments when appropriate.

	Insufficient Data	No	Yes	Specify
Ability to sleep	_____	_____	_____	_____
Ability to eat/drink	_____	_____	_____	_____
Responds to autonomic pressure (e.g., relieves self)	_____	_____	_____	_____
Self-awareness (e.g., "I" statements)	_____	_____	_____	_____
Long-term memory skills (e.g., visual, auditory, tactile, olfactory)	_____	_____	_____	_____

	Insufficient Data	No	Yes	Specify
Short-term memory skills	___	___	___	___
Reports cognitive activity	___	___	___	___
Awareness of surroundings (e.g., observations of environment)	___	___	___	___
Ability to estimate time	___	___	___	___
Ability to ambulate (e.g., voluntary movements)	___	___	___	___
Intact sensory skills (e.g., visual, olfactory, hearing)	___	___	___	___
Ability to express feelings (e.g., verbalizes anger, shows rage or fear)	___	___	___	___
Intact motor skills (e.g., grasping reflex, biting)	___	___	___	___
Withdrawal reflex from pain	___	___	___	___
Voice recognition (e.g., of victim)	___	___	___	___
Self-grooming	___	___	___	___
Ability to maintain posture	___	___	___	___
Ability to show facial expression	___	___	___	___
Rudimentary chaining of behaviors (e.g., tracking and moving toward visual stimulus)	___	___	___	___
Ability to drive	___	___	___	___
Other signs of basic self-regulation	___	___	___	___

GOAL FORMULATION

Relevant to the time before the alleged violence, goal formulation taps the ability to systematically analyze and integrate the accused's awareness of self and environment. The capability of productively elaborating from a small number of cues from the crime context is also measured. The ability to think of the violence act before it occurred, as evidenced by behaviors compatible with the idea of the violence to follow, is the central issue of this section.

	Insufficient Data	No	Yes	Specify
Marked cognitive and/or behavioral focus	___	___	___	_____
Ability to link thoughts with adaptive behavior (e.g., walking until entrance is found)	___	___	___	_____
Verbal coherence and verbal fluency	___	___	___	_____
Speaks to victim (e.g., requests money)	___	___	___	_____
Controlled conversation	___	___	___	_____
Appreciation of temporally distant need (e.g., need for more drugs to prevent withdrawal)	___	___	___	_____
Knowledge of steps or elements in violent sequence	___	___	___	_____
Cognitive mapping (e.g., navigating from home to crime scene)	___	___	___	_____
Shows capacity for reflective thought about violence (e.g., verbalizations which involve comparisons)	___	___	___	_____
Ability to think of alternatives to instant violence	___	___	___	_____
Statements to others that he or she would harm the victim (e.g., for socially undesirable behavior)	___	___	___	_____
Victim a targeted individual	___	___	___	_____
Personalizes victim	___	___	___	_____
Other signs of goal formulation	___	___	___	_____

PLANNING AND PREPARATION

Relevant to the time before the alleged crime, this refers to the ability to show cognitive preparation for subsequent behaviors. Routine rehearsals for the alleged crime are the highest form of ability in this dimension.

	Insufficient Data	No	Yes	Specify
Foreknowledge of alleged crime	___	___	___	_____
Creation of time schedules	___	___	___	_____
Temporal ordering of steps to complete task	___	___	___	_____
Ability to revise plan given new information	___	___	___	_____
Completes plan in reasonable time frame	___	___	___	_____
Ability to interpersonally relate to others as planned	___	___	___	_____
Motor or mental rehearsal of crime sequence	___	___	___	_____
Use of ruse to fool victim	___	___	___	_____
Lured victim into defense-less position	___	___	___	_____
Brings weapon and paraphernalia (e.g., "rape kit") to scene	___	___	___	_____
Telephone, lights, security devices disabled	___	___	___	_____
Other signs of planning/ preparation	___	___	___	_____

Effective Performance

Occurring during the violence sequence, effective performance reflects the notion that the accused may simultaneously observe and change his or her behavior in response to a fluctuating environment, all in accordance with the goal or desired object of the action sequence. Hypothesis testing is the highest form of effective performance, as when the accused changes his own behavior (e.g., threatens victim, puts key in lock) in order to see the reaction (e.g., victim acquiescence, door becomes unlocked) and then changes his own behavior accordingly (e.g., proceeds to rape victim, goes through door to bedroom). In essence, this skill taps the ability to show a concordance between intentions/plans and actions.

	Insufficient Data	No	Yes	Specify
Able to view environment objectively (takes abstract attitude)	___	___	___	_____
Violence did not occur close to home/work (for planned violence)	___	___	___	_____

	Insufficient Data	No	Yes	Specify
Demonstrates a variety of acts (flexible behavior as with several weapons)	____	____	____	_____
Displaying multiple sets of simultaneous motor behaviors	____	____	____	_____
Able to orchestrate multi-step, multitask scheme (e.g., long, connected chains of behaviors)	____	____	____	_____
Concerted effort in order to accomplish goal (e.g., despite victim resistance)	____	____	____	_____
Ability to show change in principle (e.g., from robbery to rape)	____	____	____	_____
Ability to show self-controlled somatic responses (e.g., sex with ejaculation, eating, drinking; all within violence sequence)	____	____	____	_____
Ability to delay responses	____	____	____	_____
Ability to monitor and self-correct ongoing behavior	____	____	____	_____
Nonstimulus boundedness (acts independent of environmental influences)	____	____	____	_____
Ability to regulate tempo, intensity and duration of behaviors	____	____	____	_____
Controlled mood during inflicting of violence	____	____	____	_____
Ability to avoid nonerratic behavior unless planned (e.g., deliberately becomes substance intoxicated)	____	____	____	_____
Hypothesis testing	____	____	____	_____
Awareness of wrongdoing during violence (e.g., from statements to victim)	____	____	____	_____
Ability to hit/penetrate vital body target (e.g., deep knife penetration, shots to head)	____	____	____	_____
Controlled cutting of victim	____	____	____	_____

	Insufficient Data	No	Yes	Specify
Ability to stop violence (e.g., response cessation with no perseveration)	____	____	____	_____
Intact self-control (retrospectively reported by accused)	____	____	____	_____
Victim bound or other restraints used	____	____	____	_____
Mouth taped	____	____	____	_____
Mouth gag used	____	____	____	_____
Blindfold placed over victim's eyes	____	____	____	_____
Absence of bite marks on victim	____	____	____	_____
No blood smearing or splattering	____	____	____	_____
Victim tied to another object	____	____	____	_____
Takes pictures of victim	____	____	____	_____
Perpetrator encourages bystanders to engage in violence to victim	____	____	____	_____
Torture of victim	____	____	____	_____
Other aggressive acts prior to death	____	____	____	_____
Obliteration or destruction of evidence during instant violence	____	____	____	_____
Other signs of effective performance	____	____	____	_____

RECOVERY PERIOD BEHAVIORS

The accused may, after the instant offense, exhibit behaviors suggestive of memory/knowledge that a possible crime had been committed. These include efforts ostensibly directed towards not getting caught for the alleged offense, or of minimizing possible aversive consequences.

	Insufficient Data	No	Yes	Specify
Moves away when help arrives	____	____	____	_____
Disposes of or hides victim's body	____	____	____	_____
Amputation of "ID" body parts (i.e., head, hands)	____	____	____	_____

	Insufficient Data	No	Yes	Specify
Disposes of victim's clothing	_____	_____	_____	_____
Other alteration of crime scene	_____	_____	_____	_____
Disposes of weapon used in offense	_____	_____	_____	_____
Disposes of other crime-related material	_____	_____	_____	_____
Takes souvenir from victim/ scene	_____	_____	_____	_____
Cleans own body	_____	_____	_____	_____
Washes own clothes used in alleged crime	_____	_____	_____	_____
Cleans/washes other material	_____	_____	_____	_____
Makes verbal statements of crime recall (e.g., spontaneous statements)	_____	_____	_____	_____
Relevant nonverbal gestures (e.g., points to victim's body)	_____	_____	_____	_____
Prevaricates incompatible behavior (e.g., makes up verifiably false story)	_____	_____	_____	_____
Writes confession	_____	_____	_____	_____
Other signs of recall for instant offenses	_____	_____	_____	_____

POST-VIOLENCE DEPRESSION PHASE

For many violent perpetrators, a period of guilt and remorse is experienced after the exhibited aggression. This is especially true for episodic or rare violent offenders. The self-control to avoid self-punitive behavior is the focus of concern here (e.g., suicidal, self-mutilative gestures). Apology and remorseful behaviors are very common here and imply little about self-control or choice at the time of the instant violence.

ROUTINE MENTAL/PSYCHOLOGICAL BEHAVIORS

Eventually, there is a return to baseline functioning for most individuals who perpetrate violence. The new baseline of routine activities and skills would also include that which is a function of violence-related learning, such as increased substance abuse, disturbed sleep patterns, and fashioning of new weapons. Some behaviors may be reduced (e.g., driving after conviction for negligent homicide, social activities which require trust and reciprocity). In the final analysis, an individual is never the same after the perpetration of substantial violence to others.

Part E: Self-control Model

The rationally based decision model below can be adapted to a wide range of instant offenses. The model represents the evaluator's post hoc decision path in coming to conclusions relevant to defendant's competencies at the time of the instant offense.

			No
Forensic Psychological Criteria	Yes	No	Opinion

1. Adequate forensic data base.
   Includes historical and
   instant offense information
   relevant to the accused,
   alleged victim(s), and crime
   context (Part A)   ＿＿＿ ＿＿＿ ＿＿＿＿

2. Presence of significant basal
   violence (two or more acts of
   threatened, attempted, or
   consummated violence; Part B)   ＿＿＿ ＿＿＿ ＿＿＿＿

3. Common themes for basal violence
   and instant offense (Part B)   ＿＿＿ ＿＿＿ ＿＿＿＿

4. Self-Regulation (Part C)
   *Considerable to substantial goal
   formation   ＿＿＿ ＿＿＿ ＿＿＿＿
   *Considerable to substantial
   planning & preparation   ＿＿＿ ＿＿＿ ＿＿＿＿
   *Considerable to substantial
   concordance between plans
   and actions   ＿＿＿ ＿＿＿ ＿＿＿＿
   *Considerable to substantial
   effective performance   ＿＿＿ ＿＿＿ ＿＿＿＿
   (To meet model requirements
   for substantial overall self-control,
   the evaluator must score Yes on 1-4
   above.)

5. The accused had substantial
   self-control at the time of the
   instant offense.   ＿＿＿ ＿＿＿ ＿＿＿＿

APPENDIX C

INSANITY REPORT FORMAT

MENTAL FITNESS AND CAPACITY REPORT

Date of Report

Honorable William Smith
First Circuit Court
State Capitol Building
Anytown, Anystate 00001

Forensic Psychological Evaluation
RE: DOE, JOHN NMI
    SSN: 000-00-0000
    DOB: Month, Day, Year
    Charge 1: Unpremeditated Murder
    Charge 2: Robbery in the First
      Degree, 5 counts

Dear Judge Smith:

This is the report of the forensic psychologist (requested/appointed) by (you/ the Court/Sanity Board, etc.) to examine and report upon the mental condition of the(defendant/client/patient/subject, etc.), John NMI Doe, SSN 000-00-0000, currently (assigned/residing/incarcerated, etc.) at (location name and address, including zip code).

FORENSIC DATA BASE: The nature of the examination consisted of (clinical interviewing/psychological testing/neuropsychological testing/interview of significant others/ward observation/records review/naturalistic observation/behavioral assessment with a functional analysis of crime-related responses/social-environmental assessment/review of medical findings/developmental assessment/ competence assessment/description from relevant demographic data/postdiction or prediction from base rates, etc.) for a total of approximately (N to N) hours of evaluation. Mr. Doe was examined both at the (place, date) and the (place, date) while he was on (pretrial confinement status/in the community on bail, etc.). In addition to (one/two/N) clinical interviews, he was administered the following psychometric instruments: (list all tests, including multiple administrations and unsuccessful attempts).

The following individuals were interviewed and/or rendered written statements to the undersigned:

(list all persons and their relationship to accused or investigation process; indicate number of interviews and location, if significant).

The following written materials were reviewed:

(list source and type, include "nonofficial" materials, such as diaries, notes from the accused to his attorney, etc.).

ASSESSMENT BEHAVIOR AND DATA BASE VALIDITY:

(Cooperative/uncooperative) and of (normal/disheveled/abnormal) appearance, this (single/separated/divorced/widowed/married), (white/black, etc.), (N) year old (vocation and rank or status within vocation) exhibited a (logical and coherent/fragmented/tangential/circumstantial/blocked stream of thought, etc.). Affect was (appropriate/inappropriate, such as laughter or rage, blandness, lability). A trend towards (somatic preoccupation/paranoid suspiciousness/rumination about past injustices, etc.) was observed. Orientation was apparent for (time/place/person/circumstance). Memory for (short/intermediate/remote) events was (intact/impaired) as evidenced by (performance on presented sequences of numbers/inquiries by examiner as to prior evaluation events/recollection of independently verified historical events), (with/without) a tendency to confabulate. Judgement was (marginal/adequate, etc.), as shown by (appropriate/inappropriate) responses to standardized comprehension questions (give examples—response to finding envelope, discovering theater fire). Abstraction ability, as reflected by responses to proverbs (give examples—response to glass houses, striking while the iron is hot), was (appropriate/concrete—if so, give response). Associational ability, as reflected by responses to similarity items was (concrete/abstract/appropriate), as shown by (give examples—orange, banana; chair, table). Reading and writing skills are (normally developed/impaired, specify). Computationally, he had (no difficulty/difficulty) counting backwards from 20 (but/and) had (difficulty/no difficulty) in (serial 7's/3's/adding/subtracting/multiplying). Fund of information was (adequate/inadequate—if so, give responses to four presidents, population of USA, senators in U. S. Senate). Overall, his intelligence appeared (normal/below normal, etc.), which is (congruent/incongruent) with his education (specify years and focus). Insight into the emotional basis of his present condition was (minimal/apparent, etc.). No (other, if applicable) pathognomonic features of his clinical appearance were noted.

(If features such as tattoos are present, state "for identification purposes...")

Distortion analysis of Mr. Doe's evaluation responses revealed, for the time of the interview, an attempt to (fake good/fake bad/invalidate results/present himself in an accurate manner—explain terms). This is based on (validity scale results/goodness of fit between test profile and clinical behavior/performance on scales or test procedures specifically designed to assess attempts at misrepresentation/discrepancy between response and established events). Distortion analysis for the time of the instant offense(s) revealed an attempt to (fake good/fake bad/confuse the crime picture/present himself in an accurate manner—explain terms if not done previously). This is based on (assessment of claimed psychopathological conditions when compared to known data, e.g., BAC/establishing the likelihood of claimed psychopathology with DSM-III diagnostic criteria/comparing similarity of current distortion to claimed psychopathology).

Interviewed others and written materials were also scrutinized for distortion. Statements by significant others may have been influenced by (a desire to assist the accused because they wish to be rejoined/a sincere desire to honestly represent the facts/the lengthy period between the instant offense(s) and the written recollection of such). Statements by the victim may have been influenced by (a desire for revenge/stress at the time of the instant offense(s)/a state of intoxication/the lengthy time between the alleged crime and investigation results, etc.).

Generally, evaluation results for Mr. Doe are considered an accurate portrayal of the accused, taking into consideration mental status, test-taking attitude, (psychological/intellectual/neuropsychological, etc.) limitations and competencies, and witnesses'/investigators' input.

DEFENDANT RECONSTRUCTION OF INSTANT OFFENSE(S):

(If available, a detailed account of the alleged crime is presented by the accused, e.g., see police investigation report/JAG files).

Generally, the accused stated, during the present assessment, that the (killing/rape/battery/etc.) was (in self-defense/accidental/deliberate, etc.) after the victim (struck him/threatened him, etc.). After the incident (witnesses stated/the accused self-described) his behavior as (describe), his affect as (describe), his cognitive functioning as (describe), his verbal remarks, in substance, as (paraphrase or quote).

[Repeat above paragraph for all charged crimes.]

(If amnesia is claimed.) Of particular interest is the claimed loss of memory (following onset of strangulation of the victim/after the second knife thrust, etc.). This amnesia, if genuine, could be caused by an elevated emotional state such as intense anger or fear, or other condition such as (head trauma/an alcoholic blackout/psychosis/dissociative reaction/substance intoxication/epileptic seizure/other organic states) at the time of the crime. For the instant offense, the claimed amnesia is most compatible with the occurrence of (type or combination, include malingering if conditions for amnesia do not meet DSM-III inclusionary criteria).

(If auditory hallucinations are claimed.) The accused also stated that he heard a "voice" to the effect that (the victim was trying to kill him, etc.). Four points are relevant here. First, volunteering that the voice was experienced at the time of the crime (did not take place until long after the accused rendered previous statements about the crime which did not include auditory hallucinations/took place at the crime scene to investigating officers, etc.). (One wonders to what extent presenting the "voice" was prompted by the demand characteristics of the accused's legal situation/Presenting the "voice" in such a spontaneous manner while under obvious stress heightens the probability that it was, in fact, genuine, etc.). Second, if instant offense events were as the accused describes, his acts (may have been in self-defense and therefore the voice is of little relevance/may have indeed been prompted by the auditory hallucination). Recall that the victim had (describe relevant behaviors) and the context was (describe relevant contextual stimuli). Third, hearing the "voice" (is/is not) tantamount to obeying it, as the accused (related a number of instances where the voice's command was disregarded; give examples/has acquiesced to it in all reported instances). Fourth, the "voice" is described as (ego systonic/ego dystonic). Given the chance to rid himself of the "voice," he (would/would not) do so because of its (describe positive or negative properties). This means that (describe implications of ego-systonic/dystonic experience).

(Describe and evaluate if other unusual features of defendant's instant offense experience are claimed.)

HISTORICAL VERSUS INSTANT OFFENSE BEHAVIORS:
(If available.)
A general history of the accused is also presented in (Dr. X's report/the presentence evaluation).

The defendant was born and raised in Anytown, Any State, the (give ordinal position) of (give number of male and female siblings).

Relevant aspects of his history which may bear upon the alleged crime include conditions which are associated with development of criminal behavior, such as arrest history/a family chronically affected by intramember friction and lack of support/a violent same-sexed parental model/abuse as a child/school problems including frequent fighting and assaults on teachers, etc.).

Medical problems include (relevant diseases/spontaneous loss of consciousness before age 10, etc.). His substance abuse history was (describe).

(If available.) Apparently, the accused dealt with the above circumstances by (describe strengths and competencies/describe helping relationships with significant others or agencies/describe diversion into areas such as sports, academics, hobbies/mention psychiatric hospitalizations or treatment).

MENTAL CONDITION:
The diagnosis(es) representing a reconstructed mental condition for the time of the alleged crime is (specify, DSM-III, NNN.NN). This is based on (specify DSM-III inclusionary criteria which apply). The diagnosis(es) for the time of the assessment is (specify, DSM-III, NNN.NN). This is based on (specify DSM-III inclusionary criteria).

(If two diagnoses are identical.) The diagnosis of (specify) for the time of the alleged crime (is temporally linked to the identical diagnosis at the time of the evaluation in the sense that both mental conditions have been continually operative during the two time points/even though identical to the diagnosis at the time of the evaluation, represents the mental condition occurring episodically with no implication of continued operation between the two temporal points).

SELF-DETERMINATION OF INSTANT OFFENSE BEHAVIORS:
(If relevant cognitive events operative.) The cognitive capacity of the accused to appreciate the wrongfulness of his acts may have been adversely affected by the following events:

(Specify those which apply.)

(1) During a delusion of imminent harm followed by self-defensive behavior (link to history, diagnosis, severity of associated conditions);
(2) Other delusions (analyze appropriateness of delusion if it were true);
(3) When experiencing hallucinations (specify, command auditory hallucinations/visual hallucinations but not illusions; link, as above);

(4) In cases of clinical retardation or in borderline conditions where cognitive abilities are especially deficit compared to performance skills (link);

(5) Other relevant conditions such as dissociative disorders and some organic states (link).

(If relevant cognitive events operative.) Cognitive capacity to appreciate the wrongfulness of his acts seems to have been present, as evidenced by the following events:

(Specify those which apply)

(1) Flexibility of response, as when the accused brought his (burglar tools/murder weapon, etc.) to the scene of the alleged crime;

(2) Interposing a stimulus to a known response, as (when the accused set his alarm clock in order to meet the victim at a certain time and location, etc.);

(3) Attempting to remove potentially aversive stimuli, as (when the accused was caught at the site of the killing attempting to eliminate incriminating evidence, etc.);

(4) Recounting the alleged crime to others (specify) which at least suggests image recall;

(5) Verbally responding or exhibiting behaviors to others suggesting he knew his acts were wrong.

(If relevant volitional events operative.) The volitional capacity of the accused to conform his conduct to the requirements of the law may have been adversely affected by the following events:

(Specify those which apply.)

(1) All specified cognitive conditions; as that which adversely influences cognition also affects volition (specify);

(2) Ingestion of the following substances: (specify);

(3) Cumulative stress and other affective experiences operative up to (several months/one year, etc.) before the instant offense and manifested by (specify and describe);

(4) Momentary stress at the time of the crime associated with (victim provocation, describe/social demand traits of the alleged crime, describe);

(5) Certain rare organic conditions (e.g., tumor in limbic system/RAS) acting on self-control abilities.

(If relevant events operative.) Events suggesting volitional capacity include the following:

(Specify those which apply.)

(1) Changing availability of a stimulus, as when the accused (gave his friend a firearm to keep in his apartment only to retrieve it prior to the alleged crime, etc.);

(2) Doing something else, as when one tightens all muscles to avoid a flinch response. For the accused, the similarity is (refusal to respond to police questions after apprehension, etc.);

(3) Statements or behaviors by the accused suggesting self-control, as when the accused (stated he "pushed" the gun to the floor before firing to avoid hitting the victim, etc.);

(4) Deprivation, as when the accused remained free of intoxicants and socially isolated himself prior to the alleged crime (demonstrate deprivation linked to choice and not other conditions).

CONCLUSIONS:

(Address all.)

(1) In my opinion, the accused is (competent/not competent) to proceed legally. He (has/does not have) an appropriate knowledge of the nature and quality of the legal proceedings, and (is/is not) aware of the possible outcomes and consequences to himself. On the (Competency Screening Test/Competency Assessment Instrument), the accused scored in a range suggestive of (competency/incompetency) to proceed.

(2) Concerning the unpremeditated murder charge, it is my opinion that the defendant (did/did not) lack substantial capacity to appreciate the wrongfulness (criminality) of his acts. Concerning the same charge, it is my opinion that the defendant (did/did not) lack substantial capacity to conform his conduct to the requirements of the law.

(For diminished capacity.) (a) Concerning the unpremeditated murder charge, it is my opinion that the accused suffered an impairment in his ability to appreciate the wrongfulness of his acts, corresponding to the highest level(s) of cognitive intent for this charge. This is based on the simultaneous operation of (specify). (b) Concerning the same charge, it is my opinion that the accused suffered an impairment in his ability to conform his conduct to the requirements of the law, corresponding to the highest level of cognitive control. This is based on the simultaneous operation of (specify).

(For additional charges not linked to an adequate data base.)

Concerning the (robbery/rape/assault, etc.) charge, no comments can be proffered regarding mental capacity as those charges are not anchored to an adequate data base. That is, the charges (relate to isolated episodes presented long after the alleged acts/were corroborated in most cases by single accusers of doubtful credibility, etc.).

(If applicable, moreover, the accused does not recall his state of mind on the specified dates; therefore, no linkage of the alleged crime to state of mind can be examined).

Thank you for this interesting referral.

Sincerely,

Harold V. Hall, Ph.D., ABPP
(List Specialization) Clinical and Forensic Psychologist
(License/Certification Status) Certified, State of Hawaii
(Diplomate Status) Diplomate, ABPP, ABFP

Appendix D

Self-control Analysis: A Case Illustration

Re: State of Hawaii v. Thomas Nakano
             Criminal Number 12345
             SSN: 123-44-5678

Dear Ms. _____:

This is the report of the clinical-forensic psychologist requested by your agency to conduct a behavioral analysis of instant offense-related behaviors relevant to the defendant in this case, Thomas Nakano, POB Waipahu, Hawaii, DOB January 19, 1957, SSN 123-44-5678, Criminal Number 12345, who is currently on bail status awaiting trial scheduled for May 23, 1987 in the First Circuit Court of Hawaii.

FORENSIC DATABASE: The nature of the behavioral analysis consisted of clinical interviewing of multiple witnesses, significant/knowledgeable others, review of relevant case materials, and inspection of the alleged crime scene and route.

THE INSTANT OFFENSE AND RELATED SEQUELAE: DESCRIPTION AND SEVERITY OF IMPACT: Alleged facts of the instant offense, including summarized events, have been presented in forensic database sources presented earlier. Briefly, on June 16, 1986 at around 2 a.m. at the Waikiki East Apartment, the accused is alleged to have killed the victim, Edward Kato, by inflicting a single shotgun blast to the left chest area. At about 8 p.m. the previous night, after working at his job as a mechanic, Mr. Nakano had driven the victim and a mutual acquaintance to Mr. Kato's apartment. There, they allegedly consumed about four beers and two "rainbows" (Tuinals) each, and shared a marijuana cigarette. The accused appeared to engage in a verbal disagreement with the victim, arguing possibly about work, drugs, and/or a female known to both of them, an Arlene Gordon, who was due to move into the victim's home the next day. The victim and the accused's disagreement progressed into a physical altercation outside the apartment, with the victim apparently the loser, ending up with minor facial injuries and possibly losing the keys to his vehicle. Irate, agitated, shouting death threats, and stating that he would return, the accused possibly went to this van and obtained a fishing spear, a bayonet, and a stick and headed back towards the victim's apartment. En route, he was intercepted by a neighbor of the victim, who, forewarned of the earlier fight and later behaviors, was armed with a baseball bat. The accused was disarmed and was accompanied to the victim's apartment, where further argument broke out between Mr. Kato and the accused. The accused left the apartment area to call a friend for assistance. His friend came and the defendant was driven home, where he ingested both beer and marijuana, and obtained several more weapons, to include an axe and a single-shot shotgun with four cartridges. He then had his friend drive him back towards the victim's home. En route, the vehicle stopped and the accused got out and fired his rifle. After discharging it into the air and towards the ocean, he returned to the jeep and was driven to a small park adjoining the neighborhood complex of the victim. He left on foot with his weapons and walked to the vicinity of the victim's apartment until the latter's return from a disco/bar. They entered the victim's apartment together, engaged in an argument, and were told by the victim's roommate to quiet down in order for the latter to get to sleep. The argument continued in a subdued fashion, with the accused terminating the interaction by asking the victim if he could bring his girlfriend into the apartment. He left, obtained his shotgun, returned to the apartment and allegedly shot the victim immediately and without conversation. He was attacked by the roommate after the latter apparently believed he was to be the next victim. The accused's firearm was pulled away from him and he fled the apartment and returned to the Jeep. He was driven to the vicinity of his mother's residence. The accused was arrested several hours later in a vehicle driven by his mother, heading toward the airport area.

The various examiners, although differing in their conclusions in regard to criminal responsibility or whether the accused suffered from a psychosis at the time of the alleged shooting, present data that at the time of the alleged shooting, the accused may have been suffering from substance intoxication and possibly an organic brain syndrome, superimposed upon a borderline personality disorder.

An analysis of instant offense events suggests the following may have occurred:

1. Violence toward another was suggested, as opposed to violence to property or self. The violence toward property that may have occurred seemed incidental to violence toward another party;
2. Threatened and attempted violence may have been exhibited to multiple persons at multiple sites. Alleged victims were either in an acquaintance relationship with the accused or were previously known to him. Stranger violence was not suggested;
3. Lethal violence was exhibited, involving the use of a firearm and multiple other weapons; the weapons may have been owned by the accused and involved no recent purchases;
4. Normal inhibitory factors, such as the presence of witnesses or the alleged unwillingness of the victim to resume fighting did not seem to prevent later alleged violence;
5. Violence may have been related to substance intoxication and/or other assumed mental/behavioral disorders. The key question is to what degree mental capacity was affected by substance intoxication, alone or in combination with other psychological conditions and cumulative/momentary stress.

Relevant History of the Accused

The background of the defendant has been presented in part by others and will not be repeated here. Instead, a few observations regarding the connection between antisocial behavior and mental/psychological conditions are in order.

1. The developmental history of the accused appeared chaotic and psychologically unstable. He may have been born out of wedlock and was the oldest of four children, all of whom, except one brother, are half-siblings. The father left the family when the accused was two years old and he was raised by his grandmother, whom he reportedly described as strict and who treated him like a "baby." His mother appeared unstable, worked as a waitress and was married five times. The defendant reported that he did not feel loved by his mother during his early years.

School grades and test scores were uneven over the years, reflecting upheaval and stress but also an ability to do well academically and to conform appropriately. Entries in the school records during the development period showed at times that he "emotionally and socially seems to feel insecure-very aggressive" (March 5, 1963), was seen as "emotionally insecure" (February 1, 1964), and needing "encouragement to do well" (April 1966). Other school notes reported good deportment. He graduated from Washington High School in June 1975 in the bottom quartile of his class. The latest year of academic testing revealed uneven performance, with STEP scores for science = 22 (percentile), social studies = 57, and listening = 9 (Fall, 1973). Standardized testing during Spring 1974 revealed average or better scores in quantitative, math, and writing areas, with below average scores in verbal and reading areas. Emotional problems may have contributed to the uneven performance as the accused performed differently in similar areas over time. The accused was described as always needing to be in control of others, which did not prevent peer bonding during those years.

In general, antisocial behavior during the developmental period is minimal in quantity, except for alleged drug buying (especially marijuana and hashish) during the last several years of high school. An interest in weapons emerged, with at least one incident involving the accidental discharge of a shotgun. An increasingly close relationship with and protectiveness toward his mother was also observed during the high school years.

2. The first few years of the young adult period were characterized by attempts to develop a stable identity and to maintain control over himself and others. He became a Jehovah's Witness for several months. He may have spent about half a year in the Marine Corps, with the defendant claiming to have left because he was a conscientious objector. He returned to polysubstance abuse as part of his young adult lifestyle. Several drug-related treatments were experienced during the period from 1974 to 1977, to include admission to Kaiser Medical Center in May 1974 and King's Medical Center and the State Hospital in March 1978. He received outpatient treatment at the Honolulu Mental Health Clinic (April to November 1975; February to July 1977), Drug Addiction Services of Hawaii (admitted June 5, 1975) and the Downtown Drug Clinic (dates unknown) following inpatient treatment earlier during those years.

The May 1974 Kaiser Medical Center admission was precipitated by a feeling that his mind was leaving his body, fear of loss of control, impulses to hurt himself or someone else, and other symptoms, followed by intense abuse of psychedelic drugs, such as LSD, MDA, and mescaline. A note here is that as the effect of the drugs wore off, his delusions and agitation increased, suggesting unresolved psychological conflicts with the function of substances to self-medicate and to escape pain (as substance abuse in post-traumatic stress disorders often operate to reduce symptoms) rather than to simply get high or to enjoy the euphoric effects. This suggestion is reinforced by witnesses observing the accused in recent years typically starting off the day with a beer and a marijuana cigarette.

The March 1978 State Hospital admission was precipitated by making out a will after planning to kill himself, followed by kicking out the windows of the police vehicle which was called to the scene. The accused had been smoking heavily and orally ingesting THC for several weeks prior to his admission. This was followed by his boss' accusation that he was stealing from his employer's account.

In general, evidence of antisocial behavior here is minimal, with the accused suffering several mental breakdowns associated with substance abuse.

3. From about 22 years of age, the period of psychiatric upheaval is somewhat subdued, with the accused holding different jobs, such as a manager for a bakery, then as a ramp agent for King Kamehameha Air Service, and then a succession of mechanic jobs. The substance abuse continued, as suggested by a February 8, 1977 arrest for Driving Without a License (police report R-12567) and Possession of Controlled Substance. Marijuana vegetation was also found within his vehicle. A March 15, 1978 arrest again involved Driving Without a License and having marijuana within his vehicle (police report B-23125). While testifying in regard to a murder trial, the accused admitted that he bought and consumed a quantity of Quaaludes on June 16, 1980. During 1981, he was reportedly involved in buying, selling, and using cocaine. His roommate at the time reported that the defendant once held a shotgun to his head after accusing him of stealing an ounce of cocaine from him. The roommate ran from the residence after allegedly being threatened repeatedly during the incident and obtained a police escort to subsequently retrieve his possessions.

The substance-abusing lifestyle continued after the instant offense, to include arrests for selling marijuana to an undercover officer (August 1986) and possession of four packets of marijuana in his vehicle (December 1986). An amber-colored vial of cocaine residue was found in the front pocket of his shorts during the last arrest.

In general, antisocial behavior during this last period appeared to have increased, with the accused firmly entrenched in a drug-oriented lifestyle. Rehabilitation efforts to control or eliminate substance abuse and other psychopathological behavior were not successful.

ASSESSMENT OF SELF-DETERMINATION FOR INSTANT OFFENSE(S) BEHAVIORS

An assessment of mental capacity can be sequentially presented for the temporal flow of the instant offense(s). This will be in terms of events which suggest cognitive and volitional impairments and abilities before, during, and after the instant offenses.

(a) Previous to the alleged shooting. (Several weeks before.):

In general, witnesses and other data sources suggest a deterioration in behavioral functioning on Mr. Nakano's part prior to the commission of the alleged offenses. Impairments were noted even though he worked at his job as a mechanic, associated with friends and family, continued to maintain his household with renters, and involved himself in other activities.

Several weeks prior to the instant offense, the accused was allegedly abusing methadrine, a stimulant drug, which made him paranoid, hypersensitive, jumpy, and irritable. His renters during these last two weeks corroborated the deterioration in behavior at home. They described the accused locking his door even to go to the bathroom, becoming irritated for no ostensible reason, and refusing to talk even when socially appropriate. Other alleged stresses during this time were reported by the various evaluators, to include quitting a job as head mechanic for another company and reconciling with his girlfriend who had been beaten by her boyfriend.

(b) Previous to the alleged shooting. (At the victim's apartment.) (approximately 10:30 p.m. to 12:30-1:30 a.m.):

For most of the above time span, the defendant was able to socialize appropriately with co-workers and friends after completing a day's work as a mechanic. Toward the end of this time, some kind of a physical altercation occurred with the victim, the alleged perpetrator having emerged the loser, sustaining minor facial injuries and possibly losing his car keys in the process. Mr. Nakano then became socially inappropriate, verbally loud, agitated, and seemingly indifferent to whether witnesses heard multiple threats to return and kill the victim (as reported by several witnesses). His aggression continued after the victim stated he did not want to continue fighting. The victim was overheard by one of the witnesses as saying, "...no like fight" or words to that effect. The accused apparently allowed himself to be disarmed after leaving and then returned shortly to the area of the victim's apartment. He went to the victim's apartment, where he engaged in further threats and angry words. Later, at a nearby telephone booth, he continued in his agitation, apparently had difficulty dialing the telephone, dropped coins, and was almost incomprehensible in speech. He allegedly said, "This is what rainbows does to you" or words to that effect. He generalized his anger to the telephone booth, banging on the telephone and yelling, and to persons who offered to help ("If you say one word, I'm going to shoot you, fuck up," and "Leave me alone if you know what's good for you" or words to that effect; other witnesses reported inappropriate behavior at that time, to include a challenge to fight). He was seen to be unsteady on his feet. In general, the limitations and impairments cited above may have occurred because of the combined effects of substance ingestion (about four beers, several tranquilizers, and possibly a marijuana cigarette), anger, and possibly other factors. The defendant became almost disorganized in speech and nonfunctional in adaptive and motor behavior, and with a pronounced tendency to generalize and displace aggression to other persons and objects in the environment.

Premorbid personality traits may also have contributed to impairments. Abilities demonstrated after the altercation with the victim included (1) flexibility of response, as when the defendant attempted to return to the victim's apartment after obtaining and carrying multiple weapons, including a (cocked) Hawaiian sling, a bayonet, and a stick; (2) long-term recall, as when the accused threatened the intercepting party that the latter would not be going to Maui because the accused was going to kill him. This also shows the displacement tendency of the accused's anger, as discussed above; (3) intermediate-term recall, as shown by his awareness and knowledge of recently occurring events within the previous hour (e.g., the fight with the victim, the ability to locate the victim's apartment after he left, the memory that he had called for assistance indicated by placing a second call to King's house and asking if help was on its way); (4) short-term recall, as shown by the ability to respond to what persons were saying a few moments before, even though the answer may have been aggressive or distancing in nature. Short-term recall was also shown by the ability to dial a sequence of telephone numbers; and (5) the ability to influence others, as when the accused on the telephone interacted with and successfully convinced a party to retrieve him from the vicinity of the accused's neighborhood and to take him home.

(c) Previous to the alleged shooting. (The period of time from leaving until returning to the neighborhood of the victim: between 12:30-1:30 a.m. and about 3:30 a.m.]).

Mr. King, as he related in his statement, picked up Mr. Nakano from the vicinity of the Waikiki East Apartments. He noticed the defendant was hard to understand and slurred his speech, had glassy eyes, smelled a little of alcohol, and was nonresponsive to questions but when he answered, would perseverate (e.g., the theme that nobody takes advantage of him "like that"). Motor agitation was pronounced, with the accused "shaking up and down," "wobbling all over." Suspiciousness and generalization of anger were evident towards the two local persons and one other who had all allegedly taken his keys and hid them from him. He affirmed taking substances earlier (i.e., "I took the fucking downers...Rainbows" or words to that effect.) He buried his shirt in a loud and somewhat strange fashion at a service station, indifferent to the appearance he created by emptying trash out of the dumpster and then covering his shirt.

This period of time may have been the most delimiting for the accused from a behavioral point of view and was possibly due to the combined effects of premorbid personality factors, ingested substances, and high emotion caused by the previous interpersonal friction.

He continued to show emotional behavior upon arrival at his house, pounding on the front door and then yelling at the renter to open up. He ingested more substances, including a beer and a marijuana cigarette.

Generalization of the anger was seen, the target of aggression expanding to a small group (e.g., "They like war, they get war" or words to that effect) with lack of insight as to his own mental condition (e.g., "I'm okay," "I stay sober" or words to that effect). Anger was shown toward the victim and two others for the remainder of the time at the house, and for the trip from the house to the victim's neighborhood. Motor agitation appeared to be reduced toward the middle and end stages of this time period.

Capacities shown by the accused during this period of time included (a) the ability to recognize and signal his friend who picked him up near the telephone booth; (b) the ability to direct others (e.g., going into the service station), count money and to twice engage in man-machine interface (i.e., to obtain cigarettes), once after the correct amount but incorrect type of coinage was used. This shows gross motor sequencing and memory skills, to include long-term recall (i.e., remembering his brand) and short-term recall (counting money), in addition to successfully modulating his behavior upon negative feedback; (c) the ability to signal for assistance at his house and to display the intermediate-term memory required to let the party know he had lost his means of ingress; (d) at his house, he displayed the ability to interact with another party with continuation of inter- mediate-term memory necessary to correctly relate events related to the earlier altercation to Mr. King, even if he may have been suspicious of the motivations of the previous actors; (e) at his house, the ability to engage in both fine-motor, short-term sequencing, and long-term recall skills simultaneously, as required when he opened the combination safe in his living room; (f) at the house, display- ing the choice to engage in further substance ingestion, drinking a beer, and directing his friend to roll a marijuana cigarette, which the accused subsequently smoked; (g) at the house, the ability to later recall long-term events (e.g., owing his friend money) and the counting skills necessary to parcel out money to pay him back, which he did; (h) the gross motor skills necessary to ambulate and obtain and hold a rifle and later an axe. The carrying of multiple weapons showed further flexibility of method in terms of multiple means of opportunity to aggress; (i) at the house, showing the ability to tell time and to delay gratification of ag- gression for a period of time until the victim was available, as when the accused was "dillydallying" around the house after obtaining the firearm in question, looking at the clock often, and then when 3 a.m. came (a short while before "last call" at the disco/bar at which the victim was present), looking at the clock once more and stating, "Oh, we gotta leave," or words to that effect; (j) the ability to state intentions of future behaviors when he stated, "I going get revenge," "I going get those guys," or words to that effect, referring to the parties involved in the earlier altercation; (k) the self-control ability shown by the defendant when he handed his friend the shotgun ("He grabbed the hatchet," "He gave me the gun to pick up the axe" or words to that effect), after telling the friend, "You're the only one can take me there," or words to that effect previous to ordering the friend out of the house to (first) transport him to the scene of the alleged crime. ("He made me walk out first," or words to that effect.) Hall (1985) stated the following in this regard: "Consider changing the availability of a stimulus, as when the accused gives a friend a firearm to hold prior to the commission of a crime. Paradoxically, this may be seen as indicating that loss of self-control is feared when it is in fact operating. The element of choice becomes obvious when the accused retrieves the firearm some time before committing the instant offense" (p. 13), (1) en route to the neighborhood of the victim, the ability to direct the driver to the specific point (e.g., "Take me to Waikiki East Apartments" or words to that effect) and to modify the usual route to that area from the house of the accused (e.g., "...he wanted me to go down to the sewage way"); (m) en route to the neighborhood of the victim, showing vigilant responses by turning around to see if they were followed; (n) the ability to progress beyond stating intentions to sequences of intended acts (e.g., "I'm going to get the haole first, man" [later] "I don't know where the haole live, but I going to check out Edward first," "I going to be right back," or words to that effect when parked in the vicinity of the victim's apartment ("haole" is a prejoritive term for a Caucasian); (o) the continued ability not only to interact with the driver but to control and intimidate him by implied force for noncompliance (e.g., "I know people who squeal and fuck it, I can blow them away," also alluding to relationships with "mafia," "hit man," and people on the mainland, "You better wait right here," or words to that effect), when parked in the vicinity of the victim's apartment; (p) the behavioral ability to rehearse the operation by discharging the firearm prior to entering the neighborhood of the victim and far enough away not to be heard by residents of that area; (q) the attempt to remove and prevent potentially incriminating evidence previous to the alleged shooting, as possibly represented by wiping the barrel portion of his firearm with dark or black socks or rags in an up and down motion (the socks or rags were over each hand, with the accused dressed completely in black) and by carrying the rifle around by the barrel with a rag; (r) the ability to locate and retrieve his axe from the back of the Jeep; and (s) the directional ability to find the victim's apartment area from the Jeep.

(d) Several minutes before the alleged shooting, acts during the instant offense, and subsequent immediate behaviors (sometime between 3:30 and 4:15 a.m.):

The accused, upon leaving the jeep, was apparently still angry at the victim and the two others, and still very likely was under the influence of multiple intoxicants as described. He may have met with the victim after the latter got out of the taxicab, went up to the room with him, engaged in further argumentation, left for a few moments, returned and shot the victim. During the struggle with roommate Anthony Kalua, who supplied most of the information in this section, the defendant may have inappropriately yelled for help and lost a slipper. During this period of time, arousal had turned generally from initial agitation to aggressive determination and then from a basic fight to flight response. Again, there was an apparent inability to confine the aggression to a single target. This assumes that the accused was not deliberately attempting to get rid of witnesses to the alleged crime (see below).

Abilities during this period included the following: (1) Ability to delay gratification: The accused may have been waiting for the victim after the accused left the Jeep and walked to the victim's neighborhood complex (e.g., the victim stated to the cab driver, "That's the guy I was fighting with," or words to that effect); (2) The ability to interact with others and to modulate his verbal behavior just prior to the instant offense, as shown by both the victim and the accused lowering their voices when requested by the roommate at the victim's apartment; (3) The ability to seemingly prevaricate when the accused stated he was going to get his girlfriend and return, instead returning to the room with a shotgun and an axe; (4) The intermediate-term memory ability to relocate his weapons, ambulate back to the apartment, and then allegedly take deliberate aim from a shoulder position, hitting the victim in the chest area; (5) The intermediate-term auditory recall ability represented by telling the roommate, "Now tell me to be quiet," or words to that effect; (6) The ability to initiate another sequence of motor behaviors based upon memory and practice, represented by pointing the shotgun at the roommate, opening the barrel, and attempting to load it before the sequence was interrupted by the roommate wresting the weapon from the accused; (7) The accused's ability to fight off his assailant and to successfully flee the scene of the instant offenses and to elude pursuit by dodging, running, and hiding behaviors (per Smith: "He was running like he was doing a sprint; he looked better than when he was walking earlier;" per Kama: "He was fast, no trouble running," or words to that effect).

(e) After the alleged shooting until arrest (approximately 4:15 to 8 a.m.):

The accused allegedly returned to the area of the Jeep and left the neighborhood of the instant offense. At this point, he was in pain caused by a possible dislocated shoulder suffered during the fight with the roommate.

He was dropped off near his mother's residence and was described by her as being in "bad shape," with his speech difficult to understand. He was difficult to arouse when he went to sleep a short time later. He then asked for a ride to the airport area. En route, he was arrested. He was found with two bullets in his pocket, thus failing to get rid of incriminating evidence. Impairments during this period of time are most likely related to a combination of pre-morbid factors, physical pain, fear generated by the flight response, the effect of multiple intoxicants and exhaustion caused by the expenditure of a large amount of energy over the previous few hours.

Abilities during this period included the following: (1) The ability to relocate the Jeep and to once again focally direct the driver (i.e., "Get the fuck out of here, man," "...to the highway," or words to that effect); (2) Ability to feel pain. This "ability" renders less likely a condition of gross alcohol or drug intoxication where pain signals are partially or completely anesthetized; (3) Attempting to avoid aversive stimuli, represented by telling the driver to look straight ahead and to drive slowly as a police car passed them en route to the crime scene; (4) Awareness of correct intended direction, as represented by the accused's cursing at his friend when a wrong turn was made (i.e., "Where in the fuck are you going?" or words to that effect); (5) Intermediate-term recall of events when responding to his friends' inquiries in regard to what had transpired (to King: "Do you think he's dead?" "history," "I got 'um , no worry," or words to that effect); (6) Ability to change plans when his friend balked at returning him home; (7) Ability to find and ambulate to his mother's residence after being dropped off; (8) Awareness and recall that he had done wrong, as represented by telling his mother that he was in trouble and later requesting transportation to the airport area.

Conclusions

1. The database is sufficient to draw some relevant conclusions with a reasonable degree of psychological certainty. Data from other examiners was considered, but all conclusions rendered were derived independently of other psychological/medical examiners who are involved in this case;

2. Database sources were assessed for suggestions of deliberate and nondeliberate distortion. Conclusions rendered are considered an accurate representation of events, taking into account report and witness limitations and competencies, the possible psychological disorder and substance abuse tendencies of the defendant, biases of input sources, and other factors.

3a. No evidence emerged that the accused has a major psychiatric disorder in that (1) no bizarre behaviors emerged at the time of the alleged crimes; (2) general level of anxiety (not anger) was not significant, except for the period after the alleged shooting; (3) there was not amnesia for alleged events, (4) delusions of a psychotic quality were not operative, even though the accused may have questioned the motives of the victim and relevant others; (5) there were no hallucinations; (6) depression, not the result of substance abuse, was not present; (7) there was no elevated or expansive mood at the time of the alleged crime; (8) the accused was understandable by the victim and others even though at times, there was an impairment of speech, especially when the accused was emotionally aroused; and (9) there was a strong to extreme expression of emotion, primarily anger, during the commission of the alleged crime, but this was appropriate to and congruous with the situation, and not psychotically incongruous. In general, there was no evidence of a formal thought disorder or major psychiatric disorder previous to, or at the time of, the alleged offense, with all former mental conditions and treatments being associated with substance abuse.

3b. Evidence emerged of polysubstance intoxication at the time of the alleged offense(s) as evidenced by (1) ingestion of alcohol and different psychotropic substances prior to the alleged shooting; (2) maladaptive behavior as evidenced by the hyper-aggressivity and assaultiveness; (3) other relevant symptoms, to include slurring of speech, impaired judgement, partial incoordination, mood changes, irritability, psychomotor agitation, and limited insight; (4) confirmatory evidence in the form of chemical test results; and (5) the above symptoms not due to any other mental disorder.

3c. Because of the absence of "a" and the voluntary nature of the substance ingestion in "b," the accused does not meet the American Law Institute (ALI) standard for the insanity defense in this jurisdiction.

4. The accused did not lose cognitive control over his behaviors in that he did not lack the ability to appreciate the criminality of his behavior. He appeared aware of transpiring events. Further, he appeared to engage in planning for the alleged shooting, which involved the use of multiple weapons, delays in time-tables, movement over distances using several modes of transportation, waiting for the victim, prevaricating to the victim, successfully fleeing the scene of the alleged crime, having backup transportation to take him out of the area, and other factors.

5. The accused was not substantially impaired in his ability to conform his behavior to the requirements of the law. He was able to substantially change, monitor, modulate, and otherwise control not only his behavior, but the behavior of others, as discussed previously. There was a definite behavioral focus and goal orientation in regard to the alleged crime. A behavioral rehearsal of the eventual firing of the homicide weapon was apparent. The level of activity required for the alleged crimes were considerable, requiring a concerted effort on the part of the accused to consummate the acts, as discussed above. In general, the accused's impairment in self-control over criminal behavior was at most mild to moderate for the above stated reasons but not substantial, meaning that the accused had the ability to refrain from the alleged shooting, although the chain of maladaptive behaviors may have been set off in an initially impulsive fashion.

Sincerely,

APPENDIX E

INTERACTIONAL REPORT: A CASE ILLUSTRATION

Re: State of Hawaii v. Anthony Barnes
             Criminal Number 12-5555
             Count I: Attempted Murder
             Count II: Assault in the First Degree

Dear Ms. _____ :

This is the report of the forensic psychologist requested by your office to ex-amine and report upon the instant case in regard to defendant-victim interaction and related behavior. A primary issue to be addressed in this report is to what extent self-control of the accused was adversely affected by extreme emotion at the time of the alleged offenses. A related issue is to what degree behavioral self-regulation was exhibited during the instant offenses, irrespective of operative emo-tion, stress, or other arousal factors.

A secondary issue concerns the credibility and mental condition of the victim

The defendant, Anthony Barnes, DOB February 16, 1953, POB Waipahu, Hawaii, SSN 555-88-9876, is presently in pretrial detainment at the Hawaii Com-munity Correctional Center (HCCC). The victim of the alleged attempted murder and assault is Carole Gordon, DOB October 18, 1962, POB Los Angeles, Califor-nia, SSN 234-99-8778. The date of the alleged crimes was August 29, 1986, with the incident occurring at the Seaview Lounge on Montgomery Street in Honolulu.

The following analysis sequentially focuses on (a) the forensic database uti-lized in terms of perpetrator, victim, and contextual stimuli; (b) an analysis of evalu-ation validity and victim/witness distortion. The mental condition of the victim is addressed here; (c) an analysis of emotional and self-control aspects of alleged crime behavior in terms of time flow; and (d) conclusions in regard to behavioral self-determination and emotion at the time of the alleged offenses.

Forensic Database: Relevant to the alleged perpetrator, the following materi-als were reviewed and/or individuals interviewed:

(1) Central Medical Center records of hospitalization (August 29 to Septem-ber 17, 1986);

(2) Kamehameha Hospital records (September 3 to 5, 1986);

(3) Records from T. E. Chang, M. D. (April 2, 1985 to April 10, 1986);

(4) Records from the Williams Clinic, Inc., Kailua (May 24, 1984 to September 6, 1985);

(5) Mililani Clinic and Hospital records of neurology examination; also containing an history of significant events, handwritten by the accused (September 18, 1986; September 29, 1986);

(6) A letter from the Office of the Prosecuting Attorney to HCCC Intake Service Center recommending high bail status (Wayne S. Song, dated September 30, 1986);

(7) Preliminary hearing transcript (October 9, 1986);

(8) Honolulu Police Department incident reports (K-11111 dated August 30, 1986; S-23232 dated December 10, 1986; P-38889 dated June 9, 1986; R-09876 dated June 12, 1986);

(9) Ex-parte petition for temporary restraining order for protection (FC-M, No. 86-0005 of July 30, 1986 for victim; FC-M No. 10029 of May 25, 1984 for wife, Tamara C. Barnes);

(10) Letters and drawings by the defendant while at HCCC to the victim (all in 1986: September 6, September 29, October 5, October 15, November 19, November 28, December 8, December 16, December 18);

(11) Pretrial Bail Report by Samuel Kane of the Intake Service Center, HCCC (dated September 16, 1986);

(12) A letter from the victim's current boyfriend to the defendant (dated November 6, 1986);

(13) An interview of Samuel Taft, witness at the crime scene (April 13, 1987, by telephone);

(14) An interview of Kevin Nielson, DOB February 5, 1952, witness and worker at the crime scene and acquaintance of the victim (April 17, 1987, by telephone);

(15) An interview of Marcus Nishikawa, investigation officer of the instant offense (April 18, 1987, by telephone);

(16) An interview of Keith D. Conley, DOB May 25, 1961, acquaintance of the accused and victim, and a witness to the instant offenses (April 18, 1987, by telephone, April 19, 1987, April 22, 1987);

(17) Victim Assistance Program records in relationship to accused-victim interaction; also in regard to Tamara Barnes, the defendant's wife. Interview of Mary Jordan, victim assistance advocate (April 23, 1987);

(18) An interview of Dennis King, Ph. D., treating psychologist at HCCC (April 24, 1987, twice by telephone);

(19) An interview of Monica Johnson, M.S.W., former director of The Safe House (April 25, 1987, by telephone);

(20) An interview of George Kam, employee at Hawaiian Photos, Waialae (April 27, 1987, by telephone);

(21) An interview of Susan Fountaine, former employee of the Sky Lounge (April 27, 1987, by telephone);

(22) An audio-visual film of the accused and others relating to the issue of family violence (*Abuse in the Family*, a four-part series prepared for local television, dated February 2, 1983);

(23) HCCC medical and dormitory adjustment records of the accused;

(24) An undated letter from the victim to the accused;

(25) Honolulu Police Department (HPD) investigation reports of the instant offenses;

(26) State of Hawaii educational records reflecting the accused's academic progress, standardized test scores, and behavioral observations;

(27) Employment application forms for several previous jobs;

(28) U. S. Navy personnel records for the accused for the period from May 30, 1972 to October 7, 1975;

(29) Clinical neuropsychological report of Michael Parker, Ph. D. (August 15, 1986); also, test protocols and notes for second examination (February 2, 1987);

(30) James Potter, Ph. D., Director of Psychology Workshops (April 23, 1987);

The undersigned's request to psychologically examine the defendant was denied by the defense attorney.

Relevant to the victim, the following materials were reviewed and/or individuals interviewed:

(31) See #2, 3, 5, 6, 7, 8, 9, 10, 11, 12, 13, 14, 15, 16, 17, 18, 21, 24, and 25;

(32) Nimitz Medical Center (NMC) records reflecting July 23, 1986 to August 9, 1986 hospitalization of the victim at that facility.

NMC outpatient clinic file contained some entries in regard to earlier medical intervention;

(33) Certificate of Live Birth of Carol Susan Carter, the victim, from Pennsylvania State Department of Health (certified as a true copy, March 30, 1980);

(34) Decree of divorce regarding Mark T. and Carol S. Thompson, (October 30, 1985, Case No. 85-P-999, District Court of King County, Montana);

(35) Parkins Medical Center records reflecting August 1-9, 1986 hospitalization at that facility;

(36) Interview of Paul O. Lowrey, DOB May 29, 1964, who assisted the victim after the alleged stabbing (April 25, 1987);

(37) Clinical interviews of the victim (May 10, 19, and 28, 1987, June 2, 1987);

(38) Bipolar Psychological Inventory (BPI) Lie Scale (administered twice: May 28, 1987, June 2, 1987);

(39) Sacks Sentence Completion Test (administered May 28, 1987);

(40) Marital Pre-counseling Inventory for the relationship with her current boyfriend (Stuart, R. B. & Stuart, R. S., 1973) (administered May 28, 1987;) Marital Pre-counseling Inventory reconstructed for the time of the victim's relationship with the accused (administered June 2, 1987);

(41) Fundamental Interpersonal Relationships [with] Others—Behavior (FIRO-B; administered June 2, 1987);

(42) Bender Gestalt Visual-Motor Test (BGVMT, with recall and Koppitz system scoring; administered June 2, 1987);

(43) Minnesota Multiphasic Personality Inventory (MMPI) Critical Items List (administered twice: May 28, 1987, June 2, 1987); MMPI, Form R (June 2, 1987);

(44) Slosson Intelligence Test (SIT) for Children and Adults (administered May 28, 1987);

(45) Booklet Categories Test (administered May 28, 1987);

(46) Wechsler Adult Intelligence Scale—Revised (WAIS-R), administered June 2, 1987);

(47) Tactual Performance Test (administered June 2, 1987);

(48) Seashore Rhythm Test (administered June 2, 1987);

(49) Speech-Sounds Perception Test (administered June 2, 1987);

(50) Finger Oscillation Test (administered June 2, 1987);

(51) Wechsler Memory Test, Form I (administered June 2, 1987);

(52) Trail Making Test, A and B (administered June 2, 1987);

(53) Reitan-Klove Sensory Perceptual Exam (administered June 2, 1987);

(54) Reitan-Indiana Aphasia Screening Test (administered June 2, 1987);

(55) Consultation with Robert King, Ph. D., Head, Neuropsychological Department, Hawaii State Hospital (June 9, 1987);

(56) Consultation with Ronald Miyake, M. D., neurologist, Central Clinic (June 10, 1987);

(57) Writing tasks to include (a) year-by-year presentation of most significant events, from birth to present and (b) list of physical symptoms attributed to the instant offenses;

(58) Consultation with David Smith, Ph. D., neuropsychologist (June 10, 1987).

Relevant to the context of the crime, the following records were reviewed or procedures implemented:

(59) See #14, 15, 16, 18, 21, and 25;

(60) Physical examination of the crime scene and escape route (May 29, 1987);

(61) Examination of photos of the victim (March 23, 1987). Diagrams and photos of the crime scene were also examined (March 27, 1987; April 26, 1987).

Assessment Behavior and Database Validity: The victim was cooperative and of attractive appearance. This white, female, 24-year-old business school student exhibited a logical and coherent stream of thought. Affect was appropriate, with some emotional behaviors such as muscle twitches and eye reddening when discussing the present incident. A trend towards fear of the accused was observed. Orientation was apparent for time, place, person, and circumstance. Memory for immediate, short-term, and long-term events was intact, as evidenced by performance on passages of words and sequences of numbers on standardized testing, and by accurate responses to inquiries by the examiner as to prior evaluation events. Episodic long-term memory involved recollection of independently verified historical events without a tendency to confabulate. Judgement was marginal, as shown by history and by some test responses. Abstraction ability was appropriate. Reading and writing skills seem normally developed but were low average in quality. Computationally, she had no difficulty counting backwards from 20 or with basic adding, subtracting, and multiplication of math problems. Fund of information and vocabulary skills were marginal, possibly reflecting her eighth grade education and some cultural-familial factors. Overall, her intelligence was measured as average on a screening test (SIT) and low average on a comprehensive intelligence test (WAIS-R). Overall verbal abilities were low average and performance abilities were average.

Distortion analysis of the victim's evaluation responses revealed, for the time of the interview, an attempt to present herself in an accurate manner. This is based on (a) goodness of fit between test profile and clinical behavior, (b) performance on scales or test procedures specifically designed to assess attempts at misrepresentation, (c) little or no discrepancy between responses and established events, and (d) consistent performance on repeated measures. Distortion analysis for the time of the instant offenses revealed an attempt to present herself in an accurate manner, but was mitigated by loss of recall after the initial knife thrusts, shock effects of the stabbing, and subsequent post-traumatic stress disorder (discussed later). Further, she reported drinking several alcoholic beverages on the night of the instant offenses and affirmed cocaine ingestion on the previous evening (August 28, 1986).

The mental conditions of the victim at the time of the evaluation are as follows:

Axis I: Post-Traumatic Stress Disorder, Acute (DSM-III Code 308.30)

A. Recognizable stressor that would evoke significant distress symptoms in almost anyone.

On August 29, 1986 at about 2 a.m., the victim was stabbed 12 times in the back and neck with another stab wound creating through and through puncture wounds of the jugular vein and carotid artery, penetrating three to four inches into the neck. She was unresponsive upon arrival at the emergency room. Deep tendon reflexes in her legs were unobtainable, toes were downgoing to bilateral plantar stimulation, and her blood pressure was 88/41, associated in part with a significant loss of blood. She received four liters of crystalloid fluids followed by two units of transfused blood upon admission.

Secondary stressors include loss of work and position, financial problems, and subsequent medical interventions.

B. Reexperiencing the trauma.

Following the stabbing, the victim experienced the following: (a) nightmares of being trapped by the accused; (b) frequent flashbacks of the perpetrator dragging her out of the lounge while stabbing her; (c) suddenly acting or feeling as if the traumatic events were reoccurring because of an environmental or ideational stimulus. In regard to the last, unresponsiveness and memory for ongoing environmental events (e.g., someone talking) has been lost on occasion, with the victim exhibiting fear-related muscle tightening and escape responses (e.g., others noting her almost going off the edge of a chair or couch without realizing it when someone was discussing an unrelated stabbing); and (d) frequent ruminating about the stabbing event. Some of the above symptoms appear to be increasing in frequency and severity as a by-product of current involvement in the instant case.

C. Numbing of responsiveness to, or involvement with, the external world, beginning some time after the traumatic event.

The victim has shown a markedly diminished interest in, or outright avoidance of, several significant activities (e.g., eating, socializing, drinking alcohol) and sites (e.g., lounges, cane fields) where violence involving the use or threatened use of a knife was experienced from the accused. Some constriction of affect is seen compared to descriptions of pre-instant offenses behaviors. Level of distrust has increased, especially toward males.

D. Symptoms of autonomic arousal or suppression and/or related signs.

These include (a) continual scanning of the environment with increased anxiety when by herself, (b) sleep pattern changes with a reduction of several hours in average total sleep time, (c) startle responses, (d) memory and concentration problems with no indication that these problems are of organic etiology, (e) guilt, to include occasional thoughts that she wished she had died during the knife assault, and (f) body image problems, relating to scarring and disfigurement from the knife wounds.

Presently, the victim is involved in training as a secretary, has a positive and satisfying central love relationship, and has substantially reduced her alcohol intake and eliminated drug abuse. Analysis of her history prior to the instant offenses, however, revealed frequent job changes and periods of unemployment. She showed an inability to maintain enduring attachments to her previous spouses and significant others in her life. There appeared to be a failure to plan ahead and some recklessness, especially when under the influence of alcohol and/or drugs. Previous abuse of alcohol appears to be significant and the substance of choice. Other personality features by history include occasional angry outbursts or tantrums, low frustration tolerance, a need to frequently receive assurance and support from others, and long-term family conflict and discord. Decision-making skills are poor.

Personality features revealed by psychological testing, exclusive of MMPI results, indicate a low to medium expression of affection toward others, with comparable (low to average) needs for involvement from others. This pattern is usually seen as a result of being "burned" in interpersonal relationships. In terms of expressed control, decision skills and perceived behavioral influence over others are low. Dependency needs are elevated. This is usually seen with individuals with low self-esteem. In terms of social interaction, social skills are intact. High anxiety is attached to many social situations where she does not feel accepted by others. Social selectivity is extremely high, meaning that she is "picky" when it comes to choosing others as (emotionally) close associates, another pattern associated with close relationships that have turned out badly. Family relationships are poor, which is congruent with a reported developmental history of frequent corporal punishment, sexual abuse by extended family members, and gross behavioral problems on the part of parents and stepparents.

Minnesota Multiphasic Personality Inventory (MMPI) and MMPI Critical Items List: Her performance yielded the following MMPI profile (015' 8246-739/:L/F'K#). Validity scale results and repeated testing on critical items over time suggested a valid profile with a high degree of consistency. This person admitted to personal and emotional difficulties, is asking for help, and is unsure of her own capabilities in dealing with perceived high current stress. Clinical scale elevations describe a person who is uncomfortable with herself and others, hypersensitive, distrustful of others, concerned about somatic functioning and physical appearance, withdrawn, and who engages in frequent ruminative behavior.

The type of profile elevation shown by the victim (high point pair 0-1) is rare and usually does not occur except when other scales are elevated, when then reflects possible additional psychopathological conditions. The social style and interactive behavior of the victim prior to the instant offenses can be characterized as active, operating within an individual who knew how to respond interpersonally in an appropriate manner. This suggests that MMPI scales known to be elevated by PTSD symptomatology (see Axis I) contributed to the mild to moderate profile elevations and the overall configuration (see above Figley, 1985 cite, all MMPI scales elevated by PTSD in some studies; others reflect elevations in F, 2, 3, 7, 8, 0). Removal of PTSD-related items would then reduce psychopathology to more normal levels. Some character features would undoubtedly remain, reflecting the chronic traits discussed in the first paragraph under Axis II considerations. Nosuggestions of a thought disorder or other psychotic process emerged upon testing.

Axis III: Physical disorders or conditions related to the instant case include (1) headaches, generalized or with a burning sensation toward the back of the head.

Nerve sensations are occasionally experienced in the chest and arms when the head is leaned forward, (2) surface numbness, from below the chin to below the knee on the right side of the body, and down the leg on the left side. Focal numbness is also experienced on the back in the area of the stab wounds. Leg stiffness is reported in the morning, (3) balance problems with falling if she is not concentrating on the synchrony required for ambulation. She loses her balance if she attempts to run, (4) occasional aphasic signs such as producing "blurred" words, or words switched around in sequence, when those verbal characteristics were not noticed prior to the stabbing.

The above signs appear to be residual symptoms from the sustained trauma. Earlier pathological signs included: (1) left hemiparesis (i.e., abnormal neurological; normal CT scan and C-spine at Kuakini); (2) residual central nervous system deficit corresponding to Brown-Sequard syndrome, resulting in loss of sensation and discrimination in certain body sites (i.e., spectrum analysis significant for turbulent flow of right carotid artery; CT scan, arch aortagram, and carotid arteriogram essentially normal; abnormal neurological); (3) right Horner's pupil; (4) equivocal Babinski on the left; (5) ataxic gait favoring the left; (6) relatively weaker left shoulder shrug; (7) weaker left compared to right arm; (8) adequate swallow reflexes with a right pull to uvula; downward left tongue protrusion; (9) positive bilateral Hoffman sign (clawing movement of fingers created by stimulating the index finger); (10) temporary blindness, accompanied by initial visual blurring and later pain on the top of her head.

In order to further pinpoint possible neuropsychological impairment, a composite neuropsychological battery plus some focal tests were administered (see Forensic Database). Mild severity of cerebral processes were revealed (Halstead Impairment Index = .3) primarily on tasks requiring motor speed, coordination of upper extremities, manual dexterity, and sensitivity to stimulation (i.e., impaired performance on Tactual Performance Test—TPT, finger oscillation, tactile finger recognition). Results suggested a primarily, not exclusively, right hemisphere involvement (i.e., left-handed finger oscillation, nondominant hand performance on TPT, left- versus right-handed TPT, left-handed tactile finger recognition). The lesion appears static (with deficits improving) as opposed to progressive (i.e., little difference in VWS and PWS weighted scores, no suppressions, intact scores for Seashore Rhythm Test and Speech-Sound Perception Test). The overall results are consistent with a cerebral circulatory dysfunction or insufficiency. In general, current neuropsychological deficits are mild and do not involve higher order cognitive processing, visual perception functioning, or long-term, short-term, or immediate recall skills.

In terms of input from significant/knowledgeable others, statements made during the present evaluation in regard to alleged crime events were generally, but not totally, consistent with earlier versions presented to various investigators; expected errors of omission occurred as a result of forgetting over time and other factors but few errors of commission, as in fabrication, were presented. Several witnesses were reluctant to be interviewed and expressed fear of retaliation from the accused. The account of the offenses by significant/knowledgeable others were concrete, clear, vivid, and contained much detailed description within the limitations of their involvement and the brief span during which the instant offenses occurred.

Accounts were original in terms of lack of stereotyping, internally consistent, and imbedded in the transpiring circumstances of the crime context and the reporting parties. The accounts contained behavioral chains of events and involved the reporting of subjective experiences and feelings. Unexpected complications and interruptions were mentioned as well as unfavorable behaviors on the part of witnesses. All of the above are fundamental or special semantic criteria which in combination are associated with truthfulness of crime accounts.

The accused's account of the instant offenses is partially presented by spontaneous statements during and subsequent to the alleged crimes. Amnesia was claimed for the actual stabbing but not for immediately preceding events (discussed later), or for the suicidal behavior. Regaining memory for instant offense events was reported in Dr. _____ 's assessment records, dated _____ .

Generally, evaluation results are considered an accurate portrayal of the temporal sequence of the instant offenses and related events, taking into consideration the mental status and condition of the victim, test-taking attitude, psychological, intellectual, and neuropsychological limitations and competencies, and witnesses' and investigators' input.

Sequential Assessment of Emotion and Behavioral Self-Regulation: Emotional level and behavioral self-regulation of the accused can be sequentially analyzed for the temporal flow of the instant offenses, based upon knowledge of the victim, the accused, significant others, and the crime context. This will be in terms of database-reported events which suggest emotional and self-control impairments and abilities before, during, and after the instant offenses.

(a) Previous to the alleged offenses: The six to seven months before and violence history.

During this time, the accused's marital relationship fell apart, with his three children being placed in foster care (March 1986), separation from his wife (April 1986), and his entering into an intimate but stormy relationship with the victim (March 1986). His job of one year was lost, with several unsuccessful attempts to reintegrate into the working field. Substance ingestion during this period consisted of alcohol, tobacco (about one pack daily), and daily use of anabolic steroids as an adjunct to his body building. Social activities consisted in part of frequent dating and socializing with friends. Possession of weapons was observed during this period, to include carrying a knife on his person, keeping a samurai sword behind his truck seat, and ownership of lethal weapons, including an assortment of knives, "numchuks," "stars," and spears.

Violent or potentially violent activities toward self or others need to be examined as part of the accused's behavioral reaction to stress and placed within a historical perspective. It is important to note that violence in recent times represents a continual pattern, to include previous violence (1) as a victim of child abuse, (2) frequent fighting with peers (e.g., see school records), (3) animal cruelty, (4) a suicide attempt by drug overdose (1982), (5) physical assaults on his wife, Tamara Barnes, especially from 1981 to 1983. Victim Assistance Program files indicate kicking his wife's back, head, and shoulders with threats to kill her (March 2, 1984). Later, his wife was punched in the face and head, resulting in black, swollen eyes, lumps on her head, red marks and bruises by her temple, and severe pains in her head (July 3, 1984). During a conjoint counseling session, the accused threatened to hit her and police were called by the therapist (August 2, 1984). A Temporary Restraining Order was obtained for the period from August 12, 1984 to February 10, 1985.

Violence toward others since 1983 is presented below.

Date	Event	Source
May 3, 1983	Spouse abuse with threats to kill	Victim Assistance Program and Family Court records
June 8, 1983	Spouse abuse	Victim Assistance Program and Family Court records
June 13, 1983	Spouse abuse	Victim Assistance Program and Family Court records
May to June 1986	Threats to kill victim	Victim and self if victim tried to leave him
May to June 1986	Told acquaintance several	Witness that if the victim left him, he would kill her
June 8, 1986	Multiple strikes with fists	TRO, Victim, HPD to victim's face/head report
June 12, 1986	Kidnapping, Assault with a Weapon (knife) and Attempt to do Bodily Harm complaints. Grabbed victim by her hair, put knife to her throat in presence of co-workers, dragged victim into vehicle and left.	HPD report
June 12, 1986	Assault on pregnant wife	Witness, Wife, HPD report
June 27, 1986	Grabbed, yanked by hair, dragged, threw and choked victim	TRO, Victim
June 28, 1986	Grabbed, punched on head four or five times, restrained victim's head with foot	TRO, Victim
June 29, 1986	Grabbed and swung victim by hair; placed loaded .45 caliber pistol to victim's head; later threatened to kill self	TRO, Victim
July 18, 1986	Took victim to cane field, put knife to her throat, threatened to cut her throat if they did not have sex; victim complied. Last contact with accused prior to the stabbing	Victim
July 21, 1986	Stabbing of the victim (instant offenses)	Witnesses

(b) Previous to the alleged stabbing: The week before.

In general, data suggests a period of high cumulative stress on Mr. Barnes' part, to include (1) a disrupted relationship with the victim. Mr. Barnes and Carol Gordon were living in separate quarters at this time; (2) the accused was sleeping in this truck and the victim was staying at a friend's apartment; (3) the defendant was not working; (4) he was in poor financial shape; (5) his pickup truck was in danger of being repossessed for nonpayment; and (6) attempts on his part to reconcile with his wife were fruitless. Retrospective self-reported depression and hopelessness were evident. Self-regulation during this period included the ability to drive his vehicle, socialize with acquaintances, and go to recreational spots during the evening, engaging in a wide variety of lounge-appropriate behavior. The accused was aware of and was due to appear in court in connection with a Temporary Restraining Order the victim had filed in an attempt to keep him away from her. A previous arrest for failure to appear at a TRO hearing should be noted.

(c) Previous to the alleged offenses: Before and after arrival at the crime scene.

For some hours prior to arrival at the Seaview Lounge, the accused allegedly consumed a large amount of hard liquor at various places with a friend or relative. Between 1:00 and 1:30 a.m. on August 29, 1986, he entered the bar with this individual and proceeded to the victim's table, where she was seated with three acquaintances. The accused introduced his companion as his brother and asked the victim if he could have his pet dog, a pit bull, back. He was polite, with no unusual behavior noted. The victim, allegedly fearing for her life, went to the lounge manager and told him of her fear. The manager then escorted the accused to the front entrance of the lounge to talk to him. At that point, the accused was observed to show signs of growing agitation and anger. He went to the bar counter area after the five- to ten-minute talk and had a beer with his "brother." He was observed to be staring at the table where the victim was seated, in what appeared to be an angry fashion, muscles tensed, eyes wide open, and head nodding up and down. The witnesses at the table commented that it was their belief that violence was imminent, but that they believed it would occur outside the bar. The victim left her table to prepare for her dance, stopped by the jukebox to play some songs, and proceeded back to her table. Upon the victim reaching her table, the accused moved toward her.

The accused's reported emotions during the portion of this time period when he was allegedly drinking with his companion were primarily depression and hopelessness. He reported that he did not mention his upset to his companion. Significant emotion, apparently anger, occurred (1) when he was talked to outside the lounge by the manager, and (2) when he was sitting at the bar subsequent to his return. Self-regulation shown during this period included (1) gross motor, fine motor, and recall abilities in order to engage in man-machine interface; (2) ability to locate the bar, ambulate to the interior, scan the environment, spot the victim, leave the bar upon the manager's request, return to the bar, locate his acquaintance, go to him, and later walk to the victim; (3) verbal behaviors and social interactive skills as evidenced by the introduction of his "brother" and other prosocial behavior at that time; (4) ability to conceal the knife; (5) immediate, short-term, and long-term auditory and visual memory which are necessary for successful execution of the above behaviors. Immediate auditory recall, for example, is required when engaging in verbal conversation, as shown when he first entered the lounge. Long-term recall, as another example, is tapped when one mentions animals another party presumably has in their possession, or to introduce a relative; (6) the ability to delay the knife attack, if in fact there was such an intent when he was at the bar or at some prior time.

(d) During the instant offenses.

At approximately 2 a.m. on August 29, 1986, the accused approached the victim from his position at the bar, stating, "Get over here," or words to that effect. At that point, the victim had arrived at the table and lifted her glass about half way to her mouth. The accused then grabbed the victim by her hair with his left hand and pulled out a double-edged knife from his clothing with his right hand, blade upright (by thumb). He proceeded to stab her multiple times while dragging her toward the bar entrance. The victim collapsed and essentially lost recall after the assault commenced but witnesses recall her screaming, "No, no, no, don't do this," or words to that effect. The initial thrusts appeared to be in the upper back and neck areas. The final stab in the throat resulted in the carotid artery and jugular vein trauma. The victim was released at a point not far from the entrance and the accused ran off.

Emotion during the instant offenses appeared to be significant for all the preceding reasons regarding cumulative stress. Other events signifying some emotion concern (1) the perseverative nature of the stabbing, (2) no material gain was realized from the victim (e.g., money, possessions), and (3) it was unlikely that the accused could get away with the crime as it was perpetrated in the presence of 30 to 40 people.

Self-regulation shown during this period include (1) the ability to verbalize, command, and follow through on statements; (2) simultaneous use of motor behaviors represented by holding, stabbing, and dragging the victim at the same time, all combined with; (3) goal-direction, as represented by dragging the victim toward the door, irrespective of what he would do with her once there; (4) ability to multiply stab a relatively circumscribed section of the body; (5) specific focus of attack to a vital area; and (6) attempts to escape, as represented by running off, implying awareness of wrongdoing.

(e) After the alleged crimes until hospitalization.

Subsequent to releasing the victim, the accused ran outside the lounge (2:00 to 2:07 a.m.), then toward the mountain across Kapiolani Boulevard, then proceeded in the direction of Hawaii Community College (HCC). Bar patrons were in pursuit in both a vehicle and on foot. He climbed a six-foot fence at the boundary of HCC and went into a side alley, attempting to conceal himself behind a vehicle. Police arrived shortly afterwards and ordered him to come out with raised hands (2:09 a.m.). The accused emerged with his hands above his head, but then fell forward, saying, "Just let me die, I want to die," or words to that effect. While lying face down, the accused stated several times, "I love her," or words to that effect (2:11 a.m.). He mentioned several times a "Jim Kalanaki" (phonetic). The police noticed lacerations on both of the accused's wrists. The knife was found several feet from his original hiding spot. He became semi-conscious and was rendered first aid. He was arrested for Attempted Murder (2:12 a.m.) and shortly after was transported the hospital (2:27 a.m.) At the hospital, he became less stuporous and offered that "They jumped my brother," or words to that effect. His wife, Tamara Barnes, came to the hospital and the accused told her that he loved the victim. He also stated that he attempted suicide because the children were out of the house and that he believed Mrs. Barnes was not planning to reconcile with him (3:00 to 3:20 a.m.). The accused then went to sleep. He entered surgery a short time later for deep cuts to both wrists (4:55 a.m.) and was out later in the morning (6:35 a.m.). Later, he admitted to physically abusing the victim over the previous several weeks (see hospital consultation record). The next day, he was formally charged with Attempted Murder and Assault in the First Degree, with the accused declining to make a statement at that time.

Emotional distress during this period appeared to be the highest of all the time blocks. Panic, fear, and self-blame appear to be the type of emotion rather than the anger of the earlier stage. High emotion during this period is manifested by (1) running away from the bar, and under circumstances likely to result in apprehension; (2) attempting to escape in a disadvantaged manner when other means were available (e.g., he ran past his truck parked on the opposite side of the street); his companion was later seen by the truck with the driver's door open; (3) attempting to kill himself in what appears to be a genuine effort at suicide; (4) spontaneous and repetitious statements in regard to the victim and others; and (5) other behaviors.

Self-regulation during this period appeared to be at the lowest. Yet, running away and hiding behind the vehicle in the alley can be construed as a continuing awareness that he had done wrong, in addition to attempting to escape detection. He had the ability to scale a tall fence, to partially comply with police instructions, and to verbalize. The ability to prevaricate was intact, as evidenced by his false statement that his brother had been "jumped." Recent and remote memory was intact, as shown by a variety of behaviors and his statements to his wife.

(f) After initial medical treatment to the present.

The accused was transferred from the hospital to pretrial detainment at HCCC. Multiple psychiatric diagnoses during the hospitalization were given, to include DSM-III Adjustment Reaction and Borderline Personality Disorder. The suicide attempt was seen as genuine, but there were many apparent attempts to manipulate the social environment through the use of further suicide threats. Although the defendant denied recall of the instant offenses, he repeatedly expressed remorse for his deeds. At other times, he stated that the victim laughed at him just prior to the attack.

Self-regulation increased with hospitalization. Attempts to control the judicial process and the victim's behavior was shown by (1) multiple contacts by a family member to the victim in attempts to get her drop the charges against the accused; (2) a series of letters by the accused with the theme that the victim must share the blame due to her presumed traits of psychological insecurity, distrust, suspiciousness, short-temperedness, greed for money, and playing "mind games" with him. He stated that he physically abused her when she made him tense, claimed no insight for the alleged offenses, and asked God to forgive both of them. He affirmed his love for the victim many times. He shared suicide ideation with the victim: "I mite as well hang myself with a strip of my sheet;" "[I'm] depressed;" "my body wants to die," "I honestly don't know what I might do to myself right now." He later told the victim that he hopes she would leave for Alaska because he might then by able to rest his mind; (3) several pictures drawn by the accused, showing what appeared to be the accused with a large knife cutting through the air, labeled "The Edge," and signed by the accused. Other aggressive drawings were sent to the victim, including one labeled, "Gardenia Gardens Lounge," the scene of a previous knife-wielding, assault, and dragging incident by the accused.

On _____, Judge James Meyer filed a report indicating that the accused had violated his TRO by contacting the victim through letters and his sister, Trudy King (HPD report #1867B).

On _____, the accused complained of his transfer to a dormitory and wrote, "Been experiencing harassment because I am gay."

On _____, the accused admitted striking another inmate in the face with his fist. Mr. Barnes stated that his wife was struck by a pimp in Waikiki and that he believed the victim-inmate was a pimp and, therefore, decided to take it out on him. The victim-inmate was transferred out of the HCCC dormitory and the accused was adjudged to have suffered an emotional break. He was placed on a suicide watch by HCCC officials.

On _____, the victim made a complaint to the HPD indicating that the accused was harassing her by issuing death threats to her and her roommate (HPD report #872A2).

Summary of Self-Regulatory Behaviors: Characteristics or behaviors of the accused which indicate both knowledge of wrongdoing and self-regulation for the time of the alleged offenses, when taken in their entirety, are as follows:

(1) As a predisposing variable relevant to basal violence, a significant violence history extended over years characterized by choice behaviors and reinforcing outcomes;

(2) As a predisposing variable relevant to intentional behaviors, multiple statements to significant others that he would kill the victim if she attempted to dissolve the relationship;

(3) As a predisposing variable relevant to opportunity factors, previous instances where the victim was assaulted by the accused where a knife was used as a threat stimulus;

(4) As a predisposing variable relevant to triggering stimuli and awareness of vulnerability, breakup in the central love relationship with both his wife and the victim;

(5) No indication of impaired intelligence or a major psychiatric disorder. Examination after the instant offenses revealed logical thought processes, no delusions or hallucinations, and present suicidal ideation. History and recent diagnoses suggest a long-standing personality disorder;

(6) Suggestions that the accused may have prepared for or at least had fore knowledge of the alleged crimes;

(7) Intact orientation, scanning, and sensory skills during the crime time sequence;

(8) Intact memory skills for both recent and long-term events;

(9) Intact interpersonal skills before the attack;

(10) Ability to delay the attack for a significant period of time;

(11) The focus of the attempted homicide should be considered specific;

(12) At least three sets of motor behaviors were exhibited simultaneously during the attack;

(13) Knowledge of wrongdoing and attempting to escape from the crime scene; and

(14) Prevarication subsequent to arrest in regard to crime events.

CONCLUSIONS:

1. The database is sufficient to draw some relevant conclusions with a reasonable degree of psychological certainty. Available data from other examiners was considered, but all conclusions rendered were derived independently of other psychological/medical examiners who are involved in this case;

2. Database sources were assessed for suggestions of deliberate and nondeliberate distortion. Conclusions rendered are considered an accurate representation of alleged crime events, taking into account report and witness limitations and competencies, the possible psychological disorders of the victim, biases of input sources, and other factors.

The victim emerged as a credible source of information, taking all factors into account. Deliberate distortion in terms of fabrication or lying was not suggested. Nondeliberate distortion created by the trauma of crime events and a subsequent post-traumatic stress disorder was taken into consideration by comparison to both cross-validating information and to the victim's own input over time and across many test procedures.

The perpetrator's credibility for reporting some crime events could not be assessed as some data was not available for cross-validation. Distortion in regard to the manner in which the alleged crime events occurred is suggested by the accused's post-arrest statements. Distortion in regard to evaluation behavior, particularly faking bad (malingering), was suggested by test procedures administered by evaluators in this case.

3. Level of emotion experienced by the accused appeared different as a function of temporal crime sequence. Mild emotion is suggested for the time he entered the crime scene until just before the stabbing. Behavioral self-regulation during this period was high and was characterized by (1) an ability to scan and orient himself to the crime scene, (2) an ability to conceal his knife, (3) normal speech patterns, (4) normal motor and other physical behaviors, (5) an ability to initiate and interact socially in an appropriate fashion, (6) an ability to delay the attack for a significant time span, and (7) adequate short- and long-term memory skills which were required to successfully execute the above.

Moderate emotion was suggested for the duration of the attack as demonstrated by (1) demanding in an angry tone of voice that the victim come to him; (2) the potentially lethal attack itself, and it occurring in the presence of others; and (3) the perseverative nature of the multiple knife thrusts. Behavioral self-regulation during this period included the (1) ability to verbalize, (2) the simultaneous multiplicity of motor behaviors shown (grabbing and holding, dragging, stabbing), (3) the goal-direction of the dragging, (4) the near-lethal knife thrust in the front part of the victim's neck as a final killing thrust, and (5) the decision to let the victim go and run from the crime scene.

Considerable to substantial emotion was suggested from the point of releasing the victim until his attempted suicide and was demonstrated by panic, escape, and self-destructive behavior. Behavioral self-regulation during this period was lowest and included running and climbing behaviors, an unsuccessful attempt to conceal himself, and partial compliance with police instructions.

In general, extreme emotion was not suggested for the time of the alleged offenses, as shown by a substantial degree of self-control and self-regulation during and especially before the attack. Further, momentary anger and long-standing resentment toward the victim, shown by previous attacks and other relevant behaviors toward her, characterized his behaviors up to the final near-fatal knife thrust. Panic and self-destructive feelings characterized his considerable to substantial level of emotion from the time he released the victim until his arrest. Overall, data suggest that the accused could have refrained from the stabbing if he had so chosen and that the highest level of emotion occurred subsequent to the attack.

(4) At the conclusion of the multiple evaluations, a Tarasoff warning was issued to the victim in this case. This was based upon (a) the violence history of the accused in general, (b) the preoccupation with the possession of multiple weapons, particularly lethal weapons, (c) pre-instant offense violence toward women and the victim in particular, (d) the apparent homicidal intent of the attack in the instant case involving the use of a deadly weapon resulting in near-fatal injuries, and (e) post-arrest intrusive and threatening behaviors toward the victim.

Sincerely,

CC: Presiding Judge
       Defense Attorney
       Prosecuting Attorney

APPENDIX F

CUT-OFF SCORES FOR CHANCE-LEVEL RESPONDING TO TESTS OF VARYING LENGTH

Total Number of Items	Cut-off score p <= .05	(Number Correct) p<= .01
7	0	0
8	1	0
9	1	0
10	2	1
11	2	1
12	2	1
13	3	1
14	3	2
15	4	2
16	4	3
17	5	3
18	5	3
19	5	4
20	6	4
21	6	5
22	7	5
23	7	5
24	8	6
25	8	6
26	9	7
27	9	7
28	10	7
29	10	8
30	10	8
31	11	9
32	11	9
33	12	9
34	12	10
35	13	10
36	13	11
37	14	11
38	14	12
39	15	12
40	15	12

Reprinted with permission from National Bureau of Standards. (1949). *Tables of the Binomial Probability Distribution.* Washington, DC: U. S. Government Printing Office.

GLOSSARY

A

Actus reus. "Guilty act"; a wrongful act. As opposed to guilty mind, "mens rea."

Acute alcoholic hallucinosis. State of alcoholic intoxication characterized by hallucinations.

Adverse witness. A witness who gives evidence which is prejudicial to the party examining the witness at the time. Commonly refers to a witness whose testimony is prejudicial to the party by whom the witness was called.

Alarm and mobilization reaction. First stage of the general-adaptation-syndrome, characterized by the mobilization of defenses to cope with a stressful situation.

Amicus curiae. "Friend of the court." A person who petitions the court for permission to provide information to the court on a matter of law that is in doubt, or one who is not a party to a lawsuit but who is allowed to introduce evidence, argument, or authority to protect one's interest.

Amnestic syndrome. Inability to remember events more than a few minutes after they have occurred, coupled with the ability to recall the recent and remote past.

Attest. To bear witness to; to affirm as true or genuine.

B

Bona. Good or virtuous.

Burden of proof. In the law of evidence, the duty of a party to affirmatively prove a fact in dispute. The obligation of a party to convince the trier of fact as to the truth of a claim by establishing by evidence a required degree of belief concerning a fact. In civil cases, proof must be by a preponderance of the evidence. In criminal cases, all crime elements must be proved by the government beyond a reasonable doubt. In some equity issues and more recent decisions of the Supreme Court the standard of proof is clear and convincing evidence.

C

Certiorari. "To be informed of." An action or writ issued by a superior court requiring an inferior court to produce a certified record of a particular case tried by the latter. The purpose of said action is to enable the higher court to inspect the proceedings to determine whether or not there were any irregularities. Most commonly used by the Supreme Court of the United States as a discretionary device to choose the cases it wishes to hear.

Civil. Of or pertaining to the state of its citizenry. Relates to an individual's private rights and remedies sought through civil action; in contrast to criminal proceedings.

Clear and convincing. A standard of proof greater than preponderance but less rigorous than reasonable doubt. Proof that should leave the trier of fact with no reasonable doubt about the truth of the matter in issue.

Collusion. The making of an agreement between two or more persons with a view towards avoiding litigation.

Compensation neurosis. Symptoms exceeding physical findings which persist long after expected recovery.

Conduct disorders. Childhood disorders marked by persistent acts of aggressive or antisocial behavior that may or may not be against the law.

Confabulation. Fabrication of information to fill in memory gaps. Associated with organic conditions.

Conspiracy. A combination of two or more persons who propose to commit an unlawful or criminal act, or to commit a lawful act by criminal means.

D

Deception. Conscious distortion of behaviors or self-report.

Default judgement. A decision of the court against a defendant because of failure to respond to a plaintiff's action.

Delusion. Firm belief opposed to reality but maintained in spite of strong evidence to the contrary.

Direct examination. The initial questioning or examination of a witness by the party who originally called the witness to testify.

Discovery. A pretrial procedure by which one party can obtain vital facts and information material to the case in order to assist in preparation for the trial. The purpose of discovery being to make for a fair trial and to allow each party to know what documents and information the opponent has in possession.

Dissociation. Separation or "isolation" of mental processes in such a way that they split off from the main personality or lose their normal thought-affect relationship.

Dissociative disorder. Psychoneurotic disorder characterized by amnesia, fugue, somnambulism, or multiple personality.

Distortion. Unintentional or intentional misrepresentation of events.

E

Exclusionary rule. The rule that defines whether evidence is admissible in a trial. In cases where evidence has been illegally obtained, it must be removed from consideration by the fact finders.

F

Fabrication. Relating imaginary events as if they were true without intent to deceive; confabulation.

Factitious disorder. Assuming the role of a patient by the voluntary production of symptoms.

Fiduciary. A person having the duty to act in a relationship of high trust and confidence for another's benefit in the capacity of trustee, executor, or administrator.

Folie à deux. A psychotic interpersonal relationship involving two people (e.g., husband and wife both become psychotic with similar or complementary symptomatology).

Frye test. A test emphasizing that the subject of an expert witness' testimony must conform to a generally accepted explanatory theory. Named after the case in which the determination was made.

H

Hearsay. A statement made during a trial or hearing that is not based on the personal, first-hand knowledge of the witness.

Hearsay rule. The regulation making a witness' statement inadmissible if it is not based on personal knowledge, unless it falls within certain exceptions.

Hypnosis. Trance-like mental state induced in a cooperative subject by suggestion.

I

Illusion. Misinterpretation of sensory data; false perception.

In camera. In chambers; in private. The hearing of a case before a judge in private chambers when all spectators are excluded from the courtroom, or when the judge performs a judicial act while the court is not in session.

Incompetency. Lacking the physical, intellectual, or moral capacity or qualification to perform a required duty.

Informed consent. A person's agreement to the occurrence of a specified event based on a full disclosure of facts needed to make an intelligent decision.

Insanity. A social or legal term indicating a condition in which a person lacks legal responsibility or capacity due to mental illness. As stated in the American Law Institute Penal Code, "A person is not responsible for criminal conduct if at the time of such conduct as a result of mental disease or defect he lacks substantial capacity either to appreciate the criminality or wrongfulness of his conduct or to conform his conduct to the requirements of the law."

J

Just-world hypothesis. The hypothesis stating that the world is fair and that victims deserve what happened to them and, therefore, do not deserve help.

L

Leading question. A question posed which is improper because it suggests to the subject a desired answer.

M

Malfeasance. The commission of an unlawful, wrongful act; any wrongful conduct that affects, interrupts, or interferes with the performance of official duties.

Mens rea. A guilty mind; having a guilty or wrongful purpose or criminal intent.

Mistrial. A trial which is terminated before its normal conclusion and declared invalid prior to the returning of a verdict. A judge may declare a mistrial due to an extraordinary event (e.g., death of a juror), for a fundamental, prejudicial error that cannot be corrected by instructions to the jury, or because of the jury's inability to reach a verdict (hung jury). In a criminal case, a mistrial may prevent a retrial under the doctrine of double jeopardy.

M'Naghten rule. In most jurisdictions, the test applied for the defense of insanity. Under this test, an accused is not criminally responsible if suffering from a mental disease or defect at the time of committing the act and not understanding the nature and quality of the act or that what was done was wrong. In order to be considered "sane" and, therefore, legally responsible for the act committed, the defendant must know and understand the nature and quality of the act and be able to distinguish between right and wrong at the time the offense was committed.

Modus operandi. Manner or mode of behavior; a criminal's typical pattern of performing crimes.

Moot. A subject for debate; unsettled; undecided. A case is "moot" when a determination on a matter is sought, which, when rendered has no practical effect on the matter under dispute.

Moral nihilism. Doctrine which denies any objective or real ground for moral beliefs and holds that the individual is not bound by obligation to others or society.

Multiple personality. Type of dissociative disorder characterized by the development of two or more relatively independent personality systems in the same individual.

Munchausen by proxy. Supplying factitious information on a child's health or manipulation of a child's health.

N

Non compos mentis. Insane; not sound of mind. A very general term including all varieties of mental derangement.

P

Path analysis. Statistical technique which takes into account how variables are related to one another through time and how they predict one another.

Perceptual filtering. Processes involved in selective attention to aspects of the great mass of incoming stimuli which continually impinges on the organism.

Perseveration. Persistent continuation of a line of thought or activity once it is under way. Clinically inappropriate repetition.

Posthypnotic amnesia. The subject's lack of memory for the period of hypnosis.

Presumption. An inference resulting from a rule of law or the proven existence of a fact which requires such rule(s) or action(s) to be established in the action. Presumptions can be irrebuttable, such as the presumption of incapacity in a person under seven years to act, or rebuttable, in which case it can be disproved by evidence.

Prima facie evidence. Evidence which, in the judgement of the law, is good and sufficient to establish a given fact or a chain of facts making up the party's claim or defense. If such evidence is unexplained or uncontradicted, it is sufficient to sustain a favorable judgement for the issue it supports; may be contradicted by other evidence.

Proximate cause. An occurrence that, in a natural and unbroken chain of events, results in an injury and without which the injury would not have occurred. The event that is closest in the causal relationship to the effect.

Pseudocommunity. Delusional social environment developed by a paranoiac.

Pseudodementia. Faking loss of intellectual abilities. A depressed state confused with brain damage, usually in the elderly.

Pseudologia fantastica. Pathological and compulsive lying. The motive is unknown or uncertain in many cases.

R

Reality assumptions. Assumptions which relate to the gratification of needs in the light of environmental possibilities, limitations, and dangers.

Resistance. Tendency to maintain symptoms and resist treatment. Uncovering of repressed material.

S

Significant others. In interpersonal theory, parents or others on whom an infant is dependent for meeting all physical and psychological needs.

Simulation. An intentional imitation of the basic processes and outcomes of a real-life situation, carried out in order to better understand the basic mechanisms of the situation. In civil law, misrepresenting or concealing the truth, as when parties pretend to perform an act different from that in which they really are engaged.

Sodium pentothal. Barbiturate drug sometimes used in psychotherapy to produce a state of relaxation and suggestibility.

Stare decisis. The legal policy of courts stating that once a principle of law is laid down, it will be adhered to and applied to all future cases in which the facts are substantially the same. Serves to ensure security and certainty of legal principles.

Suppression stage. The retraction of disclosures of sex abuse by the child. Associated with loyalty conflicts and stress.

T

Tort. A private or civil wrong or injury, excluding a breach of contract, for the court will provide a remedy in the form of an action for damages.

V

Voir dire. To speak the truth. The preliminary examination made by the court or by attorneys of one presented as a prospective juror to determine competence to serve or as a witness to determine competence to speak the truth.

W

Work product. Work done by an attorney while representing a client, such as writings, statements, or testimony in regard to legal impressions, tactics, strategies, and opinions, that are ordinarily not subject to discovery. Discovery may be obtained only when the party seeking it has a substantial need for the material to prepare the case and is unable to obtain the substantial equivalent of the material by other means without undue hardship.

INDEX

G

H

I

L

M